Women and Achievement in Nineteenth-Century Europe

D0781463

This major new history of European women organizational roles during the "long" ninete women could and could not do if they sought activity, purpose, or recognition beyond their own homes. Linda L. Clark surveys women's achievements in literature, art, music, theater, charity, education, medicine, law, and public administration, and examines the relationship between women's professional and philanthropic activity and the rise of feminist organizations. She shows that, despite continuing legal, cultural, and familial obstacles, thousands of ambitious women pursued professional activities for reasons that often combined economic need with aspirations to do meaningful work and gain public recognition. Detailing women's accomplishments from England to Russia, this unique survey enables readers to connect individual life stories with larger political, social, and economic contexts between 1789 and 1914 and is essential reading for students of modern European history, women's history, and gender studies.

LINDA L. CLARK is Professor of History, Emerita, Millersville University of Pennsylvania. Her previous publications include *The Rise of Professional Women in France: Gender and Public Administration since 1830* (2000), *Schooling the Daughters of Marianne: Textbooks and the Socialization of Girls in Modern French Primary Schools* (1984), and *Social Darwinism in France* (1983).

NEW APPROACHES TO EUROPEAN HISTORY

Series editors

WILLIAM BEIK *Emory University*
T. C. W. BLANNING *Sidney Sussex College, Cambridge*
BRENDAN SIMMS *Peterhouse, Cambridge*

New Approaches to European History is an important textbook series, which provides concise but authoritative surveys of major themes and problems in European history since the Renaissance. Written at a level and length accessible to advanced school students and undergraduates, each book in the series addresses topics or themes that students of European history encounter daily: the series embraces both some of the more "traditional" subjects of study, and those cultural and social issues to which increasing numbers of school and college courses are devoted. A particular effort is made to consider the wider international implications of the subject under scrutiny.

To aid the student reader, scholarly apparatus and annotation is light, but each work has full supplementary bibliographies and notes for further reading; where appropriate, chronologies, maps, diagrams and other illustrative material are also provided.

For a list of titles published in the series, please see end of book.

Women and Achievement in Nineteenth-Century Europe

LINDA L. CLARK

Millersville University of Pennsylvania

CAMBRIDGE
UNIVERSITY PRESS

CAMBRIDGE UNIVERSITY PRESS
Cambridge, New York, Melbourne, Madrid, Cape Town, Singapore, São Paulo, Delhi

Cambridge University Press
The Edinburgh Building, Cambridge CB2 8RU, UK

Published in the United States of America by Cambridge University Press, New York

www.cambridge.org
Information on this title: www.cambridge.org/9780521658782

First published 2008

Printed in the United Kingdom at the University Press, Cambridge

A catalogue record for this publication is available from the British Library

Library of Congress Cataloguing in Publication data

Clark, Linda L., 1942–
    Women and achievement in nineteenth-century Europe / Linda L. Clark.
      p. cm. – (New approaches to European history)
    Includes bibliographical references and index.
    ISBN 978-0-521-65098-4 (hardback) – ISBN 978-0-521-65878-2 (pbk.)
    1. Women–Europe–History–19th century. 2. Women authors–Europe–History–
    19th century. 3. Women educators–Europe–History–19th century. 4. Women social
    reformers–Europe–History–19th century. 5. Achievement motivation in
    women–Europe–History–19th century. I. Title.

    HQ1587.C53 2008
    305.48'963109409034–dc22   2007052049

ISBN 978-0-521-65098-4 hardback
ISBN 978-0-521-65878-2 paperback

Contents

List of figures   *page* vi
Acknowledgements   viii

Introduction: women and achievement, reality and rhetoric   1

1   Women and the revolutionary era: negotiating public
    and private spaces, 1760s–early 1800s   5

2   Women and literature: authorship, publication, audience   40

3   Women and the arts: creating, performance, fame   82

4   Caring and power: from charity to social reform   125

5   Extending education: learning and teaching   160

6   From education to other professions   197

7   Organizing for women's rights: leaders and supporters   240

    Epilogue: looking beyond 1914   285

Additional general studies and reference works   290
Index   292

Figures

1.1   Élisabeth Vigée-Lebrun, "Self-Portrait," 1790.
      Uffizi Gallery, Florence, Italy. Photo credit: Scala/
      Art Resource, N.Y.   *page* 13
1.2   Mary Wollstonecraft. Ann Ronan Picture Library,
      London. Photo credit: HIP/ Art Resource, N.Y.   32
2.1   Élisabeth Vigée-Lebrun, Portrait of Germaine
      de Staël, 1807. Chateau Coppet, Switzerland.
      Photo credit: Erich Lessing/ Art Resource, N.Y.   45
2.2   George Sand caricatured by A. Lorentz, *Le Charivari*,
      5 August 1842. Photo credit: Library of Congress,
      Washington, D.C.   54
2.3   Selma Lagerlöf. Photo credit: Mary Evans Picture
      Library, London.   74
3.1   Marie Bashkirtseff, "Life Class in the Women's
      Studio at the Académie Julian," c. 1881. Photo credit:
      Courtauld Institute of Art, London.   88
3.2   Clara Schumann and Robert Schumann. Photo:
      Hervé Lewandowski. Musée d'Orsay, Paris, France.
      Photo credit: Réunion des Musées Nationaux/ Art
      Resource, N.Y.   109
3.3   Friedrich August von Kaulbach, "Eleonora Duse."
      Photo: Alfredo Dagli Orti. Museo Teatrale alla Scala,
      Milan, Italy. Photo credit: Bildarchiv Preussicher
      Kulturbesitz/ Art Resource, N.Y.   118
4.1   Elizabeth Fry. From *Memoir of the Life of Elizabeth Fry,
      with Extracts from Her Journal and Letters*, edited by her
      daughters Katharine Fry and Rachel Elizabeth
      Cresswell, 2nd edn. (London, 1848).   139
4.2   Alice Salomon. Photo credit: May Wright Sewall
      Collection, Library of Congress, Prints and Photographs
      Division, LC-USZ 62-115858.   154

5.1   Helene Lange, German educator. From Helene Lange,
      Lebenserinnerungen (Berlin, 1930).   173
5.2   French student teachers at a normal school. Photo credit:
      Archives départementales du Loiret, Orléans.   178
5.3   A French teacher's science lesson. Photo credit:
      Adoc-Photos/ Art Resource, N.Y.   179
5.4   Marie Curie. Oxford Science Archive, England.
      Photo credit: HIP/ Art Resource, N.Y.   192
6.1   Florence Nightingale in the barrack hospital at Scutari.
      Oxford Science Archive, England. Photo credit: HIP/
      Art Resource, N.Y.   200
6.2   Anna Hamilton, 1900. Photo credit: Institut de
      Formation en Soins Infirmiers Florence Nightingale,
      Maison de Sant Protestante, Bordeaux.   206
6.3   Aletta Jacobs. Photo credit: University Museum,
      Groningen, the Netherlands.   219
6.4   Jeanne Chauvin. Photo credit: Mary Evans Picture
      Library, London.   226
6.5   Maria Vérone. Photo credit: Bibliothèque Marguerite
      Durand, Paris.   229
7.1   "The March of the Women," by Ethel Smyth, 1911.
      Photo credit: Museum of London.   259
7.2   Hubertine Auclert, 1906. Photo credit: Bibliothèque
      Marguerite Durand, Paris.   261
7.3   Aletta Jacobs and Carrie Chapman Catt, in South Africa,
      1911. Photo credit: University Museum, Groningen, the
      Netherlands.   277
7.4   International Council of Women meeting, 1914. Photo
      credit: May Wright Sewall Collection, Library of Congress,
      Prints and Photographs Division, LC-USZ 62-49121.   279

Acknowledgements

Historians inevitably become indebted to other historians and to specialists in other academic fields, whose works provide a point of entry into the study of a topic. This is particularly true when one ventures from an area of expertise in one national history and undertakes a comparative study. The lists of selected readings at the end of each chapter in this volume indicate the works of many of the scholars from whom I have drawn for this book and to whom I am greatly indebted for information and interpretations. Because this book is a general study rather than a scholarly monograph, it has not been possible to acknowledge many other scholars' contributions in footnotes, which are largely limited here to the identification of quotations. Any effort to list all of the colleagues who have offered advice, formally and informally, over the years would inevitably exclude many others who deserve thanks. But I do want to thank two colleagues who have done important work on the comparative history of European women and shared their findings with me for about thirty years: Karen Offen and Jim Albisetti. I also want to thank Sarah Curtis, Christine Adams, Marilyn Boxer, and Elinor Accampo for recently sharing unpublished papers with me. Whitney Walton, Anne Quartararo, Steve Hause, and Jim Albisetti generously shared illustration material. William Beik, who asked me to undertake this project, deserves special thanks for providing helpful comments on drafts. I also thank the Faculty Grants Committee of Millersville University of Pennsylvania for providing some released time from teaching that supported an early phase of work on this project, and both the Millersville and California State University Long Beach librarians who helped me secure materials from other libraries. In addition I much appreciate Caroline Howlett's copy-editing.

Other acknowledgements are more personal in nature. I began planning and reading for this book while I was completing a study of women civil servants in France, also published by Cambridge University Press. But work on the present book was deferred when my late husband Ned Newman was diagnosed with an incurable, albeit treatable, form of cancer. I thank my departmental colleagues John Osborne, Jack Fischel, Dennis Simmons, and Tracey Weis for taking over my classes on short notice when medical emergencies occurred. A few months after Ned's death, French history colleagues Mary Lynn Stewart, Rachel Fuchs, Lenard Berlanstein, Elinor Accampo, and Judy Stone took me to dinner at a French restaurant in Toronto where we remembered Ned and talked about the present and the future; I thank them all for warmly encouraging me to get back to history work when I might be ready to do so. I also thank historians Fran Malino, Gene Black, Cissie Fairchilds, Sharon Kettering, Patrick Harrigan, and Bob Weiner for support at a very difficult time. For the constant support that family members and close friends offer when a death is near and then occurs, I thank my sister and brother-in-law, Carol and Vern Mir, my mother-in-law Colette Newman, and my friends Susan Linde, Zenaida Uy, and Cynthia Dilgard. My most recent personal debt is to my husband Bill Weber, a fellow historian who has enriched both my life and my work as a historian.

Introduction: women and achievement, reality and rhetoric

What could a nineteenth-century European woman do, or not do, if she sought special activity, purpose, or recognition beyond her own home? As in other times and places, possibilities for individual women often were enhanced or restricted by many of the determinants that shaped the lives of their fathers, brothers, husbands, or sons. Social class, education, religion, ethnicity, race, and place of residence were important determinants, as was the nature of a person's upbringing and developing sense of self-worth. Unlike men, however, women also faced restrictions based on *gender* – that is, on a set of socially constructed beliefs about their physical and psychological nature and appropriate roles. Many, if not most, contemporaries believed that gender traits stemmed from biological differences created by God or nature. Accordingly, public authorities, opinion brokers, and families cited custom, law, and scientific premises to justify restricting many women to roles presumably suited to their distinctive traits. Indeed, many historians argue, nineteenth-century delineations of gender traits and roles became in some respects more rigid than in earlier eras.

During the nineteenth century, Europeans in industrializing countries increasingly defined women's sphere of activity as the private space of the household and men's sphere as the public space. Two familiar explanations for this delineation of roles and spheres highlight the legacy of the French Revolution and the impact of industrialization. The French Revolution excluded women from the new political rights awarded to men as voters, even as it promoted an ideology of universal and equal rights that some women would try to claim for their sex. Industrialization led to more separation of the home from the workplace, although the extent to which this affected and changed women's income-producing work varied by country, time period, and individuals' marital status. To these two causal explanations historians have added discussions of how elites fearful of political and economic change tried to shore up the status quo by placing new emphasis on mothers' roles as the first shapers of the values of the next generation. Historian Joan Scott, among others, also

1

has argued that the very rhetoric of separate spheres for men and women was itself a cause of new restrictions on women in the labor force.[1]

Yet despite the common rhetorical separation of the masculine and public sphere from the feminine and domestic sphere, lines between the public and private spheres were, in reality, often blurred. Thus historians must reckon with more than one kind of difference between familiar rhetoric and nineteenth-century actuality. For example, European countries, to varying degrees, noticeably expanded educational opportunities for girls and young women as well as for boys and young men. Although schools typically perpetuated familiar assumptions about appropriate gender roles, women whose mental horizons were expanded by instruction at home or in school might become uncomfortable with some, if not all, aspects of gender ideology. To justify engaging in activities that were somehow "public" in nature, women, and supportive men, frequently cited common notions about feminine qualities and argued that in certain "public" roles those special qualities might serve the general good. Such was the case with many nineteenth-century descriptions of women teachers' "maternal" work with children. Similar characterizations applied to nurses or pioneering social workers as well. Indeed, teachers and other nineteenth-century employed women from middling or lower-middle-class backgrounds often simply translated older descriptions of the activities of charitable or religious women to a professional realm. More unusual, of course, were those women who defied convention and tried not only to enter a supposedly masculine realm of activity but also to gain public recognition for their endeavors. Women authors, artists, scholars, scientists, and professionals with advanced training illustrate this kind of exceptional achievement, for which some pre-nineteenth-century precedents existed. When feminist organizations developed during the later nineteenth century, their goals commonly included improvements in women's legal status and education, plus access to more, and better paid, types of employment. For many feminists, political rights seemed a more daring goal and so were usually added later rather than sooner to organizations' formal agendas.

This book traces the ways in which European women from more than one kind of background sought to overcome the much-discussed divide between public and private spheres by seeking more recognition for the "public" value of their traditional activities and also by demanding and

---

[1] Joan Wallach Scott, "The Woman Worker," in *Emerging Feminism from Revolution to World War*, ed. Genevieve Fraisse and Michelle Perrot, vol. IV of *A History of Women in the West*, ed. Georges Duby and Michelle Perrot (Cambridge, Mass.: Harvard University Press, 1993), 419–44. See also Joan Wallach Scott, *Gender and the Politics of History* (New York: Columbia University Press, 1988).

gaining access to new opportunities in cultural and professional fields. It reveals how determined women managed to negotiate social, cultural, attitudinal, or legal restrictions on their sex and to expand the limits of what was possible for themselves and later generations of women. The focus on women and achievements often places women from middle- and upper-class backgrounds in the spotlight. Yet some women of more modest social origins also managed to achieve upward social mobility and public recognition as a result of new educational opportunities or by exercising special talents, especially in cultural endeavors. The study of "achievers" is not intended to suggest to readers that they are intrinsically more meritorious than the millions of women whose names are lost from the historical record. More on the circumstances faced by working-class women can be found in Rachel Fuchs's volume on *Gender and Poverty in Nineteenth-Century Europe* in this Cambridge University Press series. Recent historians of women have often criticized, and appropriately, earlier treatments of women's history that simply catalogued "women worthies" and ignored all of the others. But when women of achievement are studied within larger political, social, economic, and cultural con- texts, it is possible to explore how women tested the limits on restrictions long presumed to hold women back. Furthermore, the importance of women setting precedents should not be minimized. While many women did not want the notoriety often attached to public activities, such as was long the case for acclaimed actresses and singers, others could find hope for attaining their own goals precisely because someone else had already done so.

Like many studies of nineteenth-century European topics, this volume covers the "long" nineteenth century, beginning with the French Revo- lution of 1789 and concluding with the start of World War I in 1914. Chapter 1 explores the impact of the French Revolution on possibilities for women by examining some features of Old Regime society and then noting changes tied to the Revolution and the Napoleonic aftermath. Then follow chapters on women writers, women in the arts, women exerting "caring power" through charitable and reform activities, women and education, women and professions, and, finally, women's organ- izations promoting feminist agendas. Although Chapters 2 through 7 are thematic, they are sequenced to treat, first, areas in which some eight- eenth-century women had been active, such as literature and the arts, and then to examine later pursuits. Within chapters, topics are sequenced chronologically when appropriate.

Throughout the text, readers will note discussion of how women justified crossing gender barriers to enter types of activity previously closed to women or seen as unsuitable for them. At first glance, such justifications often seem to fall into two categories: the right of women to be treated as equals; or the right of women, as women, to do something that would benefit from the input of women's special qualities. The latter position is often termed one of seeking "equality in difference," as Karen Offen has noted in her studies of European feminism.[2] Frequently, however, individual women or organizations utilized a mixture of justifications, the exact emphasis depending upon the chronological moment, national setting, or audience being addressed.

Of necessity, the women and groups presented here frequently come from the more often studied major countries, or emerging nations, of France, England, Germany, and Italy, and in the cases of Austria (Austria-Hungary after 1867) and Russia, from the nationalities therein dominant. Comparative examples are also offered from the Low Countries, Scandinavia, Iberia, the Balkans, and minority nationalities in Austria and Russia, as well as from European encounters with parts of the nonwestern world. Some brief individual biographies are included to help highlight possibilities for women in a given type of endeavor or national context and to shed light on factors allowing for achievement. Appropriately, one may question how representative of other women's lives an individual story is. Nonetheless, historical work in recent years has witnessed a revival of biographical studies which allow for the capturing of complexities, in individual lives or in contexts, that are not readily apparent in works of social history emphasizing characteristics of groups and analysis of social class. The "new" biography, broadly defined, recognizes that individuals often have multiple identities and that individual lives must be understood within a large context that includes political, economic, cultural, religious, and, of course, gender realities.[3]

---

[2] Karen Offen, "Defining Feminism: A Comparative Historical Perspective," *Signs: Journal of Women in Culture and Society* 14 (Autumn 1988): 119–57; Karen Offen, *European Feminisms, 1700–1950: A Political History* (Stanford, Calif.: Stanford University Press, 2000).

[3] For example, Jo Burr Margadant, *The New Biography: Performing Femininity in Nineteenth-Century France* (Berkeley: University of California Press, 2000).

1 Women and the revolutionary era: negotiating public and private spaces, 1760s–early 1800s

Article One of the Declaration of the Rights of Man and the Citizen, issued by the French National Assembly in August 1789, proclaimed that "All men are born and remain free and equal in rights." Two years later Olympe de Gouges (1748–93), a humbly born former actress and aspiring playwright, offered a revised version in her Declaration of the Rights of Woman: "Woman is born free and remains equal to man in rights."[1]

Both statements on individual rights illustrate why the French Revolution in 1789 has long been considered the start of not only modern French history but also modern European history. Revolutionary advocacy for equal rights and individual freedom launched a new democratic era in European political and social history. By setting precedents for undercutting royal and aristocratic power, the Revolution inspired later generations of reformers and revolutionaries in France and elsewhere in Europe. French revolutionaries' theoretical commitment to equality led to the abolition of the Old Regime's legally defined class structure, the basis for inequities in its tax structure. Indeed, the widening debate over taxation and related issues of fairness and representation between 1787 and 1789 contributed directly to the start of the Revolution. In place of the previous legal division of society into the first estate (clergy), second estate (aristocracy), and third estate (commoners), revolutionaries envisioned a single category of citizens. On 17 June 1789, determined members of the third estate delegation, elected to the Estates General convened in May, called for retitling the Estates General the National Assembly, much to the dismay of King Louis XVI and many aristocrats. Also eliminated between 1789 and 1791 were distinctions between the rights of the Catholic majority and Protestant and Jewish minorities, a change paralleled by a greater

---

[1] Olympe de Gouges, "The Declaration of the Rights of Woman," in *The French Revolution and Human Rights: A Brief Documentary History*, ed. Lynn Hunt (Boston: Bedford Books of St. Martin's Press, 1996), 125.

secularization of society and attitudes. In the name of economic freedom, the Assembly in 1791 abolished guilds, which had protected artisans' interests but also restricted individuals' ability to enter various occupations. The massive revolt by slaves in the Caribbean colony of Saint-Domingue (modern-day Haiti) prompted the Convention, the more radical revolutionary body elected after the overthrow of the monarchy in 1792, to abolish slavery in 1794. Through such enactments the French Revolution, like the earlier American Revolution, launched a new political era in western civilizations.

But where do women fit into the French Revolution, the eventual exporting of the Revolution to other countries, and its aftermath? Was the Revolution as progressive a development for women as for men? De Gouges's statement on women's rights, unlike the Declaration of the Rights of Man and the Citizen, was not adopted by any revolutionary assembly. Furthermore, de Gouges herself was guillotined during the Convention's Reign of Terror (1793–94), her execution occurring nineteen days after that of Queen Marie Antoinette, to whom she dedicated her declaration. Some historians and political theorists, such as Joan Landes, see the fate of the widowed de Gouges, a butcher's daughter, as part of the evidence that the Revolution was not only less progressive for women than for men but actually diminished women's status.[2] That critical perspective on gender and the Revolution has fueled much recent debate, particularly since France's 1989 celebration of the bicentennial of the Revolution. It was not a completely novel view, however. Some women made similar observations in nineteenth-century memoirs, but over time their judgments fell into obscurity, dismissed by historians in later democratic eras as the complaints of disgruntled aristocrats or former beneficiaries of royal patronage who lost status or wealth because of the Revolution.

Weighing the French Revolution's short-term and long-term impact on women necessitates examination of multiple issues. The Revolution did not empower women as voters, but simply noting that fact does not adequately address the complexity of changes in society, the economy, and culture during the dramatic decade of 1789–99 and its aftermath. It is necessary, first, to look backward into eighteenth-century social and cultural realities, before the Revolution turned the pre-1789 Bourbon monarchy into the Old Regime (*ancien régime*). Then the revolutionaries' record on women's rights and that record's relationship to both previous realities and revolutionary pronouncements on universal rights require

---

[2] Joan B. Landes, *Women and the Public Sphere in the Age of the French Revolution* (Ithaca, N.Y.: Cornell University Press, 1988).

assessment. The French Revolution is not the first major historical development whose significance may seem different, in some respects, when assessed for its impact on women. Joan Kelly-Gadol's provocative question "Did women have a Renaissance?" similarly spurred discussion of whether ostensibly progressive features of the European Renaissance, including literary humanism, were as beneficial for women as for men between 1350 and 1600.[3]

Exceptional eighteenth-century women

What influence or power could women wield in France or elsewhere in Europe before 1789? Traditional European societies were typically hierarchical: social classes were legally defined, and rights or privileges were awarded on the basis of aristocratic birth or rank. Such practices became unacceptable to later democracies, which accord rights to individuals regardless of social status. Yet the unequal distribution of privileges in traditional societies allowed some women to become exceptions to general norms. Their exceptional activities also could provoke backlash, however, and spur efforts to tighten regulations to prevent more women from achieving renown or special status.

Some women became rulers before 1789, their status derived from birth or marriage. France's Salic law, invented during a disputed fourteenth-century royal succession, barred queens from ruling in their own right, but the reigns of England's Queen Elizabeth I (1558–1603) and the Austrian Empress Maria Theresa set different precedents. Mother of Marie Antoinette, Maria Theresa reigned for forty years (1740–80), surviving challenges to her right to rule during the War of the Austrian Succession. In Russia the 34-year reign of Catherine II ("the Great") began in 1762 after her husband, Tsar Peter III, was killed in a palace coup that she helped orchestrate; and she was not the first empress. Indeed, some historians contend that gender stereotypes were then less deeply ingrained in Russia than elsewhere in Europe, although others disagree. Peter I ("the Great") set the stage for women ruling Russia for two-thirds of the eighteenth century when his wife Catherine became his designated successor (1725–27). His niece Anna assumed the throne in 1730; and in 1741 Elizabeth, Peter's never-married daughter, began a twenty-year reign, during which she arranged for her nephew and successor to marry a young German princess – the future Catherine II. Cosmopolitan in

---

[3] Joan Kelly-Gadol, "Did Women Have a Renaissance?" in *Becoming Visible: Women in European History*, ed. Renate Bridenthal and Claudia Koonz (Boston: Houghton Mifflin, 1977), 137–64.

cultural tastes, Catherine II became known for her westernizing policies. Yet Russian elites were the primary beneficiaries of her enactments, for serfdom, largely gone from western Europe, remained deeply entrenched. Catherine's interests included upper-class girls' education, and she found a French model in St. Cyr, a girls' school started in 1686 by Françoise de Maintenon, second wife of Louis XIV.

For France, judgments about women's power or influence before the Revolution often highlight their role in the salons, those social gatherings in private residences where aristocrats and upper-middle-class people, the *bourgeoisie*, often mingled in a "republic of letters." A feature of the Parisian social landscape since the 1660s under Louis XIV, salons became a notable setting for discussing contemporary concerns, including arguments in texts by prominent eighteenth-century Enlightenment authors. By the second half of the eighteenth century, salons, like the press, were central to the development of what Jürgen Habermas termed a new "public sphere," positioned between the royal court and the larger society and important for the airing of views on numerous governmental and social issues.[4] Indeed, the term "public opinion" (*l'opinion publique*) came into usage by the 1750s. Men and women mingled in salons, as did aristocrats and bourgeois, and such women as Marie-Thérèse Geoffrin (1699–1777) and Suzanne Necker (1739–94), wife of Louis XVI's Swiss-born finance minister, were not only hostesses but also facilitators of discussion. The now familiar usage of the term *salon* to connote a kind of intellectual sociability, with hostesses designated as *salonnières*, developed somewhat later, however. Originally a salon was simply a room for social gatherings. As commentators later perceived salons' influence to be waning, the term salon, like the term Old Regime, became useful for characterizing pre-revolutionary society. Thus in 1800, Germaine de Staël, the Neckers' daughter, recalled the importance of intellectual interchanges for "distinguished men in all spheres" under the former monarchy and also women's contribution: "The influence of women is necessarily very great when all events occur in salons, and all character is revealed in words; in such a state of affairs, women are a power, and what is pleasing to them is cultivated."[5]

Because France remained the pacesetter in many areas of European culture, as it had been during Louis XIV's long reign, the salon inspired emulators in other capital cities. Reacting against earlier Russian cultural

---

[4] Jürgen Habermas, *The Structural Transformation of the Public Sphere: An Inquiry into a Category of Bourgeois Society*, trans. Thomas Burger and Frederick Lawrence (Cambridge, Mass.: M.I.T. Press, 1989).

[5] Quoted in Madelyn Gutwirth, *Madame de Staël, Novelist: The Emergence of the Artist as a Woman* (Urbana: University of Illinois Press, 1978), 4.

and religious traditions, including the social separation of the sexes, the westernizing Tsar Peter I encouraged women's presence at aristocratic gatherings in St. Petersburg. In London after 1750, Elizabeth Montagu (1720–1800), wife of an aristocrat, was among the hostesses whose gatherings invited comparison with French salons. Similar events in Madrid were called *tertulias*. Some late eighteenth-century Berlin salons brought Christians and Jews together in the homes of prosperous Jewish families, such as Henriette and Marcus Herz. French had replaced Latin as the *lingua franca* of educated European elites by 1700, and reading publics in London, Madrid, Berlin, Vienna, and St. Petersburg were familiar with leading French authors. In the wake of the seventeenth-century scientific "revolution," which replaced the Aristotelian-Ptolemaic model of an Earth-centered universe with one Sun-centered, the French and other Europeans could regard stimulating contemporary debates on philosophical, social, and political issues as indicative of an Age of Reason or a *siècle des lumières* (century of lights), termed in German the *Aufklärung* (Enlightenment) and in Italian *Illuminismo*.

The cultural prominence of salons, and women's role in them, also inspired critics. Already in 1687 the Abbé François de Salignac de la Mothe Fénelon's famous treatise on education for aristocratic girls at St. Cyr prescribed an emphasis on their future domestic duties as wives and mothers in order to counter the worldliness of Parisian salon society. Jean-Jacques Rousseau (1712–78) mocked the salon as "a harem of men more womanish" than their hostess,[6] and his pedagogical treatise *Émile* (1762) ridiculed and chastised the educated women who aspired to be men's intellectual equals. In England, learned women frequenting literary salons were mocked as unattractive "bluestockings" or *bas-bleus*, the equivalent French term. Initially a humorous label for a male scholar who attended Montagu's salon wearing working-class blue cotton stockings rather than a gentleman's dress stockings, the term also signified a serious attitude rather than aristocratic frivolity. Although Hannah More, a schoolmaster's daughter, celebrated Montagu's circle in her long poem *The Bas Bleu* (1786), the label soon became pejorative and applied only to women. The German philosopher Immanuel Kant warned in *Observations on the Feeling of the Beautiful and Sublime* (1764) that too much learning made women ugly. Mocking two French women, Anne Dacier, a translator of ancient classics, and the Marquise Émilie du Châtelet, translator of Isaac Newton's *Principia Mathematica*, Kant wrote

---

[6] Quoted in Dena Goodman, "Women and the Enlightenment," in *Becoming Visible: Women in European History*, 3rd edn., ed. Renate Bridenthal, Susan Mosher Stuard, and Merry E. Wiesner (Boston: Houghton Mifflin, 1998), 256.

that they "might as well even have a beard."[7] In Rousseau's *Émile*, Sophie, the fictional companion for the young hero, was educated for domesticity and motherhood. "A woman's education," Rousseau intoned, "must therefore be planned in relation to man," to enable her to "be pleasing in his sight, to win his respect and love, to train him in childhood, to tend him in manhood, ... to make his life pleasant and happy."[8] Restrictive as that message was, many contemporary women nonetheless saw in *Émile* a new valorization of their maternal roles, for Rousseau emphasized that mothers played a crucial part in children's moral and physical development. Some women also recognized inherent problems or dangers in his prescriptive limits for women's education and behavior, however, among them Stéphanie de Genlis.

Denunciations of women who stepped out of their prescribed social place were not novel in the later eighteenth century. They had both classical and biblical roots. In ancient Greece, Aristotle grounded separate gender roles and women's formal exclusion from public life in notions about men's intellectual, moral, and physical superiority. Defining the family as the basic unit of society, he assigned leadership of the family and civic society to men. Judeo-Christian biblical texts also provided rationales for women's subordination to men, beginning with Eve's punishment for making Adam sin. Christian texts did speak about the spiritual equality of the sexes, but the apostle Paul formally enjoined women to keep silent in churches. In ancient Rome, the satirist Juvenal compared learned matrons who voiced opinions at dinner parties to clanging bells. Although Plato had called for educating both men and women of the elite "guardian" class imagined for his ideal Republic, it was the Aristotelian gender polarities that medieval theologian Thomas Aquinas combined with the biblical in his *Summa Theologica* (1266). When the Italian Renaissance extended medieval universities' emphasis on Latin and classics for educated men, such gender polarities continued to figure in European humanists' pedagogical treatises. Admittedly, Baldesar Castiglione's *Book of the Courtier* (1528), a widely translated guide to upper-class comportment in Renaissance courts, recommended comparable instruction in letters and arts for both sexes, but Castiglione also assumed that while men's knowledge would impress princely employers, women's learning enhanced their ability to organize social gatherings. Furthermore, many religious and secular spokesmen continued to question whether such learning was useful or even morally appropriate for women, even upper-class women.

---

[7] Excerpt from Kant in *History of Ideas on Woman*, ed. Rosemary Agonito (New York: G. P. Putnam's Sons, 1977), 131.

[8] Jean-Jacques Rousseau, *Émile*, trans. B. Foxley (New York: Dutton, 1972), 328.

Knowledge of the classics, a badge of social distinction for the upper classes, was not deemed necessary for most children of either sex. Indeed, in 1800 many Europeans were not literate. Men were more often literate than women, and where literacy rates were high, they reflected a dovetailing of political, religious, and economic goals. Typically literacy in vernacular languages was prized more highly in towns and cities than in rural areas because it was useful for economic activities. The Protestant Reformation's emphasis on Bible reading to deepen piety also spurred creation of schools for both sexes in Germany, England and Scotland, the Dutch Netherlands, Scandinavia, and Switzerland, as did Counter-Reformation competition between Catholics and Protestants in some French, German, and Swiss regions. Catholic schools likewise taught reading, if not writing, as an aid to learning the fundamentals of faith, but many moralists worried that literacy exposed the "weaker sex" to ideas encouraging immoral acts, such as writing love letters. The ability to sign a marriage register was a common measurement for literacy but did not indicate depth of knowledge. In Protestant Prussia, where Kings Frederick William I and Frederick II ("the Great") called for compulsory education, about three-fourths of men and half the women were literate by 1800. English rates were comparable: 68 percent of men and 43 percent of women. In Amsterdam in 1780 Dutch male literacy reached 85 percent and female literacy, 64 percent. Yet in France in 1787, only 27 percent of women were literate, as compared to 47 percent of men. French female literacy was noticeably higher in towns, however, and the Catholic Church subsidized most day and boarding schools. In Catholic areas without strong religious rivalries, such as Spain, education often lagged as Counter-Reformation bans on vernacular editions of the Bible reinforced negative attitudes toward reading, and religious culture remained oral and visual.

Instruction at home was typically the core educational experience for upper- and middle-class European girls. By the late eighteenth century, against the backdrop of Enlightenment emphasis on developing the rational man, some governments took greater interest in schooling for boys and sometimes also for girls. Russia's Smolny Institute for Noble Girls, founded in 1764 and modeled on St. Cyr, taught religion, foreign languages, morals and good manners, music and dancing, but less history and geography. Under "enlightened despot" Joseph II, Austria's Hapsburg regime created a school for army officers' daughters in 1775 and one for civil servants' daughters in 1786, both preparing girls to become governesses should they need to work. Russia's 1786 education statute envisioned an urban network of free secondary and coeducational primary schools open to all non-serf classes, but aristocratic and middle-class boys were the major beneficiaries, schoolboys outnumbering girls ten to one in 1800. In pre-1789 Paris, schools accommodated about one-fifth of all girls. Daughters of Parisian merchants and artisans filled about 90 percent of places in day schools, while nobles' daughters often spent a few years at boarding schools.

As in Rousseau's *Émile*, teachers usually tried to prepare boys and girls for different gender roles. Like Fénelon previously, or like later critics who railed against the "new woman" of the 1890s or the "flapper" after World War I, Rousseau and other eighteenth-century critics of some women's activities issued prescriptions for correct behavior at a moment when many people realized that certain women were deviating from general norms and gaining recognition, and sometimes financial benefit, from their endeavors. By the later 1700s, biographical dictionaries of notable women appeared in various countries, their very publication confirming contemporary interest in what women accomplished in the past or present. Although gaining fame or great fortune is not most people's experience in any time or place, an exceptional man's accomplishments would not be denounced for deviating from masculine norms and thereby posing dangers to the well-being of families or the moral foundation of the social order.

In what ways did exceptional women gain attention through achievements before 1789, and how did contemporaries react to their successes? Examples from the arts, literature, and pedagogy are illustrative.

In France, the royal court, like earlier Renaissance courts, supported gifted writers, painters, and musicians. Marie Antoinette's appreciation of the talented Élisabeth Vigée-Lebrun (1755–1842), who painted flattering portraits of the queen and aristocratic patrons, provided this professional artist of modest origins with access to high society and valuable commissions, and also secured her admission to the Royal Academy of Painting and Sculpture (Figure 1.1). Instructed by her artist father at a time when the Royal Academy, like counterparts in other countries, excluded women from training in its own school, Vigée-Lebrun was not the first woman judged worthy of inclusion among artistic notables in France or elsewhere. The Florentine Academy had admitted a woman painter, Artemisia Gentileschi, in 1616, fifty-three years after its founding. Of the 450 Royal Academy members admitted between its founding in 1648 and abolition during the Revolution, fifteen were women, the first woman entering in 1663. Louis XIV declared support for "all those who are excellent in the arts of Painting and Sculpture ... without regard to the difference of sex."[9] At least 500

[9] Quoted in Ann Sutherland Harris and Linda Nochlin, *Women Artists: 1550–1900* (New York: Los Angeles County Museum of Art and Alfred A. Knopf, 1977; 6th reprinting, 1984), 34.

Figure 1.1 Élisabeth Vigée-Lebrun, "Self-Portrait," 1790.

women artists (and probably more) were active in Europe between 1400 and 1800, and the 290 identified for the eighteenth century were a larger contingent than that of any previous century. Those 500 included 212 French, 130 Italian, 67 Dutch or Flemish, 41 German, 25 English, 17 Spanish, 5 Swiss, and 3 Scandinavian women.

When Vigée-Lebrun entered the Royal Academy in 1783, two other women were already members: Marie Thérèse Reboul (1729–1805), a miniature painter and wife of a prominent artist, had entered in 1757, and Anne Vallayer-Coster (1744–1818), known for floral and still-life painting, entered in 1770, receiving the title "painter to the Queen" in 1780. Vigée-Lebrun and portrait painter Adélaïde Labille-Guiard (1749–1803) were admitted on the same day, but accompanying their entry was a royal decree making concessions to men hostile to official recognition of talented women. Henceforth no more than four women could be members at the same time. The Academy, with fifty full members, once included six women, but men had also tried to exclude all women in 1706. That attempt, like another in 1770, was invalid without the force of a royal decree. Many Academy members resisted Vigée-Lebrun's admission on the grounds that her husband's work as an art dealer disqualified her. Longstanding Academy rules excluded those engaged in such commerce, and a wife presumably shared her husband's status. But recognizing that the king and queen supported her membership, the Academy used her special case to press the king for a general rule limiting women members to four. The Academy's director argued that "this number is sufficient to honor their talent; women cannot be useful to the progress of the arts because the modesty of their sex forbids them from being able to study after nature and in the public school established and founded by your Majesty."[10] Women in the Academy, unlike male artists, could not have their own studios in the Louvre, and in 1787 the Academy reprimanded neoclassical painter Jacques-Louis David for violating the rule against instructing women pupils in his Louvre studio.

Royal Academy membership did entitle women artists to exhibit in its biennial Salon, and the ambitious Vigée-Lebrun and Labille-Guiard utilized the opportunity. For Labille-Guiard, a haberdasher's daughter instructed first by a painter living near her father's shop and later by the distinguished Maurice Quentin de la Tour, official recognition brought commissions from the royal family and an annual pension of 1,000 livres. After separating from her husband around 1779, Labille-Guiard had established a studio to give lessons to girls, and her painting of herself with two pupils, exhibited in 1785, was testimony to the practical value of artistic skills. Because social elites regarded drawing, like musical ability or needlework, as a necessary accomplishment for refined young ladies, women could earn money as art or music teachers.

In Great Britain, the talented portrait painter Angelica Kauffmann (1741–1807) and the floral painter Mary Moser were among the forty founding members of the Royal Academy of Arts in 1766. But there would be no women successors until 1922. In Sweden, portrait painter

---

[10] Quoted in Mary D. Sheriff, *The Exceptional Woman: Elisabeth Vigée-Lebrun and the Cultural Politics of Art* (Chicago: University of Chicago Press, 1996), 105–06.

Ulrica Pasch (1735–96) was among the fifteen initial members of the Royal Academy of Fine Arts, recognized by King Gustaf III in 1773, and the Royal Danish Academy of Fine Arts elected one woman in 1780 and another in 1790. Spain's Royal Academy of Fine Arts, founded in 1752, also admitted women to its three membership categories, and by 1808 33 women constituted eight percent of those admitted. Yet before 1789, the Imperial Academy of Arts in St. Petersburg, dating from 1757, accepted only one woman, French sculptress Marie-Anne Collot (1748–1821). Brought to Russia in 1766 by her mentor Étienne Falconet, she worked with him on an equestrian statue of Peter the Great and produced busts of Empress Catherine, earning a substantial income during a twelve-year stay.

Hostility to women artists in France during the 1780s extended beyond limiting Academy membership or excluding women students from studios in the Louvre. When four women exhibited works at the Fall 1783 Salon, one reviewer faulted Vigée-Lebrun's portrait of herself holding a palette and brushes and also mocked her ambitious efforts to paint historical subjects. The less prestigious genres of portraiture and still-life were deemed the appropriate ones for women. Since the Renaissance, education in the classics was considered a prerequisite for artists' rendition of historical and mythological subjects, and few women received such an education. Women were also presumed to lack the rationality or self-control that producing historical paintings required. Discussing Vigée-Lebrun's allegorical "Peace Bringing Back Abundance," the critical reviewer opined that she could not be a real history painter because, "The arms, the head, the heart of women lack the essential qualities to follow men into the lofty region of the fine arts. If nature could produce one of them capable of this great effort, it would be a monstrosity"[11] The Academy refused to recognize the ambitious Vigée-Lebrun as a painter of historical subjects, and she discovered that gaining public attention also entailed public ridicule. Nonetheless, she was more successful than any previous woman artist in France. Remembered for paintings of Marie Antoinette with her children, she also painted many other prominent men and women and could charge high prices. Unsurprisingly, she was later among the women who, having lived through the revolutionary era, preferred the Old Regime.

Teaching also provided women from suitable backgrounds with employment in court circles. Countess Stéphanie de Genlis (1746–1830), daughter of an impoverished noble and wife of a marquis, became the governess of the daughters of the Duke de Chartres (later the Duke

[11] Quoted in ibid., 191.

d'Orléans). Regretting the inadequacy of her own education, the largely self-taught Genlis developed an instructional program influenced by her reading of Enlightenment philosophers but also critical of their attacks on religious institutions. She favored "useful" learning in history, geography, foreign languages, and mathematics, and on-site visits to workshops and farms, and in 1777 she was provided with a secluded locale to test her educational theories. In 1782, by which time she had published more than a dozen pedagogical volumes, her job title was changed from governess (*gouvernante*) to governor (*gouverneur*), signifying the unprecedented, and not uncontroversial, assumption by a woman of supervision of Orleanist boys' education as well. Several male tutors resigned in protest from the Orléans household. One of her pupils, the future King Louis-Philippe (b. 1773), remembered her as a stern taskmaster. Genlis's publications included the popular and widely translated *Adèle et Théodore* (1782), with prescriptions for girls' education that partly matched and partly countered Rousseau. She agreed that marriage and motherhood were women's destiny but argued that Rousseau's restrictions on female learning would hinder their ability to become the moral mothers he prized. Her stories in *Veillées du Château* (1784) included attention to women artists, past and present, and a timely defense of Vigée-Lebrun. Presenting a mother discussing art with two daughters when they visit a Salon exhibition, Genlis had one girl call Vigée-Lebrun a "superior genius." The mother then recounts the harsh criticism directed at Vigée-Lebrun, yet adds reassuringly, "But the public is just and cannot be prevented from praising whatever pleases and strikes [it]." Genlis herself experienced public ridicule along with fame. The poem "The Enigma, or Portrait of a Famous Woman," published in a literary review in 1782, depicted her as a hermaphrodite: "Physically I am of the feminine type/ But mentally, morally I am of the masculine."[12] Yet she also claimed in her later memoirs that philosopher Jean d'Alembert suggested during the early 1780s that she and three other women might become the first of their sex to join the official literary greats in the *Académie Française* (French Academy), founded in 1635, if only she would stop criticizing some philosophers for doubting religious tenets.

Jeanne Campan (1752–1822), Genlis's contemporary, avoided such controversy before 1789. The daughter of a Foreign Ministry official, she shared her brother's lessons from male tutors and excelled in music. At

---

[12] Quotations in Anne L. Schroder, "Going Public Against the Academy in 1784: Mme de Genlis Speaks Out on Gender Bias," *Eighteenth-Century Studies* 32.3 (1999): 379; and Sheriff, *Exceptional Woman*, 184.

the age of fifteen, she became a "reader" (*lectrice*) in the household of Louis XV's daughter. Marriage to the son of a secretary to the Queen positioned Campan to become a lady-in-waiting to Marie Antoinette, experience facilitating her earning of a living as an educator after the monarchy fell. Economic necessity dictated her employment before 1789 and later, for her husband, like Vigée-Lebrun's husband, was an unreliable spendthrift, and Campan had a young son to support.

Less well known to French high society than women directly connected to the court was another exceptional working woman benefiting from royal support, Angélique Marguerite Le Boursier du Coudray (d. 1794), the "king's midwife." The government supported her work as an instructor in midwifery techniques, which she toured France to demonstrate from 1760 to 1783, using a model of the female pelvis that she marketed and sold, along with a textbook that she authored. She and her associates trained about 10,000 women, thereby perhaps contributing to the post-1750 population increase from 20 million to 26 million, usually attributed to greater agricultural productivity and the decline of plague. Du Coudray's instruction of women helping women clients set a precedent for later regimes' selective hiring of women in positions of responsibility when such assignments could be justified as requiring knowledge and sensibilities deemed uniquely feminine and, for reasons of modesty or propriety, be better filled by a woman. By the late eighteenth century, however, many male physicians questioned midwives' competence, citing new scientific and medical literature that linked women's presumably lesser intellectual capacities or suitability for roles other than mothering to their physical differences. Better understanding of the female reproductive organs had replaced the ancient notion of woman as a less developed man. Although du Coudray's adopted niece followed in her footsteps, there were evidently no others comparably recognized. The precedent for a French woman traveling in an official capacity also was often forgotten, for in 1900 critics still claimed that the state's employment of women inspectors who traveled to evaluate schools or public assistance providers set dangerous new precedents.

In Russia, Princess Ekaterina Dashkova (1743–1810) was the first woman, other than an empress, to hold an important official post. Unlike du Coudray, who needed to support herself, Dashkova was wealthy and privileged. Educated in the home of her uncle, Chancellor Mikhail Vorontsov, she married at the age of fifteen and was widowed within six years. She met the future Empress Catherine in 1759 and participated in the court conspiracy that brought her friend to power in 1762. Dashkova's memoirs portrayed their friendship as that of the only two women "who did any serious reading." Catherine herself was a prolific writer, authoring twenty-five plays and many articles and children's stories. In 1783, after Dashkova's return from extensive travels, including a sojourn in Edinburgh where her son attended the university, Catherine appointed her to head the Russian Academy of Sciences, founded under Peter I and with censorship responsibilities. Although Dashkova wrote that she accepted the role reluctantly because "God himself, by creating me a woman, had exempted me from accepting [such] employment," she soon proposed creating a Russian literary academy, modeled on the Académie Française.[13] She directed both academies for eleven years, founded two scholarly journals, and oversaw completion of the first official dictionary of the Russian language. No woman attained full membership in the French Academy of Sciences until 1979 or entered the Académie Française until 1980, although each awarded prizes to accomplished women long before that.

Apart from the prestigious national academies, hundreds of learned societies and academies existed in cities or smaller states, some officially sponsored and some privately organized. Some included women. As with art academies, Italian learned societies provided a model for the rest of Europe. The first Italian literary academy to admit women was the Arcadian Society (*Accademia degli Arcadia*), founded in 1690 and based in papal Rome. It reserved at least six memberships each year for women, and as of 1728, 74 women were just under 3 percent of 2,419 members. Most of these women came from aristocratic or upper-class families, and the poetess Maria Maddelena Morelli was crowned poet laureate on the Capitoline Hill in 1776, a ceremony reminiscent of the honoring of the early Renaissance poet Petrarch in 1341.

In Spain, more than fifty local societies participated in discussions of reform characteristic of the Enlightenment during the 1770s and 1780s. Josefa Amar y Borbón (1749–1833), daughter of a court doctor and wife of a jurist, became the first woman admitted to the Economic Society of Aragon, to which her husband belonged, in 1782. To request membership she submitted her translation of an Italian treatise on Spanish literature. Enjoying the recognition membership provided, although she did not regularly attend meetings, she sent an essay on the intellectual equality of the sexes to the prestigious Economic Society of Madrid in 1786. The leading center for discussion of reforms, the Madrid Society had just admitted two women on an exceptional basis. One was the

---

[13] Ekaterina Dashkova, *The Memoirs of Princess Dashkova*, trans. and ed. Kyril Fitzlyon (London: John Calder, 1958), reprint, introduction by Jehanne Gheith, afterword by A. Woronzoff-Dashkoff (Durham, N.C.: Duke University Press, 1995), 31, 201.

young María Quintana Guzmán y la Cerda (1768–1803), a child prodigy already named as the first, and only, honorary woman member of the Royal Academy, Spain's counterpart of the Académie Française, and also awarded a doctorate in letters by the University of Alcalá. As the Madrid Society debated admitting other women, Amar complained in her essay that "men, not satisfied after having reserved for themselves positions, honors, compensations for their work ... have also deprived the members of our sex of the satisfactions of having an enlightened mind."[14] Better education could remedy deficiencies perceived in women's intellectual abilities, she argued. The Madrid Society subsequently opted for placing women on a separate and subordinate women's committee, confirmed by a decree from Charles III in 1787. That committee, launched with fifteen aristocratic members, soon welcomed Amar. Its activities included supporting the municipal orphanage and promoting women's education and vocational training.

Amar y Borbón was not the only published woman author in late eighteenth-century Spain, but women writers were more numerous in England and France. English women had a relatively easier time than French women in publishing their work, even though they numbered only about 4 percent of published English authors during the 1780s, as compared to 2 percent in France. One study of 913 English women who published between 1660 and 1800 notes a marked increase for the decades after 1760, when literacy rates were rising and some women authors' success inspired emulators. Because France had a population triple that of England, the contrast between 78 women with works in print in France during the 1780s and 119 English women publishing for the first time during the 1770s, or another 166 publishing for the first time during the 1780s, is all the more striking. Many prominent French women writers were aristocrats like Genlis, and most of the others came from bourgeois families. Such origins are not surprising because family support was crucial for young women's access to education, whether at home or in a convent school.

Many successful English women authors came from middle-class backgrounds. The widowed Catherine Macaulay (1731–91), whose father was a landowner and mother a banker's daughter, gained renown with her eight-volume *History of England from the Accession of James I* (1763–83), a work critical of the monarchy and published when reformers were advocating extension of the right to vote for the House of

---

[14] Quoted in Eva M. Kahiluoto Rudat, "The View from Spain: Rococo Finesse and Esprit versus Plebeian Manners," in *French Women and the Age of Enlightenment*, ed. Samia I. Spencer (Bloomington: Indiana University Press, 1984), 403.

Commons. Macaulay tackled history even though novels, poetry, or pedagogical works were considered more appropriate literary genres for women, and she impressed the younger Mary Wollstonecraft as "the woman of the greatest abilities that this country has ever produced." Manon Roland, among her French admirers, admitted in her memoirs that she would have liked "to be the Macaulay of my country."[15] Like counterparts elsewhere, English women authors approached publication with concern about its impact on their personal reputations. Thus Fanny Burney (1752–1840) disguised her handwriting on the manuscript of *Evelina* (1778), her first successful novel, because printers of manuscripts that she had copied for her father, an organist and music historian, knew her hand. A brother and a male cousin negotiated with her publisher. Because income from writing was inadequate for the unmarried Burney's needs, she accepted the Queen's offer of a court post as Second Keeper of the Robes in 1786, resigning after five years, with the award of an annual pension of £100.

Among German writers, Sophie von La Roche (1730–1807) is often designated the first professional woman author. A physician's daughter who gained aristocratic status through marriage in 1753 to an official in the courts of Mainz and Trier, she attracted attention with her first novel, *The History of Lady Sophia Sternheim* (1771, *Geschichte des Fräuleins von Sternheim*). After her husband's reformist views led to his dismissal in 1780, she produced educational fiction for women. Late in life she helped educate her granddaughter Bettina, a future author.

A decade after La Roche's *Sophie Sternheim*, Betje Wolff (1738–1804) and Aagje Deken coauthored the first Dutch novel, *Sarah Burgerhart* (1782), issued in three editions within four years and translated into English and French. Telling their story through letters (a format popular in England), Wolff and Deken exposed the Dutch middle class's values and vices, warning that without proper education, "the best girls" were "in danger of falling into lamentable tragedies."[16]

Like successful women authors and artists, some actresses and women concert performers enjoyed considerable fame. Yet work on the stage also carried connotations of immorality. Here again, national context made a difference. The Catholic Church then refused to administer sacraments to actors and actresses, judging their assumption of someone

---

[15] Quotations in Joanne Shattock, *The Oxford Guide to British Women Writers* (Oxford: Oxford University Press, 1993), 273; and Mary S. Trouille, *Sexual Politics in the Enlightenment: Women Writers Read Rousseau* (Albany: State University of New York Press, 1997), 188.

[16] Quoted in Henk Vynckier, "Elizabeth Wolff-Bekker," in *An Encyclopedia of Continental Women Writers*, ed. Katharina M. Wilson, 2 vols. (New York: Garland, 1991), II: 1352.

else's identity on stage to be immoral. Sarah Siddons (1755–1831), the expressive English actress, avoided notoriety, however, and carefully cultivated an off-stage image of domesticity and maternal devotion to her seven children. Her fame and respectability exceeded that of any previous or contemporary actress, and her reputation benefited not only from theater critics' praise but also artists' flattering images. Joshua Reynolds painted her as "the tragic muse" in 1784. The essayist William Hazlitt pronounced her "the stateliest ornament of the public mind."[17]

In sum, certain women successful in creative endeavors and the occasional women rulers gained considerable public attention before 1789. Yet women with a claim to fame also risked drawing criticism or mockery for stepping into the limelight, as Rousseau's and Kant's critiques indicate. Such critiques set the tone for the next generations' discussions of suitable activities for women in public or quasi-public settings.

The impact of the French Revolution

The French Revolution's promises of reform inspired many men and women, but its outbreak and eventual radicalization posed problems and dangers for people closely linked to the Bourbon monarchy. A Parisian crowd's takeover of the Bastille prison on 14 July, 1789 and Louis XVI's yielding to demands of the National Assembly prompted the King's younger brother and some aristocrats to begin an emigration that intensified after August 1792. Vigée-Lebrun and Genlis were but two of the more than 14,000 women (at least 2,506 of them aristocrats) who emigrated between 1789 and 1799. After the October Days of 1789, when a large Paris crowd, including many women, marched to the royal palace at Versailles and forced the royal family to take up residence at the Tuileries palace in Paris, Vigée-Lebrun fled to Italy with her daughter. Genlis, by contrast, shared the enthusiasm of the Orléans family for the constitutional plans of the Assembly, which also moved into Paris. She did not find Paris threatening until 1791, after the King and his family's failed effort to flee from the capital. Among the authors fueling the mounting anti-royalist sentiment was Louise Kéralio-Robert (1758–1821), who targeted the *Crimes of the Queens of France, from the Beginning of the Monarchy to Marie-Antoinette*.

Debate among historians about the Revolution's significance for women rests, of course, on more than the fate of once-privileged

---

[17] Quoted in Robyn Asleson, "'She Was Tragedy Personified': Crafting the Siddons Legend in Art and Life," in *Sarah Siddons and Her Portraitists*, ed. Robyn Asleson (Los Angeles: J. Paul Getty Museum, 1999), 90.

individuals. At issue are the relationship between gender and the very nature of the new political ideology, and also the content of specific laws. The French Revolution, like the American Revolution, offered the western world a political theory of universal rights. Yet each also incorporated gendered language in their basic statements of principles and did not extend new political rights to women. The Declaration of Independence of 1776 proclaimed that "all men are created equal" and endowed with "inalienable rights" to "life, liberty and the pursuit of happiness." The French Declaration of 1789 was titled "The Rights of Man and the Citizen." Most revolutionary leaders did not envision extending the right to vote for public officials to women, although the Marquis de Condorcet, Marie-Jean Caritat, had advocated this in 1788, and the state of New Jersey allowed unmarried women meeting qualifications for voting to do so until 1807, when they were excluded. Women's exclusion from political rights required justification, for which two rationales loomed large. One rationale, echoing Rousseau, termed women's roles in the domestic sphere "natural" for their sex and thus branded their activities in the public or political sphere unnatural. Medical and scientific authorities provided a second rationale: the idea that biological differences between the sexes "naturally" led to different societal roles.

During the French Revolution, nonetheless, some women tried to expand women's rights more fully than was the case in the new American republic before 1800. Other advocates besides Gouges included the Dutch-born Etta Palm d'Aelders, who started a revolutionary women's club, and Théroigne de Méricourt, born in the Austrian Netherlands. Pauline Léon, an actress, and Claire Lacombe, a chocolate maker educated by her father, founded the Society of Revolutionary Republican Women in Paris in May 1793, its members proclaiming themselves "women citizens" (*citoyennes*). Women also participated in revolutionary crowds. As the history of more than one modern revolution reveals, people living through moments of change often expect, as old institutions crumble and laws are discarded, that more will be altered than proves to be the case, especially when forces for change are countered by supporters of the older order. Yet before the Reign of Terror silenced many independent voices, women across France founded more than fifty pro-Revolution clubs between 1789 and 1793, and individual women made proposals to enhance women's roles and possibilities.

Etta Palm d'Aelders (1743–99) envisioned a supervisory role for women in many public services that the revolutionary state planned to establish as it took over the education, poor relief, and medical care previously managed by Catholic orders. In February 1790 the National

Assembly abolished monastic orders, in part as a cost-cutting measure because the state had taken control of church property, but also because many revolutionaries shared the view of Enlightenment precursors who thought cloistered establishments served no socially useful purpose. The dissolution of convents meant the end, for the moment, of a distinctive women's space. Yet because many religious women had helped staff Catholic hospitals, other charitable institutions, and girls' schools during the Old Regime, Palm's advocacy was not completely novel. Her proposal to the Assembly of the Friends of Truth in 1791 cited familiar assumptions about women's "maternal" nature to argue that women were well suited to investigate poor people's requests for public assistance and to supervise education and the hiring of wet nurses. She was also president of the Society of Women Friends of Truth.

Two years later, the revolutionary Convention dashed many hopes and expectations of women like Palm, who fled back to the Netherlands in 1793. France had been at war with anti-revolutionary Austria and Prussia since April 1792, and in August 1792 a Parisian crowd overthrew Louis XVI, who was perceived as sympathetic to the enemy. The fall of the monarchy also doomed the Legislative Assembly, elected under the terms of the Constitution of 1791. A new constitutional Convention now proposed to replace the previously restricted right to vote with universal manhood suffrage. As the number of states warring with France increased in 1793 and the war took a greater toll on resources – a toll exacerbated by the outbreak of civil war in western France in March 1793 – the Jacobin bloc in the Convention demanded harsher measures against internal enemies of the Revolution. The ensuing Reign of Terror, legitimized by the Law of Suspects in September 1793, soon silenced many critics of the Jacobin leaders and resulted in the arrest of a half million suspected enemies of the Revolution and the deaths of at least 35,000 of those suspects, including 16,000 sentenced by revolutionary courts. Women were about 14 percent of those arrested in Paris (1,305 of 9,294), about 9 percent (1,332) of those sentenced to death in the entire country, and 20 percent of executed aristocrats (226 of 1,158).

In the climate of mounting repression, even some women sympathetic to the Revolution fared poorly. The Convention, reacting to a clash between the Society of Revolutionary Republican Women and a group of market women whom the Society wanted to compel to wear the red liberty bonnet, outlawed women's political clubs on 30 October 1793. Convention deputies embraced Jean-Baptiste Amar's argument, on behalf of the Committee of General Security, that women should not meet in "political associations" because they would "be obliged to sacrifice to them more important cares to which nature calls them," namely the "private" or domestic functions in the social order that result "from the difference between man and woman." The ill-fated Marie Antoinette had gone to the guillotine on 16 October (nine months after Louis XVI), and execution of two other politically prominent women followed in November: Gouges and Manon Roland (b. 1754), a former Girondin minister's wife whose salon had furthered his political career. When some women wearing red liberty caps subsequently approached the Paris city government, asking to be heard, city councillor Pierre Chaumette denounced such public action as "contrary to all the laws of nature." He also cited the chilling examples of the recently executed Roland, "that haughty wife ... who thought herself suited to govern the republic," and the "shameless" Gouges "who abandoned the cares of her household to involve herself in the republic" before her head "fell under the avenging blade of the laws."[18] Jeanne Dubarry, mistress of Louis XV, was executed in December. In May 1795 the post-Terror Convention banned women from all political meetings and forbade groups of more than five women from assembling in the streets.

The references to "nature" as the basis for the differences between the societal roles of men and of women loom large in some historians' and political theorists' contention that modern republicanism, drawing on precedents in ancient Athens or Rome as well as on scientific pronouncements on sexual difference, was by definition wedded to designating the new rights of citizens as for men only. Condorcet, who offered the opposing argument that there was no "natural difference between men and women that can legitimately found [women's] exclusion from a right," was in a distinct minority among revolutionaries.[19] And Condorcet, too, became a victim of the Revolution, killing himself in prison in 1794 rather than waiting for execution.

The harshness of revolutionaries' words and deeds regarding politically active women in 1793 should not obscure more positive aspects of the Revolution for women. To a limited extent, women benefited legally from revolutionaries' professed commitment to equality. The reform of inheritance law in 1791 eliminated the practice of primogeniture (the eldest son obtaining the bulk of an estate) and stipulated that daughters should share equally with brothers in a parental legacy. The divorce law of 1792, another challenge to the Catholic Church which did not recognize divorce, was also egalitarian in permitting both sexes to seek divorce on exactly the same grounds. Furthermore, the Constitution

[18] Amar and Chaumette statements in Lynn Hunt, ed., The French Revolution and Human Rights: A Brief Documentary History. (Boston: Bedford Books of St. Martin's Press, 1996), 137–39.

[19] Excerpted in Hunt, ed., *French Revolution*, 121.

of 1791 envisioned free public primary schools for all children, even though plans for implementation assumed some differences between what boys' schools and girls' schools would offer. Charles-Maurice de Talleyrand-Périgord, for example, emphasized that girls' schools should teach the "virtues of domestic life" and "talents useful in the government of a family."[20] Yet by also recognizing that what mothers taught children was vital for imbuing the next generations with France's new political values, revolutionaries assigned new significance to girls' schooling. To educate future mothers, both the constitutional monarchy of the early Revolution and the subsequent republic assumed the need for public schooling. Other concerns took priority after France went to war, however, and limited educational progress.

The Revolution did not exclude women from activity in some cultural arenas where they had gained recognition previously. In the case of women's authorship, revolutionary policy had positive features, as historian Carla Hesse demonstrated. Whereas 78 women had works in print in France between 1777 and 1788, 329 women had works published between 1789 and 1800. Nearly all of the latter were living authors (17 died before 1789), and the majority (198) were married. Women authors, like their male counterparts, benefited from the Revolution's ending of Old Regime censorship (however ineffective that sometimes was) and the consequent expansion of the literary marketplace. The pace of political change after 1789 also heightened readers' demand for commentary on current developments. Writing for an audience was, of course, a kind of public activity, even if done at home, and in 1793 Jacobin leaders insisted that women did not belong in the public arena. Yet it was not the act of writing but rather controversial political views that doomed Gouges and Roland. And women did not shy away from writing political commentary. Of 657 publications by women during the revolutionary decade, 251 were political pamphlets, a genre certainly not deemed as "feminine" as the novel. Women's other published works included 96 novels, 49 plays, 39 educational treatises, and 38 volumes of poetry.

The very act of writing was important as self-assertion, a testimony to an individual's awareness of having something to say to a larger public than one's immediate family. Manon Roland's example is instructive. Although she once had written an essay on women's education for a contest sponsored by the academy of Besançon (unpublished until 1864), she stayed in the background when her husband's political

---

[20] Quoted in Linda L. Clark, *Schooling the Daughters of Marianne: Textbooks and the Socialization of Girls in Modern French Primary Schools* (Albany: State University of New York Press, 1984), 7.

associates gathered in her salon, from which she excluded other women. She also knew that many people held negative opinions of women authors who gained public attention. But when imprisoned after the Jacobins ousted the Girondins from the Convention in June 1793, Roland wrote her *Appeal to Impartial Posterity*, combining personal history and political commentary. First published in 1795 after the Terror, her memoir ended with the prediction, "And I too will live on for future generations." Gouges also anticipated that her patriotic self-sacrifice would keep her name alive "in full glory among future generations."[21]

Less statistically impressive than women's publishing record was a small increase in performances of women's opera librettos or opera music during the Revolution. Between 1770 and 1788, an average of only one woman's work per year was performed, and that became two per year between 1789 and 1800. The ending of controls on musical theater in 1791 facilitated this trend, for by 1795 there were five times as many halls as in 1789. Julie Candeille's *Catherine, or the Beautiful Farmer*, which opened in December 1792, was the most successful of the women's musical works. Instructed by her father, a composer and singer, Candeille (1767–1834) was an accomplished vocalist, pianist, and harpist who had appeared before the king in her early teens. She also acted in Paris and provincial cities. In 113 performances of the tale of the virtuous Catherine, Candeille dominated the cast, singing and accompanying herself on the piano and harp. Justifying her career in 1795, she denied being motivated by "pride" or "pretension" and instead cited economic necessity, a more suitable explanation for a woman: "Submissiveness and necessity led me to the theatre: a propensity for such work and a love of it emboldened me to write. These two resources, united, are my sole means of survival."[22]

Women artists also continued professional activity during the Revolution, Vigée-Lebrun's example of voluntary but well-advised exile notwithstanding. Vigée-Lebrun was evidently the only painter attached to the old court who was repeatedly slandered in print during the Revolution – as was her patron Marie Antoinette. The Revolution's leading official painter, David, certainly disliked Vigée-Lebrun. Her husband, after trying to justify her absence in Italy as that of an artist traveling to a traditional mecca for study and training, secured a divorce in 1794 because laws on the confiscation of émigré property threatened his assets.

[21] Quotations in Trouille, *Sexual Politics*, 315.
[22] Quoted in Judith Tick, "Women in Music, II, 3: Western Classical Traditions, 1500–1800," in *New Grove Dictionary of Music and Musicians*, 2nd edn., ed. Stanley Sadie and John Tyrrell, 29 vols. (London: Macmillan, 2001), XXVII: 525.

Labille-Guiard did not experience comparable difficulties, even though the Royal Academy responded to her proposal to drop its quota on women members by excluding women from discussions of its reorganization and reducing their status in 1791 to that of honorary members. She lost patrons associated with the court but found new commissions. Her portraits of eight revolutionary deputies, including Talleyrand and Maximilien Robespierre, were among the canvases by twenty-two women (along with 773 by men) that were displayed at the Salon of 1791, the first Salon open to artists not in the Royal Academy. The enterprising Labille-Guiard continued giving lessons to girls until 1793, and she suggested starting a school to teach poor girls artistic skills with industrial applications, a project endorsed by Talleyrand but not implemented. She was also among the first women to obtain a divorce.

After the Royal Academy was abolished in 1793, at David's urging, its replacements included the Popular and Republican Society of the Arts, which Labille-Guiard joined, as did twenty other women painters, two women sculptors, and four engravers. But when the Convention banned women's political clubs, male artists voted to exclude women because they were "different from men in every respect" and should not take jobs destined for men. One republican complained that Vigée-Lebrun had inspired too many women who "wished to busy themselves with painting although they should only occupy themselves with embroidering the sword-belts and caps of the police."[23] Nonetheless, some women continued to paint revolutionary heroes and patriotic scenes. Soon after the Convention ended the Terror in July 1794, the Society of the Arts reversed itself and allowed women members to return, but four months later the government dissolved this and other popular societies. Women were not eligible for full membership in the Fine Arts section of the new Institut de France, the official body established in October 1795 to replace pre-revolutionary academies and later reorganized by Napoleon Bonaparte. Yet Labille-Guiard managed in 1795, with support from a senior administrator of museums, to obtain lodging and a studio in the Louvre, benefits denied women under the Old Regime. She also received an annual pension of 2,000 livres. Although women seeking artistic training still faced significant obstacles (see Chapter 3), women artists' exclusion from a new official academy, like women writers' exclusion from the Académie Française, mattered far less in practical terms than their ability to reach a commercial market. Artists found buyers through Salon exhibitions, and in 1801 the 192 Salon exhibitors included 28 women.

---

[23] Quoted in Harris and Nochlin, *Women Artists*, 45–46.

Actresses' status at the Comédie Française, the first official state theater, also became an issue during the Revolution. The Catholic Church had excommunicated actors and actresses, and the royal government barred actors from holding local public offices. Yet, since the seventeenth-century, performers enjoyed royal patronage, the Comédie Française becoming known as the house of Molière, whose comedies Louis XIV enjoyed. In 1786 the Conservatory of Dramatic Arts was started. Legal discrimination against thespians ceased with the Revolution, one aristocratic deputy crediting "the Enlightenment, the love of the arts, and reason" with undercutting old prejudices against actors.[24] The ending of restrictions on opening commercial theaters in 1791, like the freeing of the press, also paved the way for reaching larger audiences. But actresses' participation in the internal governance of an official troupe was controversial. Previously actresses at the Comédie Française and Comédie Italienne had gained the same rights as actors to par-ticipate in their troupe's general assembly, although those rights were eroded before 1789. A royal decree in 1766 empowered a committee composed only of actors to evaluate scripts and make recommenda-tions on what to stage to the full troupe. The troupe's general assembly lost its remaining role in screening scripts in 1780, but the screening committee included two actresses and six actors. In 1789 some actors proposed removing women from their general assembly, arguing that the law excluded women "from all virile functions," but the measure failed because no actress voted for it.[25]

Revolutionary rhetoric often contrasted the immoral private lives of the Old Regime's privileged aristocrats with the presumed morality of humble citizens in a new republic of virtue, and some writers after 1789 still claimed that actresses were more responsible than actors for making the theater immoral. Yet Rousseau's political heirs treated most harshly the actresses or actors tainted by royalist or counter-revolutionary alle-giances. By 1791, the Comédie Française was split between consti-tutional monarchists and republicans, and the latter formed the Theater of the Republic that thrived under the Jacobins. Some more conservative actors and actresses (fifteen men, fourteen women) were arrested in September 1793, after an audience applauded a play with the lines, "the most tolerant are the most reasonable," and persecutors are

---

[24] Count de Clermont Tonnerre, excerpted in Hunt, ed., *French Revolution*, 87.
[25] Lenard R. Berlanstein, *Daughters of Eve: A Cultural History of French Theater Women from the Old Regime to the Fin-de-Siècle* (Cambridge, Mass.: Harvard University Press, 2001), 75.

"reprehensible."[26] The incarcerated included Françoise Raucourt and Louise Contat, known for her role as Suzanne in Beaumarchais's *Mariage de Figaro* (1784), a play mocking class privilege before the Revolution. Also endangered was Marguerite Brunet, better known as Mlle Montansier, France's first woman theater director, who had managed the Theater of Versailles and enjoyed Marie Antoinette's backing in the 1770s and 1780s. Montansier opened a new theater in Paris in 1790 and later renamed it the Theater of the Mountain (after the high seats, the *montagne*, occupied by Jacobins in the Convention), but this nod to political leaders did not spare her from arrest in November 1793. Nonetheless, Marie-Madeleine Guimard, another actress with ties to Marie Antoinette, received a certificate of good citizenship from authorities during the Terror. In the social gatherings of the Thermidorean Reaction (1794–95) and Directory (1795–99) that signaled a relaxation of fear and tension, Montansier and various actresses could again mingle with respectable men and women.

After the Terror, the Convention opened several new schools in late 1794 for the advanced training of male elites, including the École Polytechnique for engineers and École Normale Supérieure for educators, but provided nothing comparable for young women. Some enterprising women then launched schools that they hoped would attract families in the social strata whose daughters formerly attended convent schools. Jeanne Campan left the village where she had hidden during the Terror and opened a boarding school in Saint-Germain-en-Laye. Her own circumstances made her acutely aware that some middle-class women needed to earn money, for her husband had considerable debts and she was supporting her son and three nieces in her care after her sister's suicide during the Terror. Campan's curriculum would suit leisured ladies, but her hiring of skilled instructors in language, art, and music also enabled well-trained young women to become teachers of these subjects. Indeed, one new official institution, the Paris Conservatory of Music, opened in 1795, offered female pupils separate classes and briefly employed Countess Hélène de Nervo de Montgeroult as professor of piano. Musical accomplishment held out the less respectable possibility of a public singing career as well.

In many areas of French cultural and social life, as in political life, General Napoleon Bonaparte's leadership after the November 1799 coup toppling the Directory introduced new organizational features and controls, and Napoleonic law had significant negative aspects for

---

[26] Quoted in F. W. J. Hemmings, *Theater and State in France 1760–1905* (Cambridge: Cambridge University Press, 1994), 84–85.

women. Yet a limited number of women were on the Bonapartist state payroll, and actresses in the reconstituted Comédie Française and other official theaters were not alone in this regard. The well-connected Campan, whose school had been attended by Napoleon's stepdaughter, Hortense Beauharnais, was positioned for a unique educational role.

Women elsewhere in revolutionary Europe

As the Revolution in France heralded liberty and equality and undermined royal privilege and legally defined social classes, other Europeans watched with admiration and fear, even before war began in 1792. In other countries, as in France, some women had expressed opinions on public issues before 1789, and sometimes also acted upon them. For example, English aristocratic women like the Duchess of Devonshire were involved in campaigning before Parliamentary elections. Voting for the House of Commons was limited then to about 5 percent of men, who might be influenced by a powerful local noble. During the Dutch Patriot rebellion in 1786–87 against the stadtholder from the House of Orange, some women also took public stances. Author Betje Wolff wrote pro-Patriot pamphlets, discarding her previous belief that politics was not an appropriate concern for women. The Patriots' arrest of the stadtholder's daring wife Wilhelmina prompted her brother, King of Prussia, to intervene militarily to suppress the rebellion. Wolff and Deken then fled to France, remaining there for a decade. Rebellion against Hapsburg control in the Austrian Netherlands, adjacent to France, began in December 1789, as privileged groups led by Henri Van der Noot and more democratic elements led by Jan Vonck joined forces against Austria, before splitting over differences in their goals. There women played more active roles in the conservative reformers' camp, as exemplified by Countess Anne Thérèse d'Yves, who wrote pamphlets and maintained a Brussels salon, and by Jeanne de Bellem, Van der Noot's mistress, who also authored pamphlets during his exile before the revolt.

Advocacy of improved education for women, or at least for women from those social classes presumed to benefit from learning, predated the Revolution. Addressed by Renaissance humanists, it also concerned pioneering English women writers like Mary Astell (1666–1731) and drew more attention during the Enlightenment. In 1673 François Poullain de la Barre pronounced that "the mind has no sex," but many disputed that idea. As an issue, women's education entailed discussion of whether their intellectual abilities were equal to those of men and also what women from different social classes could or should do with their learning. Louise d'Épinay (1726–83) and Genlis were among the French women entering that discussion, each challenging Rousseau's restrictions, even while sharing his view that women were more governed by feelings than were men. In 1786 Amar y Borbón contested the views of Francisco Cabarrús, a kind of Spanish Rousseau, and in 1790 published her *Discourse on the Physical and Moral Education of Women*, which criticized the aimlessness of many middle- and upper-class women's lives. Amar's book reflected her extensive reading and included an annotated bibliography on women's education from Greek antiquity to the present. She argued that women's reason could be as fully developed as men's and that some would profit from learning Greek and Latin, but she also carefully added that extended learning would not divert women from their domestic roles, as critics alleged. Instead, it would benefit their husbands and children. She did not question existing social class divisions, commenting that for "women of the vulgar class ... it is sufficient to know how to perform the mechanical tasks of the house." Although Spain's monitoring of publications intensified in response to the French Revolution, a censor found Amar's volume "in complete conformity with Catholicism and with the State," predicting that better female education would benefit the government.[27]

Mary Wollstonecraft's *Vindication of the Rights of Woman* (1792) was bolder with regard to what women might do with a better education (Figure 1.2). The work of a former teacher from a struggling middle-class English family, it has become the best-known text from the 1790s on women's abilities and rights, even though Wollstonecraft's language and demands were milder than those that some of her French counterparts proffered. Wollstonecraft (1759–97) had already penned a defense of the Revolution in reply to Edmund Burke's denunciation of its extensive ambitions in his *Reflections on the Revolution in France* (1790), and she took up women's rights after being disappointed by revolutionaries' unequal treatment of girls' education and of women. Although she assumed that most women would remain engaged primarily with domestic duties and utilize more education to become better mothers and wives able to share in their husbands' concerns, she also saw education as the key to new employment opportunities for women needing to support themselves. Moreover, like Gouges, she advocated political rights for women.

English reception of Wollstonecraft's *Vindication*, with its discussion of rights, was inevitably colored by growing distaste among political and social elites for what the Revolution came to represent. The year 1793

---

[27] Quotations in Bridget A. Aldaraca, *El Angel des Hogar: Galdós and the Ideology of Domesticity in Spain* (Chapel Hill: University of North Carolina Press, 1991), 48, 50.

Figure 1.2 Mary Wollstonecraft.

brought the execution of Louis XVI, closure of French churches, and England's entry into the war against France. Indeed, Wollstonecraft's sympathies lay with the Girondins, not the Jacobin leaders of the Terror. In a climate of general backlash against discussion of extending the rights of men or women in England, Wollstonecraft's reputation as a worthy critic of the status quo also suffered from her husband William Godwin's revelations about her private life following her death after childbirth in 1797. Needing money, Godwin, known as a radical thinker, published parts of her letters and diaries, revealing not only her sojourn in France in

1793–94 but also her affair with an American and the birth of an illegitimate child. For decades to come, critics dismissed Wollstone-craft's credibility on women's issues by treating her as an immoral woman offering nothing of value to respectable women. The less famous author Helen Maria Williams (1762–1827) experienced similar assaults on her reputation because of her lifestyle and pro-revolutionary accounts from France. Preferring the Girondins to Robespierre, she was among the British subjects arrested in Paris in 1793 but did not lose her enthusiasm for the Revolution and chose to remain in France. England's *Anti-Jacobin Review* reviled her, and the *Gentleman's Magazine* judged that she had "debased her sex, her heart, her feelings."[28]

Yet even as backlash against revolutionary ideas spread outside France, some women in parts of Germany, the Dutch Netherlands, and Italy welcomed changes brought by victorious French armies. Several women publicly supported the short-lived revolutionary republic in Mainz in 1792, including widow Caroline Böhmer (later Schlegel-Schelling), and were arrested when Prussia suppressed it in 1793. France's egalitarian program inspired Theodor von Hippel (1741–96), a Prussian administrator, to offer sweeping recommendations for making women equals in *On Improving the Status of Women* (1792), but the Prussian legal code of 1794 took a different stance. Terming the husband the head of the household, it gave him final authority over a couple's joint affairs. It also required healthy women to nurse their babies but allowed husbands to tell them when to stop.

In the Dutch republic of 1795–1800, established as a sister regime by the French Directory, specific women's issues appeared in political debate, and women's clubs were founded. Palm d'Aelders, back from France, joined this debate, although she was also arrested as a suspected spy for the House of Orange. Wollstonecraft's *Vindication* was translated into Dutch in 1796 by a sympathetic man, and, as in 1786–87, some women wrote in support of political change. Maria Paape's "Republican Prayer of a Patriotic Woman" (1795) matched the views of her husband Gerrit, who imagined an ideal society where men and women would be fully equal. The blind Petronella Moens directed the periodical *Woman Friend of the Fatherland* in 1798–99 and, like Wolff, identified education as the key to more freedom for women. Although overt anti-revolutionary action was limited in the Dutch setting, some women were executed as counter-revolutionaries, including the aristocrat van Dorth tot Holthuisen.

---

[28] Quoted in Janet Todd, ed., *A Dictionary of British and American Women Writers 1660–1800* (Totowa, N.J.: Rowman and Littlefield, 1987), 325.

In Italy, Napoleon and his generals also replaced old governments with sister republics and found local supporters, including women. Carolina Airenti Lattanzi (1771–1818) insisted in her *Slavery of Women* (1797) that the two sexes should have the same rights and duties in the new Cisalpine republic. The poet and publicist Eleonora Fonseca Pimentel (1758–99), wife of a marquis and former lady-in-waiting to the queen, endorsed the Parthenopian republic in the former kingdom of Naples and edited the official pro-revolutionary newspaper until defeat of the republic doomed her and a hundred other revolutionaries to arrest and hanging. Although she had argued forcefully for equality of rights, regardless of social background, she did not explicitly address women's rights. Queen Marie-Caroline, Marie Antoinette's sister, helped determine Fonseca's fate.

Princess Dashkova's experiences in Russia further illustrate the backlash during the 1790s against reforms and prominent women. Empress Catherine was angered by her approval of the performance of a play somewhat critical of authority, and Dashkova withdrew from, but did not resign, her Academy posts. Tsar Paul formally removed her after his mother died in 1796. He also changed the royal succession by decreeing that the male ruler shall be "preferred to the female," thus setting the stage for four male rulers before the Romanov dynasty fell in 1917. But such misogyny did not deter the court from commissioning Vigée-Lebrun, in St. Petersburg from 1795 to 1801, to do a portrait of Paul's wife, and the Imperial Academy of Arts made her an honorary associate. After Paul's murder in 1801, Dashkova, previously exiled to an estate, attended Alexander I's coronation and heard his advisers disparage Catherine, insisting that "a woman could never govern an Empire."[29] Dashkova's memoirs, penned in French in 1804, defended Catherine and justified her own court role and travels as a mother's activities undertaken to further her children's interests.

The Napoleonic regime and women

The backlash in France against women's demands for greater freedom or equality continued after Napoleon took over the government. Even before his civil code imposed new restrictions on women, some women detected changes in their social position. The outspoken Germaine de Staël complained in *On Literature* (1800) that "since the Revolution men had found it politically and morally useful to reduce women to the most

[29] Dashkova, *Memoirs*, 279.

absurd mediocrity."[30] Napoleon soon banished her from Paris and later from France. Vigée-Lebrun, allowed to return to France only after 255 artists signed a petition for her repatriation in 1801, recorded in her memoirs that the status of salon hostesses had greatly declined. At social gatherings, she remarked, men and women now stayed on opposite sides of a room, no longer mingling freely. Yet salons and their hostesses did retain an important place in nineteenth-century French social and political life, historian Steven Kale reminds us, even as new political institutions provided men with outlets unavailable before 1789.

Napoleon's education policy reflected common assumptions about gender differences and corresponding societal roles. In 1802 he introduced *lycées*, public secondary schools with a rigorous academic program for males likely to become military leaders or administrators. No girls' *lycées* existed before 1880. Several schools for daughters of men in Napoleon's Legion of Honor did set a precedent for state-funded girls' education that offered more than an elementary curriculum, but training for careers was not their ostensible purpose – some ambitions of their directress Campan after 1807 notwithstanding. Scorning the "weakness of women's brains, the changeableness of their ideas," Napoleon wanted the Legion of Honor schools to offer practical subjects to prepare "useful women" able to run a household.[31] He relegated elementary education to local and religious authorities, expecting that most girls would receive only limited instruction. He also favored nuns as elementary teachers, believing that religion instilled docility in females.

Napoleonic rulings restricted or abolished freedoms granted during the Revolution in more than one category. He restored slavery in French colonies in 1802 but could not reconquer rebellious Haiti. Workers were controlled through mandatory passbooks (*livrets*) recording employment histories. Women's rights were limited by the civil code of 1804. Although it enshrined the revolutionary principle of equality before the law, which had replaced class-based privileges, women, and especially married women, were not the legal equals of men. Article 213 in the section on "respective rights and duties of husband and wife" specified that a wife owed "obedience to her husband" while he owed her "protection." Because of past regional differences concerning property ownership, the code did allow couples to choose between joint ownership of property brought into the marriage or the wife's dowry remaining

---

[30] Quoted in Madelyn Gutwirth, *The Twilight of the Goddesses: Women and Representation in the French Revolutionary Era* (New Brunswick, N.J.: Rutgers University Press, 1992), xvi.

[31] Quoted in *Nouveau dictionnaire de pédagogie*, ed. Ferdinand Buisson (Paris: Hachette, 1911), s.v. "Légion d'honneur (Maisons d'éducation de la)," and "Filles (Instruction primaire, secondaire et supérieure des), Première partie, De 1789 à 1870."

her own property. Nonetheless, a husband had to consent if his wife wanted to give away her property, acquire property, work, make a will, or bring a lawsuit, even if she was a "public tradeswoman." The rationale, Napoleon's legal adviser explained, was that "nature determines their [women's] fate. Women need protection because they are weaker; men are free because they are stronger."[32]

From the Revolution, Napoleonic law preserved the principle of equal division of inheritances and also divorce, but added restrictions. Henceforth a person could bequeath one quarter of an estate as he or she pleased (and more than a quarter if there were fewer than three children), and a surviving spouse did not automatically share in the inheritance. Catholic moralists and other conservative critics would condemn the inheritance law for creating incentives for limiting births because families often wanted to limit division of property. France's birthrate after 1800 did decline more rapidly than that of other countries but, note demographers, this trend started before 1789. Preservation of the Revolution's requirement of a civil marriage ceremony, with a religious ceremony optional, further displeased Catholics, as did the possibility of divorce. Napoleon's wish for a male heir after his wife, the widow Josephine Beauharnais, was beyond childbearing age evidently contributed to his retention of divorce in a Catholic country, his courting of the Church through the Concordat with the pope in 1801 notwithstanding. He also intervened in his Council of State's legal deliberations to insist on reinforcing patriarchal authority, perhaps influenced by his experience with Josephine's infidelity. The Napoleonic code's treatment of marital infidelity and divorce enshrined the proverbial "double standard." A husband could seek divorce if his wife was unfaithful, but she could do so only if his adultery reached the extreme of bringing another woman into their home. Furthermore, an adulterous woman might be jailed for up to two years, but a man who kept his mistress in the family home faced only a fine. Undoing the Revolution's liberal divorce law, the code essentially restricted the grounds for it to adultery; flagrantly abusive treatment, such as wife-beating; and conviction for crime and a sentence of degrading punishment.

Because Napoleon exported law codes to other parts of Europe under French sway, his legal legacy continued in more than one place after his downfall in 1814. Divorce, however, was eliminated in France in 1816 by the Bourbon Restoration, closely allied with the Catholic Church.

---

[32] Jean-Etienne Portalis, quoted in Marcel Garaud and Romuald Szramkiewicz, "The Civil Code and the Family," in *Napoleon and His Times: Selected Interpretations*, ed. Frank A. Kafker and James M. Laux (Malabar, Fla.: Robert E. Krieger, 1989), 313.

Looking ahead

Important aspects of Napoleonic law, like English common law, disadvantaged women in ways that some women and men would criticize and seek to remedy during the nineteenth century. We shall see that as such critics framed arguments favoring change, they drew upon both traditional and newer notions regarding gender and the rights of individuals. Many would embrace arguments that recent historians have labeled "maternalism."[33] Like traditionalists opposing extensions of women's rights, maternalists cited biological differences between the sexes and the importance of mothering roles, for which women were presumed to be emotionally suited. But maternalists also claimed that precisely because of mothers' importance to the well-being of society, women deserved more or all of the rights accorded to male citizens.

The Revolution of 1789–99 did not give women equal rights of citizenship. Yet it was because of the Revolution that many arguments about equality, for women as well as men, circulated in Europe and acquired plausibility for later generations. In turn, the counter-revolutionary backlash against equal rights for men continued to operate powerfully against equal rights for women. As industrialization altered the economic landscape of nineteenth-century Europe and increasingly separated workplaces from the home, other arguments for the inappropriateness of women working or leaving the home also came to the forefront. How determined and talented women, like some creative eighteenth-century women, maneuvered for positions, recognition, or reforms in this ideological climate is addressed in subsequent chapters.

Further reading and reference works

Applewhite, Harriet B., and Darline G. Levy, eds. *Women and Politics in the Age of the Democratic Revolution*. Ann Arbor: University of Michigan Press, 1990.

Applewhite, Harriet B., Darline G. Levy, and Mary D. Johnson, eds. *Women in Revolutionary Paris, 1789–1795*. Urbana: University of Illinois Press, 1979.

Barker, Hannah, and Elaine Chalus, eds. *Gender in Eighteenth-Century England: Roles, Representations and Responsibilities*. London: Longman, 1997.

Dashkova, Ekaterina. *The Memoirs of Princess Dashkova*. Translated and edited by Kyril Fitzlyon. London: John Calder, 1958. Reprint: Introduction by Jehanne Gheith. Afterword by A. Woronzoff-Dashkoff. Durham, N.C.: Duke University Press, 1995.

---

[33] Seth Koven and Sonya Michel, eds., *Mothers of a New World: Maternalist Politics and the Origins of Welfare States* (New York: Routledge, 1993).

Desan, Suzanne. "'Constitutional Amazons': Jacobin Women's Clubs in the French Revolution." In *Re-Creating Authority in Revolutionary France*, ed. Bryant T. Ragan Jr. and Elizabeth A. Williams, 11–35. New Brunswick, N.J.: Rutgers University Press, 1992.

    The Family on Trial in Revolutionary France. Berkeley: University of California Press, 2004.

Gelbart, Nina Rattner. *The King's Midwife: A History and Mystery of Madame du Coudray*. Berkeley: University of California Press, 1998.

Goldsmith, Elizabeth C., and Dena Goodman, eds. *Going Public: Women and Publishing in Early Modern France*. Ithaca, N.Y.: Cornell University Press, 1995.

Goodman, Dena. *The Republic of Letters: A Cultural History of the French Enlightenment*. Ithaca, N.Y.: Cornell University Press, 1994.

Gutwirth, Madelyn. *The Twilight of the Goddesses: Women and Representation in the French Revolutionary Era*. New Brunswick, N.J.: Rutgers University Press, 1992.

Harris, Ann Sutherland, and Linda Nochlin. *Women Artists 1550–1950*. New York: Los Angeles County Museum of Art and Alfred A. Knopf, 1977; 6th reprinting, 1984.

Hesse, Carla. *The Other Enlightenment: How French Women Became Modern*. Princeton, N.J.: Princeton University Press, 2001.

Heuer, Jennifer Ngaire. *The Family and the Nation: Gender and Citizenship in Revolutionary France, 1789–1830*. Ithaca, N.Y.: Cornell University Press, 2005.

Hufton, Olwen H. *Women and the Limits of Citizenship in the French Revolution*. Toronto: University of Toronto Press, 1992.

Hunt, Lynn, ed. *The French Revolution and Human Rights: A Brief Documentary History*. Boston: Bedford Books of St. Martin's Press, 1996.

Hyde, Melissa, and Jennifer Milam, eds. *Women, Art and the Politics of Identity in Eighteenth-Century Europe*. Aldershot: Ashgate, 2003.

Kale, Steven. *French Salons: High Society and Political Sociability from the Old Regime to the Revolution of 1848*. Baltimore: Johns Hopkins University Press, 2004.

Keener, Frederick M., and Susan E. Lorsch, eds. *Eighteenth-Century Women and the Arts*. Westport, Conn.: Greenwood Press, 1988.

Knott, Sarah, and Barbara Taylor, eds. *Women, Gender and Enlightenment*. New York: Palgrave Macmillan, 2005.

Landes, Joan B. *Women and the Public Sphere in the Age of the French Revolution*. Ithaca, N.Y.: Cornell University Press, 1988.

Laqueur, Thomas. *Making Sex: Body and Gender from the Greeks to Freud*. Cambridge, Mass.: Harvard University Press, 1990.

Letzter, Jacqueline, and Robert Adelson. *Women Writing Opera: Creativity and Controversy in the Age of the French Revolution*. Berkeley: University of California Press, 2001.

Madariaga, Isabel de. "The Foundation of the Russian Education System by Catherine II." *Slavonic and East European Review* 57 (July 1979): 369–95.

May, Gita. *Elisabeth Vigée-Le Brun: The Odyssey of an Artist in an Age of Revolution*. New Haven, Conn.: Yale University Press, 2005.

Meehan-Waters, Brenda. "Catherine the Great and the Problem of Female Rule." *Russian Review* 34 (July 1975): 293–307.

Melzer, Sara E., and Leslie W. Rabine, eds. *Rebel Daughters: Women and the French Revolution*. New York: Oxford University Press, 1992.

Messbarger, Rebecca. *The Century of Women: Representations of Women in Eighteenth-Century Italian Public Discourse*. Toronto: University of Toronto Press, 2002.

Nash, Carol. "Educating New Mothers: Women and the Enlightenment in Russia." *History of Education Quarterly* 21 (Fall 1981): 301–16.

Peruga, Mónica Bolufer, and Isabel Morant Deusa. "On Women's Reason, Education and Love: Women and Men of the Enlightenment in Spain and France." *Gender and History* 10 (August 1998): 183–216.

Schroder, Anne L. "Going Public against the Academy in 1784: Mime de Genlis Speaks Out on Gender Bias." *Eighteenth-Century Studies* 32.3 (1999): 376–82.

Sheriff, Mary D. *The Exceptional Woman: Elisabeth Vigée-Lebrun and the Cultural Politics of Art*. Chicago: University of Chicago Press, 1996.

Smith, Theresa Ann. *The Emerging Female Citizen: Gender and Enlightenment in Spain*. Berkeley: University of California Press, 2006.

Spencer, Samia I., ed. *French Women and the Age of Enlightenment*. Bloomington: Indiana University Press, 1984.

Sullivan, Constance A. "The Quiet Feminism of Josefa Amar y Borbón's 1790 Book on the Education of Women." *Indiana Journal of Hispanic Literatures* 2 (Fall 1993): 49–73.

Todd, Janet, ed. *A Dictionary of British and American Women Writers 1660–1800*. Totowa, N.J.: Rowman and Littlefield, 1987.

Trouille, Mary S. *Sexual Politics in the Enlightenment: Women Writers Read Rousseau*. Albany: State University of New York Press, 1997.

Vega, Judith A. "Feminist Republicanism: Etta Palm-Aelders on Justice, Virtue and Men." *History of European Ideas* 10.3 (1989): 333–51.

2 Women and literature: authorship, publication, audience

Writing is an act of self-assertion, whether in the private form of diaries and letters or for publication. Creation of a text may enable an author to gain understanding of self or display mastery of knowledge, sway or mold opinions, or simply entertain others. Because they could write in the private space of the home, many nineteenth-century women authors worked in a setting judged appropriate for their sex, albeit one where household duties often interrupted writing. Yet women who published and attracted readers also placed themselves in a kind of public realm. In the wake of the French Revolution, the woman author continued to elicit varied reactions from commentators, including the increasingly numerous professional literary critics. Stéphanie de Genlis thus thought it wise to state in 1811 in her book on women's influence on French literature that women's writing was compatible with domestic duties.

Women authors appeared well before the nineteenth century, of course. Fragments of poetry by Sappho survive from ancient Greece, and the more numerous women's manuscripts from the Middle Ages include those of Hroswitha of Gandersheim, the nun often termed the first German woman writer. The widow Christine de Pisan, possibly the first professional woman author, turned to writing to support herself and her three children, finding patrons at the French court where her Italian father had worked. Contending in her *Book of the City of Ladies* (c. 1405) that the intellectual equality of the sexes would be evident if women were appropriately educated, she has sometimes been called the first feminist, although the term "feminist" was not used until the 1880s. By 1800 numerous women had written in a variety of genres: poems, religious and pedagogical tracts, short stories and novels, drama, biographies and autobiographies, and some histories and scientific texts. The novel, as it emerged during the later seventeenth and eighteenth centuries, became increasingly popular, and many considered it a quintessentially feminine literary genre, regardless of an author's sex. Plots centering on human relationships and private life appealed to women, and literate women of the aristocracy and middle classes had the money to buy novels and leisure time to read them.

Historians of various national literatures underscore the importance of individual women in the development of the novel. Marie-Madeleine Pioche de La Vergne, Countess de Lafayette, is credited with writing the first modern French novel, *La Princesse de Clèves* (1678), which was quickly translated into English. By the time that Samuel Richardson gained fame in England for his popular novels *Pamela* (1740) and *Clarissa* (1747–48), tales in epistolary format of young women defending their virtue when beset by rakes, English women such as Aphra Benn, Delarivière Manley, Penelope Aubin, and Eliza Haywood had already ventured into the genre, sometimes with scandalous plots. Between 1750 and 1770, six of the twenty most popular English novelists were women. Sophie von La Roche has been credited with creating the modern German novel, and Betje Wolff and Aagje Deken, the first Dutch novel. Yet perceptions of the novel as a feminine genre also meant that it was long considered a lesser genre than poetry, the essay, history, or philosophy. Many men in the Age of Reason presumed that women's preoccupation with love, feelings, and private life gave women authors distinctive emotional insights expected by readers of novels – the success of Rousseau's novel, *La Nouvelle Héloïse* (1761), reprinted seventy times by 1800, notwithstanding. Novelists gained greater prestige during the nineteenth century, when critics rated some novels as serious literature and not simply amusing stories.

Although the market for books expanded from the later 1700s onward, both their high cost, relative to today's standards, and lack of widespread literacy limited the size of the reading public. Women's literacy rates of 40 percent or more in England and Prussia in 1790 were not matched even in 1890 in Spain (25 percent) or Russia (14 percent). As the population of literate women increased, especially in urban areas, periodicals intended for women also appeared, including *The Female Spectator* (1744–46) in England; the *Journal des Dames* (1759–78) in France; *La Pensadora* (Woman Thinker) (1763–64) in Spain; the *Giornale delle Dame* (1781) in Italy; and *Amalia's Leisure Hours, Dedicated to Germany's Daughters* (1790–92) in Germany.

During the nineteenth century more women published their writing than ever before. In France, for example, women's representation among authors with works in print increased from 2 percent in 1784 to 4 percent in 1821, at least 299 women having published between 1811 and 1821. Women were perhaps half of all English novelists before 1840, and in 1859 one German critic stated that women predominated as novelists. By 1900, thousands of women across Europe had published in a variety of literary genres, including over 4,000 women who wrote in German and a comparable number in French. Some women authors also became well-known public personalities whose success inspired other women but sometimes provoked disapproval as well.

Highlighting women authors from successive generations, this chapter begins with examples from France and England, where a female literary tradition had already developed by 1800, and then turns to other countries or linguistic areas. In the early nineteenth century, the nation-state such as France, England, or Spain was not yet the typical European political model. When Napoleon subjected many once-independent regions to French control, he not only continued the Revolution's undercutting of the older political and social order in areas beyond France but also provided impetus for new nationalist, anti-French ambitions in German- and Italian-speaking areas, among others. Literature contributed to the imagining of new national communities, and women authors played a role in the process. In the multinational Hapsburg Empire, where the language of the court and central government was German, the revival or creation among Slavic groups or Hungarians of a sense of unique national identity entailed efforts to develop or extend a literary tradition and common historical narrative. Literature was also a means of preserving Polish identity after an independent Poland disappeared in 1795, due to partitions by Russia, Austria, and Prussia.

The examples of notable women authors considered here represent only a tiny fraction of the thousands of women who published. Yet individual successes provided models for aspiring authors of later generations to emulate. Individual trajectories also reveal issues that were critical for women authors trying to find their voice and an audience. When and why did women decide to write? What was their educational preparation? Were members of their immediate families – parents, siblings, husbands – supportive or resistant? What themes and topics did women tackle? What literary genres did they favor, and in which ones was achieving success most likely? What influence did pressing public issues – social, economic, political, nationalist, religious – have on choices of subject matter? What self-perceptions did women authors reveal, and how did they explain or justify their writing ambitions? And how did critics review women's publications? The writers discussed represent each decade of the nineteenth century, and the works highlighted are largely novels and autobiography, genres especially revealing of authors' thoughts about women's circumstances.

Germaine de Staël and contemporaries

During the first decade of the nineteenth century Germaine de Staël (1766–1817) was probably better known, or more notorious, than any other living woman author. Her publications, colorful life history, and travels made her an international figure. Her social background, upper-middle-class (bourgeois) and eventually aristocratic, also exemplified the privileged milieus from which women authors more often emerged around 1800, as compared to the later decades of the nineteenth century.

Aristocratic and upper-middle-class daughters were nearly always educated, usually at home and not necessarily systematically. The importance of parental encouragement of learning, particularly by fathers, is a recurring theme in many women authors' biographies, as is that of sisters benefiting from tutors hired for brothers. Some girls also attended schools, in Catholic countries typically convent schools, or in England, day or boarding schools run by men or lay women. The quality of instruction in schools varied enormously, as noted in Chapter 5. Some offered a respectable array of academic subjects, while others were remembered by pupils for their emphasis on piety, social graces, and feminine "accomplishments" in needlework, drawing, and singing. Publicly funded schools, where they existed before passage of compulsory education laws, usually provided only elementary instruction and served the children of parents with modest means, such as artisans, lower-level employees, workers, or farmers. Gaye Tuchman's study of English novelists born between 1750 and 1865 reveals that only a minority of women authors experienced schooling outside the home (15 percent of those born before 1815, 25 percent of those born later), whereas formal schooling was the norm for male authors (70 percent of those born before 1815, 83 percent of those born later). Extensive reading provided many young women who became writers with their first literary models.

Crucial formative influences in de Staël's life predated the French Revolution. Her mother, the *salonnière* Suzanne Necker, only child of a Swiss pastor, knew Latin and worked as a tutor before marrying the rich banker Jacques Necker. Familiar with Rousseau's educational prescriptions, Mme Necker decided that her only child should be brought up like Émile, not Sophie. By the age of twelve, the privately instructed Germaine was reading Montesquieu, Rousseau, and Voltaire. She was allowed to express her opinions in her parents' salon and began developing self-confidence that served her well as an author. Yet some features of this indulged child's life could also stifle her ambitions. Necker, whom she adored, mocked his adolescent daughter's writing and discouraged his wife's plans to write about Fénelon. Germaine at age nineteen still accepted her father's judgments, writing in her diary: "How little are women cut out to follow the same career as a man ... A woman ought not to have anything of her own and should find all her pleasures in those she loves."[1] But her marriage in 1786 to an older Swedish diplomat was not a love match. Arranged by her parents, it provided an aristocratic title and status, typifying the upper-class tradition of marriage based on calculations of economic and social advantage, not individuals' emotional happiness. A year later a daughter was born.

The Revolution changed de Staël's life. She saw her father humiliated when Louis XVI fired him in July 1789, but then, after the Bastille fell, witnessed his triumphant return as Parisians applauded his advocacy of tax reform. Her salon in the Swedish embassy attracted supporters of a constitutional monarchy. After Louis XVI was overthrown, she fled to her parents' home in Switzerland and gave birth to a son fathered by the Count de Narbonne. The end of the Terror allowed a return to Paris and salon life; her husband was again an ambassador and her new lover Benjamin Constant sought influence. Still embracing the Revolution's ideals, de Staël supported the Directory, an elite republican regime, even as she, Constant, and others continued debating how best to reconcile individual liberty and social order, often admiring England's representative institutions.

De Staël also grappled with reconciling notions of liberty and ideas she had internalized about women's appropriate roles. In *On Literature, Considered in Its Relations with Social Institutions* (1800) she offered her much-cited formulation that in a republic, philosophy would remain the domain of men, whose reasoning powers were superior, but women, endowed with greater sensibility and feeling, would claim literature. Her claim was but one example of how many nineteenth-century women tried to turn common notions about gender differences to their advantage, arguing that women's unique traits made them better suited than men for certain roles, including roles other than the strictly domestic. As de Staël acquired literary fame after 1800, no longer publishing anonymously, she also provoked Napoleon. In 1802, after Constant and others angered by Napoleon's assaults on liberty were ousted from the legislative Tribunate, de Staël addressed her novel *Delphine* to the "enlightened" public now silenced. Literature had become a "weapon of the human spirit" during the eighteenth century, she wrote in *On Literature*. When Napoleon exiled her, she became a symbol of defiance to his increasingly dictatorial regime. Set during the Revolution, *Delphine*'s treatment of marriage, divorce, and duplicitous religious figures disturbed people eager to reembrace traditions after great upheaval.

---

[1] Quoted in Madelyn Gutwirth, *Madame de Staël, Novelist: The Emergence of the Artist as a Woman* (Urbana: University of Illinois Press, 1978), 39.

Figure 2.1 Élisabeth Vigée-Lebrun, portrait of Germaine de Staël as Corinne, 1807.

The heroine presented an ambiguous message. De Staël opened the novel by quoting her mother: "A man must know how to defy opinion, a woman to submit to it."[2] Yet Delphine sometimes defied convention, before committing suicide when unable to be with the royalist man she loved.

In *Corinne, or Italy* (1807) de Staël created a new type of heroine, as literary scholars have emphasized (Figure 2.1). Unlike previous women characters whose struggles centered on preserving their virtue or surviving economically, Corinne was a talented woman who courted

[2] Ibid., 101.

fame. She was a gifted poet feted by the Roman populace, just as male poets had been honored. But by having the crowd shout "Long live genius! Long live beauty!" de Staël made creative talent compatible with femininity. Daughter of an Italian mother and English father, Corinne experienced travails which contemporaries compared to those of de Staël, and she met a sad end, like Delphine. Corinne's English father told her that proper English women had no other vocation than "domestic duty," and Oswald, the English lord she loved, married her more conventional half-sister. Emotionally devastated because she had chosen Oswald and love over "the independent destiny" that once made her happy, Corinne could no longer write, or live, and she wasted away. De Staël's novels placed her in the company of other successful contemporary French women authors – notably Sophie Cottin, Genlis, Adélaïde de Flahaut, and the Dutch-born Isabelle de Charrière. Vigée-Lebrun painted de Staël as Corinne, and *Corinne* was quickly translated into English by Isabel Hill and into German by Dorothea Mendelssohn Veit Schlegel.

De Staël's interest in national differences in culture, signaled in *On Literature* and *Corinne*, was central to *On Germany* (1810, *De l'Allemagne*). The theme was timely, for French incursions into German and Italian states, long politically disunited, were stimulating a new national consciousness. Presenting German Romanticism to French readers, de Staël characterized it as concerned with inner personal truths, in contrast to French preoccupation with social conventions. She had visited Germany, met Johann Wolfgang von Goethe, Friedrich von Schiller, and Alexander von Humboldt, and hired August Schlegel to tutor her younger children. Her sympathetic treatment of German literature enraged Napoleon, who banned her book in France but could not prevent its reissue in Leipzig after his disastrous Russian campaign of 1812. De Staël returned to Paris after Napoleon's defeat, married the much younger John Rocca, and before her death in 1817 worked on a book on the French Revolution, planning to highlight her father's work.

Commentary on de Staël's life and literary work long continued. More than forty French editions of *Corinne* appeared between 1807 and 1872. The 7,000 copies sold between 1816 and 1820 put it in twentieth place among French bestsellers for those years. Twenty years later it ranked tenth among bestsellers, and in each instance only one other woman, Cottin, figured on bestselling lists, usually headed by seventeenth-century classics like La Fontaine's *Fables* or Fénelon's *Télémaque*. De Staël's example influenced younger women authors, including George Sand and Delphine Gay in France; Cristina Belgiojoso in Italy; Charlotte Brontë, George Eliot, Jane Carlyle, Anna Jameson, and Elizabeth Barrett Browning in England; and Margaret Fuller and Harriet Beecher Stowe in the United States. Yet there were also negative aspects to her continuing reputation. Some women and men found her life immoral. The Romantic poet Alphonse de Lamartine once praised her as "a male genius in female form ... uniting within herself Corinne and [the revolutionary] Mirabeau!," but he later doubted that it was "appropriate for women to write and to aspire to glory in the world of letters," stating that de Staël became "no longer a woman, but a poet, and orator." More fittingly, she was remembered at an 1893 international women's congress for inaugurating "a new era of vigorous writers among women."[3]

The life of contemporary English novelist Jane Austen (1775–1817) differed in important respects from that of the *salonnière* de Staël. The sixth of seven children, Austen was the shy daughter of a scholarly country rector who instructed her. Never married, although not without suitors, she resided with family members. Similarly, about a third of a group of eighty-seven better-known English women authors born before 1800 remained single. Austen read widely – particularly novels by Richardson, Henry Fielding, and women authors Fanny and Sarah Burney, Mary Brunton, Maria Edgeworth, Anne Grant, Elizabeth Hamilton, Laetitia-Matilda Hawkins, Anna Maria Porter, Jane West, and Helen Williams. She also admired *Corinne*. Austen began writing as a teenager, like de Staël, and drafted three novels by the age of twenty-five. But she published nothing until she was in her thirties, family members' earlier efforts to interest publishers proving unsuccessful. Her first books appeared anonymously, the title pages of *Sense and Sensibility* (1811) and *Pride and Prejudice* (1813) simply identifying the author as "a lady."

Austen's witty novels have entertained generations of readers, but they also contain a serious message about the dilemmas of middle-class women who lacked economic resources and might not marry. In *Pride and Prejudice* heroine Elizabeth Bennet was one of five daughters, without prospects of inheritance, whom the parents hoped to marry off. She rejected a man she did not love, unlike her desperate friend Charlotte. Eventually Elizabeth found love, overcoming her own pride and the snobbish prejudices of her upper-class husband. Women's emotional and economic need for love and marriage also figured in Austen's other novels, even as she often mocked bickering spouses. Her six novels, published between 1811 and 1818, were usually well received, and several quickly appeared in French translations, but demand for English editions long remained limited. During her lifetime the most that she

---

[3] Quotations in ibid., 280–81, 290–91; and Helen P. Jenkins, "Madame de Staël," in *The Congress of Women*, ed. Mary Kavanaugh Oldham Eagle (Chicago: W. B. Conkey, 1894), II: 690.

earned from one book was £310 for *Mansfield Park* (1814), far less than the £2,000 paid to Burney for *Camilla* (1796) or the £2,100 for Maria Edgeworth's *Patronage* (1814). An 1833 edition of Austen's novels and occasional reprints satisfied demand until a nephew's *Memoir* in 1870 launched a Jane Austen cult, prompting new editions and bestowal of literary classic status. By then, Austen's theme of unmarried women's lack of economic options engaged feminists in England and other countries, but the later label "Janeites" for admirers of her novels also signified appreciation of her renditions of country life in a past era untroubled by the ills of industrial society.

Unlike the once less famous Austen, Maria Edgeworth (1768–1849), also unmarried, was the most commercially successful and prestigious early nineteenth-century English woman author. Her Anglo-Irish land-owner father had encouraged her writing, and the two collaborated on educational treatises, initially inspired by the need to instruct her many younger siblings. As a teenager she translated Genlis's *Adèle et Théodore*, and in 1800 published her first novel, *Castle Rackrent*. Its success and subsequent novels brought contacts with leading authors. Austen, an admirer, sent her a copy of *Emma*. The success of women like Edgeworth also convinced male contemporaries that writing fiction could be prof-itable, as county clerk Walter Scott demonstrated with his popular his-torical novels, starting with *Waverley* (1814).

By the time de Staël and Austen died in 1817, post-Napoleonic Europe was enjoying the first extended peace since 1792. Conservative politics colored the Restoration period from 1815 to 1830, so termed because of the Bourbon monarchy's return in France and parallels in Spain and the Kingdom of the Two Sicilies. Rulers with less lofty titles resumed control of Italian states south of Austrian-controlled Lombardy and Venetia and of some smaller German states surviving after Napoleon's abolition of the Holy Roman Empire and many German political entities. Governments' fears of new revolutions or demands for reform led to repressive measures like the English Six Acts of 1819, or the Carlsbad Decrees of 1819 insti-gated by Austrian minister Metternich and applied in the states loosely joined in the German Confederation (1815–66). Innovative cultural trends were linked to Romanticism, with its emphasis on feeling rather than the reasoning which conservatives blamed for leading eighteenth-century minds astray. Rebellious Romantics asserted their right to break free from the constraints of previous cultural styles, but many early Romantic writers' political leanings dovetailed with conservative Restoration politics and glorification of past eras like the Middle Ages as times of ideal stability. In France, the young Victor Hugo praised the Bourbons, and only in 1830 did he famously proclaim that Romanticism was "liberalism in literature."

The Restoration era's climate of opinion and conformity did not welcome rebellious women. Alliances between Throne and Altar linked two pillars of public order, and political and religious leaders alike enjoined women to focus on their domestic and maternal roles. As "mother-educators," women could imbue children with respect for existing institutions. The 1820s lacked another de Staël, but some women did work remarkable social critiques into fiction and non-fiction.

In Restoration France, Claire de Duras (1777–1828) penned *Ourika* (1823), a novella with a compelling critique of racial prejudice and, indirectly, of slavery. Educated in a convent school, Duras was the daughter of an aristocrat supportive of the Revolution but executed during the Terror. She and her mother fled to her mother's native Martinique, where wealthy owners of sugar plantations had avoided the slave rebellion gripping Saint-Domingue. She married a fellow émigré in London, eventually returning to France during Napoleon's rule. In an evidently loveless marriage to a man eager to use her wealth, Duras found compensation with her two daughters. Socially prominent, she maintained a salon that supported her husband's role at court and attracted François René de Chateaubriand, the Romantic author and government minister. Duras began writing extensively in 1822, when she withdrew to her country estate and produced five manuscripts. Writing provided creative release from her sadness and entertainment for friends. *Ourika,* read first to salon guests, recounted the travails of a young African woman brought to France as a small child by an officer who saved her from slavery. The story had a basis in real life, but Duras embellished it. A kind aristocratic woman saw to Ourika's education, but her happiness as a teenager was shattered when she overheard a conversation making her aware that a white man would not marry her because of her black skin. The Revolution's promise of liberty gave her hope until the Terror made that seem a cruel hoax, and she condemned Haiti's rebel slaves who committed murders. In despair after her patroness's son married another woman, Ourika entered a convent and wasted away. The first black heroine of a novel set in Europe and first African female narrator in French literature, Ourika shared the fate of Corinne. Like de Staël, Duras looked back nostalgically on social life under the Old Régime, despite noting its injustices, but her disillusion with the Revolution was greater. *Ourika* was first published anonymously, but interest in it prompted new editions in 1824, totaling more than 5,000 copies. One edition was published in St. Petersburg. Four plays based on the novel were produced, and the court artist François Gérard painted an image of Ourika. Goethe wrote that the novel overwhelmed him. Yet Duras's success had a downside, for critics circulated verses mocking her creative pretensions.

No German women novelists before 1830 would enjoy the same lasting fame as de Staël or Austen, despite La Roche's earlier success. Caroline de la Motte Fouqué (1775–1831) has a place in German Romanticism as the well-known author of at least twenty novels, some of them translated into English. More typically, however, contemporary German women recognized for literary talent appear in later accounts as translators, journalists, educators, minor poets, letter writers, or facilitators of male intellectuals' careers in salons. Yet among twenty-seven better-known German literary women born between 1755 and 1799 and writing during the 1790s or after 1800, a number of life stories broke the conventional mold of marriage and domesticity for women. Eleven were aristocrats by birth or marriage, a social status not typical of most later German women authors. Another seven came from the middle-class households of university professors and pastors, homes which provided books and exchanges of ideas. All but four married, but ten would divorce, a possibility in Protestant German states or under Napoleonic-era legal reforms in Catholic states, and another separated and lived with a lover. Two of the single women committed suicide. Of the twelve who remained married, seven became widows. Rahel Levin experienced several romantic disappointments before marrying aristocrat Karl Varnhagen von Ense, fourteen years younger, and converting from Judaism to Christianity to do so in 1814. Dorothea Mendelssohn Veit Schlegel and Henriette Herz also came from prominent Jewish families and later converted, Mendelssohn when she remarried and Herz as a widow.

Rahel Varnhagen (1771–1833), whose biographers include twentieth-century philosopher Hannah Arendt, was best known for her Berlin salons, one dating from 1790 to 1806 (ended when the French army reached Berlin) and the other from 1819 to 1832. The daughter of a jewelry merchant, she hired tutors to improve her command of foreign languages and mathematics when she realized the deficiencies in her education. Her literary skills were evident in her letters, which were sometimes read aloud in salons by recipients and later familiar to a wider public because her husband published them posthumously as *Das Buch Rahel* (1833–34), creating a kind of Rahel cult. The writer Fanny Lewald, among the younger women inspired by her example, admired her overcoming of adversities with "something masculine, solid and audacious in her spirit."[4]

---

[4] Quoted in Patricia Herminghouse, "Women and the Literary Enterprise in Nineteenth-Century Germany," in *German Women in the Eighteenth and Nineteenth Centuries: A Social and Literary History*, ed. Ruth-Ellen B. Joeres and Mary Jo Maynes (Bloomington: Indiana University Press, 1986), 91.

Bettina von Arnim (1785–1859), granddaughter of La Roche, did not become a recognized author until the age of fifty. Like Varnhagen and Fouqué, she moved in the stimulating milieu of famed male Romantic writers. But the Romantics' praise for works of individual genius, by a Goethe or a Ludwig van Beethoven, did not usually extend to recognizing female talent as equally exceptional. For example, Dorothea Mendelssohn Schlegel (1763–1839), whose second husband was the writer and philosopher Friedrich Schlegel, helped support their household by writing the novel *Florentin* (1800), the authorship of which was first credited to him, as was her translation of *Corinne*. Von Arnim was the sister of the Romantic poet Clemens Brentano and the wife of Achim von Arnim, a poet and novelist. The mother of seven children, she conducted a long correspondence with Goethe but ventured into publication only after her husband's death. Henriette Herz (1764–1854) was also a widow when she translated Wollstonecraft's *Vindication of the Rights of Woman* in 1832. Von Arnim's fictionalized *Goethe's Correspondence with a Child* (1835), drawn from her admiring letters and published after Goethe's death, became a bestseller and made her salon popular. In *Die Günderrode* (1840) she told the sad story of her friend Caroline von Günderrode (1780–1806), a poet who committed suicide after romantic disappointments. Clemens reacted to his sister's renown by criticizing her for damaging her reputation with excessive self-revelation, but she persisted with writing.

Private and public issues: from Romanticism to Realism, 1830s–1850s

For some women authors, the decade of the 1830s was a new moment of opportunity, or so it seemed in retrospect, in comparison to the 1840s and 1850s when critics' backlash against women's literary ambitions and successes became more pronounced. Contemporaries in France sensed a more liberal climate of public opinion after the three-day July 1830 Revolution in Paris toppled the Bourbon monarchy and produced modest changes in the 1814 constitution, although press censorship continued under the ensuing July Monarchy of the Orleanist king Louis-Philippe. In this time of transition in literary history from Romanticism to Realism – coinciding with greater industrialization and urbanization – women wrote in a variety of genres and made new forays into journalism. The issues they addressed included women's status in private and public life, and the impact of political and economic changes.

Novelist and essayist Aurore Dupin Dudevant (1804–76), using the pseudonym George Sand, became the most celebrated French woman author of the 1830s and 1840s. Her background straddled two classes, as she noted in her autobiography, *Histoire de ma Vie* (1854–55). Her paternal grandmother had married a minor aristocrat and owned a château at Nohant. Her mother Sophie, of humble origins, married her father, a Napoleonic officer, shortly before her birth. After his death in 1808, Aurore's sophisticated grandmother took charge of her, sending Sophie back to Paris. Her education began with lessons from a tutor, in the company of her half-brother. She entered a convent school in Paris, returning to Nohant at age seventeen to help her dying grandmother. Her grandmother's library included works by Rousseau, Shakespeare, and women authors Sévigné, Lafayette, Châtelet, Genlis, and de Staël. In 1822, she married Baron Casimir Dudevant, a retired army officer whom she left after eight years and the birth of two children. She hoped to earn a living in Paris by writing, for her husband legally controlled her inherited wealth and gave her only a small allowance.

Aurore Dudevant's literary fame began with *Indiana* (1832), published under the name of G. Sand and, because of its plot, soon provoking speculation about the author's sex. She adopted the pseudonym George Sand for multiple reasons. Although many women already had published under their own names, some other earlier or contemporary authors chose anonymity or female pseudonyms to avoid bringing notoriety to their families. German women writers employed some 1,500 pseudonyms during the nineteenth century. Sand's husband and mother-in-law forbade her use of the Dudevant name, and they had the force of law behind them. Women's adoption of masculine pseudonyms was relatively new and reflected concerns about the literary marketplace, for many assumed that publishers and readers took male authors more seriously. Later, when Sand's sex was no secret, the male pseudonym, along with sometimes wearing masculine attire or smoking, was likely part of a strategy for attracting attention to herself and thus to her books. She also wanted to counter the negative bluestocking image associated with women authors, telling a friend in 1832, "Never call me *femme auteur* [woman author]" and later bemoaning being "tainted by the label *femme de lettres*."[5] Contemporaries employing masculine pseudonyms included Delphine Gay de Girardin, whose commentary in her husband's newspaper appeared under the byline of the "Vicomte de Launay" and Marie d'Agoult (1805–76), who wrote as "Daniel Stern" and, with Sand's encouragement, began writing her autobiographical novel *Nélida* (1846) when depressed by the ending of her relationship

---

[5] George Sand, letters, 27 January 1832, 22 March 1834, in George Sand, *Correspondance*, ed. Georges Lubin (Paris: Garnier, 1964–91), II: 16, 546.

with composer Franz Liszt. In contrast to Sand's dislike of the label woman author, the conservative Annette von Droste-Hülshoff (1797–1848) addressed a polemical poem to other German *Schriftstellerinnen* (women authors), advising them to shun male literary models and find their own female voice.

The plot of *Indiana*, like many of Sand's sixty other novels, treated themes of social and legal injustice. Exposing prejudices concerning sex, class, and race, it also had autobiographical elements. Indiana Delmare, married at a young age to an older army officer, was trapped in a loveless marriage and emotionally dead until Raymon, a seductive aristocrat, awakened her feelings. Raymon had already impregnated Indiana's maid, who committed suicide after he refused to marry her because "a working girl was not a woman." Indiana's rigid, narrow-minded husband somewhat resembled Casimir Dudevant, and her floundering to make sense of her life in an arranged marriage seemed a version of Sand's younger self. Sand attributed Indiana's ignorance of the world to inadequate education, designed by male relatives. She underscored Indiana's legal situation through Colonel Delmare's references to a wife's obligation to obey – a parroting of the civil code at a time when divorce had been abolished and would not be restored until 1884. Indiana's attempts to express her feelings and claim personal freedom prompted Delmare to mock her for sounding like a character in a novel – the genre still being identified with women. Numerous comparisons between the situation of women and that of slaves marked the narrative. Indiana told her husband in one memorable scene that he might control her body but could not control her mind. She found happiness after his death, fleeing with her cousin Ralph to an island in the Indian Ocean where they devoted their resources to freeing slaves. The success of *Indiana* created a market for Sand's next novels about women, *Valentine* and *Lélia*, and six other novels published by 1837. In the meantime, her literary success and liaisons with writers Jules Sandeau and Alfred de Musset angered her husband, who physically attacked her in the presence of others while she was at Nohant in 1835, prompting her to obtain a legal separation.

Critics heaped both praise and ridicule on Sand as she gained literary status (Figure 2.2). In 1835 Charles-Augustin Sainte-Beuve noted fellow critics' abuse of "the most eminent woman in literature" since de Staël, a judgment Sand mirrored when she wrote that de Staël "was insulted just as much as I am in the press." Etienne de Jouy asked, "Are you a man, a woman, are you an angel, a demon?" Novelist Honoré de Balzac admired her as an "artist" who was "great-hearted, generous, devout," but added, "she has the main characteristics of a man; *ergo*

MIROIR DROLATIQUE.

Si de **Georges Sand** ce portrait
Laisse l'esprit un peu perplexe,
C'est que le génie est abstrait,
Et comme on sait n'a pas de sexe.

Figure 2.2 George Sand caricatured by A. Lorentz in *Le Charivari*, 5 August 1842.

she is not a woman."[6] Particularly insulting was the epithet "female ink pisser" (*pisseuse d'encre*). Sand countered by repeatedly justifying her writing as driven by needing to support herself and her children. Only in the 1850s in her autobiography did she confess to liking the creative process of writing and enjoying fame, admitting her long hesitation to reveal this.

Hesitancy to admit ambitions considered unfeminine also characterized many English, American, and German women's self-presentations until well into the twentieth century. Women's private writing, unsurprisingly, often revealed more about ambition than their published works. Well before Droste-Hülshoff's first volume of poetry appeared in 1838, when she was forty-one and not yet ready to attach her full name to it, she had wanted to be famous. Austen's letters indicate delight in earning money from her writing, yet her brother insisted after her death that she had sought neither fame nor profit.

Despite controversy, Sand received praise from many eminent male literary figures and became a new role model for women writers in France and elsewhere, as she realized by 1837. Her writing impressed French authors Hugo and Balzac; British writers William Makepeace Thackeray, G. H. Lewes, and John Stuart Mill; German poet Heinrich Heine; Polish poet Adam Mickiewicz; and Russian novelists Ivan Turgenev and Fyodor Dostoevsky. Cuban-born writer Gertrudis Gómez de Avelleneda (1814–73) discovered Sand before her family moved to Spain in 1836, and her first novel *Sab* (1841) resembled *Indiana*, with themes of the oppression of slaves and women. Thirty-seven translations of Sand's works appeared in Spain by 1851. Elizabeth Barrett Browning (1806–61), the reclusive English poet, addressed Sand in verse in 1844 as "Thou large-brained woman and large-hearted man", and "True genius, but true woman."[7] Browning had endured her father's hostility to her efforts to write about the development of genius, a subject he thought beyond her ability. Her famous novel-in-verse "Aurora Leigh" drew from both de Staël's and Sand's examples. Germans coined the term *Georgesandismus* (George-Sandism) for the combination of literary concerns and independent lifestyle that Sand created, and Russians

[6] Quotations in Isabelle Nagasinki, "Germaine de Staël among the Romantics," in *Germaine de Staël: Crossing the Borders*. ed. Madelyn Gutwirth, Avriel Goldberger, and Karyna Szmurlo (New Brunswick, N.J.: Rutgers University Press, 1991), 181–82; and Christine Battersby, *Gender and Genius: Towards a Feminist Aesthetics* (London: The Women's Press, 1989), 22.
[7] Elizabeth Barrett Browning, "To George Sand, A Desire," and "To George Sand, A Recognition," in *The Norton Anthology of Literature by Women: The Tradition in English*, ed. Sandra M. Gilbert and Susan Gubar (New York: W. W. Norton, 1985), 263–64.

referred to *Zhorzhzandovshchina*. Elena Gan (1814–42) and Maria Zhukova (1804–51), among the first Russian women to publish a significant amount of fiction, wrote about society's stifling of intelligent women. Gan, wife of an army captain and mother of four, recorded that other military wives reacted negatively to her writing. Zhukova, separated from a spendthrift husband, began publishing stories in 1837 to support herself and a son. Although Sand's popularity in Russia, ruled by the highly conservative tsar Nicholas I, may seem surprising, women and men could read her tales as commentaries on unhappy private lives, not threatening to public order. Some Russian moralists saw danger in Sand's emphasis on love, however, just as they questioned the role of women like the poet Karolina Pavlova (1807–93) in literary salons, which fostered the development of Russian as a literary language but also reflected the importance of French in upper-class education and society.

By the early 1840s Sand extended her fictional attacks on social injustice to the condition of the working classes, a stance placing her in the company of socialists like Michel de Bourges, Pierre Leroux, and Félicité de Lamennais. With such advocacy Sand also disputed the notion that she was simply a *femme auteur* writing for other women. She became the patroness of several male working-class authors celebrated by Lamartine and the literary elite when worker-poetry was in vogue. Like Flora Tristan, who exposed English working-class miseries in *Promenades dans Londres* (1840), she believed that articulate workers would help lead in creating a more just society. Artisan-writer Agricol Perdiguier, model for Sand's hero in *Le Compagnon du Tour de France* (1840), benefited from the largesse her earnings made possible. That nearly all the acclaimed worker-poets were men was a sign that deficiencies in working-class education were even more marked for women than for men. Yet Antoinette Quarré (1813–47), the relatively well-educated illegitimate daughter of a middle-class mother in provincial Dijon, found in the vogue for worker-poetry an opportunity to gain renown. She refashioned her identity, presenting herself as a humble dressmaker, and profited from literary patrons' willingness to aid talented workers.

Whereas Sand drew many humble characters from an artisanal rather than industrial milieu, English novelist Elizabeth Gaskell (1810–65) provided notable renditions of the largely unregulated factories of the early industrial era, farther advanced in England than elsewhere. Married to a Unitarian minister and mother of four daughters, Gaskell moved from writing short pieces to longer works after her only son died in infancy. *Mary Barton* (1848) and *North and South* (1855) presented troubling aspects of the Manchester industrial setting, but her heroines played woman's traditional role of conciliator, trying to bring employers and workers together. Gaskell was also the first biographer of Charlotte Brontë (1816–55), whose acclaimed semiautobiographical novel *Jane Eyre* (1847), published under the pseudonym of "Currer Bell," recounted the travails of an orphan who became a governess.

Sand's and Gaskell's wideranging interests in matters political, social, and economic challenged some commentators' assumptions that most women's concerns were, or should be, limited to private family matters. More than one study of British literature has pinpointed the 1840s as the moment when male authors began vying noticeably with women for prestige as novelists, in the process multiplying critiques of women's literary abilities. After Walter Scott's success, more men took up what had been considered a woman's genre, translations of his books evidently also inspiring more men elsewhere in Europe to write novels. Stendhal, initially known for essays and biography, published his first novel in 1827 and his classic *The Red and the Black* in 1831. Balzac's realistic novels exposed the greed, pettiness, and other foibles of the French from all social classes, and contemporary critics often compared Sand favorably to him. Yet as more men competed with women for recognition as novelists, many critics and male authors insisted that certain topics were inappropriate for women, for moral reasons or because of their presumed ignorance, and so advised women to stick to sentimental domestic fiction and not try to emulate the social realism of writers like Charles Dickens. The French backlash against women authors included nasty caricatures as well as negative book reviews.

In such an atmosphere it is not surprising that successful women writers like Sand or, later, George Eliot disparaged many women's intellectual abilities, making comments that now seem unduly hostile. Although inspired by Sand's example, Mary Ann Evans ("George Eliot") published "Silly Novels by Lady Novelists" in the progressive *Westminster Review* in 1856. The young Fanny Lewald (1811–89), also influenced by Sand, distanced herself from what she saw as trivial in other German women's fiction. Writing was Lewald's release from personal unhappiness, including conflict with her domineering merchant father, who long resisted her pleas to allow her to publish anonymously. Her first novels, *Clementine* (1842) and *Jenny* (1843), presented dilemmas in women's lives, yet her biting satire *Diogena* (1847) mocked aristocratic women's travails in novels by Countess Ida Hahn-Hahn. In a different vein, women socialists complained that novels diverted readers from thinking about serious problems and ways to effect social change.

Despite much criticism, more women managed to publish their work and gain recognition by the mid-nineteenth century. Earning a living from writing was always chancy, but more women did so, including larger numbers of single women. Of a group of 144 English women authors born between 1800 and 1880, 44 percent (64) were single. Authors benefited from new publishing formats and the increased numbers of readers produced by the expansion of schooling. Magazine editors lured readers with serialized novels, as did French newspaper editors like Émile de Girardin, who in 1836 introduced the *feuilleton*, a segment of a novel on the lower half of a page or two of the daily paper. Writers, like other nineteenth-century professionals, also sought to protect their economic interests. French writers started the Société des Gens de Lettres (Society of Authors) to safeguard published authors' rights to their intellectual property and provide modest financial security. Between its founding in 1837 and 1870, 91 women were among 246 members. The General Association of German Writers had only 4 women among 150 members in 1880, and a British authors' group that emerged in 1883 did not admit women until 1889.

Male authors' resistance to competition from women mirrored the general critique of women's work in the larger society. The shrill insistence that women properly belonged in the private space of the home, not in public spaces, was connected to several developments. As industrialization increasingly altered economic structures, moving more production from homes or small shops to larger factories, many commentators deplored women's work in factories. Critics objected to the immorality of mixing the sexes in the workplace, often overlooking the economic need that drove women to seek work and accept less pay than men. Doctors and scientists objected that arduous physical labor was too taxing for many women and might impair childbearing ability, and some claimed that women's excessive use of intellectual powers caused nervous strain and might have similar dire results. Political developments also made an impact. The revolutions of 1848, like the revolution of 1789, triggered a wideranging backlash against advocates of radical, or even gradual, reform and reinforced the rhetoric about the separateness of masculine and feminine spheres – even though in reality many women's lives were not rigidly separated from public issues or activities.

Many women authors took political stances in reaction to the more than fifty revolutions that swept across France, the Italian peninsula, German states, and the multinational Austrian Empire in February and March 1848. Sand acted on her democratic ideals by writing publicity releases for the provisional government of the Second Republic that replaced the Orleanist monarchy. She refused, however, to allow a group of women to submit her name as a candidate for the constitutional assembly, after their newspaper *La Voix des Femmes* heralded her as a "genius" whose candidacy men would accept because she "has become a man through her courage, but remained a woman in her maternal nature." As violence in Paris undercut support for the new order in June 1848, she began retreating from politics. After Louis Napoleon Bonaparte's election as president of the democratic republic and later coup to perpetuate himself in power, Sand turned to writing novels about rural life. During the 1860s, when several authors proposed nominating her for a place among the forty literary "immortals" of the Académie Française, she demurred, writing that "In our time women's place is no more in the Academy than in the Senate, the legislative body, or the army."[8] While Sand withdrew to Nohant, Marie d'Agoult wrote an account of the 1848 revolution and attracted opponents of Napoleon III's Second Empire (1852–70) to her Paris salon.

The failure of liberal political reforms or nationalist projects also affected literary women in Austrian regions and Italian and German states. The Italian aristocrat Cristina Belgiojoso, who organized medical care in the short-lived Roman Republic in 1849, could not safely return to her estate in Austrian-controlled Lombardy and from exile wrote travel accounts about the Near East before moving to France. The divorced countess Hahn-Hahn became more conservative. Once dubbed a German George Sand, she had written popular novels about independent women, like *Countess Faustine* (1840), and women's miseries in marriage. In 1850, after her male companion died, she converted to Catholicism, endowed a convent, wrote on religious themes, and shunned novel writing until 1860. Lewald's account of the 1848 revolution in Berlin, the Prussian capital, suggested that its leaders tried to change too much too quickly. Louise Aston and Claire von Glümer mixed critiques of angry German crowds with their own support for democratic goals in novels published, respectively, in Baden and Saxony, not in Prussia which led the military repression. Glümer's *Fata Morgana* (1851), set in 1848, featured romance, but Aston created a politically active woman in *Revolution and Counterrevolution* (1849). Aston had written previously about emancipating herself and in 1848 started a journal in Berlin, soon banned, but she ceased publishing after marriage in 1850.

Bozena Nemcová (1820–62), celebrated as the first important Czech woman author, was part of the literary revival of the Czech language that preceded the failed Prague uprising against Austro-German control in 1848. Wife of a minor Czech official moved from post to post, she incorporated folklore in her published stories and gained fame with

---

[8] Quotations in Donna Dickenson, *George Sand: A Brave Man, the Most Womanly Woman* (Oxford: Berg, 1988), 70, 72.

Babicka (1855, Grandmother), a novel based on her own childhood experiences with her grandmother in a village. Nemcová was the illegitimate daughter of servants in a noble household, or perhaps a noblewoman's daughter. Life with her parents was unhappy, and marriage at the age of seventeen to an older, sometimes violent, man brought new difficulties. Writing provided an escape from travails, and certain intellectuals' early encouragement reinforced her commitment to it. Poetry "awakened" her to life, she once wrote, and using her mind let her be "independent" of her husband. When she "seized the national idea with my whole heart," she hoped that it too would satisfy her "yearnings" for more than the joy her children provided. Yet Nemcová was often cautious. Her famous poem "To Czech Women" (1843) emphasized that while men fought with weapons, women served by educating children, although her poem "Glorious Morning" (1845) did call on women to become "regiments of warriors," emulating mythical past heroines. *Babicka* became a Czech classic, praised by nationalist historian František Palacký and translated into French, Russian, German, and English. Celebrating a traditional hard-working Czech woman and family customs, it was a veiled nationalist protest and also comparable to Sand's literary renditions of humble peasants. The Czech grandmother refused to be awed by noble privilege when she encountered a duchess. Although Nemcová became increasingly independent, she challenged traditional gender roles less than social class barriers. Woman, she wrote in *Village in the Mountains* (1856), "must be raised to the ruler's seat next to man, not to judge, not to punish, but as an angel of peace between him and the world."[9] Among the younger women she inspired was the successful novelist Karolina Svetlá.

Scandinavian women wrote in a less politically repressive atmosphere than Nemcová but also bemoaned familial and societal repression of women's aspirations. Fredrika Bremer (1801–65), Sweden's first major woman novelist, was the daughter of a wealthy landowner who hired a governess and tutors to educate his daughters, their lessons including French, German, and English. Allowed to read English novels when she was fifteen, Fredrika thought Lovelace's exploitation of women in Richardson's *Clarissa* appalling. The Bremers and their daughters often traveled but, despite diversions, Fredrika found life dismal. She began

---

[9] Quotations in Wilma Abeles Iggers, *Women of Prague: Ethnic Diversity and Social Change from the Eighteenth Century to the Present* (Providence, R.I.: Berghahn Books, 1995), 74, 75, 80; and Jitka Malecková, "Nationalizing Women and Engendering the Nation: The Czech National Movement," in *Gendered Nations: Nationalisms and Gender Order in the Long Nineteenth Century*, ed. Ida Blom, Karen Hagemann, and Catherine Hall (Oxford: Berg, 2000), 303.

writing while depressed and first published stories anonymously. She used family settings for *Familjen H* (1831), *Hemmet* (1839, Home), and other realistic novels like *Nina* (1835) and *Neighbors* (1837). Soon she was a popular writer, awarded a medal by the Swedish Academy and her identity no secret. Bremer's depictions of women evolved, as her conventional self-sacrificing women gave way to showing in *Hemmet* that parents and society thwarted daughters' efforts to develop themselves. Rejecting marriage proposals, she studied English political economy and corresponded with Maria Edgeworth and Harriet Martineau, author of *Illustrations of Political Economy* (1832–34). Translations of her stories into German, English, French, Dutch, and Danish let her realize a childhood dream of becoming important for Sweden. During a long trip to the United States in 1849–51, she heard that her books were nearly as popular as Dickens's novels.

Bremer's American sojourn also afforded contact with the women's rights activity developing since 1848. She was impressed by women who conducted public meetings where they compared women's situation to that of slaves in southern states. Visiting England in 1851 reinforced her interest in reform work, reflected in her novel *Hertha* (1856), later called a starting point for Swedish feminism. The heroine and her sisters suffered from a cold father's domineering ways – a situation mirroring Bremer's own life. Hertha was entitled to an inheritance from her mother, but her father controlled it. Bremer herself could not control her finances, including income from writing, until she was almost forty. The capable Hertha, convinced that Jesus's message was one of equality between the sexes, decided to help other women and urged them to seek a larger purpose in life. Initially townspeople found her strange, but after a catastrophic fire they applauded the relief work she undertook with other women. Hertha met a soul mate, engineer Yngve Nordin, but her father delayed consent to their marriage, and as a dutiful daughter, despite her independent ideas, she would not sue to gain legal independence and protect her inheritance. The father agreed to the marriage only when Yngve lay dying, and when the father died, there was no inheritance left. Hertha, in the meantime, opened a girls' school and held "conversations" with older girls to develop their self-reliance and awareness of social problems. A grateful town preserved Hertha's legacy after her death. Bremer's depiction of women's legal inferiority helped influence the passage of laws in 1858 and 1863 that improved unmarried women's status, and a Swedish feminist association created in 1884 was named after her.

Norwegian author Camilla Collett (1813–95) also figured in Scandinavian feminism. Daughter of a politically prominent father and sister of Norway's leading Romantic poet, she had an education shaped by her father's liking of Rousseau's *Émile*. Her brother Henrik Wergeland studied a wide range of subjects, but her destiny at age thirteen was the finishing school, first in the capital Christiania (renamed Oslo in 1924) and then in Germany. Collett published her famous first novel, *The District Governor's Daughters* (1854–55, *Amtmandens Døttre*) anonymously. Like most contemporary women novelists, she presented marriage as the desirable destiny for women, provided that it was based on mutual love, not financial arrangements. Her father and brother had thwarted her own first romance and compelled her sister to marry someone she did not love. After ten years of marriage to a lawyer, Collett was widowed with four sons in 1851 and then began publishing stories and articles. *The District Governor's Daughters* told of a young love blocked by parents and by chance, its heroine accepting marriage to an older man. Collett called it "the long suppressed cry from my heart," and in 1862, abandoning anonymity, published a revealing memoir. Responses to her commentary on women's status evolved from hostility to greater receptivity. The King of Sweden and Norway (then jointly ruled) awarded her a gold medal, and famed playwright Henrik Ibsen called her prose "the best to be found in Norway."[10] By the time that Ibsen's controversial character Nora in *A Doll's House* (1879) became an internationally known symbol of the miseries of housewives who felt trapped in middle-class comfort, Collett's *From the Camp of the Mutes* (1877) had indicted centuries of literature for relegating women to inferior status. She became more radical as she recognized that making marriage partners truly equal required legal and social changes as well. Considered Norway's first feminist, she wrote an essay on Norwegian women's status for *The Woman Question in Europe* (1884), a volume edited by the son of American women's rights pioneer Elizabeth Cady Stanton.

Women and the high culture / popular culture divide

George Eliot (1819–80) gained a place among the authors of nineteenth-century English classics, along with Dickens and Thackeray – a rare accomplishment for a woman writer. Her novels that became part of the canon of English literature fit into what arbiters of taste term "high culture." As newspapers and periodicals proliferated and many print materials became cheaper, contemporaries, including literary critics, began speaking of a distinction between "high culture" and "popular

---

[10] Quotations in Kirsten Seaver, "Translator's Introduction," to Camilla Collett, *The District Governor's Daughters* (Norwich: Norvik Press, 1992), 7, 13.

culture," an enduring dichotomy. Matthew Arnold and Eliot were among the intellectuals using the term "high culture" by the 1850s and 1860s. A similar dichotomy for visual and musical arts was identified as the mass production of images increased and musical venues multiplied. Publications that arbiters of taste placed in the high culture category included scholarly works in philosophy and history, among other disciplines, and serious fiction and essays by recognized authors whose works rated inclusion in various countries' canons of literary classics. Although popular culture could include oral traditions, publications designated "popular" were often mass-circulation newspapers and magazines which offered serialized stories of romance or adventure to lure readers into buying the next issues. Success in a serialized format could determine whether fictional works later appeared as books.

Eliot, born Mary Ann Evans, began her literary career with translations and criticism before publishing the novels that made her famous. An avid reader, she attended boarding schools and received private lessons in German, Italian, Greek, and Latin. Her stern father was an estate manager, whose household she ran after her mother died in 1836. They conflicted during the 1840s when she refused to attend church because she doubted certain religious tenets. Influenced by recent German scholarship placing the Bible in historical context, she translated David Friedrich Strauss's controversial *Life of Jesus* and Ludwig Feuerbach's *Essence of Christianity*. A small annuity received after her father's death in 1849 enabled her to move to London, where she wrote for, and helped edit, the *Westminster Review*, and became part of a literary circle that included philosopher Herbert Spencer and writer George Henry Lewes. Her long liaison with Lewes, who was married and legally unable to divorce (evidently because he had condoned his wife's adultery), lasted from 1853 until his death in 1878, the irregularity of their household causing family members to shun her. With Lewes's encouragement, Evans began writing fiction, first using the pseudonym George Eliot in 1857 – although the Feuerbach translation had appeared with her own name. Her first novel, *Adam Bede* (1859), was a great success. Then followed *The Mill on the Floss*; *Silas Marner*; *Romola*; *Felix Holt*; *Middlemarch*, usually judged her greatest novel; and *Daniel Deronda*. She realistically depicted farmers, tradesmen, and the lower middle classes of the English Midlands. More than one male character, including Adam Bede and *Middlemarch*'s Caleb Garth, resembled her father. There were also autobiographical elements in the intelligent, intense heroine of *The Mill on the Floss*, Maggie Tulliver, ostracized by her brother and the community after her reputation was unjustly compromised. Critically acclaimed during her lifetime as a major novelist, Eliot enjoyed financial success.

Eliot's fictional women and plots have elicited a variety of comments, as has her complicated relationship to contemporary reform efforts on behalf of women. In 1855 she published (anonymously) a sympathetic article about the ideas of American writer Margaret Fuller, and by treating Wollstonecraft as Fuller's precursor she drew attention to the *Vindication of the Rights of Woman*, often vilified or ignored since 1800. Because many of Eliot's women characters lived deadening lives and endured economic hardship, due to limited education, social prejudice, and male cruelty, some recent commentators underscore feminist themes in her fiction. Mrs. Transome in *Felix Holt*, for example, stated that "God was cruel when he made women." Eliot was friendly with the reformer Barbara Bodichon for nearly three decades and in 1856 signed a petition for improving married women's property rights. Yet she refused to support women's suffrage when John Stuart Mill and others advocated it in 1866. Like the positivist philosopher Auguste Comte, she and Lewes believed that social progress required the cooperation of men and women, each making distinctive contributions. Women's "exquisite type of gentleness, tenderness, possible maternity" was part of their "peculiar constitution for a special moral influence," which entering the public arena could harm, she argued.[11] Her ambivalence on women's rights was possibly influenced by her father's contempt for many reformers after the French Revolution, as well as by reluctance to take on additional public controversy when many judged her relationship with Lewes scandalous.

Eliot wanted to see herself as superior to the "silly" lady novelists she had discussed in 1856. Unfairly discounting previous generations of English women writers, she also asserted that "in France alone woman has had a vital influence on the development of literature ... in France alone, if the writings of women were swept away, a serious gap would be made in the national history."[12] Many critics separated Eliot from the category of "women" novelists whom they took less seriously. Popular author Margaret Oliphant echoed many male reviewers when she judged in 1885 that Eliot's books were "less definable in point of sex than the books of any other woman who has ever written" because of their size, "freedom of style, an absence of that timidity" of many other women. Yet unlike Austen, whose reputation grew over time, Eliot's reputation after her death was somewhat diminished by male critics who increasingly

---

[11] Eliot quoted in Bonnie Zimmerman, "George Eliot and Feminism: The Case of *Daniel Deronda*," in *Nineteenth-Century Women Writers of the English-Speaking World*, ed. Rhoda B. Nathan (Westport, Conn.: Greenwood Press, 1986), 231, 232.

[12] Quoted in Eva Martin Sartori and Dorothy Wynne Zimmerman, eds., *French Women Writers* (Lincoln: University of Nebraska Press, 1994), xv.

chastised women for venturing into supposedly masculine subjects. Leslie Stephen, father of novelist Virginia Woolf, complained in 1888 about Eliot's "feminine tendency ... to accept philosophers at their own valuation."[13] Some twentieth-century critics also thought that Victorian moralizing marred her art, but many still consider that Eliot's depth and complexity makes her England's greatest woman novelist. Most nineteenth-century women authors were not so highly regarded.

Margaret Oliphant in England and Eugenie Marlitt in Germany were among the popular women authors profiting from initial publication of their work in serialized formats. Both wrote to earn a living, as did many other women who suffered changes in financial circumstances. Oliphant (1828–97) was a prolific writer who excelled at telling stories. The daughter of a minor customs official, she was educated at home in Scotland and published her first novel by the time she was twenty-one. In 1852 she married a stained-glass artist and went to live in London. His death in 1859 left her with debts and three young children, and she returned to Edinburgh. Her *Autobiography* (1899), published posthumously, recorded how she stayed up at night to write the first novel in the series *The Chronicles of Carlingford* (1862–76), which established her literary reputation. She noted, "I don't think I have ever had two hours uninterrupted ... during the whole of my literary life."[14] Each *Carlingford* volume was first serialized in *Blackwood's Magazine*. Oliphant's novels totaled nearly one hundred, many with plots about unhappy marriages or strong women who support weak or ineffective husbands, fathers, or brothers. She wrote biographies, histories, and travel books as well, and edited Blackwood's foreign classics series, for which she wrote volumes on Dante and Cervantes. The Macmillan Publishing Company also contracted for her work and paid her about £500 a year between 1870 and 1891. All told, her literary production amounted to 250 volumes.

Friederike Eugenie John (1825–87), who first published as E. Marlitt to mask her sex, was born in a small central German town, the daughter of a failed businessman. Her mother recognized her vocal talent and helped her sixteen-year-old daughter obtain support from the ruling family. Princess Mathilde von Schwarzburg-Sonderhausen arranged for further training. John spent three years in Vienna and made her singing debut in Leipzig in 1846, but a loss of hearing cut short her operatic

---

[13] Oliphant and Stephen quoted in Gaye Tuchman, with Nina S. Fortin, *Edging Women Out: Victorian Novelists, Publishers, and Social Change* (New Haven, Conn.: Yale University Press, 1989), 186, 187.

[14] Quoted in Virginia Blain, Isobel Grundy, and Patricia Clements, eds., *The Feminist Companion to Literature in English* (New Haven, Conn.: Yale University Press, 1990), 813.

career. In 1853 she began ten years of employment as her patroness's companion. When Mathilde, divorced, could no longer pay her, she lived with her brother, a teacher, and turned to her pen at the age of thirty-eight. Marlitt's success was tied to the magazine *Die Gartenlaube* (The Arbor), with a circulation of more than 325,000 by the early 1870s. It was advertised as a family magazine, but Marlitt's stories appealed especially to women. The popularity of her first short story in 1865 and first novel in 1866 created demand for her next manuscripts, published in *Die Gartenlaube* before appearing as books and sometimes translated into English, French, Spanish, Portuguese, Italian, Swedish, or Russian. Although her fiction lacked the explicit protests found in Sand, she often showed women overcoming adversity before a happy ending. For example, in *Goldelse* (1866) a middle-class woman married an aristocrat, a crossing of class barriers less unusual by the mid nineteenth century. In *Die Zweite Frau* (1874, The Second Wife) an impoverished aristocrat bowed to her mother's wishes and married an arrogant aristocratic widower seeking a wife to care for his son. Marriage ended her need to earn money illustrating books, and she devoted herself to domestic duties. Because of her exemplary dedication and pleasing personality, her initially indifferent husband became loving and her stepson's behavior improved. This Cinderella tale of leaving poverty for riches, happiness, and secure social position offered readers an escape from humdrum existences, and such plots kept readers from all social ranks, including working women, eager for Marlitt's next books. Indeed, a shortened version of *Second Wife* remained in print in 1991. Marlitt, never married, produced ten novels, plus short stories, and bought a villa in 1871.

In Russian-ruled Poland Eliza Pawlowska Orzeskowa (1841–1910), daughter of a landowning family, became a successful professional writer, authoring popular novels and non-fiction. Her complete works occupy fifty-two volumes. First educated by governesses, she also attended a Catholic boarding school in Warsaw where she met her life-long friend Maria Konopnicka (1842–1910), later Poland's leading woman poet. She married Piotr Orzesko, a landowner twice her age, with whom she became part of the failed Polish uprising of 1863. His deportation to Siberia and the confiscation of his estate necessitated that she earn money. Mindful of Russian censors and police, Orzeskowa penned realistic novels about provincial life, compared by some critics to Balzac's fiction. Her characters in *Waclawa's Journals*, *Marta*, *Eli Makower*, *Meir Ezofowicz*, and *Dziurdziowie* included women, gentry farmers, peasants, and Jews. A nationalist, she created heroines and heroes who rose above the prejudices or interests of their social class or ethnic group to act for the good of the entire community. *Marta* (1873), translated into fifteen languages, struck a responsive chord with many readers. It chronicled the dilemmas of a young widow trying to support herself and a child but lacking vocational skills and the social status enjoyed while her prosperous husband was alive. Unable to do other work after she lost a sewing job, she resorted to begging and stealing, and died when hit by a horse-tram. The plot had autobiographical elements, for Orzeskowa divorced her husband after his return from exile and believed that her marital status, coupled with literary work, made her a social outcast. *Marta* reputedly prompted hundreds of young women to seek more education, some of them leaving Poland to attend universities. Orzeszkowa credited Sand's novels with influencing Polish women's ideas about emancipation and, like Collett, contributed an essay to Theodore Stanton's *Woman Question*. She used an inheritance to open a publishing house in Vilnius, but Russian officials closed it in 1882 after the assassination of Alexander II, and confined her to her home, where she then taught local girls. During the political thaw after the Russian revolution of 1905 she edited the *Lithuanian Courier* and was honored by women's groups.

The life stories of Oliphant, Marlitt, and Nemcová, among others, are those of successful women writers after 1850 from backgrounds other than the aristocratic or upper-middle-class milieus of many predecessors, particularly predecessors not from England or parts of northern Europe. Nonetheless, the educational advantages and sense of one's social importance that came with upper-class status still figured in some aristocratic women's paths to gaining literary recognition, as with the Austrians Marie Ebner-Eschenbach and Berta von Suttner, and the Spaniard Emilia Pardo Bazán.

The socially prominent Ebner-Eschenbach (1830–1916), born Marie von Dubsky, believed that German women authors had more difficulty gaining acceptance than French and English women. She recorded in *Meine Kinderjahre* (1906), her autobiography to the age of fourteen, the importance of her governess's encouragement of her writing when many relatives voiced hostility to it. Eventually encouragement also came from a stepmother and from her aristocratic husband, an older cousin whom she married in 1848. Nonetheless, he and others worried that the failure of her first plays, including one about Madame Roland, reflected badly on the family name. The childless Marie persisted, and after her first successful collection of stories in 1875, more literary hits followed. Her novel *Das Gemeindekind* (1887, Child of the Parish) exposed social class prejudice, provoking comparisons with Dickens's *Oliver Twist*. In this story about two children left alone after their father committed murder and their mother was jailed, a baroness gave the girl, Milada, the seeming advantage of a convent education but rejected the boy, Pavel. Milada, mistreated by nuns, wasted away; Pavel, at a simple village school, enjoyed a kind teacher's tutelage. Not forgetting her own struggles to gain recognition, Ebner-Eschenbach joined the Austrian Women Writers' and Artists' Union, founded in 1885 to help women become established professionally. Her own literary network included Ida von Fleischl-Marxow, poet Betty Paoli, and novelists Louise von François and Enrica von Handel-Mazzetti. She also supported the Association for Extended Women's Education. Ebner-Eschenbach's novels typically placed women in domestic settings, but her critiques of marriages arranged for economic advantage, as in *Zwei Komtessen* (1883, Two Countesses), and depiction of strong women overcoming adversity won plaudits from feminists, who considered that her achievement bolstered their cause, even though she did not join a feminist association. Feminists often quoted her aphorism, "The woman problem was born when a woman learnt to read."[15] Regarded by 1900 as Austria's leading woman author, she received messages for her seventieth birthday signed by 10,000 women, and in 1910 became the first woman awarded an honorary doctorate by the University of Vienna.

The younger Berta von Suttner (1843–1914), daughter of an Austrian general, rebelled against her family's military tradition and embraced pacifism. Well educated, she became the governess of Baron von Suttner's daughters in 1873, and eloped with his son Arthur in 1876. Highly independent and progressive thinkers, they lived in Russia for nine years, he working as an engineer and journalist while she taught. Berta published her first novel in 1883 and another seven before *Die Waffen Nieder* (1889, Lay Down Your Arms) made her famous throughout Europe. The heroine's life, traced from childhood to the Franco-Prussian War, had autobiographical elements. Martha von Tilling, at seventeen, was enthusiastic about the Austro-Sardinian War of 1859, but by 1871 the horrors of war had destroyed her happiness. In a much-quoted statement, Russian author Leo Tolstoy likened the impact of Suttner's antiwar novel to that of Harriet Beecher Stowe's antislavery classic, *Uncle Tom's Cabin*. By 1914, forty editions and translations in sixteen languages had appeared. Suttner spearheaded the founding of the Austrian Peace Society in 1891 and encouraged peace groups elsewhere, but fewer Europeans joined such associations than read her book. A symbol of international peace efforts as arms races

[15] Quoted by Harriet Anderson, *Utopian Feminism: Women's Movements in Fin-de-Siècle Vienna* (New Haven, Conn.: Yale University Press, 1992), 144.

intensified, she received the 1905 Nobel peace prize, one of the annual awards that had recently been created by the legacy of Swedish millionaire Alfred Nobel.

Emilia Pardo Bazán (1851–1921), Spain's leading woman novelist, was the only child of provincial nobles who nurtured her intellectual development but imposed some restrictions. Her mother directed her early education; her politically moderate father considered that women's intelligence was the equal of men's, yet also controlled her reading as an adolescent. When the family left provincial Galicia to spend winters in Madrid, Emilia attended a school where, she recalled, the French directress treated students "worse than galley slaves" and made them speak only French. She found books in her father's library "more beneficial" than some of her tutors, and would have preferred to study Latin instead of the piano, against which she "secretly rebelled," but her preferences were ignored. When she reached age fourteen, her parents allowed more choice of books, letting her read moralistic novels by Fernán Caballero (pseudonym of Cecilia Böhl de Faber) but only after she produced acceptable needlework. They regarded major French novelists as too "pernicious for a young lady," but the curious Emilia took a copy of Hugo's *Notre Dame de Paris* from a friend's house and read it at night. By the time of her marriage, at age sixteen, to a Galician noble studying law at the University of Santiago de Compostela, she recognized deficiencies in her education and began extensive reading in philosophy, also securing tutoring in mathematics and sciences. Only 19 percent of Spanish women were literate by the 1870s, as compared to 47 percent of men, and Pardo Bazán saw that men with access to advanced schooling did not understand how difficult it was for a woman "to teach herself and fill the gaps in her education."[16] Most contemporary Spanish women authors came from the same background as their readers, the landowning and professional classes, only 15 percent of the population. For leisure reading, Pardo Bazán chose French, English, and Spanish novels, and during this time of intellectual self-development did not have the parental concerns later brought by three children, born between 1876 and 1881.

Pardo Bazán published her first poetry and essays in journals and newspapers during the late 1860s and 1870s and a first novel in 1879, but her literary celebrity came in the 1880s with several more novels and her essays on French literary naturalism, *La Cuestión Palpitante* (1883, The Burning Question). The latter was a defining event in her life and career.

---

[16] Emilia Pardo Bazán, "Autobiographical Sketches" [1886], in *The House of Ulloa*, trans. Roser Caminals-Heath (Athens: University of Georgia Press, 1992), 268, 271, 273, 274, 282.

The controversial essays, first published in a Madrid newspaper, drew condemnation from the pulpit, for naturalist Émile Zola's exposés of the seamy side of human life – alcoholism, prostitution, workers living like animals – challenged older notions that art should uplift and moralize. Conflict with her socially prominent husband also ensued. After he gave her an ultimatum to stop writing, she left him. *La Dama Joven* (1885) recounted a similar conflict between a young wife's ambitions and a husband's demands, but in the story an actress renounced her career to pacify her mate. Women paid an emotional price for pursuing creative ambitions, Pardo Bazán wrote in 1895: "What for a man are flowers are for us thorns. Each step toward art costs us some pain and some injury."[17]

In the naturalist novel considered Pardo Bazán's masterpiece, *Los Pazos de Ulloa* (1886, The House of Ulloa), the central woman character Nucha was the long-suffering wife of a crude, brutal, philandering aristocrat. Living on an isolated rural estate, where her husband's mistress and illegitimate son were servants, she was yet another literary commentary on the naivete of many young women entering marriages dictated by parents. The plot was equally an indictment of aristocratic decadence, featuring an arrogant landowner blind to economic ruination ahead. Nucha found solace with her daughter and a resident priest, who first counseled acceptance of female duty but later tried to help her flee. Her fate was to waste away and die, leaving her daughter to grow up neglected and in tatters. The controversial novel drew much critical acclaim, but some who praised it also complained that its revealing autobiographical prologue was in poor taste. Other critics denigrated its brutal naturalism, prompting Pardo Bazán to counter that her work, unlike French naturalism, was compatible with Spanish Catholic traditions, which she respected.

As a major novelist, Pardo Bazán belonged to a generation of Spanish writers better able than predecessors to earn a living by writing, Benito Pérez Galdós most notable among them. Although she had inherited wealth and received money from her husband, she wanted to project the image of a woman who could support herself and exist independently. After beginning an affair with Galdós in 1888, she sensed her life undergoing "a kind of transposition from the condition of woman to that of man."[18] She welcomed public recognition, becoming the first woman member of the Ateneo, Madrid's leading literary group, and was

[17] Quoted in Ruth El Saffar, "Emilia Pardo Bazán (1851–1921)," in *Spanish Women Writers: A Bio-Bibliographical Sourcebook*, ed. Linda Gould Levine, Ellen Engelson Marson, and Gloria Feiman Waldman (Westport, Conn.: Greenwood Press, 1993), 380.

[18] Quoted in Stephen Miller, "Pardo Bazán, Emilia (1852 [sic]–1921): Reception of Her by Male Colleagues, 1870–1921," in *The Feminist Encyclopedia of Spanish Literature*, ed.

dismayed when the Royal Academy rejected her candidacy after a nasty debate. Not surprisingly, Pardo Bazán's journal articles often detailed the difficulties facing women. At her own expense she founded the review *Nuevo Teatro Crítico* (New Critical Theater), using it during the 1890s to discuss not only literature but also women's education and roles. In an essay on Spanish women published in the London *Fortnightly Review* in 1889, she complained that "the social distance between the two sexes is today greater than it was in old Spain. Men have gained rights and privileges in which women have no share."[19] Although Pardo Bazán's nineteen novels, thirty volumes of non-fiction, and more than 1,500 newspaper columns brought her into the public arena, she recognized, like French women a century earlier, that the political liberalism which made Spain a constitutional monarchy did not grant women all of the rights enjoyed by men. Even in 1916, after the education minister named her to a chair at the University of Madrid, students boycotted her classes and she stopped lecturing. The academic appointment indicated, nonetheless, her status as the author of contemporary classics.

The identification of the "new" woman: authors and heroines

During the 1890s the term "new woman" entered vocabularies. Coined by English novelist Sarah Grand, it signified the attitudes and lifestyles of women who chose careers or love on their own terms. Like the term "feminism," first widely used during the 1890s after decades of discussion of women's rights, the term "new woman" or its French equivalent, *la femme nouvelle*, well described choices already made by many women. Literary women in the public limelight were not a novelty by the 1890s, nor was their addressing of many public issues, including restrictions, formal and informal, on women's lives. Women authors' attention to women's issues mirrored ongoing controversy about marital relationships, women's entry into previously all-male professions, and new demands for women's suffrage. Their sensitivity to women's dilemmas was often rooted in personal experience, as was true for earlier generations. Some of the women who gained literary renown around 1900 had also benefited from more advanced formal education.

Janet Pérez and Maureen Ihrie, 2 vols. (Westport, Conn.: Greenwood Press, 2002), II: 461.
[19] Emilia Pardo Bazán, "The Women of Spain," *Fortnightly Review* 45 (January–June 1889): 879–904, quotation, 883.

German authors Gabriele Reuter and Ricarda Huch, who published their first important novels during the 1890s, came from comparable middle-class backgrounds. Reuter (1859–1941), born in Egypt where her father had business interests, had to leave school in Germany at the age of thirteen, after his death reduced the family's circumstances. Residing with her ailing mother in Weimar, she read widely and was introduced by her uncle, a painter, to various writers and artists. She already had two novels in print when *Aus Guter Familie* (1895, From a Good Family) made her famous. Subtitled *The Sufferings of a Young Woman*, it traced the stifling of Agathe Heidling's interests, talents, and desires in a middle-class milieu, where her father restricted her reading and thus her ability to think, and wrecked her chances to marry by using her dowry to pay her unworthy brother's debts. After spending two years in a mental institution, Agathe emerged broken in spirit and consigned to a living death. *Aus Guter Familie*, in its eighteenth edition by 1908, started Reuter's lucrative writing career. She published nineteen other books by 1914. Her most popular novel, *Ellen von der Weiden* (1900; 62nd edition, 1923), underscored the psychological suffering of a doctor's wife unfulfilled by domesticity and driven to divorce. Biographies of *Marie von Ebner-Eschenbach* and *Annette von Droste-Hülshoff* responded to growing demand for histories of women and reflected her own interest in how other women had realized literary ambitions. Her most controversial novel, *Das Tränenhaus* (1909, House of Tears), was set in a home for unwed mothers, its heroine a successful author abandoned by an irresponsible man. Reuter herself had a daughter but never married, and she sympathized with reformers' efforts to improve single mothers' situation.

The university-educated Ricarda Huch (1864–1947) was among the "new women" holding academic credentials long the preserve of men. Born into a wealthy Protestant merchant family in Braunschweig, she went to Switzerland to study in 1887 because German universities did not yet formally admit women. She also had to overcome familial resistance: her grandmother feared that scientific study threatened religious faith, and her father was hesitant but unable to stop her while he was in Brazil on business. After receiving a doctorate in history in 1891, Huch first worked in a library and taught in a girls' school in Zurich. She published poetry under the pseudonym Richard Hugo, but it was the neoromantic novel *Erinnerungen von Ludolf Ursleu dem Jüngeren* (1893, Reminiscences of Ludolf Ursleu the Younger) that made her famous. Semiautobiographical, it recounted the decline of a mercantile family, a plot anticipating Thomas Mann's *Buddenbrooks* (1901), and one segment featured women university students. Huch returned to Germany in 1896, expecting to teach, and while in Vienna for research met an Italian dentist whom she married. Their two years in Trieste, where a daughter was born, supplied the setting for her second novel, *Aus der Triumphgasse* (1902), about the poor residents of a squalid area. Settling in Munich in 1900, she continued the writing career that outlasted her first marriage and brief second marriage. She also returned to historical and literary subjects. Huch's books on German Romanticism, published in 1899 and 1902, combined discussion of aesthetic values and creative genius with biography and attention to women's role in literary salons. Her studies of the Thirty Years' War (1618–48) and nineteenth-century Italian unification mixed narration of grand events with psychological profiles and scenes of everyday life, real or imagined, with the result that critics often found her histories amateurish. Yet her essaying of a wide range of subjects built her reputation as the most important German woman writer of the early twentieth century.

For Swedish writer Selma Lagerlöf (1858–1940), formal education also played an important role in shaping ambitions (Figure 2.3). Born in a manor house and sheltered as a child, she experienced her studies at a teacher-training college in Stockholm during the 1880s as a watershed, enabling her to become independent. Financial reverses had necessitated the sale of her family's property, and Lagerlöf taught for ten years at a girls' school, until her literary earnings increased. Her first novel, *Gösta Berlings Saga* (1891), told the story of a defrocked minister and "romantic genius" who eventually reformed his life, aided by his wife. The massive *Jerusalem* (1901–02) opened in a Swedish farming community and progressed to Jerusalem, after a pastor persuaded townspeople to resettle in Palestine. Critics compared *Jerusalem* to Homeric epics or Shakespearean drama, and Lagerlöf received the Nobel prize for literature in 1909, the only woman so honored before 1914.

Training in a teachers' college was also an important formative experience for French author Gabrielle Reval and Italian authors Matilde Serao and Ada Negri. Serao (1856–1927) preferred to work in a state telegraph office and then in journalism, but her "scuola normale femminile" figured in a successful autobiographical story, published in 1885, that featured a new group of professional women teachers and also looked critically at their working conditions, as did some of her other stories about women's workplaces. Reval (1870–1938), a graduate of France's elite institution for training female secondary school professors, published four novels about students and teachers between 1900 and 1910.

For the poet Negri (1870–1945), education was the key to both new social status and a literary career. Unlike the many women authors from upper- or middle-class backgrounds, she came from a working-class

Figure 2.3 Selma Lagerlöf, first woman to receive the Nobel prize for literature.

family in northern Italy. Her grandmother, once a personal maid, was a concierge; her father was a manual laborer; and her mother worked twelve-hour days in a textile factory. Her mother's hard work and sacrifices enabled Ada to continue her education and become an elementary school teacher. At the age of eighteen, she began teaching in a remote village and also published several poems in a Milan newspaper. Her successful first volume of poetry, *Fatalità* (1892, Fate) went through five editions in two years, brought sudden fame, and, like *Tempeste* (1895, Storms), made her the first recognized Italian writer of either sex from working-class origins. There had been no Italian version of the French or English worker-poet movements of the 1830s and 1840s. Publication also led to promotion and a post in a "preparatory" school. Negri's poems described northern Italy's industrial centers, with strong images of factory conditions, dismal working-class dwellings, and workers' feelings of hopelessness. Depictions of workers' physical suffering and strikes violently suppressed reminded readers of French miners in Zola's *Germinal* (1885), but Negri's tone was less pessimistic. Her poetry was popular, author Sofia Bisi-Albini opined, because of its modern and democratic qualities. Success with *Tempeste* allowed Negri to stop teaching and move to Milan, where she married a businessman and gave birth to a daughter whom she adored, as verses in *Maternità* (1904, Motherhood) record. Later separated from her husband, she went to Switzerland, where she wrote poetry expressing the sadness of a woman betrayed.

Contemporaries identified another Italian "new woman" in Sibilla Aleramo's controversial autobiographical novel, *Una Donna* (1906, A Woman), which drew international attention. Aleramo, the pen name of Rina Faccio (1876–1960), attended public school in Milan, but after her father moved the family south in 1887 her formal education ended because the town where he managed a factory had no advanced girls' school. Intellectually progressive, he encouraged her independent study. In *Una Donna* a woman took up writing as an escape from marital unhappiness and provincial boredom. The title character, like Aleramo herself, was raped as a teenager, did not disclose the incident, and agreed to marry the rapist, who worked for her father. Both character and author also sought to justify leaving a young son, a troubling decision necessitated by laws awarding fathers custody when parents separated. After starting to publish articles in magazines, Aleramo moved to Rome in 1902, likening her relocation to Sand's move to Paris. The poet Giovanni Cena, her lover, introduced her to literary circles and encouraged her to write *Una Donna*. Translated into French and English, it received international acclaim for its feminist message, and was often compared to Ibsen's *Doll's House*. Detractors alleged that it encouraged female degeneracy, finding confirmation in Aleramo's 1911 essay characterizing women's literary creativity as a unique transformation of maternal and erotic desires. Later known as much for a flamboyant lifestyle as for literary talent, she never replicated *Una Donna*'s success.

Anastasiia Verbitskaia (1861–1928), author of the first bestselling Russian "women's novels," also introduced a "new woman" into Russian fiction. She was the most popular Russian woman writer of her day but certainly not among the few women whom Russian critics around 1900 finally deemed first-rate authors – such as the symbolist poet Zinaida Gippius. Attracting readers in small towns as well as in St. Petersburg or Moscow, Verbitskaia attributed her success "to the new reader who appeared in the 1890s from the lower classes."[20] From a gentry family on her father's side, she grew up in a home where actors, artists, and writers gathered. Her autobiography presented her grandmother, mother, and sister as the most influential people in her life. She attended a girls' school in Moscow and studied at the Moscow Conservatory, all the while reading European and Russian authors. Although she once envisioned an operatic career, she had to work as a governess and music teacher after her father's death. Her husband, an engineer, also discouraged her performing ambitions but wanted her to earn money, even after three sons were born. She became a journalist during the 1880s and turned to fiction in 1894, when her own life was increasingly unhappy. Depicting women journalists, teachers, medical students, and even labor organizers, Verbitskaia challenged women's restricted place in the family and society in novels like *She Freed Herself* (1899) and the bestselling *Spirit of the Time* (1907–08), set during the 1905 Revolution. After 1899, her own company published her novels and also translations of foreign novels about women. The six volumes of *Keys to Happiness* (1909–13), her most famous novel, were each issued in editions of about 35,000, at a time when few press runs exceeded 10,000. Its theme was Russia's need for "new" ideas and "new" people, including new women. The bold character Mania, an internationally successful dancer, claimed the right to happiness in love and work, and had two lovers, but she scandalized readers less than the lesbians in Lidia Zinov'eva-Annibal's *Thirty-Three Abominations* (1907). In her autobiography Verbitskaia blurred the line between her own life and those of her heroines, evidently trying to maintain readers' interest in her fiction. Its dedication "To My Reader" in 1908 exemplified her often florid prose: "I want like-minded readers ... who, in the affirmation and growth of the individual, see the

---

[20] Quoted in Natasha Kolchevska, "Anastasiia Verbitskaia," in *Russian Women Writers*, ed. Christine D. Tomei (New York: Garland, 1999), I: 612.

dawn of a distant, new, and glittering life ... [and] feel the value of
the isolated individual's protest and ... the most trivial victory of the
spirit."[21] Testimony to the presence of "new women" in eastern as well as
western Europe, that individualistic message displeased the Bolsheviks
after the 1917 revolution.

Conclusion

By the early twentieth century European women's involvement with
literature was wideranging, as estimates for numbers of women authors
reveal. For example, compilations of information on women authors,
made around 1900 and more recently, record 4,000 to 5,000 women
writing in German, their publications including not only fiction, poetry,
biography, history, and travel accounts but also textbooks, religious
devotional materials, cookbooks, household manuals, etiquette books,
and countless newspaper and magazine articles. Women writers organized their own associations in Vienna (1885), Leipzig (1890), and Berlin
(1896, 1898), with one Berlin group claiming 230 members in 1911. For
France, comparable statistics range from 1,200 to 5,000 women writers,
the latter figure matching German counterparts and equating about 20
percent of all French authors in print in 1902. England, France, the
Netherlands, Belgium, Scandinavia, and Germany, as well as German-
speaking areas of Austria-Hungary, all approached near-universal literacy
rates for adult women as well as men by 1910. Some 418 nineteenth-
century Italian women writers could be identified by 1875; and in Spain,
where lower demand for publications correlated with high illiteracy rates,
the number of nineteenth-century women writers nonetheless reached
more than 600. At least 250 Russian women published works between
the 1790s and 1914. Women writers were often underrepresented in
official statistics, however. The German census of 1882 listed only 350
women among 19,380 professional writers, and the British census of
1911 tabulated only 385 women authors and journalists.

Numbers do not, of course, reveal the qualitative dimensions of
women's place in literary history. Male critics still disparaged many
women's writing and often thought that they complimented writers like
Eliot, Sand, Pardo Bazán, Huch, or Lagerlöf, whom they took seriously, by
terming their work unlike most women's writing or more like that of men.
That many women writers produced stories focused on love and family life

---

[21] Anastasiia Verbitskaia, "To My Reader," in *Russia Through Women's Eyes:
Autobiographies from Tsarist Russia*, ed. Toby W. Clyman and Judith Vowles (New
Haven, Conn.: Yale University Press, 1996), 336.

helps explain critical tendencies to identify women's writing as a separate, and lesser, category. So, too, did the content of successful new magazines for women and girls, such as *Femina*, with a circulation of 135,000 in France by 1906. Becoming a bestselling author also could have a different meaning for a woman than for a man, and intellectuals often doubted that popularity was compatible with seriousness. Hedwig Courths-Mahler (1867–1950), a former servant and sales clerk who began publishing in 1905, remained on bestseller lists because of romance novels, such as *Was Gott Zusammenfügt* (1913, What God Has Joined Together), which sold 402,000 copies by 1919 – far more than any book by Huch, whose best-seller, *Ludolf Ursleu*, sold 41,000 copies by 1925, before she became the first woman writer elected to the Prussian Academy of Arts. The Swedish Academy had welcomed Nobel prize winner Lagerlöf in 1914.

Although many women writers criticized their societies for disadvan-taging women, many others, including authors of household manuals, pedagogical literature, or religious texts, did not. Isabella Beeton's *Book of Household Management* (1859), an English bestseller, sold two million copies during the first decade after publication. Expansion of public schooling and compulsory education increased demand for books for young readers, and the French Third Republic's most popular textbook, *Le Tour de la France par Deux Enfants* (1877), sold more than eight million copies. Written by "G. Bruno" (pseudonym of Augustine Fouillée), it told the patriotic story of two orphan boys crossing France. More than 1.5 million copies of Marie Robert Halt's *Suzette* (1889), used in French girls' schools, were printed by 1920. *Jessica's First Prayer* (1867), the story of a slum child by English author Hesba Stretton (pseudonym of Sarah Smith), sold more than 1.5 million copies and was widely translated, Alexander II ordering copies for Russian schools. Some of Agnes Sapper's popular German children's stories reached several hundred thousand readers.

By 1914, women writers as a group were better educated and more widely read than women writers of 1800, and they essayed an impressive array of issues. Novels about women suffering from prejudices and legal disabilities based on gender and class, and essays on women's rights were among the publications advocating reform in various countries. Women's entry into formerly all-male professions also supplied new models for fictional heroines. In England novels and stories with feminist themes multiplied between 1880 and 1920. Women's rights congresses between 1888 and 1914 also celebrated women authors as exemplars of women's achievements in many countries. Admittedly, some women authors, such as Laura Marholm (1854–1928) in Germany, Mary Ward (1851–1920) in England, and Colette Yver (1874–1953) in France, rejected demands for equality of the sexes, particularly political equality, on the grounds that engaging in politics could harm the special attributes of womanhood. Yet the literary success of such antifeminist women entailed tackling public as well as private issues and placed them in a public arena – as their critics, like popular novelist Hedwig Dohm (1831–1919), author of *Die Antifeministen* (1902), readily noted. Women also addressed many issues that were not gender-specific. Suttner's antiwar novel struck responsive chords at a time when European powers were forming opposing alliances. Women socialists treated the injustices and poverty besetting workers, and the first volume of socialist Lily Braun's memoirs, published in 1909, became a bestseller. Women's publications also helped support demands for national independence and celebrated newly independent states, such as Greece and Romania. As women's range of pursuits widened, there was virtually no literary genre or area of knowledge into which some women writers did not venture. Women authors' focus on women's lives in fiction and memoirs did much to raise awareness of women's issues before feminist organizations ever emerged.

Further reading and reference works

Catling, Jo, ed. *A History of Women's Writing in Germany, Austria and Switzerland.* Cambridge: Cambridge University Press, 2000.

Charnon-Deutsch, Lou, and Jo Labanyi, eds. *Culture and Gender in Nineteenth-Century Spain.* Oxford: Clarendon Press, 1995.

Clyman, Toby W., and Judith Vowles, eds. *Russia through Women's Eyes: Autobiographies from Tsarist Russia.* New Haven, Conn.: Yale University Press, 1996.

Davies, Catherine. *Spanish Women's Writing 1849–1996.* London: Athlone Press, 1998.

Dickenson, Donna. *George Sand: A Brave Man, the Most Womanly Woman.* Oxford: Berg, 1988.

Diethe, Carol. *Towards Emancipation: German Women Writers of the Nineteenth Century.* New York: Berghahn Books, 1998.

Fergus, Jan. *Jane Austen: A Literary Life.* London: Macmillan, 1991.

Finch, Alison. *Women's Writing in Nineteenth-Century France.* Cambridge: Cambridge University Press, 2000.

Flint, Kate. *The Woman Reader 1837–1914.* Oxford: Clarendon Press, 1993.

Forsås-Scott, Helena. *Swedish Women's Writing 1850–1995.* London: Athlone, 1997.

Garton, Janet. *Norwegian Women's Writing 1850–1990.* London: Athlone, 1993.

Gilbert, Sandra M., and Susan Gubar. *The Madwoman in the Attic: The Woman Writer and the Nineteenth-Century Literary Imagination. 2nd edn.* New Haven: Yale University Press, 2000.

Glenn, Kathleen M., and Mercedes Mazquiarán de Rodríguez, eds. *Spanish Women Writers and the Essay: Gender, Politics, and the Self*. Columbia: University of Missouri Press, 1998.

González-Arias, Francisca. *Portrait of a Woman as Artist: Emilia Pardo Bazán and the Modern Novel in France and Spain*. New York: Garland Publishing, 1992.

Gutwirth, Madelyn. *Madame de Staël, Novelist: The Emergence of the Artist as a Woman*. Urbana: University of Illinois Press, 1978.

Gutwirth, Madelyn, Avriel Goldberger, and Karyna Szmurlo, eds. *Germaine de Staël: Crossing the Borders*. New Brunswick, N.J.: Rutgers University Press, 1991.

Heldt, Barbara. *Terrible Perfection: Women and Russian Literature*. Bloomington: Indiana University Press, 1997.

Hemingway, Maurice. *Emilia Pardo Bazán: The Making of a Novelist*. Cambridge: Cambridge University Press, 1983.

Holmes, Diana. *French Women's Writing 1848–1914*. London: Athlone, 1996.

Holmgren, Beth. "Gendering the Icon: Marketing Women Writers in Fin-de-Siècle Russia." In *Russia–Women–Culture*, ed. Helena Goscilo and Beth Holmgren, 321–46. Bloomington: Indiana University Press, 1996.

Iggers, Wilma Abeles. *Women of Prague: Ethnic Diversity and Social Change from the Eighteenth Century to the Present*. Providence, R.I.: Berghahn Books, 1995.

Joeres, Ruth-Ellen. *Respectability and Deviance: Nineteenth-Century German Women Writers and the Ambiguity of Representation*. Chicago: University of Chicago Press, 1998.

Joeres, Ruth-Ellen B., and Mary Jo Maynes, eds. *German Women in the Eighteenth and Nineteenth Centuries: A Social and Literary History*. Bloomington: Indiana University Press, 1986.

Nathan, Rhoda B., ed. *Nineteenth-Century Women Writers of the English-Speaking World*. Westport, Conn.: Greenwood Press, 1986.

Norton, Barbara T., and Jehanne M. Gheith, eds. *An Improper Profession: Women, Gender, and Journalism in Late Imperial Russia*. Durham, N.C.: Duke University Press, 2001.

Ozouf, Mona. *Women's Words: Essay on French Singularity*. Translated by Janet M. Todd. Chicago: University of Chicago Press, 1997.

Peterson, Linda H. *Traditions of Victorian Women's Autobiography: The Poetics and Politics of Life Writing*. Charlottesville: University Press of Virginia, 1999.

Stephens, Sonya, ed. *A History of Women's Writing in France*. Cambridge: Cambridge University Press, 2000.

Tomei, Christine D., ed. *Russian Women Writers*. 2 vols. New York: Garland Publishing, 1999.

Tuchman, Gaye, with Nina E. Fortin. *Edging Women Out: Victorian Novelists, Publishers, and Social Change*. New Haven, Conn.: Yale University Press, 1989.

Vollendorf, Lisa, ed. *Recovering Spain's Feminist Tradition*. New York: Modern Language Association, 2001.

Walton, Whitney. *Eve's Proud Descendants: Four Women Writers and Republican Politics in Nineteenth-Century France*. Stanford, Calif.: Stanford University Press, 2000.

Winegarten, Renee. *Accursed Politics: Some French Women Writers and Political Life, 1715–1850*. Chicago: Ivan R. Dee, 2003.

Biographical dictionaries

Blain, Virginia, Isobel Grundy, and Patricia Clements. *The Feminist Companion to Literature in English: Women Writers from the Middle Ages to the Present*. New Haven, Conn.: Yale University Press, 1990.

Bloom, Abigail Burnham, ed. *Nineteenth-Century British Women Writers: A Bio-Bibliographical Sourcebook*. Westport, Conn.: Greenwood Press, 2000.

Clyman, Toby W., and Diana Greene, eds. *Women Writers in Russian Literature*. Westport, Conn.: Praeger, 1994.

Frederiksen, Elke P., and Elizabeth Ametsbichler, eds. *Women Writers in German-Speaking Countries: A Bio-Bibliographical Critical Sourcebook*. Westport, Conn.: Greenwood Press, 1998.

Hardin, James, ed. *German Fiction Writers, 1885–1913*. 2 vols. Detroit: Gale Research, 1988.

Hardin, James and Donald Daviau, eds. *Austrian Fiction Writers, 1875–1913*. Detroit: Gale Research, 1989.

Ledkovsky, Marina, Charlotte Rosenthal, and Mary Zirin, eds. *Dictionary of Russian Women Writers*. Westport, Conn.: Greenwood Press, 1994.

Levine, Linda, Ellen Engelson Marson, and Gloria Feiman Waldman. *Spanish Women Writers: A Bio-Bibliographical Source Book*. Westport, Conn.: Greenwood Press, 1993.

Pérez, Janet, and Maureen Ihrie, eds. *The Feminist Encyclopedia of Spanish Literature*. 2 vols. Westport, Conn.: Greenwood Press, 2002.

Russell, Rinaldina, ed. *The Feminist Encyclopedia of Italian Literature*. Westport, Conn.: Greenwood Press, 1997.

Italian Women Writers: A Bio-Bibliographical Sourcebook. Westport, Conn.: Greenwood Press, 1994.

Sartori, Eva Martin, and Dorothy Wynne Zimmerman, eds. *French Women Writers*. Lincoln: University of Nebraska Press, 1994.

Shattock, Joanne. *The Oxford Guide to British Women Writers*. Oxford and New York: Oxford University Press, 1993.

Wilson, Katharina M., ed. *An Encyclopedia of Continental Women Writers*. 2 vols. New York: Garland Publishing, 1991.

3   Women and the arts: creating, performance, fame

Creative activities in the visual arts, music, or theater brought public recognition to some talented women before and after 1800. Drawing and singing, like the ability to converse intelligently, had been prized for women of higher social status since the Renaissance. By the late eighteenth century, successful middle-class families also valued such talents and expected governesses or girls' boarding schools to combine academic lessons with what the English termed "accomplishments" or the French, *arts d'agrément*. Sketching, singing, playing the piano, and conversing, as well as sewing and needlework, were all desirable skills for wives and dutiful daughters in the home. But upper- and middle-class women were not expected to pursue artistic activities on a professional basis that would place them in the limelight.

As women artists, singers, and theatrical performers became less of a rarity during the eighteenth century, their work was often deemed problematical. Stage performers' virtue was repeatedly questioned. If women sought recognition in the visual arts or music, they faced negative judgments about female abilities or lack of feminine modesty, just as women writers did. Impressionist painter Pierre-Auguste Renoir's disparaging distinction in 1888 between women as creators and as performers in the arts still typified many contemporary views. He opined that "women are monsters who are authors, lawyers and politicians, like George Sand ... and other bores who are nothing more than five-legged beasts," adding that the "woman ... artist is merely ridiculous, but I feel that it is acceptable for a woman to be a singer or a dancer." Performance was acceptable because "gracefulness is a woman's domain and even her duty."[1] Although Renoir ridiculed women's creative talents, his comments suggest an important evolution in attitudes toward 1900, for he accepted and appreciated the woman performer instead of vilifying her for immorality. His mocking of women artists was also, in fact, a

[1] Quoted in Barbara Ehrlich White, "Renoir's Sensuous Women," in *Woman as Sex Object*, ed. Thomas B. Hess and Linda Nochlin (London: Allen Lane, 1973), 171.

recognition of and reaction to the larger numbers of women then pursuing artistic training and careers. Nineteenth-century women's achievements in the visual arts, music, and theater, as well as obstacles to achievement, are treated in this chapter.

Women and the visual arts

The international fame of Vigée-Lebrun and Kauffmann before 1800 was exceptional for women painters, but their success inspired other women, just as de Staël and Burney inspired women writers. Their emulators included amateurs and women hoping to make a living from art. Indeed, the increasing numbers of women artists paralleled the increase in professional women authors, demonstrating art's appeal for women and possibilities for earning money from patrons' commissions, sales at exhibitions, and teaching. Already in 1831, painter Charles Gabet's dictionary of contemporary artists of the "French school" included 160 women along with more than 1,400 men. Although Gabet included both professional and amateur artists, his listings for women usually noted their public exhibitions and teaching of students in studios, private homes, or boarding schools. The British census recorded 278 women professional artists in 1841, and 1,069 in 1871. By the 1860s women were perhaps a quarter of some 4,000 French painters, the majority based in Paris. At least 200 women artists were active in nineteenth-century Denmark, and the Italian census of 1911 listed 693 women painters and sculptors.

Training

Training, money to buy materials, and space to work were essential for developing artistic talent, and here women faced obstacles. Long excluded from art schools attached to prestigious national or local academies, they typically relied on private instruction from family members and friends, or other artists. Paying for lessons required resources which poor women usually lacked. Frequently paternal nurturing of talent occurred because art was the family business. Artist fathers were the first teachers of Vigée-Lebrun, Kauffmann, and Pasch. Marguerite Gérard (1761–1837) lived with her sister and brother-in-law, the painter Jean-Honoré Fragonard, her teacher, and amassed considerable wealth. Especially before the 1850s familial instruction remained important in women's art education, and it afforded work space and advice on earning a living. English artist Rolinda Sharples (1793–1838) learned from both parents but primarily from her father, also her mother

Ellen's teacher. Two brothers became artists as well. Ellen (1769–1849), widowed in 1811, was one of a limited number of professional women artists then in England, and Rolinda was among the first English women to paint large groups of people. German painter Johann Stuntz taught his talented daughter Maria Electrina (1797–1847), and Dutch painter Henriette Ronner-Knip (1821–1909) began her long career by copying her father's sketches. French painter Raymond Bonheur, struggling financially, trained daughters Rosa and Juliette and two sons. Lessons from fathers or other male painters might also include advice offered as practical but actually restrictive. Rosa Bonheur's father advised her against competing with male painters but challenged her to surpass Vigée-Lebrun as the most talented woman painter. She later rejected his advice to avoid subjects deemed unsuitable for women.

In the hierarchy of established artistic categories, paintings of historic scenes and classical allegories were considered the most prestigious and, in turn, the province of men with the requisite classical education, whereas portraiture, still-lifes, floral paintings, and scenes of everyday life (termed genre painting) were judged appropriately feminine. Traditional artistic training for women featured line drawing and using crayon, pastels, or watercolor washes. Some women also insisted on doing oil-painting, technically more complex, messy, and smelly. Like the novel in the early nineteenth century, portraiture was judged less worthy, English essayist William Hazlitt calling it "the prose of art." Portrait painting was, nonetheless, a major source of income. Women painters were in demand for portraits of women and children, and many found male patrons. Some women did landscape painting, despite concerns about their safety when working outdoors or unchaperoned. Notions about appropriate social spaces for women thus influenced and restricted their choices of artistic media and subjects, even though many considered, privately if not publicly, that women's talents were not inferior to men's and could improve with access to better training.

For sculptresses, parental training was also crucial because many artists thought sculpture unsuited to women, due to assumptions about their limited physical strength and the impropriety of their developing skills by working with unclothed models – the latter notion also an obstacle for women painters. The first important English woman sculptor, the wealthy and unconventional Anne Damer (1748–1828), managed to study with Giuseppe Ceracchi and took anatomy lessons from a doctor; and Teresa Benincampi (1778–1830) learned from the Italian neoclassical master Antonio Canova. English sculptress Mary Thornycroft (1809–95) was trained by her father, and she and her husband (also his student) made sculpture a family business. She did portrait busts of women and children, small works being judged more suitable for sculptresses than big multi-figure works or equestrian statues. French sculptress Hélène Pilate Bertaux (1825–1909) learned from her stepfather and Augustin Dumont, and later produced nude figures. In Florence, Amalia Dupré (1842–1928) trained by working with her father.

Before art schools, private or public, became more accessible to women during the second half of the nineteenth century, many took lessons from established artists, individually or with other pupils in studios. French and British professional women artists and prominent amateurs born between 1750 and 1830 – more numerous than their counterparts in other countries – often received training outside the family circle, even if first taught by a parent. Many artists welcomed fee-paying students of either sex, for securing commissions could be chancy, and nineteenth-century artists were adapting to a decline in royal and aristocratic patronage, as well as to competitive commercial art markets. Vigée-Lebrun seldom gave lessons because her commissions were lucrative, but Labille-Guiard had many pupils, including Gabrielle Capet (1761–1818), a servant's daughter, who honored her teacher (deceased in 1803) by painting a "Studio Interior" (1808) featuring Labille-Guiard at her easel, aided by Capet, while prominent men, including artists, looked on. David instructed Marie Benoist, Constance Charpentier, Constance Mayer, Angélique Mongez, and Sophie Frémiet Rude – teaching Rude while exiled in Brussels after 1815. Mongez and Rude, a sculptor's wife, tried history painting and included nude figures in classical scenes. Several other painters set up separate teaching studios in Paris for men and women, their wives or sisters supervising the women. Portraitist Caroline Bardua (1781–1864), among the relatively few German women earning a living as an artist in 1814, studied with artists in Weimar and Dresden. The best-known female pupil of Spanish master painter Francisco de Goya was Rosario Weiss (1814–43), perhaps his daughter.

Artists who could afford it often journeyed to Italy or France. Paris had the lure of an international art capital, and many artists, particularly sculptors, visited Rome and Florence to practice copying works from antiquity and the Renaissance. Dusseldorf and Munich also attracted Scandinavian and eastern European artists, and several German and Swedish women gained exceptional access to academies formally closed to women. A church official secured entry into the Munich Academy in 1813 for Maria Ellenrieder (1791–1863), who paved the way for Louise Seidler (1786–1866). Both also studied in Rome. Elisabeth Ney, a stone-carver's daughter, became the first woman to study sculpture at the

Munich Academy in 1852. The Swedish Academy allowed painter Amalia Lindegren (1814–91) and two other women to attend classes in 1848. Lindegren, previously taught by a family friend and by artist Sophie Adlersparre, could draw at the Academy from plaster casts of sculpture but was excluded from life classes. Government grants later supported her study in Paris and Rome, and she became a popular portrait and genre painter.

By mid-century, particularly in England, numerous demands for opening or expanding institutional training for women artists figured in a larger discussion of improving young women's education. Advocates cited women's increasing need to prepare to earn a living and also argued that talented individuals deserved opportunities, regardless of sex. Paris had a school of applied arts for young women, the École Gratuite de Dessin, started privately in 1803 and state-supported since 1810. Preparing women to work on textiles, ceramics, fans, wallpaper, and graphics, it lacked the prestige of the École des Beaux-Arts (School of Fine Arts), which admitted only men. In England, art programs at new Mechanics Institutes, opened to women in 1830, also served working-class or lower-middle-class students, as did the Female School of Design, opened in 1843. Henry Sass's private art school in London admitted women by 1832, as did Dickinson's and a section of the Society of British Artists' school during the 1840s. Painter Eliza Fox (1824–1903), whose father long refused her pleas for formal training, attended Sass's school from 1844 to 1847 and started classes for women wanting to draw from nude models. She and Barbara Bodichon, an active reformer and artist, supported the new Society of Female Artists and in 1859 drew up a petition requesting "properly qualified" women's admission to the Royal Academy schools, which were free. The 38 women artists who signed it cited the participation by 120 women in recent Academy exhibitions. While Academy members debated the issue, one petitioner, Laura Herford, who had trained in Fox's classes, gained admission in 1860 by submitting work with only initials for her name. The Academy accepted thirteen more women before halting their admission in 1863, a decision that was not reversed until 1868. Women's admission came with inequities. They could sketch from casts of classical sculpture in the Antique School and draw from draped models in the Painting School, but could not attend life classes with nude models. When their drawing of lightly clad models was finally allowed in 1893, they remained in a separate class. By then, other schools offered women life drawing classes, and the Academy had less prestige. Women were a quarter of its students in the 1890s, but more studied at London's Slade School of Fine Arts, founded in 1871.

Milestones in women's art training in other countries also brought differential treatment. The Swedish Academy school opened a women's department in 1864, by which time the Academy had made Lindegren an associate member (1850) and then full member (1856), a status the British Royal Academy denied to women successors of founders Kauffmann and Moser until after World War I. The Danish Academy of Fine Arts lacked a women's school until 1888 but gave portraitist Bertha Wegmann (1847–1926) membership in 1883. In the Netherlands, the Rotterdam Academy admitted women in 1861, followed by the Rijks (Royal) Academy in Amsterdam in 1863 and The Hague Academy in 1872. Painter Suze Robertson (1855–1922) became the first woman allowed to draw from a nude model at the Rotterdam Academy in 1877, and the Rijks Academy created a women-only life drawing class in 1895. Russian women, admitted to the new St. Petersburg Drawing School in 1842, later audited some classes at the prestigious Academy of Arts, but were not eligible for the "artist" title conferred by the Academy until 1891. In 1896, it counted 34 women among 388 students. Madrid's School of Painting, Sculpture, and Engraving enrolled five women by 1878, but women were rarely more than 5 percent of students before 1914, far fewer than at less prestigious arts and crafts schools.

The resistance to admitting women to the École des Beaux-Arts in Paris, also based on objections to women taking classes with men or drawing from nude models, finally gave way in 1897, after extensive campaigning by established women artists led by Hélène Bertaux. Bertaux, who had started sculpture classes for women in 1873 and a school in 1879, founded the Union of Women Painters and Sculptors in 1881 to provide women with an opportunity to display work at a non-juried exhibition. Paris was an international mecca for women art students who could afford to attend artists' private schools, like that of Rodolphe Julian, who ran separate classes for men and women, charging women, who had fewer options, twice as much. The talented Marie Bashkirtseff (1860–84), Russian-born, did a memorable painting of a Julian Academy studio, depicting women sketching while a partly draped young male posed (Figure 3.1); and after her early death, Bertaux's Union featured 230 of her works at its 1885 exhibition. To press for opening the tuition-free Beaux-Arts school to women, Bertaux, as Union president, launched an appeal at a women's congress in 1889 and continued it in the Union's journal, seconded by painter Virginie Demont-Breton. Women artists deserved better training, Bertaux contended, because they contributed something unique to French culture, their feminine and maternal sensibilities. That argument for women's "equality in difference" was also an effort to counter perceptions of

Figure 3.1 Marie Bashkirtseff, "Life Class in the Women's Studio at the Académie Julian," Paris, c. 1881.

women artists as direct competitors with men. By creating "that which consoles the heart, charms the mind and appeals to the eye," women could fulfill "a truly feminine mission" and help art "become again a civilizing force," Bertaux claimed.[2] Although arguments based on gender difference could also justify continued separation of the sexes, they mirrored the professional ethos then defined for women teachers. Cries of "down with women" were male students' angry response in May 1897 to the legislature's opening of the École des Beaux-Arts to women, and the school closed for a month. Thereafter women could attend general lectures but took separate anatomy and drawing classes, and they remained excluded from individual artists' ateliers, to which advanced students progressed, until further legislative action in 1900.

Where official academies remained closed, new art schools for women offered alternatives to private lessons. A coalition of socially prominent women and women artists spurred the creation in 1868 of the Berlin School for Women Artists, under the aegis of the Berlin Academy of Art. Similar schools opened in 1882 in Munich – its Academy remained

[2] Quoted in Tamar Garb, *Sisters of the Brush: Women's Artistic Culture in Late Nineteenth-Century Paris* (New Haven, Conn.: Yale University Press, 1994), 160.

closed to women until 1919 – and in Karlsruhe in 1885. Austrian officials justified excluding women from Vienna's Academy of Fine Arts by claiming that "with rare exceptions they lack creative spirit in the area of great art" and "stand helpless before serious tasks" required in independent artistic activity.[3] Painters Olga Prager, Rosa Mayreder, Tina Blau, and allies secured private support to open the Art School for Women and Girls in 1897, and Blau taught landscape and still-life painting there. It became the state-supported Women's Academy in 1910, existing until the traditional Academy admitted women in 1920.

Exhibitions and sales

Artists earned a living through commissions from private patrons or public authorities, arrangements with commercial art dealers, and teaching. To establish a professional reputation and create demand for one's work, public exhibition was crucial. Women's art was increasingly on display and in a growing number of settings during the nineteenth century. The British Royal Academy exhibition was open to professionals and amateurs of both sexes, if a jury accepted their submissions, and the official French Salon was open on similar terms from 1791. Women produced 11 to 13 percent of works displayed at the annual Salon between 1801 and 1840, and the number of women participating rose from 25 out of 180 exhibitors in 1800 to 149 out of 873 in 1831. Growth in the art world paralleled expansion of commercial publishing. In 1833 a woman commentator noted that 111 of 191 women exhibiting at the Salon were unmarried, remarking that women who earned money did not have to depend on men, "a sad and almost always disastrous necessity."[4] At Royal Academy exhibits in London, 6 to 10 percent of works displayed between 1800 and 1840 were by women. During the 1850s and 1860s, at a time of backlash against women's public activities, both French and British women artists experienced setbacks. Only 5 percent of works displayed at the 1855 Salon were by women. The English Old Watercolour Society ended full memberships for women in 1850, relegating them to lesser status until 1890. Women contributed only 6 percent of works at the Royal Academy show in 1860, and their frustration with rejections by the Academy and the Society of British Artists was one reason for founding the Society of Female Artists in

[3] Quoted in Helga H. Harriman, "Olga Wisinger-Florian and Tina Blau: Painters in *Fin de Siècle* Vienna," *Woman's Art Journal* 10.2 (1989–90): 24.

[4] Quoted in Gen Doy, *Women and Visual Culture in Nineteenth-Century France, 1800–1852* (London: Leicester University Press, 1998), 80.

1857, with its own exhibition. By the 1880s, women's participation at both the Royal Academy shows and Salons increased noticeably, reaching 20 percent in 1895. Women's exhibition record demonstrates that by the time some prestigious academies admitted women students, many were already making a living as artists, even if critics often labeled them "women artists" to imply limited skills and choices of subjects.

By 1900, many innovative artists of both sexes were shunning the Salon and Royal Academy, associated with neoclassical and realistic art, and exhibiting in other venues, as the Impressionists did. Alternate venues were not necessarily more welcoming to women, however. At the French Society of Independent Artists' annual show, started in 1884, fewer than 10 percent of works displayed before 1900 were by women, and women fared no better at the more avant-garde Salon d'Automne (Autumn Salon), begun in 1903. Most British art societies restricted women to "honorary" or "lady" member status before 1900, if they even had such categories, and the New English Art Club, founded in 1886, was little better.

Few artists, male or female, made a living solely from government purchases of their work, but official appointments and commissions could be lucrative and useful for attracting other clients. French governments, regardless of political leanings, purchased art, especially at the annual Salon. Women artists Benoist, Marie-Eléonore Godefroid, and Pauline Auzou did work enhancing the image of Napoleon I's regime, and under the Bourbon Restoration Mme Lizinka de Mirbel was designated a royal painter of miniatures. Such recognition prompted the journal L'Artiste to complain in 1844 that the Fine Arts administration gave peintresses (women painters) too many commissions, and women artists, like women writers, were sometimes caricatured as "bluestockings." Napoleon III's government purchased Bertaux's "Young Gallic Prisoner," a male nude figure, and her more traditional sculpture "Assumption of the Virgin." The Third Republic provided her and Claude Vignon with commissions for decorating public buildings. Henriette Browne (1829–1901), wife of an aristocrat and, like Vignon, among a limited number of women artists using a pseudonym, received 6,000 francs from Empress Eugénie for her painting "The Puritans" and 12,000 francs for "Sisters of Charity," purchased in 1859 as a prize for a charity lottery. Such sums far exceeded teachers' annual salaries. Scenes of everyday life like Browne's, long judged a minor genre, were more popular when public tastes turned toward artistic and literary realism. Yet France's leading realist painter, Gustave Courbet, who termed his depictions of humble people "democratic" art, was scorned by Napoleon III.

Elsewhere in Europe, state patronage benefited Ellenrieder, named court painter in Baden in 1829, and Seidler, who taught drawing at the court in Saxe-Weimar and was named court painter in 1835, having done many portraits and paintings for churches. Rosario Weiss taught drawing to Spain's young Queen Isabella II in 1842. Henrietta Ward painted the English royal children and provided them with lessons, residing with her painter husband near Windsor Castle because of his royal commissions. Lea Ahlborn became Sweden's first woman civil servant in 1855, appointed to the Royal Mint to design money and medals. Ney (1833–1907) was one of the few German sculptresses to receive official commissions, completing a bust of Otto von Bismarck, architect of German unification, before moving to the United States. Hungarian-born Vilma Parlaghy (1863–1923) gained renown as a "woman painter of great men"; German emperor Wilhelm II gave her commissions and attended her solo exhibition in Berlin in 1895.[5] The Dutch portraitist Thérèse Schwartze (1851–1918) painted Queen Emma and Princess Wilhelmina, and attracted many private patrons, amassing a large fortune. Maria Wiik did official portraits of Finnish cultural figures during the 1880s and later, works reflecting Finns' determination to maintain autonomy, despite Russian rule. In Norway painter Asta Norregaard was the only woman awarded an official commission before 1900. The Danish and Swedish national galleries also bought women's work, and museums in Geneva, Bern, and Lausanne bought paintings by Louise Breslau, daughter of a University of Zurich professor.

Notable careers

Rosa Bonheur (1822–99), the most famous French woman painter after Vigée-Lebrun, prospered from official recognition and the private art market, choosing subjects other than the portraits, still-lifes, and genre scenes associated with women's art. After her first Salon showing in 1849, she specialized in painting animals and landscapes, and the Second Republic commissioned her "Ploughing in the Nivernais" (1849). She also succeeded her father at the École Gratuite de Dessin, which she and her sister headed until 1859. To complete her most famous painting, "The Horse Fair" (1853), she went twice a week to the Paris horse market, wearing trousers – attire practical for negotiating mud and muck but requiring special authorization because of a ban, since 1800, on women so dressing in public. The success of "The Horse

Fair" enabled Bonheur to exhibit whatever she chose at future Salons, without jury approval, a privilege usually limited to members of the Legion of Honor and Academy of Beaux-Arts. Dealer Ernest Gambart, whose London gallery specialized in French art, purchased "The Horse Fair" and arranged for Bonheur's visit to England, where George Eliot said of her famous painting, "What power! This is the way women should assert their rights."[6] Bonheur bought a château near Fontainebleau in 1860, where she lived with her friend Natalie Micas and sketched many animals kept on the property. "The Horse Fair" was one of the most widely reproduced nineteenth-century paintings, and in 1865 Bonheur became the first woman artist brought into the Legion of Honor. She proved, Empress Eugénie said, that "genius has no sex."[7] The award prompted painter Jules Breton to advise his daughter, whom he instructed, to make Bonheur her role model. Virginie Demont-Breton (1859–1935) became the second woman painter awarded the Legion of Honor in 1894, but her subjects – mothers, children, heroines like Joan of Arc – were more traditional for women.

English painter Henrietta Ward (1832–1924) also believed that gender did not restrict talent, writing in her memoirs, "there is no sex in art," and complaining that "pure [male] selfishness" excluded women from the Royal Academy."[8] Her grandfather, great-uncle, and uncle had been Academy members, and her parents, both painters, were her first instructors, as was Edward Ward, whom she married when she was sixteen. The Wards had a working partnership, and four daughters became artists. Henrietta's painting, not innovative, often celebrated Victorian middle-class domesticity, as in "God Save the Queen," shown at the Royal Academy in 1857 and featuring a mother at the piano instructing three children. When she essayed historical painting, Ward, mother of eight, applied domestic touches, placing subjects like Mary Queen of Scots in familial settings. Yet she recognized difficulties facing professional women artists and signed the 1859 women's petition to the Royal Academy. After her husband's death, she opened an art school and in 1897 served on the central committee of the major women's suffrage association. The never-married Emily Osborn also signed the 1859 petition and, like Ward, was among 2,000 signers (including 85 women artists and musicians) of an 1889 suffrage petition. Daughter of a clergyman, Osborn began painting

[6] Quoted in Deborah Cherry, *Beyond the Frame: Feminism and Visual Culture, Britain 1850–1900* (London: Routledge, 2000), 56.

[7] Anna Klumpke, *Rosa Bonheur: The Artist's (Auto)biography*, trans. Gretchen van Slyke (Ann Arbor: University of Michigan Press, 1997), 173.

[8] Quoted in Jane Sellars, "Henrietta Ward," in *Dictionary of Women Artists*, ed. Delia Gaze, 2 vols. (London: Fitzroy Dearborn, 1997), II: 1427.

professionally during the 1850s, doing portraits and genre scenes. Her "Nameless and Friendless" (1857) depicted a poor woman entering a shop to try to sell a painting, the only woman in a masculine commercial setting. Osborn sold it for £250, and Queen Victoria purchased her "Governess" (1860), shown at the Royal Academy.

Elizabeth Thompson (1846–1933), later Lady Butler, came from a more privileged background than Ward and Osborn but, like Bonheur, painted subjects and large canvases not usually associated with women. Trained at the Female School of Art in South Kensington and able to study independently in Italy, she had parents who encouraged their daughters' achievements. Her mother was a concert pianist, and her sister Alice Meynell became a writer. Thompson gained fame in 1874 with the Royal Academy showing of her battle painting, "Calling the Roll after an Engagement, Crimea," which Queen Victoria insisted on buying, although a manufacturer had commissioned it. Even critic John Ruskin, dubious about mass taste and notorious for insisting that no woman could excel in art because "the woman's intellect is not for invention or creation but sweet ordering, arrangement," praised Thompson.[9] She continued painting military scenes after marriage to Major (later General) William Butler. The Royal Academy considered her for membership in 1879 but narrowly voted against it. Cultivating the image of a devoted wife accompanying her husband from post to post, even as six children were born, she later said that the Academy had wisely closed the door to women. Butler was not the only Victorian-era woman to combine a conventional appearance with unconventional achievement. As the first woman known for battle paintings, she figured in feminists' assemblage of evidence of women's abilities to achieve in new areas.

Kate Greenaway (1846–1901), who once shared a studio with Butler, became a famous illustrator. The daughter of a wood engraver who encouraged her talent and stressed the need to earn a living, she benefited from the expanding market for children's books. Her father enrolled her in art classes when she was eight, and she helped him with some projects. During her career she illustrated more than 150 books, 90 magazines, and many sets of greeting cards, creating the "Greenaway child" image replicated in children's clothing, playing cards, paper dolls, and wallpaper. A business arrangement with printer Edmund Evans produced her bestselling *Under the Window* (1878), which combined her own verses with illustrations and sold more than 100,000 copies, including 30,000 in French and German translations. One of the most

---

[9] Quotation (1867) in Rozsika Parker and Griselda Pollock, *Old Mistresses: Women, Art and Ideology* (London: Routledge, 1981), 9.

widely imitated Victorian artists, Greenaway also exhibited some fifty paintings over the course of thirty years.

Greenaway's commercial success set the stage for other women illustrators, such as Jenny Nyström (1854–1946), a teacher's daughter who studied at the Swedish Royal Academy and private art schools in Paris, exhibiting in the 1884 and 1885 Salons. To earn a living, before and after marriage and the birth of a son, she painted portraits, genre scenes, and landscapes, but was best known for illustrating more than 1,000 books and magazines, mostly for children, and also for holiday cards introducing her enduring image of Father Christmas. Many illustrations were for books by women writers and teachers. Nyström said that she "successfully specialized in the realm of childhood."[10] English illustrator Beatrix Potter (1866–1943) also created children's classics, beginning with her *Tale of Peter Rabbit* (1902). By 1913, she had produced nineteen picture books peopled by Peter and other animals, and with her earnings purchased large farms.

Portraiture and commercial illustration provided livelihoods for many women artists, but during the later nineteenth century some ventured into new styles not always appreciated by traditional critics or artists. The beginning of "modern" art is typically dated from the Impressionists, who developed a style of painting with dabs or strokes of color to capture light at a particular instant. The resulting images, less well modeled than forms prized by neoclassical and realist painters, began the transition from representational to nonrepresentational, or abstract, art. At a time when photography, first developed in France by Louis-Jacques Daguerre, could produce more accurate images than painters, Impressionists challenged old ideas about artists' obligation to represent forms realistically. The label Impressionist was initially pejorative, coined by a critic of Claude Monet's "Impression of Sunrise," which was displayed at the innovative group's first show in 1874, but the public and artists soon used it to describe the inviting Parisian and country scenes painted by Monet, Camille Pissarro, Edgar Degas, Renoir, and others. Four women had ties to major French Impressionists, but only the American Mary Cassatt became known internationally. From a wealthy family, she studied at the Academy of Fine Arts in Philadelphia before going to Paris in 1865. After meeting Degas and adopting Impressionist techniques, she did many paintings of mothers and children which made her famous. Remaining in Europe, she never married, unlike three French women Impressionists whose careers were affected by that life choice.

---

[10] Quoted in Barbro Werkmaster, "Jenny Nyström," in Gaze (ed.), *Dictionary of Women Artists*, II: 1034.

Berthe Morisot (1841–95) participated in seven of the eight Impressionist exhibitions between 1874 and 1886. She and two sisters had received private art lessons, one teacher warning their mother that Berthe and Edma were talented enough to become real painters, something he termed "revolutionary" or "almost catastrophic" in the "upper-class milieu to which you belong." They practiced copying works in the Louvre, and Berthe and Edma had work accepted for the Salon of 1864. Berthe also received guidance from family friend Édouard Manet, whose brother she married in 1874. Devoted to her only daughter, she often painted women relatives, children, and friends. The Impressionists' first commercial dealer, Paul Durand-Ruel, began buying some of her paintings during the 1870s, but she did not have a solo commercial exhibition until 1892, and the state did not purchase one of her paintings until 1894. Pissarro called Morisot "a splendid feminine talent," but her reputation dwindled until interest in women artists was renewed during the 1960s.[11] The promising career of Eva Gonzalès (1849–83), a novelist's daughter also guided by Manet, was cut short by death soon after childbirth. Different circumstances halted the artistic activity of Marie Bracquemond (1840–1916). From a modest background, she studied in Jean-Auguste-Dominique Ingres's Paris studio, where she and her mother, her chaperone, were offended to hear the master artist claim that Rosa Bonheur lacked talent. In 1869 she married engraver Félix Bracquemond, soon artistic director of the Haviland porcelain works, and the two worked together, Marie designing china decoration. But the overbearing Félix also criticized her submissions to Impressionist exhibitions and painting outdoors, and according to their son, an artist aware of her ambition and his father's jealousy of her talent, Félix's belittling so wore her down that she stopped painting in 1890.

Although many contemporaries had a low opinion of Impressionism, the new French style influenced artists from other countries, including, among women, the Norwegians Harriet Backer and Kitty Kielland, the Danes Wegmann and Anna Ancher, and the Dutch Thérèse Schwartze – all of whom studied in Paris – as well as the Austrian Blau, British painter Ethel Walker, and Spaniard Marcelina Poncela Ontorio. Impressionism also became a catalyst for more experimentation with drawing and coloration, which resulted in exaggerated renditions of subjects' shapes or facial expressions and, finally, in a fully abstract modern art.

In Germany, where Emperor Wilhelm II scorned foreign influences on art, rebellious artists developed the Expressionist style to depict strong

---

[11] Quotations in Kathleen Adler and Tamar Garb, "Berthe Morisot," in Gaze (ed.), *Dictionary of Women Artists*, II: 978, 980.

emotions aroused by people and events. They used intense dark colors (unlike Impressionist pastels) and distorted shapes and facial features, often producing unsettling messages of social protest, which they contrasted to pleasing Impressionist renditions of people enjoying modern life. Three women Expressionists, Käthe Kollwitz, Paula Modersohn-Becker, and Gabriele Münter, now loom large in art histories, but graphic artist Kollwitz was the most recognized during her lifetime. From a family of freethinkers who encouraged her artistic ambitions, Kollwitz (1867–1945) studied at the women's art school in Berlin, as did the younger Becker (1876–1907). Reading Bashkirtseff's frank admissions of ambition in a diary published posthumously motivated Becker to persist with art, despite parental pressure to become a teacher. Kollwitz married a doctor whose clinic was in a working-class district, where they resided, and, as the mother of two sons, found time for art and teaching by employing household help. Zola's naturalist novels inspired her, and she later wrote, "The proletariat was my idea of beauty," not Greek images.[12] Her first fame came from lithographs and etchings based on Gerhart Hauptmann's play *The Weavers* (1893), about a workers' uprising in 1844. These images, exhibited in 1898, angered Wilhelm II, who blocked the awarding of a medal to Kollwitz. He later had her poster of a tired woman worker removed from an exhibition, his actions indicative of his regime's opposition to democratization and its anger about growing support for the German Socialist party, the largest socialist party in Europe. Kollwitz's most famous images are of a mother with a dead child the first of them dating from 1903. She was a symbol of protest against the Second Empire, which ended with Germany's loss of World War I, and in 1919 became the first woman elected to the Prussian Academy of Arts. Modersohn-Becker produced at least 400 paintings, including self-portraits in primitivist style, but sold few canvases during her often unhappy lifetime. Münter (1877–1962), from a well-to-do family, exhibited paintings in Paris and Cologne, and in Munich helped found the New Artists group in 1909 and Blue Rider group in 1911. Russian avant-garde artist Wassily Kandinsky, her teacher and lover, was sometimes hypercritical of her work but praised her 1913 solo exhibition for being "free from any trace of feminine or masculine coquetry."[13] The Nazis later branded all Expressionist art "degenerate."

Münter was not the only woman in avant-garde art movements who experienced male artists' negative reception of her work. Many men

---

[12] Quoted in Olga S. Opfell, *Special Visions: Profiles of Fifteen Women Artists from the Renaissance to the Present Day* (Jefferson, N.C.: McFarland and Co., 1991), 120.

[13] Quoted in Shulamith Behr, *Women Expressionists* (New York: Rizzoli, 1988), 48.

broke with official art circles or old styles to create artistic "secessions" in Vienna, Munich, or Berlin in the 1890s or later saw themselves affirming the artist's right, as a unique creator, to follow an inner voice and, like earlier generations, often doubted that women possessed comparable creativity. The Swedish artists known as "Young Ones" excluded women from 1909 to 1911 before relenting. Among the Fauves (literally, "wild beasts") in Paris, whose painting resembled Expressionism, as well as among the more abstract Cubists and Futurists, women artists often felt marginalized. The founders of the Salon d'Automne included only four women. In such circumstances, Émilie Charmy and Jacqueline Marval, both first trained for schoolteaching in the provinces, appreciated Berthe Weill's promotion of their work. Weill opened a gallery in Paris in 1901 and was one of the few women art dealers. The eventual success of Suzanne Valadon (1865–1935), whom Degas encouraged, was a rare rags-to-riches story among women artists, whose backgrounds were usually middle class. The illegitimate daughter of a maid, she began working at the age of eleven and was an artist's model before starting to paint. Sculptress Camille Claudel (1864–1943) received much praise from Auguste Rodin, once her teacher and lover, and gained critical acclaim by the 1890s, but she also encountered controversy because of the nudity and sexuality in some pieces. Problems with having work accepted for exhibitions and disappointing earnings contributed to the depression that eventually led to her confinement in mental institutions. Yet despite obstacles facing women artists, study in Paris or German cities and contacts with foreign artists were often crucial to the professional development of the first notable generation of Russian women artists, including sculptress Anna Golubkina and avant-garde painters Alexandra Exter, Nadezhda Udaltsova, and Liubov Popova. Newer art circles in St. Petersburg and Moscow also encouraged experimentation, Natalia Goncharova commenting before her 1913 exhibition that Russian art was "incomparably more profound and important than anything that I know in the West."[14]

Women artists' situation by 1914

In 1914, as in 1800, a woman seeking recognition as an "artist" was often regarded as a "woman artist," a label that suggested her difference from male artists in both subject matter and ability. Not surprisingly, ambitious women's attitudes toward the women-only art

---

[14] Quoted in Alison Hilton, "Domestic Crafts and Creative Freedom: Russian Women's Art," in *Russia–Women–Culture*, ed. Helena Goscilo and Beth Holmgren (Bloomington: Indiana University Press, 1996), 364.

groups of the later nineteenth and early twentieth centuries varied considerably. These offered professional connections and opportunities for exhibition when other artistic venues were limited, but were less prestigious than older male-dominated organizations. Hence the annual exhibitions of the British Society of Female Artists (retitled Lady Artists in 1872 and Women Artists in 1899), the oldest of such groups, showed great variations in the numbers of works submitted. There were 358 works at its first exhibition in 1857, and 582 in 1858, but only 255 in 1864; the total reached a prewar high of 862 in 1903, but dropped to 472 in 1913. The last drop occurred even as some women artists banded together in the Artists' Suffrage League or Suffrage Atelier to make posters for women's suffrage campaigns. The French Union of Women Painters and Sculptors avoided such sharp variations, the works displayed at its annual show rising from 94 submissions by 38 artists in 1882 to 942 by nearly 300 artists in 1897. The Union had 450 members by 1900, and its exhibition benefited when Bertaux persuaded officials who purchased art work for state collections to add it to their roster of shows visited. Elsewhere women artists joined together in the St. Petersburg Ladies Art Circle (1882), Austrian Association of Women Writers and Artists (1885), Polish Women Artists Society (1898), Norwegian Association of Women Painters (1907), German and Austrian Women Artists Union (1908), and Association of Swedish Women Artists (1910).

Women creating art and doing so professionally were more numerous in 1914 than in 1800, as the multiplying of references to women art students and artists in Paris and other capital cities indicates. One recent dictionary of women artists born before 1900 identifies some 21,000 individuals, the great majority born after 1750. Yet making a living and gaining recognition in the art world did not come easily. American-born British portrait painter Louisa Starr told the International Council of Women in 1899, "Women are heavily handicapped in Art, as in all else, by the fact of our womanhood and its duties, and ... when a woman has a profession, it means in most cases that she has two professions." She knew that many women artists combined careers with family obligations, as wives, mothers, or daughters. Art dealer Berthe Weill spoke not only of herself but also of women artists when she commented, "A woman's struggle is hard and requires an exceptionally strong will."[15]

---

[15] Starr quoted in Deborah Cherry, *Painting Women: Victorian Women Artists* (London: Routledge, 1993), 33; Weill quoted in Gill Perry, *Women Artists and the Parisian Avant-Garde: Modernism and "Feminine" Art, 1900 to the late 1920s* (Manchester: Manchester University Press, 1995), 89.

Musical careers

Women pursuing musical careers also needed the combination of talent and determination characteristic of successful women in the visual arts, for assumptions about gender routinely affected their professional possibilities, whether in performing, teaching, or composing. Yet like women artists and writers, women musicians became more numerous during the nineteenth century. British censuses recorded a sixfold increase in numbers of musicians and music teachers between 1841 and 1891, with women's representation rising from 14 percent (900 of 6,600) to nearly 50 percent (19,100 of 38,600). The 1907 German census counted 12,500 women musicians and music teachers, double the number in 1882, but only a fifth of some 60,600 musicians.

Teachers of singing or piano were the most familiar women musicians. Many gave lessons in pupils' homes, usually assuming that pupils would remain amateurs. Indeed, of the 4,700 British women musicians and music teachers enumerated in 1861, or the 23,400 in 1921, about two-thirds taught. Some secured appointments in new national or local conservatories, although often not on the same terms as men. Performing as singers continued earlier traditions, especially for women from families whose livelihood was music. Instrumental performance posed different issues. There also remained a distinction between the respectability of singing or playing the piano in a family parlor and doing so to earn a living. Professional musical performance was more in the public eye than the creation, as opposed to exhibition, of art, and issues of personal reputation dogged musical and dramatic performers. Many musical performers came from relatively modest backgrounds, more often than was true for writers or artists. Most difficult for women musicians to achieve was recognition of their talent for composing.

Performing careers: singers and instrumentalists

By 1789, in an increasingly secularized Europe, women performers were more familiar figures than they had been when religious authorities excluded them from church choirs, Catholic and Protestant, because of moral concerns about mingling the sexes or letting the alluring qualities in women's voices be heard. Many convents long prized musical training, nonetheless. Women also sang in courts and aristocratic residences, and on the stage in operatic roles. Hundreds of women singers' careers between 1600 and 1800 have been documented. Part of Italian opera from its origins, women singers gradually replaced castrati, young males castrated before puberty to preserve their soprano or contralto voices and in demand for choirs, and while the Counter-Reformation papacy tried to ban women from the Italian stage. Castrati numbered perhaps 4,000 during the 1700s and still appeared in Austrian and German operas of the 1780s, but they were uncommon in France, where Louis XIV had preferred women's voices in female roles and accepted mixed choruses. By the late 1700s, women were more prominent in Italian operas, as the term "prima donna" for the leading female singer indicated. Although a Napoleonic ban on castrati in Italian conservatories was overturned in 1815, important new operas lacked major roles for castrati after 1825.

Before and after 1800, singers often received training, at least initially, from family members, male and female. Many were Italian, German, Austrian, or French by birth but frequently pursued careers in more than one country. Three of the four daughters of the singer, violinist, and organist Fridolin Weber became sopranos, Constanze Weber marrying composer Wolfgang Amadeus Mozart. Italian contralto Josephina Grassini (1773–1850), who also sang in London and Paris, was inspiration for nieces Guiditta and Giulia Grisi, whose musical education she supervised after retiring in 1823. The German star soprano Wilhelmine Schröder-Devrient (1804–60) was the eldest child of a leading baritone and his actress wife, who schooled her in movement and diction. At a time when few singers' dramatic talent equaled their vocal skills, Schröder-Devrient became known as the "Queen of Tears," opera composer Richard Wagner stating that she inspired his vocation and provided the model for a powerful singer-actress. Singer and actress Franziska Sontag was the first teacher of her daughter, popular soprano Henriette Sontag (1806–54). Schröder-Devrient's and Sontag's operatic debuts in Vienna at the age of sixteen, after minor stage roles, were not unusually early, but vocal strain could hurt young voices, as in the sad case of Cornélie Falcon. Sontag, bowing to social expectations, left the stage in 1830 after marrying a Piedmontese diplomat but returned in 1849 when the change of monarchs due to the 1848 revolution ended his job and necessitated that she earn money. Schröder-Devrient sang her last operatic role in 1847 but continued giving concerts, telling Clara Schumann, "I have loved my art, and practiced it with a hallowed enthusiasm."[16]

New music conservatories provided an alternative or supplement to family training. Although women as well as men could study at a private singing school in Leipzig in 1771 and another in Berlin in 1790, the Paris

[16] Quoted in Susan A. Rutherford, "Wilhelmine Schröder-Devrient: Wagner's Theatrical Muse," in *Women, Theatre and Performance: New Histories, New Historiographies*, ed. Maggie B. Gale and Viv Gardner (Manchester: Manchester University Press, 2000), 76.

Conservatoire, created in 1795 to replace the Royal Music School, was the main model for other conservatories. Initially enrolling pupils between the ages of eight and thirteen as well as advanced students, and also offering dance and drama, the Conservatoire always admitted large numbers of girls and young women but segregated many classes by sex. Young women were 34 percent of its 330 pupils in 1807, and 44 percent of 558 in 1849. Although in some years more young women than men entered to study singing, piano, or acting, women were never a majority of the student body because their access to training for composition and some instruments was restricted. Administrative centralization made the state-funded Conservatoire the model for other French cities' music schools, but private entities often created conservatories in other countries. For example, the Society of Friends of Music founded the Vienna Conservatory in 1817, and the Russian Musical Society opened the St. Petersburg Conservatory in 1862, which soon received court protection. The Royal Academy of Music, started privately in London in 1823, emulated the Conservatoire by admitting males and females, consigned to separate classes. Similar conditions faced young women in conservatories opened in Milan (1807), Vienna, Brussels (1832), Leipzig (1843), Cologne (1845), Dresden (1856), Bern (1857), St. Petersburg, Berlin (1850, 1869), Naples (1872), and Frankfurt (1878). Because women students might become teachers or perhaps performers, but presumably not composers or conductors, they were expected to study voice, piano, or harp, rather than advanced musical theory. String, wind, or brass instruments were long considered unsuitable for women. The Paris Conservatoire engaged 26 women among its 345 teachers between 1795 and 1859, but limited women's assignments to singing, keyboard, or solfeggio (application of musical syllables sol to fa to a scale or melody). There were also expectations or requirements, as in Paris, that young women be chaperoned. The Brussels Conservatory instructed young men and women on different days of the week, and its star piano teacher Marie Pleyel, unlike her male colleagues, was allowed to instruct only women.

In light of the varied dates for conservatory openings, it is unsurprising that familial or private instruction remained typical in many musical biographies. Nonetheless, by the 1830s the Paris Opera, Comic Opera, and other French musical theaters drew many, if not most, of their leading women singers from the Conservatoire. Soprano Laure Cinthie (1801–63) sang secondary roles at the Théâtre Italien at the age of fifteen, soon performed at other theaters, and joined the Opera company in 1825. Italianizing her name to Cinti (later Cinti-Damoreau), she became the Opera's best-paid woman singer but left in 1835 for the Comic

Opera and leads in Daniel Auber's productions. Soprano Cornélie Falcon (1814–97) also quickly gained fame at the Opera, debuting in 1831, but she lost her voice during a performance in 1837 and never fully regained it. Although most prima donnas did not fade into obscurity in such a highly publicized way, many did not remain in the limelight for more than ten years. Marriage and family responsibilities often determined career decisions, and the press could be unkind to aging divas. Critics frequently wrote about a woman performer's youth and beauty before evaluating her singing. Cinti-Damoreau's thirty-year career, like Pauline Viardot's long career, was the exception, not the rule. After leaving the stage in 1841, Cinti-Damoreau continued giving recitals and concert tours. She also taught at the Conservatoire as of 1833, her pedagogical work providing the basis for her singing manual published in 1849.

There were other musical venues for women singers besides the opera stage. The London Philharmonic Society, founded in 1813, became the most prestigious English setting for the performance of older works regarded as musical classics, as well as for new compositions. Women soloists appeared on the Society's programs from its first year, but the Society restricted full membership to men, relegating women to associate or honorary membership until after World War I. Yet of the nearly 500 singers featured in its concerts between 1813 and 1912, 62 percent (303) were women, many of them professionals and some amateurs. Most women appeared only once, but twenty-seven women starred in nine or more concerts, including Maria Caradori-Allan, who performed forty-two times between 1822 and 1847, and Eliza Salmon, who made thirty appearances by 1824 and was in such demand that she reportedly earned £5,000 in 1823. Many soloists were English, by birth or marriage, but leading foreign singers like Schröder-Devrient, Sontag, and Viardot appeared. Women also predominated among vocal soloists at the Société des Concerts in Paris, founded in 1828, with ties to the Conservatoire. Seven women singers, including Cinti-Damoreau, were among its 94 founding members, and 13 more (including two accompanists) figured on a roster of 186 by 1840. Nonetheless, the Société excluded women from full membership in 1843, citing the "difficulty" of active members' obligations. Creating an adjunct membership for women, it limited adjuncts to eight.

Two celebrated musical sisters, Maria Malibran (1808–36) and Pauline Viardot (1821–1910), exemplified possibilities for women gaining fame as singers by the 1830s. Their father, Spanish tenor and composer Manuel Garcia, was a demanding teacher who also trained his son Manuel, later a singing teacher at the Conservatoire and in London. Their mother provided additional training. Malibran, born in Paris, made her debut as a mezzo-soprano at age seventeen in London and performed with her father's company in New York City, evidently the first Italian opera company to tour the United States. After several years of alternating between London and Paris, she sang throughout Italy between 1832 and 1836 in operas by Rossini, Bellini, and Donizetti. Her vocal power and range drew rave reviews, and her romantic travails and early death after falling from a horse became part of a legend, perpetuated by at least six books about her published before 1900.

The younger Pauline became her father's studio accompanist and, after his death when she was eleven, also studied composition with Antoine Reicha and piano with Franz Liszt. A mezzo-soprano, she made her singing debut in Brussels at age sixteen, and soon performed in Paris and London. Engagements followed in Russia, Spain, German cities, and Austria, and her husband Louis Viardot, an older writer whom she married in 1840, usually traveled with her. Although he, like her father, guided her career, she was a forceful personality. Their home in Paris became an important artistic and literary salon, featured in the popular magazine *L'Illustration*. George Sand modeled the singer heroine of *Consuelo* (1842) on Pauline, and Giacomo Meyerbeer created a role in *Le Prophète* (1849) specifically for her. That operatic performance moved composer Hector Berlioz to call her "one of the greatest artists ... in the past and present history of music," and Dickens praised her "sublime acting."[17] Gustave Vapereau's 1861 biographical dictionary lauded Viardot's musical talent, command of five languages, and helpfulness to others pursuing musical careers. She was the mother of four children and, although aided by her mother and hired caregivers, was ready by 1857 to curtail performing, even as she continued teaching and composing. She published about a hundred songs, a folksong collection compiled with Sand, and a singing manual. Her four operettas were first performed by her students at her weekly salon, and she taught at the Conservatoire from 1871 to 1875 before giving only private lessons. When traveling became tiring and voices weakened, the turn to teaching was common in many women singers' biographies, their earlier fame attracting students. Like her parents, Viardot also shaped her children's careers: daughter Louise Héritte became a contralto, teacher, and composer, and son Paul a violinist, conductor, and composer. Louise's memoirs recounted the family history, including her parents' arrangement of her unhappy marriage, and the discrimination facing women composers.

[17] Quotations in James Ard and April Fitzlyon, "Pauline Viardot," in *The Norton/Grove Dictionary of Women Composers*, ed. Julie Anne Sadie and Rhian Samuel (New York: W. W. Norton, 1994), 475.

In the Anglo-American world, Jenny Lind (1820–87) was better known than Viardot. From a modest background, Lind entered the Royal Opera school in Stockholm at the age of ten and had minor stage roles before her first lead in 1838 in Weber's *Der Freischütz*. At twenty, she was a star soprano, an official court singer, and member of the Swedish Royal Academy of Music, but vocal problems temporarily halted her career. She consulted Paris Conservatoire teacher Manuel Garcia, who first imposed silence and then taught her how to strengthen her voice and extend her range, and thus avoid Falcon's fate. New triumphs followed in Stockholm in 1842 and later in Berlin, Leipzig, Vienna, and other German cities. In London in 1847 Queen Victoria and Prince Albert attended a performance, and an adoring public dubbed her the "Swedish nightingale." There followed an American tour of ninety-three cities, arranged by circus entrepreneur P. T. Barnum, who presented her as more a natural phenomenon than a highly trained artist. During the tour she married her accompanist Otto Goldschmidt, settling first in Dresden and in 1858 in London. As Lind prospered, she devoted part of her earnings to charities and music scholarships in Sweden and England, and in 1859 gave a concert to raise money to cover debts of the Society of Female Artists. Limiting performances after 1870, she last sang publicly in 1883 but taught singing at the new Royal College of Music.

Commentators often cited Lind's exemplary private life as a reason for women performers' improved reputation later in the nineteenth century. For Adelina Patti (1843–1919), however, the scandal of leaving her husband and an affair with a married tenor did not alter her status as an international celebrity and the highest-paid singer in opera history. This daughter of a Sicilian tenor also delighted British audiences by often singing "Home Sweet Home," which well matched the tone of Victorian domesticity. She became a British citizen in 1898. Talent and good press coverage also brought celebrity status in Russia to Anastasiia Vial'tseva (1871–1913), the daughter of poor peasants, who went on stage at the age of thirteen. Famed for singing popular romantic tunes, not opera arias, she gave concerts in provincial cities as well as in Moscow and St. Petersburg. She was the only Russian woman whom the *Petersburg Gazette* in 1910 could identify among performers earning at least 100,000 rubles a year, a group also including international stars Patti and Sarah Bernhardt. During the Russo-Japanese War Vial'tseva made a well-publicized trip to the front to nurse her wounded husband, an army officer, and also sang for the troops. Her funeral procession in St. Petersburg drew 150,000 people.

Women instrumental soloists, in comparison to vocalists performing in operas and concerts, appeared less often and were usually less famous.

Many women played the piano, but acceptance of their playing in public lagged behind appreciation of it at home gatherings. Although women were eventually nearly a third of all pianists performing at the prestigious Leipzig Gewandhaus between 1781 and 1881 (84 of 261), only 14 had appeared by 1830. Nonetheless, Clara Wieck Schumann set a record there with 74 concerts, a feat most closely approached by Felix Mendelssohn's 47 concerts. At the London Philharmonic Society, 44 women were 30 percent of 150 featured pianists between 1813 and 1912, but 33 of them appeared after 1870. Moreover, only 13 played three or more times. Lucy Anderson (1797–1878), wife of a violist, appeared nineteen times between 1822 and 1862 and was the first to play Beethoven's demanding "Emperor" concerto with the Philharmonic orchestra. The German-born Louise Dulcken (1811–50) performed ten times and was a successful teacher whose pupils included Queen Victoria, previously taught by Anderson. Arabella Goddard (1836–1922) made seventeen Philharmonic appearances (1856–78), toured the British Empire during the 1870s, and taught at the Royal College of Music. Schumann's thirteen appearances between 1856 and 1888 were part of an exemplary career detailed below. In comparison to the Leipzig and London venues, women pianists found slower acceptance at the Paris Society of Concerts, where only four of twenty-one soloists were women between 1828 and 1859.

Notions about gender often colored critics' reviews of women pianists' playing. As women's solo or concerto performances became somewhat more frequent during the 1840s, Parisian critics routinely coupled comments on musicianship with observations on their appearance or use of the body, often terming aspects of a performance masculine or feminine. Compositions were also characterized as suitable or unsuitable for women. Pieces that were loud and forceful or necessitated much finger movement were often seen as masculine, those that were softer and less demanding of keyboard reaches, as feminine. Whether women should tackle Beethoven's ambitious and "sublime" works or limit themselves to playing less complicated and lighter pieces was debated. The men's piano class at the Conservatoire might play Beethoven for an annual competition; the women's assignment was more likely to be something by Haydn, Bach, or, later, Chopin. Because many male pianists performed their own compositions, while women usually did not, women's performances also occasioned comments on their lack of creativity.

Critics' evaluations of Belgian pianist Marie Pleyel and Czech pianist Wilhelmine Szarvády illustrate the praise and the scorn greeting women pianists. Trained in Paris where her parents had settled, Pleyel (1811–75) began giving concerts as a teenager and continued teaching after she married piano manufacturer Camille Pleyel, telling a friend that she still valued her independence. After a legal separation in 1835, she resumed performing, her concerts in Paris in 1845 prompting an admiring critic to pronounce "the beginning of a new era .... the [repeal] of the Salic Law in the art of the piano." He named nine women pianists in this breakthrough, placing Pleyel at the top of a list also featuring the queen's pianist, Catherine de Dietz. Another critic, Henri Blanchard, rated Pleyel "the queen of the seductive pianists," while also praising her control of the keyboard. "Madame Pleyel imitates nobody; she is calm at the piano: her eyes are almost always fixed on the keyboard; and when she raises them, her look has an unbelievable expression of audacity .... [H]er beautiful curved figure ... does nothing to betray the prodigious work of her fingers: it is the highest musical poetry coming from a soul shaped by all the experiences of life." Appearing feminine, Pleyel nonetheless commanded respect for her technical skill and artistry, and the Brussels Conservatory engaged her as a piano teacher from 1848 to 1872. The younger Szarvády (1834–1907) did not always fare as well with critics. Of her debut in Paris in 1851, Blanchard noted, "Her pink dress ... [which] revealed the entire naked length of a very pretty arm ... does not detract from the quality of her playing." Yet another critic soon faulted her playing for an "exaggeration of power, which too often precludes grace and simplicity, that poetry of women."[18] Disparagement of her playing as too masculine persisted, one critic mocking her as the George Sand of piano. Because women pianists not only had to perform skillfully but also to cope with critics' sometimes scornful characterizations of their appearance or playing style, the cultural milieu imposed a psychological toll, contributing to other women's decisions to curtail performing careers.

Women violinists with professional ambitions faced more obstacles than pianists. The violin was long thought too difficult for women to master, and many people believed that the posture used to hold and play it rendered women ugly – unlike the harp, played by women in salons and now sometimes with orchestras. In Paris, Mlle Ottavo was the only woman among 33 solo violinists featured by the Society of Concerts in 1859. London Philharmonic Society concerts included 18 women among 131 violin soloists before 1913, but only four appeared before the 1870s. None debuted there between 1850 and 1872, and only one performed more than once or twice. The great exception was Wilma

---

[18] Quotations in Katharine Ellis, "Female Pianists and Their Male Critics in Nineteenth-Century Paris," *Journal of the American Musicological Society* 50 (Summer–Fall 1997): 359, 367, 368, 374.

Neruda (1838–1911), another daughter of a famous musical family, who played in thirteen London Philharmonic concerts between 1849 and 1907. Czech organist Josef Neruda was the first violin teacher for his talented children Wilma, Marie, and Franz, with whom he formed a quartet; two other children were pianists. To provide his children with other music teachers, Josef moved to Vienna. In 1848 he started the family concert tours which took them to Germany, England, Russia, and Scandinavia, the quartet lasting until Wilma married. The Nerudas' Scandinavian tour during the early 1860s resulted in the Swedish king's appointing Wilma chamber virtuoso, and after her marriage to Swedish composer and conductor Ludvig Norman, she taught violin at the Royal Academy of Music in Stockholm until 1870. Leaving Norman, she began annual visits to London and also gave solo concerts elsewhere. She did some teaching after settling in Berlin in 1900.

By 1880, English contemporaries credited Neruda with ending the taboo on women's violin playing, and by the 1890s nearly as many young women studied the violin as studied the piano in London conservatories. Indeed, as women's piano playing became "democratized," playing the violin evidently acquired greater social status as an accomplishment. Neruda paved the way for younger performers, such as Marie Hall (1884–1956), a harpist's daughter born into poverty in Newcastle but discovered as a child prodigy by patrons who financed her education and facilitated her attaining celebrity status. May Mukle (1880–1963) pioneered as a woman cellist, learning as a child to play an instrument long thought too big for women to handle and developing her skills at the Royal Academy of Music. Her lengthy career included many solo performances and touring with her pianist sister and American violinist Maud Powell.

Major orchestras did not yet feature women playing brass or wind instruments, however. There were objections that playing them made women unattractive because cheeks were puffed out, as well as fears that extended playing could permanently distort their mouths. Brass instruments also were associated with impoverished street performers or the Salvation Army, which included women in its brass bands. Singing and the piano offered women performers more opportunities than other instruments.

Composing

The remarkable career of Clara Wieck Schumann (1819–96) displayed both virtuoso performing and composing, a combination that music critics long valued more highly than performance alone, but piano playing made her reputation. Recognized for many years as Europe's leading woman "classical" pianist and dubbed "Queen of the piano," she was sometimes judged the peer of Liszt, Sigismond Thalberg, and Anton Rubinstein. Her parents were music professionals who divorced in 1824. Friedrich Wieck taught piano and singing and ran a music business; her mother was a singer and piano soloist who also gave lessons. Clara was a child prodigy, nurtured by her domineering father, who had custody of her. She performed in the Leipzig Gewandhaus at the age of nine, made a solo debut there at eleven, and played in Paris at twelve. By 1837–38 she earned several thousand thaler from concerts in Vienna and critical acclaim for "epochmaking" performances displaying "the highest level of artistic skill combined with the greatest genius."[19] In 1840 she married composer Robert Schumann, one of her father's former pupils, their nuptials preceded by a famous lawsuit because she was defying her father, who feared that marriage would end her career. The mother of eight children by 1854, she often did subordinate her work to her husband's but still managed to give 139 concerts between 1840 and 1854, frequently introducing his compositions because, unlike Liszt or Chopin, he did not also perform (Figure 3.2).

Clara Schumann's early career gave her great confidence at the piano, but she was far more tentative about her compositional skills, which she judged inferior to Robert's. Her father encouraged her composing, but already in 1839 she wrote in a diary: "I once believed that I had creative talent, but I have given up this idea: a woman must not wish to compose – there never was one able to do it." She rated her piano trio of 1846 as "still women's work, which always lacks force and occasionally invention." Her self-doubts echoed contemporary judgments like that of Viennese author Caroline Pichler, who contrasted women's artistic and literary successes with their lack of achievement in musical composition. Although most of Clara Schumann's many songs and piano pieces were published and often well reviewed, she did little composing after Robert died. His hospitalization in 1854, after a suicide attempt, and death in 1856 left her needing to support a large family. She taught piano and gave concerts, her solo appearances between 1828 and 1891 totaling nearly 1,300. The London Philharmonic Society awarded her honorary membership in 1887, but only once did she play one of her own songs there. She also routinely took charge of business arrangements for her concert tours, negotiating

---

[19] Quotations in Nancy B. Reich, "Clara Schumann," in *Women Making Music: The Western Art Tradition, 1150–1950*, ed. Jane Bowers and Judith Tick (Urbana: University of Illinois Press, 1986), 249.

Figure 3.2 Clara Schumann, internationally prominent concert pianist, and her husband, the composer Robert Schumann.

fees, hiring supporting players, checking instruments, scheduling rehearsals, and having programs printed. The Frankfurt Conservatory appointed her chief teacher of piano in 1878, two daughters assisting her until she retired in 1892. Some contemporaries dubbed this highly demanding teacher and star performer the "priestess." She recognized that her artistic ambitions had necessitated reordering personal priorities, telling music critic Marie Lipsius: "People have no idea that if anything significant is to be achieved in art, one's education, one's entire course of life must differ from that of people in ordinary situations."[20]

In an environment where women's creative abilities were often disparaged, it was no surprise that women doubted their composing skill and subordinated it to other musical activities. Although recent biographical dictionaries identify more than a thousand women who wrote songs or instrumental pieces between the 1780s and 1914, teaching or performance provided the livelihood or renown for most of them. When women succeeded as composers, it was often for songs, a genre considered more suited to their abilities than operas or orchestral works. Other German women besides Schumann wrote *Lieder* sung at home or at public concerts. Hamburg singing teacher Louise Reichardt (1779–1826) composed more than 90 songs and choruses, Stuttgart pianist and teacher Emilie Zumsteeg (1796–1857) wrote about 60 songs, and Josephine Lang (1815–80) some 150. All three were professional musicians, unlike Fanny Mendelssohn Hensel (1805–47), whose wealthy father and famous composer brother Felix discouraged her from publishing her 250 songs. Although Felix insisted that publishing would disrupt her domestic duties, she had encouragement from her husband, a painter, and finally published one song collection shortly before her death. Maude Valerie White (1855–1937), trained at London's Royal Academy of Music and in Vienna, gained fame by composing some 200 Victorian ballads suitable for home singing and playing, and also profited from sheet music sales. At the Paris Conservatoire, where young women's choice of classes had been restricted, some women eventually joined male students in classes on counterpoint and fugue, and by the 1870s were winning prizes for composition.

Despite family or institutional opposition, then, some women persisted with composing, often able to do so because they had financial security. Such was the case for several French women. Louise Farrenc (1804–75), from a family of royal artists, studied composition and orchestration with a teacher from the Conservatoire and married a flautist whose music publishing business printed her first piano compositions between 1825 and 1839. She taught women piano students at the Conservatoire from 1842 to 1872, gaining a professorial title but long paid less than comparable men. Nonetheless, the Conservatoire in 1845 adopted thirty "études" by her as required study in piano classes. Farrenc also composed for orchestra and chamber ensembles and won some prizes, but not all of her compositions were published. The younger

---

[20] Quotations in Nancy B. Reich, *Clara Schumann: The Artist and the Woman* (Ithaca, N.Y.: Cornell University Press, 1985), 228–29; and Reich, "Clara Schumann," 276.

Augusta Holmès (1847–1903), daughter of an Irish officer residing in France, wrote operas, symphonic works, and choral pieces, including a famous ode celebrating the centennial of the French Revolution in 1889. An admirer of Wagner, she frequented Parisian musical and literary salons, and was best known for her songs. The talented Cécile Chaminade (1857–1944) received her first music lessons from her mother, an amateur pianist and singer, but her upper-middle-class father opposed her attending the Conservatoire, agreeing reluctantly to private lessons with some of its faculty. Nearly all of her 400 compositions were published, and her songs and short piano pieces were the most popular. Performances in England and praise from Queen Victoria, as well as the founding of Chaminade clubs in the United States and a financially successful American tour in 1908, highlighted her international reputation, and in 1913 she became the first woman composer awarded the Legion of Honor.

English composer Ethel Smyth (1858–1944) also faced parents' opposition to her musical ambitions, but at seventeen she prevailed in her battle with them and began formal instruction, going on in 1877 to the prestigious Leipzig Conservatory, being evidently among the first women allowed to study composition there. At its founding in 1843, Mendelssohn proposed a mission of "higher" musical education, and Leipzig, unlike older conservatories, usually admitted pupils who already had some training. It required a three-year course in theory for males but deemed a two-year course adequate for women's needs. Women were, nonetheless, nearly a third (445) of the 1,420 Leipzig graduates during its first twenty-five years. Smyth, a general's daughter, recognized, as her memoirs indicate, that her family's means permitted her training and pursuit of a nonlucrative career that poorer women could not afford. She progressed from writing songs, which she first published without asking a fee, to more ambitious orchestral works and operas. An orchestral piece and a mass were performed in London in 1890 and 1892, with financial help from the exiled Eugénie, but she could not get her operas produced in England until they were first performed in Germany. Smyth's Der Wald (1902, The Wood) was the first opera by a woman that New York's Metropolitan Opera House staged. The English production of The Wreckers (1906), her masterpiece, was delayed for three years after Leipzig and Prague debuts. Smyth commented astutely that if a woman writer found just one publisher and the public liked her work, she could overcome negative critics, but a composer could not develop a reputation without performances of her work which, if large-scale, required the resources of an orchestra, opera house, or chorus. Negative reviews of a first performance made securing resources for repeat performances difficult.

Smyth wanted her work to be accepted on the same terms as music by men, but some other women musicians, like some women artists, sought acceptance by arguing that they brought special feminine qualities to music. Unlike Sand, who despised the label woman writer, the Conservatoire-trained composer and pianist Juliette Toutain (b. 1877) readily presented herself as a woman artist. She wanted women artists and musicians to be allowed to compete for the Prix de Rome – whose winners obtained state funding to study in Rome – but she denied that women musicians competed directly with men because "in music as in anything else, woman maintains such a different personality from man." Woman's "capacity to feel very deeply and very quickly the slightest things, her gifts of assimilation prove the woman as a being particularly able to seize and render the beauty of forms and sounds," she wrote in 1903. English composer Katharine Eggar proclaimed that the Society of Women Musicians, which she helped found, was dedicated to "purifying musical life," a goal resembling Bertaux's mission for French women artists. After the French education minister opened Prix de Rome competitions to women in 1903, sculptress Lucienne Heuvelmans won a grand prize in 1911, and the young composer Lili Boulanger (1893–1918) was the first woman musician to do so in 1913. Lili and her talented sister Nadia were guided by their father, himself a Prix de Rome winner and professor at the Conservatoire, where their mother also had studied. Lili Boulanger's "modest and simple bearing" drew approval in the French press, one newspaper also contrasting her deserved professional victory with English suffragettes' militancy.[21]

Both the women's suffrage campaign and the Society of Women Musicians attracted Smyth. The Society was created in 1911, six years after the Society of British Composers had been founded without women members. An earlier Royal Society of Female Musicians had started in 1839 in reaction to women's exclusion from the Royal Society of Musicians, founded in 1838, but the two groups merged in 1865. By 1912, the new Society had 152 women members and 20 male associates and was campaigning for women's inclusion in symphony orchestras. Smyth joined the Women's Social and Political Union in 1911 and composed the music for the suffragettes' stirring anthem, "March of the Women," its words written by actress Cicely Hamilton. Some other women musicians preferred suffrage groups more cautious about tactics, however.

[21] Quotations in Annegret Fauser, "*La Guerre en Dentelles*: Women and the *Prix de Rome* in French Cultural Politics," *Journal of the American Musicological Society* 51 (Spring 1998): 102–03, 126; and (for Eggar) Paula Gillett, *Musical Women in England, 1870–1914: "Encroaching on All Man's Privileges"* (New York: St. Martin's Press, 2000), 219.

Elsewhere women sometimes contributed music to nationalist movements or other reform efforts. Norwegian composer Agathe Backer Grondahl (1847–1907), sister of painter Harriet Backer, studied piano in Berlin and Weimar, and combined a performing career, marriage, and family obligations with the composition of 190 songs and piano pieces. Most of her work was considered cosmopolitan, but she also did folksong arrangements, at a time of Norwegian national revival before independence from Sweden. Composer Valentina Serova (1846–1924) wrote articles advocating access to music education for more Russians and set her last opera, *They Roused Themselves*, against the backdrop of political unrest in 1904–05.

Actresses: from scandal to professional status

Actresses occupied an important place in the theater before the nineteenth century, unlike many women artists and musicians who were still seeking recognition as professionals rather than amateurs. Like playwrights and actors, French actresses benefited from Louis XIV's support for a royal troupe, and succeeding regimes maintained the Comédie Française and other state theaters. In Restoration England in 1661, Charles II ended the ban on women performers in place in Shakespeare's day. Actresses also worked in German theaters by the 1680s. Although accusations of immorality dogged performers, male and female, in both Catholic and Protestant states, the French Revolution's treatment of actors as full citizens signified greater social acceptance in a more secular era. By the 1880s various commentators noted the enhanced status and respectability of theater productions and performers. Indeed, the best actors and actresses were termed "artists." Actresses remained subjects of controversy, however, when they portrayed rebellious females or inverted societal roles by playing male characters.

English commentators traced actresses' path to respectability back to Sarah Siddons and her niece Fanny Kemble. Helena Faucit (1817–98), an actress favored in Victoria's court and wife of Albert's official biographer, believed that actresses' portrayals should set high moral standards for the public. The actress's duty, she wrote, was to show audiences "the types of noble womanly nature ... revealed by our best dramatic poets, and especially by Shakespeare."[22] Many actresses were young and

---

[22] Quoted in Christopher Kent, "Image and Reality: The Actress and Society," in *A Widening Sphere: Changing Roles of Victorian Women*, ed. Martha Vicinus (Bloomington: Indiana University Press, 1977), 99.

single, but others married and continued working, especially if husbands were actors. Siddons and Kemble were among the many actresses who, like women musicians, came from enterprising families of performers. Kemble and her younger sister Adelaide were part of the family's fourth performing generation. Indeed, as many as two-thirds of all actresses who debuted before 1860 came from theater families, whereas that was true for only 35 percent of those debuting after 1880. Theater families frequently toured, and until mid-century many audiences expected a performance to offer a mixture of dramatic scenes rather than a single play. Kemble's father, an actor and theater manager, persuaded his reluctant daughter to go on stage in 1829 when he had financial problems. The first successful English actress to tour the United States, Fanny (1809–93) married a plantation owner and had two children, but returned to England alone in 1845, denouncing slavery and determined to show through her writing that actresses were serious and intelligent. There was no theater tradition, however, in the middle-class background of Helen Taylor, daughter of Harriet Taylor Mill, wife of John Stuart Mill. Helen insisted on trying an acting career, much to the Mills' displeasure, and took the stage name of Miss Trevor. Her mother's death in 1858 brought her back home to be Mill's secretary, and she later became an active reformer.

By the 1880s, bigger middle-class audiences, which included larger numbers of women, enhanced the theater's respectability. So did the innovation of the matinee, heavily attended by women. Actresses' improved reputation coincided with larger numbers of women working outside the home, and employment in acting and women's place in it increased noticeably. In the 1841 English census, 310 women were 21 percent of 1,463 thespians; by 1881, actresses were just over half of that job category (2,368 of 4,565), as they were also in 1911 (9,171 of 18,247). Women were nearly half of all actors in Germany as well by 1907. In turn, English actresses' memoirs changed in emphasis. Their efforts to justify careers once considered dubious gave way to proud chartings of professional development and successes. Increasingly British actors and actresses came from middle-class backgrounds. One study of 409 actors and 241 actresses working between 1890 and 1913 reveals that among those starting careers after 1889, 46 percent of women and 59 percent of men had fathers in middle-class professions, a rarity for those debuting earlier. For France, historian Lenard Berlanstein suggests a correlation between the political empowerment of men in the democratic Third Republic and the improved reputations of theater women, formerly associated with aristocratic immorality but now enjoying broader public appeal. French actresses' memoirs presented self-justifications and emphasized personal commitments to art, family, and love. But like the famed Sarah Bernhardt, many French actresses did not cultivate the English image of married respectability. In the case of English actress Ellen Terry, an adoring public and critics overlooked an irregular private life. Prejudice against the theater plagued actresses in Russia longer than elsewhere because before serfdom was abolished in 1861, actors and actresses were often serfs, whether on nobles' private stages or in imperial theaters. Serfs were ordered to become performers, and actress-serfs could be compelled to be sexually available. After 1861, acting in imperial or new commercial theaters still bore the stigma of work for people in bondage.

Ellen Terry (1848–1928), like Bernhardt or Eleonora Duse, was part of a phenomenon of theatrical stardom that surpassed anything previously enjoyed by stage players, although she toured only in the Anglo-American world. The daughter of actor Charles Kean and his actress wife, she, three sisters, and a brother all followed their parents onto the stage, Ellen debuting at the age of nine. Married at sixteen to a much older painter, she returned to her parents within a year and from 1867 to 1874 stopped acting while she lived with architect E. W. Godwin and had two children, future stage designer Gordon Craig and playwright Edith Craig. Leaving Godwin, she returned to the stage and became London's leading Shakespearean actress. She married actor Charles Kelly in 1878, wanting respectability for her children. Reviewers frequently commented on her femininity and beauty, as well as her talent, and American author Henry James characterized her in 1881 as "wholesome and English and womanly." Whereas theater managers and company heads long wielded great power over performers, the star system, in combination with publicity in a mass circulation press, gave fortunate individuals more control over pay and working conditions. Huge differences existed, of course, between the unprecedented level of earnings for the best paid and the salaries of most performers, who would be lucky to earn as much as artisans. Terry, earning £200 a week by 1884, was then reputedly the highest-paid woman in England, but the popular Lillie Langtry (1853–1929), among the first "society" women to go on stage, soon commanded £250, and Terry later sometimes received £300. Thespians at the time considered £10 to £25 good weekly pay. Terry worked at actor Henry Irving's theater for twenty-four years, costarring with him in twenty-seven plays and enjoying the security of the arrangement. She did eight tours in the United States between 1883 and 1907. At a gala celebrating her fifty-year career, more than fifty actresses paid homage to her, and Winston Churchill praised her for elevating and sustaining "the quality and distinction of theatrical art in England during long years when it had been discreditably neglected by the state."[23]

The new star system in France, marked by the appearance of the word "celebrity" around 1840, created opportunities for ambitious women like Rachel or Bernhardt, who bridled at restrictions imposed by national companies like the Comédie Française, which offered members secure employment and pensions. France, unlike England, also provided state-funded dramatic training at the Conservatoire, typically drawing students of modest means who aspired to the security of a national troupe. Comédie Française actresses long helped make decisions about productions, until the Second Empire limited that decision-making to men in 1853. Rachel (1821–58), the Comédie Française star born Élisa Félix, daughter of a Jewish peddler, prospered at the state theater and also turned it to her own purposes. Indeed, the French star system really began within national troupes, as competition from commercial theaters necessitated higher pay for assertive leading performers. Rachel earned 4,000 francs at the Comédie Française in 1838, but 60,000 francs in 1841. The Second Empire's freeing of theaters from many state regulations further enhanced successful private French theaters' appeal to thespians, as did Russia's ending of an imperial monopoly on theater in 1882.

More has been written about Sarah Bernhardt (1844–1923) than any other nineteenth-century actress, the massive publicity starting during her lifetime, with input from Bernhardt herself. She began her career in French state theater before striking out independently to capitalize on her fame. She was evidently the first actress whose image was used to advertise pills, potions, and lotions. Daughter of a Dutch Jewish woman and her lover, Bernhardt (born Henriette Bernard) was convent educated before entering the Conservatoire in 1859. The Comédie Française hired her in 1862, later firing her for slapping another actress. She joined the Odéon theater, where she remained for six years before returning to the Comédie, paying a fine of 6,000 francs (a year's salary) for breaking her Odéon contract. After a successful tour with the Comédie in 1879 in London, where her exotic and histrionic reputation had preceded her, she left it for the potentially more lucrative commercial theater, this time being fined 100,000 francs and losing a pension. Her two-year tour of Europe and North America generated revenue to buy a theater, and she

---

[23] Quotations in Michael R. Booth, "Ellen Terry," in *Bernhardt, Terry, Duse: The Actress in Her Time*, by John Stokes, Michael R. Booth, and Susan Bassnett (Cambridge: Cambridge University Press, 1988), 69; and Sandra Richards, *The Rise of the English Actress* (New York: St. Martin's Press, 1993), 135–36.

leased another, using the name of her son (born in 1864) on legal documents. By 1883, when the term "diva" came into use in English, contemporaries linked it to Bernhardt's image as "the divine" leading lady whose grand entrances onto a stage riveted attention on her. Her romances were also legendary. She made another world tour in 1891–93, and in 1899 leased a theater from the city of Paris. Renamed the Sarah Bernhardt theater, it staged French classics and Shakespeare, plus Romantic-era plays. Bernhardt memorably portrayed romantic heroines, notably in Dumas's *La Dame aux Camélias* and Hugo's plays, but also performed at least twenty-five male roles, including Hamlet. Some nasty critics treated her cross-dressing roles as evidence that she was neither feminine nor masculine, but her popularity held with a large public, other than vicious anti-Semites. In 1906, when the mass-circulation daily paper *Le Petit Parisien* asked readers to name the ten most important people from the last century, Bernhardt was placed fourth. She had made herself a kind of French cultural ambassador to the world. She toured the United States nine times between 1880 and 1918, offering spectacles of stylized gestures and melodramatic crying and dying, which audiences enjoyed even when they did not understand French. Toward the end of her 62-year career she also appeared in silent films, the first in 1912, and continued performing after a leg was amputated.

The Italian actress Eleonora Duse (1858–1924) was perceived by many contemporaries as a rival to Bernhardt in the international arena (Figure 3.3). Both were strong personalities who defied convention, assumed managerial roles, and handled finances. Duse, born into a theatrical family, went on stage at the age of four with her parents' touring company. She had little formal education but read widely and made a lifelong friend of the writer Mathilde Serao, whom she met in Naples at a difficult time in her life. Seeing Bernhardt's performances celebrated in Italy inspired her to aim for more recognition. Psychologically realistic and passionate portrayals, as opposed to Bernhardt's highly stylized and declamatory acting style, became Duse's trademark. More than one biographer has termed her "the first modern actor," echoing judgments made as early as 1879. Duse married an actor in 1882 and had a daughter, whom she sent to boarding school and kept away from theatrical life, refusing later to let her grandchildren see her perform. In 1886 she established her own theater company, which introduced Ibsen's *Doll's House* and *Hedda Gabler* in Italy. Her tours throughout Europe and North and South America proved lucrative. Duse's most famous romantic relationship was with the younger writer Gabriele d'Annunzio, whose plays she produced, incurring heavy losses which necessitated additional tours. Proud of her international renown

Figure 3.3 Eleonora Duse, leading Italian actress.

and aware that some critics, such as George Bernard Shaw, rated her more highly than Bernhardt, Duse told her acting company in 1906 that she had "done more than anyone else to enhance the reputation of Italian drama throughout the world."[24] She retired in 1909 and opened a gathering place and library for actresses in Rome in 1914, but soon,

[24] Guido Noccioli, *Duse on Tour: Guido Noccioli's Diaries 1906–07*, trans. and ed. Giovanni Pontiero (Amherst: University of Massachusetts Press, 1982), 58.

unable to afford upkeep, she donated the books to the National Council of Italian Women.

Other actresses drew inspiration from Bernhardt's and Duse's successes, and critics often compared other women's performances to those of international stars. Maria Savina (1864–1915), the first Russian actress around whom a personality cult developed, dominated the imperial Aleksandrinski theater in St. Petersburg for nearly forty years. Dubbed the "tsarina of Russian theatre," she recognized that "fame and notoriety are like oxygen for an actor." Her style and marketing ability prompted comparisons to Bernhardt, sometimes by critics disliking her promotion of western European works. Highly paid, Savina also had a social conscience and was an officer in an organization aiding needy performers. At the Maly state theater in Moscow, Maria Ermolova (1853–1928) became a popular tragic actress, one enthusiastic critic terming her performances "apologies for women, artistic refutations of all the slander against the female heart and soul." Duse was the model for the younger Vera Kommissarzhevskaia (1864–1910), a star at the St. Petersburg state theater before she left for private theater. Asserting her wish to "fulfill the demands of my artistic individuality," she exemplified the permeation of Russian urban culture by western individualism and modernism before 1914.[25]

Recognition in the form of official decorations also came to actresses, as it did to women artists and musicians, but not so rapidly as it came to actors. The first French Legion of Honor award to an actor, in 1864, was for his Conservatoire teaching; the first for an actor's stage ability was delayed until 1883. Actress Marie Laurent's charity work was honored in 1888, but only in 1904 did Legion of Honor recognition for acting excellence go to a woman, Julia Bartet, who was more self-effacing than Bernhardt. In 1910 republican administrators ended the 1853 exclusion of women from the Comédie Française program committee. Bernhardt waited until 1914 for the Legion of Honor, and Terry was designated "dame of the British Empire" only in 1925, the second actress so titled. The first British actor was knighted in 1895.

By the time that leading actresses received official recognition, some feminists had already recognized actresses' contribution to making women's work and public roles more widely accepted. At an international women's congress in Chicago in 1893, English-born actress Julia Marlowe (1866–1950) boasted that "the actress has advanced the whole cause of woman, since every individual triumph raises the estimation in which the

---

[25] Quotations in Catherine A. Schuler, *Women in Russian Theatre: The Actress in the Silver Age* (London: Routledge, 1996), 56, 85, 170.

intellectual achievements of a whole class are held. Woman is better understood because she has been faithfully portrayed; she is more highly regarded because of her ability to make that portrayal; and that faithful portrayal has ... a powerful moral influence in an educational sense."[26] Actresses, feminists, and other commentators warned, nonetheless, that most aspiring thespians were unlikely to gain fame and fortune, and instead faced limited incomes and uncertain employment. Kittie Carson and 60 other English actresses started the Theatrical Ladies Guild in 1891 to aid needy performers and their children, and its membership soon reached 700. Some actresses also identified with feminist issues, especially in England where the Actresses' Franchise League, founded in 1908, claimed 900 members by 1913, including Terry, Hamilton, and Langtry. Other actresses feared, however, that such advocacy might alienate audiences or financial backers. Actresses also wrote and staged suffragist plays, such as *Votes for Women* (1907) by Elizabeth Robins (1862–1952) or Cicely Hamilton's *Pageant of Great Women* (1909), produced by Terry's daughter Edith Craig (1869–1947). Craig started a political theater, the Pioneer Players, in 1911, staging *The First Actress* by Hamilton (1872–1952) and Chris St. John, who traced theater women's struggles against discrimination since 1660. French actresses, like French women in general, were slower to support feminists, but the former Comédie Française actress Marguerite Durand founded a feminist newspaper, *La Fronde*, in 1897 and later embraced women's suffrage, as did the hesitant Bernhardt by 1911.

Summation

That some women artists, musicians, and actresses, like some women writers, supported feminist efforts is not surprising, for all faced obstacles as they struggled for professional acceptance – even though singers and actresses usually did not face the difficulties in acquiring training that often beset women artists, instrumentalists, or composers striving to move beyond amateur status. Talented performers also did not face judgments that they lacked the requisite combination of reason, self-control, and imagination needed for creativity and innovation in the visual arts or musical and literary composition. But if fame came more readily to women performers, they still faced negative judgments about their respectability. Performers on tour were not exemplars of middle-class domesticity, but many eventually used the press to balance their

---

[26] Julia Marlowe, "Woman's Work upon the Stage," in *The World's Congress of Representative Women*, ed. May Wright Sewall, 2 vols. (Chicago: Rand, McNally, 1894), I: 191.

stage image with a more typically feminine one as wives, mothers, and supporters of charity. Private lives varied considerably, from the conventional to the sexually unconventional, whether defiantly or sadly, but many women in the arts managed to withstand the withering public gaze and earned a living and professional recognition. The last British census before World War I tabulated nearly 50,000 women working in art, music, and theater, a statistic that combined creative roles with supporting services but nonetheless recorded women as nearly one-third of all those so employed.

Stardom in artistic endeavors was, of course, the exception, not the norm, and some feminists saw risk as well as benefit in celebrating exceptional women. Suffragist actress-author Elizabeth Robins warned in 1913 that the "exceptional woman" could also figure as an obstacle to feminist efforts because men tried to divide women and dismiss complaints about discrimination as baseless by pointing to exceptional women's achievements.

Further reading and reference works

Visual arts

Behr, Shulamith. *Women Expressionists*. New York: Rizzoli, 1988.

Borzello, Frances. *A World of Our Own: Women as Artists since the Renaissance*. New York: Watson-Guptill Publications, 2000.

Chadwick, Whitney. *Women, Art, and Society*. London: Thames and Hudson, 1990.

Cherry, Deborah. *Beyond the Frame: Feminism and Visual Culture, Britain 1850–1900*. London: Routledge, 2000.

Painting Women: Victorian Women Artists. London: Routledge, 1993.

Doy, Gen. *Women and Visual Culture in Nineteenth-Century France 1800–1852*. London: Leicester University Press, 1998.

Garb, Tamar. *Sisters of the Brush: Women's Artistic Culture in Late Nineteenth-Century Paris*. New Haven, Conn.: Yale University Press, 1994.

Women Impressionists, Oxford: Phaidon Press, 1986.

Harris, Ann Sutherland, and Linda Nochlin. *Women Artists 1550–1950*. New York: Los Angeles County Museum of Art and Alfred A. Knopf, 1977; 6th reprinting, 1984.

Heller, Nancy G. *Women Artists: An Illustrated History*. Revised edn. New York: Abbeville Press, 1987.

Higonnet, Anne. *Berthe Morisot*. New York: Harper and Row, 1990; paperback, 1991.

Klumpke, Anna. *Rosa Bonheur: The Artist's (Auto)biography*. Translated by Gretchen van Slyke. Ann Arbor: University of Michigan Press, 1997.

Morawinska, Agnieszka, "Polish Women Artists." In *Voices of Freedom: Polish Women Artists and the Avant-Garde, 1880–1990*, 13–39. Washington, D.C.: National Museum of Women in the Arts, 1991.

Opfell, Olga S. *Special Visions: Profiles of Fifteen Women Artists from the Renaissance to the Present Day*. Jefferson, N.C.: McFarland and Co., 1991.

Orr, Clarissa Campbell, ed. *Women in the Victorian Art World*. Manchester: Manchester Univesity Press, 1995.

Parker, Rozsika, and Griselda Pollock. *Old Mistresses: Women, Art and Ideology*. London: Routledge, 1981.

Perry, Gill. *Women Artists and the Parisian Avant-Garde: Modernism and "Feminine" Art, 1900 to the late 1920s*. Manchester: Manchester University Press, 1995.

Weisberg, Gabriel P., and Jane R. Becker. *Overcoming All Obstacles: The Women of the Académie Julian*. New York: The Dahesh Museum, and New Brunswick, N.J.: Rutgers University Press, 1999.

Wichstrom, Anne. "At Century's End: Harriet Backer, Kitty Kielland, Asta Norregaard." In *At Century's End: Norwegian Artists and the Figurative Tradition 1880–1990*, 21–66. Washington, D.C.: National Museum of Women in the Arts, 1995.

Witzling, Mara R., ed. *Voicing Our Visions: Writings by Women Artists*. New York: Universe, 1991.

Yeldham, Charlotte. *Women Artists in Nineteenth-Century France and England: Their Art Education, Exhibition Opportunities and Membership of Exhibiting Societies and Academies, with an Assessment of the Subject Matter of Their Work and Summary Biographies*. 2 vols. New York: Garland, 1984.

Music

Bowers, Jane, and Judith Tick, eds. *Women Making Music: The Western Art Tradition, 1150–1950*. Urbana: University of Illinois Press, 1986.

Citron, Marcia J. *Gender and the Musical Canon*. Cambridge: Cambridge University Press, 1993.

Ehrlich, Cyril. *The Music Profession in Britain since the Eighteenth Century: A Social History*. Oxford: Clarendon Press, 1985.

Ellis, Katharine. "Female Pianists and Their Male Critics." *Journal of the American Musicological Society* 50 (Summer–Fall 1997): 353–85.

Fauser, Annegret. "*La Guerre en Dentelles*: Women and the *Prix de Rome* in French Cultural Politics." *Journal of the American Musicological Society* 51 (Spring 1998): 83–129.

Gillett, Paula. *Musical Women in England, 1870–1914: "Encroaching on All Man's Privileges"*. New York : St. Martin's Press, 2000.

Holoman, D. Kern. *The Société des Concerts du Conservatoire 1828–1967*. Berkeley: University of California Press, 2004.

McReynolds, Louise. "'The Incomparable' Anastasiia Vial'tseva." In *Russia– Women–Culture*, ed. Helena Goscilo and Beth Holmgren. 273–94. Bloomington: Indiana University Press, 1996.

Pendle, Karin. "A Night at the Opera: The Parisian Prima Donna, 1830–1850." *Opera Quarterly* 4 (Spring 1986): 77–89.

Pendle, Karin, ed. *Women and Music: A History*. Bloomington: Indiana University Press, 1991.

Reich, Nancy B. *Clara Schumann: The Artist and the Woman*. Ithaca, N.Y.: Cornell University Press, 1985.

Solie, Ruth A., ed. *Musicology and Difference: Gender and Sexuality in Music Scholarship*. Berkeley: University of California Press, 1993.

Theater

Berlanstein, Lenard R. *Daughters of Eve: A Cultural History of French Theater Women from the Old Regime to the Fin-de-siècle*. Cambridge, Mass.: Harvard University Press, 2001.

Brownstein, Rachel M. *Tragic Muse: Rachel of the Comédie-Française*. New York: Alfred A. Knopf, 1993.

Davis, Tracy C. *Actresses as Working Women: Their Social Identity in Victorian Culture*. London: Routledge, 1991.

Gale, Maggie B., and Viv Gardner, eds. *Women, Theatre and Performance: New Histories, New Historiographies*. Manchester: Manchester University Press, 2000.

Gardner, Vivien, and Susan Rutherford, eds. *The New Woman and Her Sisters: Feminism and Theatre 1850–1914*. Ann Arbor: University of Michigan Press, 1992.

Hemmings, F. W. J. *Theater and State in France 1760–1905*. Cambridge: Cambridge University Press, 1994.

Richards, Sandra. *The Rise of the English Actress*. New York: St. Martin's Press, 1993.

Schuler, Catherine A. *Women in Russian Theatre: The Actress in the Silver Age*. London: Routledge, 1996.

Sheehy, Helen. *Eleonora Duse*. New York: Knopf, 2003.

Stokes, John, Michael R. Booth, and Susan Bassnett. *Bernhardt, Terry, Duse: The Actress in Her Time*. Cambridge: Cambridge University Press, 1988.

Stowell, Sheila. *A Stage of Their Own: Feminist Playwrights of the Suffrage Era*. Ann Arbor: University of Michigan Press, 1992.

Biographical dictionaries

Cohen, Aaron I. *International Encyclopedia of Women Composers*. 2nd edn. 2 vols. New York: Books and Music, 1987.

Gaze, Delia, ed. *Dictionary of Women Artists*. 2 vols. London: Fitzroy, Dearborn, 1997.

Hixon, Don L., and Don A. Hennessee. *Women in Music: An Encyclopedic Biobibliography*. 2 vols. 2nd edn. Metuchen, N.J.: Scarecrow Press, 1993.

Sadie, Julie Anne, and Rhian Samuel, eds. *The Norton/Grove Dictionary of Women Composers*. New York: W. W. Norton, 1995.

Sadie, Stanley, and John Tyrrell, eds. *The New Grove Dictionary of Music and Musicians*. 2nd edn. 29 vols. London: Macmillan, 2001.

Petteys, Chris, ed. *Dictionary of Women Artists: An International Dictionary of Women Artists Born before 1900*. Boston: G. K. Hall, 1985.

4   Caring and power: from charity to social reform

The life stories of women who dedicated themselves to helping others through charity or social reform efforts might, at first glance, seem lacking in the individual ambition exhibited by many women in professional endeavors. Yet deep commitments to serving the larger society, whether inspired by religious conviction or secular humanitarianism, required a marshaling of energies which brought some women into positions of leadership. Within Catholic religious orders or the less numerous Protestant sisterhoods, women held administrative roles and tried to inspire followers by articulating a mission, through talks or publications. Similarly, many lay women who undertook charitable or reform activities exercised leadership and, in the process, entered a kind of public arena. Indeed, some women's commitments to alleviating the suffering of others or advocating social reforms merit comparison with efforts by better-known male political or social reformers. Such women exercised what recent historians have aptly termed "caring power."[1] Caring power entailed recognizing the value of working with others to make an impact and also giving people assisted the ability to alter or control aspects of their lives.

Religiously inspired charity was an old tradition, of course, and lay people as well as religious orders provided it. But in the wake of the Enlightenment and related efforts to improve secular society, lay organizations without religious ties gained more prominence. Indeed, in 1793 French revolutionaries proclaimed a "right to assistance" for the needy. Providers of charity traditionally hoped that recipients, grateful for aid, also would remain accepting of the established political and social order. During the nineteenth century, however, many philanthropists tried to combine aid to the needy with broader reform efforts to remedy social ills, hoping not only to change and improve individuals'

---

[1] Annemieke van Drenth and Francisca de Haan, *The Rise of Caring Power: Elizabeth Fry and Josephine Butler in Britain and the Netherlands* (Amsterdam: Amsterdam University Press, 1999).

behavior but also to alter aspects of society. Some reform organizations, such as antislavery groups, aligned their goals with religious tenets, as they understood them, but others adopted more secular approaches. Contemporaries often used the terms "charity" and "philanthropy" interchangeably, but in some traditionally Catholic countries, notably France, Belgium, and Italy, the term "philanthropy" carried the connotation of aid provided by lay people acting without a religious agenda, or in a nonsectarian way supported by people of more than one faith. Although men often led nineteenth-century volunteer organizations and managed their finances, men and women sometimes worked together, and all-women groups emerged as well.

This chapter focuses on women as aid-givers, not recipients, and on how involvement in causes taking them beyond their households affected their lives. As in other aspects of social and cultural life, organizational patterns for charity and reform varied according to national, religious, political, and economic traditions, and timetables of activity varied as well. Social class, gender, and sometimes race also shaped experiences with caring power. Philosopher Michel Foucault and his scholarly disciples have argued that the nineteenth-century expansion of such public institutions as prisons, mental asylums, and schools enabled both governments and social elites to wield greater control over populations, even as they touted such institutions' humanitarian benefits.[2] Similarly, philanthropists and reformers, typically from upper- and middle-class backgrounds, often hoped that projects helping the less fortunate, such as alleviating poverty or rehabilitating former prisoners, would contribute as well to the stabilization of society. Europeans also took this mindset to overseas colonies where they governed peoples from other cultures and races. The patronizing attitudes often displayed by philanthropists and reformers toward less privileged classes or nonwhite races readily aroused negative reactions from those whom they sought to help, and certainly warrant criticism. Yet many philanthropists and reformers genuinely believed that their projects were essentially humanitarian, and not instruments of social control.

Upper- and middle-class women's participation in new manifestations of caring power became more widespread as the century unfolded, and the consequences were significant. Through efforts to aid women in need, women volunteers often developed an awareness of how society and laws seriously disadvantaged women, including women of their own

---

[2] Michel Foucault, *Madness and Civilization: A History of Insanity in the Age of Reason*, trans. Richard Howard (New York: Vintage Books, 1973); Jacques Donzelot, *The Policing of Families*, trans. Robert Hurley (New York: Random House, 1979).

social class. Moreover, involvement in one cause often led women to related projects. Indeed, women's volunteer experience contributed to the later development of feminist organizing. Groups addressing such problems as poverty or disease and their effects on women and children also sometimes became advocates for turning caring activities into paid employment for women, at a time when some governments were assuming responsibilities once left to charities and volunteers. Frequently the advocacy for expanding women's role in such work, in private or public agencies, relied on arguments that recent historians label "maternalism."[3] Maternalist reformers contended that women's special nurturing qualities could benefit not only families but also the larger society. They used traditional ideas to justify women's assumption of new public roles.

The tracing of women's caring power in this chapter begins with examples of religious charities and of organizations supported by upper-class women, including members of ruling dynasties and aristocrats. Certainly aristocrats and middle-class people sometimes worked for the same causes or groups, but the involvement of middle-class people – including women – grew noticeably where industrial and commercial economies expanded. The realities of gender relations also were apparent as men and women interacted in volunteer organizations and as women's organizations dealt with political leaders or senior male administrators in public bureaucracies handling issues that concerned volunteer groups. Select examples of women leaders of charities and related reform efforts will dramatize the possibilities for women's empowerment in an arena that broadened from traditional to newer female concerns, its associations engaging more women than any other kind of formal organization before 1914. Philanthropy and reform brought individual women into organizations where they worked with others, sometimes with men, sometimes in all-women associations. In 1889, an international conference in Paris on women's organizations highlighted hundreds of French charities, religious and secular, in which women played a leading role. By 1893, at least 500,000 English women participated in charitable activity, and 20,000 earned a living working for charitable societies, the latter total not including nurses. At least 4,000 charitable organizations existed in Russia in 1901, many with women members and about 300 of them run by women or focused on women's needs. Hungarian women then led about 800 charities. Nearly 900,000 German women belonged to Red Cross affiliates by 1912. Certainly many women's charities

[3] Seth Koven and Sonya Michel, eds., *Mothers of a New World: Maternalist Politics and the Origins of Welfare States* (New York: Routledge, 1993).

supported the status quo and regarded suffering as part of a divine plan for human life. Others, however, increasingly tried to remedy inequities, legal and social, and in the process some members became concerned about inequality between the sexes.

Religion, charity, and reform

As with much else in Europe, the French Revolution produced a rupture in religious charitable activity until the Napoleonic regime and royal restorations promoted a return to older practices. Even before the Revolution's abolition of the religious orders comprising half of the first estate, the monarchy had exiled Jesuits and imposed controls on other orders, a policy with Austrian parallels under Joseph II. Clerical resistance to the loyalty oath imposed in 1790, church closures in 1793–94, and the flight from France of clergy, nuns, and wealthy donors halted much Catholic charity. Revolutionaries expected state and local authorities to take over providing aid to the needy, medical care, and schools. To reverse the church–state hostility of the 1790s, Napoleon concluded a Concordat with the papacy that regulated French church–state relations from 1801 to 1905. Catholic orders began returning to France, and new congregations emerged. In reaction to Enlightenment critiques of religious superstition, early nineteenth-century Romantics like the royalist Chateaubriand celebrated the emotionally soothing nature of religious services in cathedrals where worshipers felt connected with the past. On the other side of the political spectrum, some early socialists linked their programs to religion by emphasizing Jesus's concern for the poor, suggesting that Christianity favored greater political and social equality. Conservatives also favored Christian charity, of course, but linked it to moralizing the poor and inculcating respect for existing state authorities. Both men and women participated in religiously oriented charities, but women's increasingly prominent role demonstrated what many historians term the feminization of religion, Catholic and Protestant, during the nineteenth century as men embraced more secular values.

In France between 1800 and 1880, some 400 women's congregations or orders were created or refounded, attracting about 200,000 sisters. Indeed, nuns were a larger percentage of France's female population in 1880, when they numbered about 127,000, than before 1789, when they numbered about 40,000. At least four-fifths of them were apostolic sisters whose mission was service to the laity, unlike contemplative sisters committed to a strictly cloistered existence organized around prayer and meditation. In Germany in 1912, some 72,000 nuns worked in caregiving or education; only 500 were in contemplative orders. The Italian tabulation of 42,664 nuns in 1861 did not distinguish between the cloistered and the more active, but women religious then staffed many schools, orphanages, and hospitals. Piedmont, the northern Italian kingdom leading national unification, suppressed some religious orders because of Pope Pius IX's hostility to unification, which ended the Papal States' centuries-old political independence by 1870. As Spanish governments seized congregations' property and dissolved some orders, the number of women religious fell to 11,000 by mid-century, only half of the 1797 total. Female orders fared better than male orders, however, because secular authorities valued them as teachers and nurses. After the Spanish tumult of 1868–75 a Catholic revival under the restored monarchy brought new recruits, and in 1904, 40,000 women were in religious orders, as compared to 11,000 men.

The largest female congregation in France, the Daughters of Charity, had aided the urban poor since its founding during the Counter Reformation by the widow Louise de Marillac and her spiritual adviser Vincent de Paul. Reauthorized by Napoleon, it had 9,100 members by 1878. The Society of the Sacred Heart of Jesus, founded by Sophie Barat (1779–1865), taught children from all social classes. Barat, daughter of a Burgundian farmer, was encouraged by her older brother, a priest, and his superior, and secured support for opening a convent in 1802. As head of the order for 63 years, Barat, with papal backing, worked to establish more Sacred Heart convents in Europe, Africa, and North America, the total reaching 100 by the time she died. Both her status as a superior general deriving authority directly from Rome, rather than from a local bishop, and the centralized organization that she led were new features of Catholic institutional life for women. Anne-Marie Javouhey (1779–1851), also from Burgundy, shared Barat's dismay about the Revolution's treatment of clergy and taught children in her village before founding the Sisters of Saint Joseph of Cluny in 1807 to aid poor children and provide work for young women. A decade later she focused on efforts abroad, her congregation creating missions in Africa, South America, and the Caribbean. She became known as *la mère des noirs* (mother of the blacks) because her missionary nuns – European and African – advocated the abolition of slavery.

Women heading religious orders were leaders in more than one respect. With or without male superiors' supervision, they oversaw the administration of convents and allied schools, refuges, hospitals, or charities, and they set an institutional tone through frequent and encouraging reminders to subordinates about their mission. They spoke of serving God and the secular world, using traditional religious language and emphasizing women's devotion to serving others. Vows of chastity and poverty did not attract most nineteenth-century women, but Catholic orders offered members security in a female community and drew many sisters from social origins more modest than was previously the case. Jeanne Jugan (1792–1879), for example, was a former servant, the daughter of a poor sailor who died when she was six. She founded the Little Sisters of the Poor, who ran shelters for abandoned children and the aged, and were recognized in 1842. The minority of orders that were contemplative provided places for women like the Carmelite nun Thérèse Martin (1873–97) of Lisieux, who believed that through prayer and self-deprivation she could help save the sinful world. At a time when republican France was expelling some Catholic orders and preparing the 1905 separation of church and state, her posthumously published autobiography about self-sacrifice, *Story of a Soul*, became a bestseller translated into more than thirty languages by the time of her canonization. The papacy's response to mounting anticlericalism around 1900 was expanded control over Catholic forces, which affected women's orders through reinforcement of bishops' or Rome's supervision of finances and activities, and bans on individual nuns going out alone.

In largely Protestant England, fewer than 20 Catholic convents existed before 1840, but by 1900 there were about 500, representing 62 congregations, two-thirds French or Belgian in origin. Many ran day or boarding schools, often drawing Irish immigrants' children. In English-controlled Ireland, nuns became essential for Catholic charities and schools. The number of Irish convents rose from eighteen in 1800 to ninety-five by 1851, and continued increasing, owing partly to donations from wealthy women like Catherine McAuley (1787–1841). She used a legacy from her Protestant adoptive parents to open a residence for poor women and school for orphans and poor children, taking vows in 1831 and founding the Religious Sisters of Mercy, eventually one of the English-speaking world's largest congregations. Yet, some historians argue, convents' prominence also deterred Irish Catholic laywomen from charity work.

Religious convictions drew both Catholics and Protestants into missionary work overseas. Such efforts predated 1800, but the nineteenth-century expansion of European empires opened new areas for proselytizing. Missionaries varied in their sensitivity to established religious and cultural practices in places where they tried to make conversions. To reach indigenous populations, they often opened schools or provided medical care, but the accompanying Christian teaching also kept away people they hoped to reach. Catholic sisters frequently went to locales where priests already had established missions. French troops, sent to conquer Algeria, brought along nuns as nurses in 1832, and in the 1840s Aglaée Hamonet became one of the first sisters to care for poor Arab women in remote areas. Nuns sometimes recruited African women for their orders, but apparently these Africans often received little education and did household chores for European nuns. Orders like Our Lady of Missions, founded in Lyon in 1861 by Euphrasie Barbier, demonstrated that Catholic women's missionary work was well under way by the time that the papacy ordered all religious orders to maintain missionaries. Nonetheless, orders not specifically designated as missionary congregations usually sent relatively few members to colonies, and many missionaries focused efforts on European settlers instead of trying to cross racial or cultural divides.

Protestant denominations sent single men, married couples, and some single women as missionaries. In India, British women might have contacts with women that men could not make in locales where social segregation of the sexes prevailed. Missionaries pursued *zenana* education, so called after the women's section of upper-class Indian houses, particularly in Muslim communities. The British and Foreign School Society sent its first woman teacher to Bengal in 1821, and women doctors and nurses arrived as medical missionaries later in the century. More Indian women than men, especially widows or single women, embraced Christianity. For unmarried Protestant women missionaries, work overseas might offer a wider range of activities than the home country. This was true for Mary Slessor (1848–1915), a mill worker as a girl in Scotland, who decided at the age of twenty-eight to teach under Presbyterian auspices in Nigeria. Probably the most famous British woman missionary, she lived in southeastern Nigeria for forty years. Once there, she often rated conversions to Christianity a lower priority than trying to end such practices as slavery, human sacrifice after important persons died, or killing twins, whose birth was called an ill omen. Improving women's lives was also a concern. To succeed, Slessor often needed British civil and military officials' support, and after the British Niger Coast Protectorate was established, she was appointed vice consul in 1898 and later became a judge in a local court. Probably the first woman magistrate in the Empire, she was empowered to make decisions based upon local law and imperial policy. She developed relationships of trust with the indigenous people among whom she lived, and also helped to extend British colonial rule.

However sincere their motivations, missionaries' intrusion into other cultures has seemed problematical in the post-colonial era since World War II. European men in colonial armies and administrations were the obvious agents of imperialism, but women missionaries and officials' wives also played a role, even as they defined their efforts in religious or humanitarian terms and found some indigenous women receptive to their efforts to lessen hardships. Indeed, even before 1914, experience led some missionaries to question notions of western superiority, among them Elise Kootz-Kretschmer, a Moravian sent to German East Africa who had more egalitarian attitudes than did many German Lutheran missionaries.

Pious laywomen also did extensive charitable work, and in Roman Catholic countries often acted in conjunction with nuns. In Russia, however, the Orthodox Church long emphasized individual giving rather than benevolent associations. There members of the imperial family, notably Catherine II and her daughter-in-law Maria Feodorovna, created the first women's charities. In post-revolutionary Paris, which grew rapidly with an influx from rural areas, women participated in at least thirty-nine charity associations by mid-century and ran seventeen of them. The Society of Maternal Charity, founded in 1788 with Marie Antoinette's patronage and revived in 1801, involved prominent aristo-cratic and bourgeois women in aiding poor women and young children. To receive its aid, women had to be married or widowed and their children legitimate. In 1810 Napoleon brought the Paris group under the umbrella of the Imperial Society of Maternal Charity with forty-four provincial branches, his interior minister noting that the Society, pre-sided over by Marie-Louise, Napoleon's new wife, offered a way for "the commendably ambitious to distinguish themselves."[4] The most socially prestigious women's charity, it received large subsidies from the Paris city government and still had eighty-one branches in the late 1800s. Because the Society wanted to aid only women married in church, and not simply in the civil ceremony required by the state, the Third Republic cut off subsidies to branches maintaining religious require-ments. Already by mid-century the Society assisted fewer people than did the lay Ladies of Charity, reconstituted in 1840. They worked with the Daughters of Charity (cited above) whom the Paris city government engaged to administer much of the public aid to the needy and sick. Adding recruits after the 1848 revolutionary unrest, the Ladies of Charity claimed 630 members by 1853. Members had to donate 50 francs annually or visit the poor, and many did both.

Home visiting was a forerunner of the case work done by twentieth-century social workers. Consistent with the nineteenth-century

---

[4] Quoted in Christine Adams, "The Provinces versus Paris: The Case of the Society of Maternal Charity of Bordeaux," *Proceedings of the Annual Meeting of the Western Society for French History* 23 (1996): 421.

philanthropists' emphasis on helping needy people learn to improve their lives, instead of simply giving them money or material aid, home visiting let volunteers judge the moral worthiness of the people aided. Previously many lay Catholics had limited their charitable involvement to donations to religious orders, but after the 1790s they, like Protestants, put more emphasis on individual activity. Typically religious charities aided churchgoers and married people. Both religious and secular charities wanted to monitor uses of their aid, and in theory, though not necessarily in reality, home visitors could also educate aid recipients by word or example. Whatever their actual impact on the beliefs and habits of the poor, home visits gave women from charities or Protestant Bible societies new awareness of social problems linked to urbanization and industrialization.

Protestants and Jews in various countries shared the goals of moralizing and stabilizing society pursued by Catholics. Since the Protestant Reformation English laypeople and clergy had cooperated in charitable work, local donors supplementing tax-supported poor relief. What was new during the nineteenth century was women's greater participation in organized charity. In Paris three young women founded the Protestant Association of Charity in 1825. In Vienna Jewish women started a charitable society in 1816, six years after Austrian aristocratic women had founded the Society for the Advancement of the Good and Useful. Lady Louise Rothschild created the first independent Jewish women's philanthropic associations in London in 1840, the Jewish Ladies' Benevolent Loan Society and the Ladies' Visiting Society. Betty de Rothschild became a leader of Jewish women's charity work in Paris.

French Protestant and Catholic women and men cooperated during the late 1820s to start the first nursery schools for very young children of working mothers in urban areas. Their model was the British "infant school." Protestant Émilie Mallet (1794–1856), daughter of a manufacturer and wife of a prosperous banker, was their most energetic woman promoter, along with Catholic philanthropist Jean-Denys Cochin. Begun in Paris and originally called *salles d'asile* – literally "rooms of asylum" – these schools combined child care, moral instruction, and simple lessons. They proved so successful that the state soon assumed administrative control, although philanthropic women retained a role as volunteer inspectresses or patrons until the Third Republic. Nuns' teaching in nursery-school classes reduced the Catholic hierarchy's initial resistance to an institution with Protestant sponsors and precedents in Protestant England. The July Monarchy's higher commission for nursery schools, appointed in 1837, was unique among advisory bodies attached to government ministries because most of its members were women. These women presented the nursery schools' mission as one of "faith, charity and maternal love," a message suiting women teachers and local school patronesses with whom the commission maintained contact.[5] It was also the message of Eugénie Chevreau-Lemercier, hired in 1837 as the "general delegate" to inspect these schools, the central government's first appointment of a salaried woman inspector, although Paris provided a municipal precedent.

In more than one country, nursery schools for children of poor women working outside the home began as philanthropic projects that eventually became public institutions, but governmental support or public approval of them varied considerably. In contrast to the French government's early embrace of nursery schools, renamed *écoles maternelles* (maternal schools) in 1881, German authorities were suspicious of kindergartens and the mission framed for them by Friedrich Froebel and women who helped introduce them. Unlike infant schools opened by religious groups since the 1820s, Froebel kindergartens encouraged religious tolerance and children's independent activities. After the 1848 revolution, Prussia banned kindergartens from 1851 to 1860, judging that Froebel's pedagogy encouraged dangerous individualism and also being wary of independent women's role in them. Aristocrat Bertha von Marenholtz-Bülow, an early sponsor, left Germany to promote kindergartens elsewhere.

Less controversial was German women's aid to the sick and needy, especially during crises like the Napoleonic wars, when women nursed wounded soldiers. Local authorities and male citizens had dominated organized charity since the Reformation, but during the cholera epidemic of 1831 Amalie Sieveking (1794–1859) volunteered to care for women in Hamburg, and she created the Female Association for the Care of the Poor and the Sick in 1832. Sieveking, from one of Hamburg's leading families, hoped to benefit not only those assisted but also the volunteers visiting homes. For "the upper classes," she said, "household and other domestic responsibilities do not offer the female side of the family a sufficient arena for the sum of their energies."[6] Although she found it difficult initially to raise funds and recruit women, 4 other cities had similar groups by 1837, and by 1847, 45. At least 250 German women's associations of different sorts existed by the early 1840s.

---

[5] Quoted in Jean-Noël Luc, ed., *La petite enfance à l'école, XIXe–XXe siècles* (Paris: Institut national de recherche pédagogique/Economica, 1982), 18.

[6] Quoted in Catherine M. Prelinger, "Prelude to Consciousness: Amalie Sieveking and the Female Association for the Care of the Poor and the Sick," in *German Women in the Nineteenth Century: A Social History*, ed. John C. Fout (New York: Holmes and Meier, 1984), 119.

Already in 1837 Sieveking's work prompted pastor Theodore Fliedner to request her help with a community of Protestant women that he had founded at Kaiserswerth, near Düsseldorf, in the Rhineland. Inspired by English women's volunteer work, notably Elizabeth Fry's projects that he encountered when he visited England, Fliedner envisioned a community of deaconesses ministering to the sick and needy, just as Catholic women's orders did. He intended to play a leading role in the community but wanted a woman supervisor of deaconesses. His wife Friederike (1800–42) and, later, his second wife Caroline filled the role which Sieveking refused because of her other work. Friederike Fliedner's contribution to the new organization was fundamental, her husband praising both her "masculine energy" and "native gentleness."[7] The deaconess community drew from Catholic models, but with important differences. Instead of lifetime vows and surrendering of personal resources to the community, single women promised five years of unpaid service, after which they could leave Kaiserswerth or renew their commitment. Forms of address within the community were familial: Fliedner was "father," his wife "mother," and the deaconesses "sisters." Women remaining for a lifetime were promised care in their old age. At a time when single women had limited possibilities for respectable employment, Kaiserswerth appealed to Protestants with deep religious convictions. Many early entrants were rural women from humble backgrounds, including servants, and daughters of artisans soon arrived. Although primarily known for nursing and nurse training, deaconesses sometimes taught poor children or cared for working women's children. By the 1850s, in addition to the deaconesses in Kaiserswerth institutions, more than 150 Kaiserswerth-trained nurses worked in other hospitals, and by 1900, 30 "daughter houses" in Germany and other countries were tied to Kaiserswerth. About 20,000 German deaconesses belonged to various orders by 1912.

Communities of deaconesses also appeared elsewhere in northern Europe. In 1841 women philanthropists and a pastor founded a Paris institution, directed by Mlle Malvesin, the first French deaconess, for twenty-six years. It soon included a refuge for released women prisoners, correctional facilities for delinquent girls, an infirmary, and a nursery school. In the Netherlands, where Catholic sisters had long done sick nursing, four women in Utrecht spurred the creation of a deaconess house in 1844. Other Dutch towns had comparable facilities, sometimes

---

[7] Quoted in M. Adelaide Nutting and Lavinia R. Dock, *A History of Nursing: The Evolution of Nursing Systems from the Earliest Times to the Foundation of the First English and American Training Schools for Women*, 4 vols. (New York: G. P. Putnam's, 1907–12), II: 21.

linked to Kaiserswerth. In Bern, Switzerland, Sophie von Wurstemberger started a small facility for the poor, the forerunner of the Deaconesses' Hospital. The first Swedish deaconess facility opened in Stockholm in 1851, its nursing course headed by a woman trained at Kaiserswerth. By 1909, 296 deaconesses were attached to the venture, which included a school, children's home, home for the aged, and hospital. A male director was also appointed. Swedish efforts inspired a Danish project in 1863, encouraged by Crown Princess Louise, who sent its directress to Stockholm for training. A Finnish deaconess house opened in Helsinki in 1867, supervised by a doctor's widow trained in a deaconess facility in St. Petersburg.

In England, new charitable orders of Anglican sisters emerged, encouraged by members of the High Church. Reverend E. B. Pusey guided the creation of the Sisterhood of the Holy Cross in 1845, and his friend Priscilla Sellon led the Sisterhood of Mercy, founded in Devonport and Plymouth in 1848. The first Anglican sisterhood devoted exclusively to nursing worked at the St. John's House Training Institution, founded in 1848. Nonetheless, Florence Nightingale insisted on going to Kaiserswerth in preparation for what became her lifelong commitment to turning nursing into a respected, paid occupation for women and one that women could lead (see Chapter 6).

Extending philanthropy and reforms

Both religious and secular convictions about fundamental human equality drew English women and men into campaigns to abolish slavery in overseas colonies. Quakers and Unitarians, both religious minorities, were heavily involved, but so were many Anglicans and Methodists. Abolitionism was one of the causes that took women beyond traditional charities and into reform projects aimed at relieving suffering by changing laws and public policy. Men led the first abolitionist groups and sometimes welcomed women members. In due course, women also created their own organizations. Although the backlash against the French Revolution hampered the first antislavery groups, abolition of the British slave trade in 1807 reawakened interest in the cause. A new abolitionist society that revived the campaign in 1823 excluded women, but in industrial Birmingham, a center of reform activity, women created the Ladies' Society for the Relief of Negro Slaves in 1825. As reformers debated the merits of gradual timetables for abolition or requiring apprenticeships before slaves were freed, Quaker Elizabeth Heyrick published an influential tract arguing that slavery was an evil requiring immediate abolition. To gain support, women highlighted slave women's suffering, asking women to imagine being unable to marry or experiencing their children being taken away. Publication of the autobiography of Mary Prince, a West Indian slave who escaped from her masters in London in 1830, dramatized such suffering and drew more women to the cause. More than 70 women's abolitionist associations were eventually organized, and 187,000 women signed an antislavery petition presented to Parliament in 1833. In the aftermath of the 1832 Reform Act enlarging the electorate, Parliament abolished slavery in 1833, allowing a transition period until 1838.

With the exception of the United States, no other country witnessed the same degree of antislavery organizing, and after 1833, some British abolitionists shifted their focus to other nations. The World Anti-Slavery Convention in London in 1840 had consequences unforeseen by organizers, who barred women from full participation. Women's separate seating and exclusion from addressing the meeting heightened awareness of women's own second-class status – most famously for Americans Lucretia Mott and Elizabeth Cady Stanton, attending with their husbands and in 1848 prominent in the first women's rights meeting in the United States. Contact with English abolitionists aroused Dutch interest as well, but a women's antislavery society targeting the colony of Surinam was not founded until the 1850s. French reformers also condemned slavery, often as part of programs criticizing injustices facing the working classes, but the Association Law of 1834 restricted organizing. The ending of slavery in French colonies during the 1848 revolution provided a second compelling national example heartening American abolitionists before the Civil War.

Charitable and reform efforts expanded noticeably during the second half of the nineteenth century, as men and women responded not only to continuing social dislocations accompanying urbanization and industrialization but also to upheavals during revolutions in 1848 and later wars. In England, Sir James Stephen heralded "the era of charitable societies" in 1849. Building on past traditions, British Protestants created three-quarters of the philanthropies started between 1850 and 1900. In the process, rivalries in the charitable arena continued among Protestant denominations and between Protestants and Catholics. Protestant–Catholic competition also occurred in the Netherlands and in many German states, but in traditionally Catholic countries the rivalries were often between religious and secular charities, with the latter sometimes tied to anticlerical politics. In France, the conservative and middle-class backlash against the crowds of 1848 promoted an expansion of Catholic activity to remedy social ills causing unrest. Empress Eugénie's patronage of charities and nursery schools was emblematic of Catholic resurgence under the Second Empire, whereas secular philanthropy stagnated until the Third Republic.

In the multinational Austrian Empire, the 1848 upheaval ended the last vestiges of serfdom, and Russia followed suit on a massive scale in 1861. Tsar Alexander II believed that abolishing serfdom was essential for stabilizing society after Russia's defeat in the Crimean War in 1856. As the Hapsburg monarchy's recovery in Austria dashed reformers' and nationalists' hopes, more women turned to charitable activity. Conservatives wanted to lessen social ills provoking anti-government protests, while political reformers sought safe outlets for effecting modest changes in German or other ethnic communities. The reign of Alexander II (1855–81) witnessed the founding of several hundred Russian charitable societies. After the 1848 revolutions elsewhere in Europe, Nicholas I, notoriously suspicious of individuals acting independently of official authorities, had banned the formation of voluntary organizations, but Alexander lifted the ban. The new flourishing of charities matched the reforming spirit of the 1860s and 1870s, before another government backlash against radicals and revolutionaries. Once dominated by royalty and the aristocracy, as in the Imperial Philanthropic Society founded in 1816, Russian charity now also engaged the middle classes, limited in size but growing. Several well-known women philanthropists in St. Petersburg started the Society for Cheap Housing and job training for poor women. In Moscow, Princess N. B. Trubetskaia founded the Brotherly Love Society in 1862 and oversaw its housing project until the 1890s. Such efforts were a response to population movements from country to city that accompanied the end of serfdom. Famine in 1891 spurred other relief efforts, and some 1,700 new organizations were created during the next decade, nearly half of all charities existing by 1901. Most Russian charities included men and women, and few were all-male groups like those long common in Protestant or Roman Catholic countries.

Philanthropy elsewhere in Europe also increasingly extended beyond traditional efforts to help the poor, sick, aged, and orphans, and attempted to reach others on the margins of society. Wanting to help and moralize the unfortunate or deviant, both volunteers and public officials framed new programs to address juvenile delinquency and aid adults, including prostitutes, who fell foul of the law. Many reformers worked to improve prison conditions and assist released prisoners, convinced that help in learning new work habits could rehabilitate individuals. Frequently a joint public-private effort, such projects enlisted many women, including Elizabeth Gurney Fry and Concepción Arenal, both internationally recognized.

The English Quaker background important to abolitionism influenced Fry's belief that women should engage in useful works of charity

Figure 4.1 Elizabeth Fry, advocate for reform of women's prisons in Britain and on the continent.

rather than "trifling" pursuits. Daughter of a rich banker and sister of a banker and reformer, Fry (1780–1845) married a London merchant, became the mother of a large family, and in 1810 undertook preaching (Figure 4.1). A visit to London's Newgate prison for women started her lifelong commitment to improving prison and asylum conditions and founding refuges for the homeless, and her husband's bankruptcy in 1828 did not deter her. In 1818 she became the first woman other than a queen to provide information to a committee of the House of Commons. Fry's association for improving Newgate laid the basis for her Ladies' Society for Promoting the Reformation of Female Prisoners, the first national women's organization in Britain, founded in 1821. Her speeches and pamphlets also advocated hiring women to staff and inspect women's prisons. Humanizing the prisoners and prostitutes they hoped to help instead of dismissing them as sinners, Fry and her coworkers emphasized the societal causes of lawbreaking, including poverty and abuse by men.

Fry's influence in England and elsewhere "accustomed" her "to power," as her daughters noted.[8] Her international activity extended to Holland, France, Switzerland, and some German states. She made five continental visits between 1838 and 1845, motivating women to create societies for prison visiting and also urging officials to replace male guards with women. France effected that change in 1839, often by employing nuns, and the Netherlands followed suit in 1841. The French Interior ministry also appointed an inspectress, Antoinette Lechevalier, for women's prisons and detention houses for adolescent girls, using the rationale that a woman could deal more effectively than men with the nuns staffing the facilities and with women incarcerated. Lechevalier came to her post in 1843 with experience as secretary of a charity aiding former women prisoners and as director of its correctional school for girls. The Steenbeck refuge for former Dutch women prisoners, started by a clergyman in 1848, was managed by deaconess Petronella Voûte and other women. Although not the first Dutch effort to rehabilitate women prisoners, it became a model for other refuges and inspired women's groups like the Ladies' Association for Pentitents in Amsterdam. Women prison visitors, claimed Sweden's head of penitentiary administration in 1900, influenced women prisoners more than men could because they better understood women, and through their maternal or sisterly interest motivated prisoners to change their behavior.

Rehabilitation of young offenders became the special concern of Mary Carpenter (1807–77), daughter of a Unitarian minister and oldest of six children. Like Fry, she was part of an English denomination much involved in reform work. Educated by her father who greatly influenced her, she became a teacher, opened a school with her mother in Bristol in 1829, and in 1846 started a school for poor children. Then followed a reformatory for boys and one for girls (both financed by philanthropists) and a vocational school. Yet the active Carpenter long hesitated to speak publicly at large meetings, remaining silent at an 1851 conference on

---

[8] Quoted in Van Drenth and de Haan, *Rise of Caring Power*, 64.

reform schools because she thought speaking inappropriate for a woman at predominantly male gatherings. Never married, she dedicated herself to continuing her father's religious and humanitarian mission. Like other volunteers, she saw herself as becoming a substitute parent for "moral" orphans. The well-intentioned Carpenter nonetheless exemplified the kind of middle-class intervention into the lives of poor families that made parents resent reformers' assumption that they could not properly rear their own children. She later visited India four times and shifted her concerns to education for Hindu girls.

Concepión Arenal (1820–93), wife of a progressive Spanish lawyer and journalist, plunged into philanthropic work after being widowed in 1855 and losing one of her children. Among Spanish women of her generation, she was the best known internationally. The daughter of a Spanish liberal in disfavor after 1815, Arenal was educated at a Madrid finishing school, which she criticized for curricular deficiencies in her book *Woman of the Future* (1861, *La Mujer del Porvenir*). On her own she studied French, Italian, and philosophy. Like Fry, she became influential through word and deed. She joined the St. Vincent de Paul Society in 1860, and, with allies, established organizations to aid women and poor families. Her manual *Visitor of the Poor* (1860) was translated into 5 languages, and in 1870 she started the biweekly *Voice of the Poor*, contributing 474 articles during its 14 years of publication. Arenal's twenty published volumes treated juvenile delinquency, prisons, and women's lives and education. From volunteer work she moved on, albeit briefly, to official roles comparable to those of the French inspectress Lechevalier. She was appointed a provincial prison visitor in La Coruña in 1863, and in 1864 founded a society to aid released women prisoners. Her published *Letters to Delinquents* (1865), which also recommended changes in prisons, led to her dismissal, but new leaders in power after Queen Isabella's overthrow in 1868 appointed her an inspectress of women's prisons, a first for a Spanish woman. Removed in 1873 after a civil war and another change in government, she continued with reform work. Arenal contributed to international prison congresses attended by government officials and reformers, and the American E. C. Wines included her essay on Spanish prisons, written for a Stockholm congress, in his *State of Prisons and of Child-Saving Institutions in the Civilized World* (1880). Her articles also appeared in the *Bulletin* of the French General Society of Prisons, and her manual for volunteer prison visitors, published in Spain in 1891, was translated into French and sold by the Society for Aiding Women Prisoners released from Saint-Lazare, led by Isabelle Bogelot. In the protracted international debate over whether crime resulted from heredity or social factors, Arenal took the latter, more progressive position but cautioned reformers to keep expectations realistic. Adults could at best modify bad behavior, she believed, but young people might be "transformed" if their misdeeds resulted from a "lack of equilibrium" as their faculties were developing.[9]

That women who joined together to do charitable work often experienced ridicule affected Arenal's views on what women's status was and should be. Through publications and talks she counseled that women needed better education to be effective in performing their public duty to help the needy, because otherwise volunteers would be like missionaries sent to help people whose language they could not understand. Improved education, she insisted, would enhance women's ability to apply to charity their distinctive qualities of sensitivity, compassion, love, religious belief, and endurance of suffering. Women in the English-speaking world also learned of Arenal through her chapter in Theodore Stanton's *Woman Question in Europe* (1884), where she gloomily recorded Spain's backwardness with regard to women's status but also identified some signs of change, such as new girls' schools and more women teachers. She predicted that the decline of priestly influence would weaken religious restraints on women, yet she praised many nuns' work. Her son commemorated her work and ideas at an international women's congress in Paris in 1900, and a volume published in Argentina presented 200 testimonials to her accomplishments from men and a few women on four continents. Its editor, Francisco Mañach, rated her the greatest woman of the nineteenth century.

As philanthropies multiplied, some leaders called for coordinating efforts to avoid needless duplication of activities and share information about what worked best to help the needy. In Victorian England philanthropists and reformers founded the Charity Organisation Society (COS) in 1869. Octavia Hill was the only woman on its first governing council. The COS wanted to make charity more efficient and effective through better training for volunteers and some paid staff, who determined who merited aid and also provided self-help advice. Its leaders firmly believed that individuals and private groups could do a better job than public agencies in teaching the needy new habits to end their dependency. The COS relied heavily on volunteer visitors, mainly women, but over time, and often reluctantly, also hired paid staff, placing more men than women in major supervisory posts. Its first *Charities Register and Digest* in 1882 was a 900-page listing. Women's financial contributions were also important: 632 women constituted a third of COS subscribers by 1900.

---

[9] Quoted in C. de Corny, "*Manuel du Visiteur des Prisonniers* par Mme C. Arenal," *Revue Pénitentiare* 17 (1893): 505.

Angela Burdett-Coutts, founder of a women's shelter and endower of churches, was a prominent donor until marriage in 1881 limited her philanthropy because she lost control of much of her wealth. A history of the COS published in 1914 by Helen Dendy Bosanquet, who worked for it before her marriage, recorded 1,500 cooperating associations in London, helping 258,000 individuals, and also 47 provincial registration committees. Many organizations shunned ties to the COS, however, preferring their independence or rejecting the harshness of the COS position on denying aid to people deemed unworthy.

The COS inspired imitators elsewhere. After visiting London, Anna Hierta-Retzius decided to use the resources of a charity founded by her late mother to start the Society for the Organization of Charity in Sweden. Its Stockholm office, opened in 1890 with support from 800 donors, directed applicants for aid to appropriate charities, after verifying need and rating them deserving. The founding of the Central Office of Charitable Organizations in Paris came after an 1889 congress aroused philanthropists' concerns about an extension of government control over private charity. Like the COS, it had male leaders. In Sweden, however, the Organization of Charity, briefly under a male director, turned in 1892 to Mrs. Montelius, who supervised its work without compensation. She proved, Ellen von Platen told an international women's meeting in 1900, that "a woman leader possesses the organizational skill" needed to get results and, as the "Soul of the Society," could inspire coworkers.[10]

The COS emphasis on self-help suited Octavia Hill (1838–1912), the eighth daughter of a banker who lost his money in 1840, for she grew up appreciating her mother's ability to cope economically. Octavia later managed a toy-making workshop started by her mother, thus learning how to organize workers and keep accounts. From an interest in educating poor children, she moved on to her famous efforts to improve working-class housing and preserve open spaces in urban areas. Ruskin helped fund Hill's first housing projects in London, where her organization bought and renovated slum housing. Her competence attracted other wealthy benefactors, including funders of the National Trust, launched in 1895 to preserve land and historic buildings.

Although Hill and others in the COS remained convinced that private charity was more effective than public aid, particularly if the latter placed the needy in degrading workhouses, many women were eager to become Poor Law guardians who monitored tax-supported poor relief at the local

---

[10] Ellen de Platen, "L'Organisation de la Charité Réformée," in *Deuxième Congrès International des Oeuvres et Institutions Féminines*, ed. Mme Pégard (Paris: Charles Blot, 1902), II: 224.

level. Women became eligible to serve in the unpaid position during the 1870s, and more than a thousand did so by 1898. Among them was the never-married Louisa Twining, who had visited workhouses since 1853 and organized the Workhouse Visiting Society in 1857. Elected to the Kensington Board of Guardians in 1884, she insisted that public projects benefited from women's nurturing qualities, and she regretted in 1898 that 300 of 648 Poor Law boards still lacked women members.

The emphasis on teaching the poor to help themselves was not unique to Great Britain, although no other country matched its scale of volunteerism. Typifying middle-class philanthropy across Europe, the self-help goal also turned many charitable workers into advocates of better education for the poor. They sponsored programs to promote basic literacy and training for work, and pressured governments to provide more schools. In St. Petersburg, for example, Nadezhda Stasova (1822–97), Maria Trubnikova (1835–97), and Anna Filosofova (1837–1912) started Sunday schools for workers and sewing workshops for poor women. Helping women to become self-supporting, these workshops were models for one in Nikolai Chernyshevsky's famous novel *What Is To Be Done?* (1863). Women's groups in other countries also sponsored job-related training, but where higher living standards for much of the population prevailed, denunciations of women's work as harmful to family life were common. In Russia such condemnations were rarer, and many philanthropists accepted women's need to work, even if they were married or mothers. Filosofova, wife of a government official, devoted more than fifty years to charity and reform, in 1895 helping to found the Women's Mutual Philanthropic Society, which soon had 1,600 members and concerns that ranged well beyond the purely charitable but could not be publicly labeled feminist in tsarist Russia.

The Salvation Army was a different kind of organization with a wide reach in England and eventually beyond. It was created by William Booth and his wife Catherine (1829–90), herself a talented preacher whose funeral drew 36,000 people. Indeed, recent studies highlight Catherine's invaluable contribution to their joint cause, noting her insistence on important roles for women in the organization and support for women's suffrage. With missionary zeal the Salvation Army tried to help people beyond the reach of traditional churches, through a combination of preaching and material aid. The COS excoriated it for giving aid indiscriminately, but it helped the downtrodden, including the homeless and alcoholics, dismissed as incorrigible by other charities. Donations from both the rich and the poorer supported this "Army," which had 2,900 centers in 34 countries by 1890. The Booths' eight children seconded the effort, Evangeline Booth becoming a "commander" in Canada and in the United States.

By the time that Booth's uniformed volunteers became a familiar sight, temperance organizations in Britain and elsewhere were publicizing the links between poverty and excessive consumption of alcohol, which affected breadwinners' health and ability to work. The temperance cause, dating from the 1820s, struck its deepest roots in the Anglo-American world and enlisted men and women, with men often its first leaders and public speakers. Women also started organizations, and the Woman's Christian Temperance Union (WCTU) in the United States, led by Frances Willard, pushed for global organization in 1891. Margaret Parker was the first president of the British Women's Temperance Association (BWTA), founded in 1876 and claiming 157,000 dues-paying members in 1910. Sweden had the largest WCTU affiliate in a non-English-speaking country, with 6,000 members in 1913. More Scandinavian women belonged to temperance organizations with both men and women members, however. The German Federation of Women Abstainers had 2,600 members by 1912, but the older German Association for the Prevention of Abuse of Intoxicating Beverages, which accepted moderate alcohol consumption, claimed 39,000 adherents. Even when temperance advocates called for moderation rather than prohibition or total abstinence, accepting wine and beer but not "hard" liquor, they found limited support in countries with wine-drinking traditions. Catholics and Anglicans, after all, used wine in the sacrament of the Eucharist. At the International Council of Women's congress in Rome in 1914, Russian, Swedish, Finnish, French, Belgian, and Dutch women spoke about their combat against alcoholism, but they represented groups much smaller than Anglo-American counterparts.

Among English women reformers with international visibility after 1870, Josephine Grey Butler (1828–1906), a leader of campaigns to abolish legalized prostitution, was the best known. Wife of an Anglican cleric-educator and mother of three sons, she joined the campaign against the British Contagious Diseases Acts while recovering emotionally from the death of her daughter. Parliament had passed three Contagious Diseases (CD) Acts between 1864 and 1869, in an effort to limit British soldiers and sailors' contracting of venereal disease. Implemented in towns with military installations, such as Liverpool where the Butlers then lived, the acts allowed police to stop women who aroused suspicion on the streets and subject them to medical examination. Opponents like Butler saw these laws as an assault on the dignity of all women, pointing out that police sometimes targeted women who were not prostitutes and also that women were being punished for men's misdeeds. Bringing the sexual double standard into focus, some women insisted that men should adopt a higher standard of morality. The London *Daily News* on 31

December 1869 published a protest against the CD Acts sent by 124 women, including Butler, Nightingale, Carpenter, and Martineau, and other papers reprinted it. Although critics of the effort complained that proper ladies should not publicly discuss sexual matters, a movement had been launched. Butler, a charismatic speaker, led the Ladies' National Association for Repeal of the Contagious Diseases Act (LNA), which had its own journal. As a devout Anglican, she effectively conveyed her belief that the campaign was a "great crusade," and in her memoir with that title indicated her conviction that God called her to this work. Previously involved in promoting women's education and a signer of a women's suffrage petition, she enjoyed her husband's steady support as she traveled throughout Britain and to the continent. She also drew male reformers to the cause by emphasizing working-class women's vulnerability in cities.

Butler was not the only woman who found her public voice during the LNA's repeal drive, and some LNA members later embraced other reform efforts on behalf of women, including suffragism. After Parliament repealed the CD Acts in 1886, a related international campaign against prostitution continued, as did British women's efforts to halt the CD Acts in India. Butler spoke of Indian women as sisters wronged by the law, but she also argued that repeal in India would strengthen England's presence there. Generally supportive of imperial goals, she warned, "Nothing so surely produces a spirit of rebellion as trampling on the womanhood of a subject race by its conquerors."[11]

Butler's trip to the continent in 1875 led to the founding of the British and Continental Federation for the Abolition of Government Regulation of Vice, later called the International Abolitionist Federation (IAF), with headquarters in Switzerland and supporters, male and female, throughout Europe and the British empire. The Federation attacked legalized prostitution and the "white slave trade" in women and children that abetted prostitution. It targeted the system of licensed brothels and police and medical inspection of prostitutes, developed in Napoleonic France and exported to or emulated by other countries. After the first IAF conference in Geneva in 1877, Dutch men and women created an affiliate, attracting some members of an older association aiding "penitent fallen women." Another Dutch group, the Women's League to Elevate Moral Conscience, as its first public act, collected 15,000 women's signatures on a petition denouncing the traffic in women's

---

[11] Quoted in Antoinette Burton, *Burdens of History: British Feminists, Indian Women, and Imperial Culture, 1865–1915* (Chapel Hill: University of North Carolina Press, 1994), 148.

bodies, submitting it to the legislature in 1885. Several Italian women also attended the 1877 IAF meeting, voicing opposition to the regulation of prostitution established by the Cavour Decree of 1860, so called after Piedmont's leader of Italy's unification. Anna Maria Mozzoni, who agreed to head a Milan IAF branch, spoke in Geneva about links between prostitution and women's difficulties in finding adequately paid work. Alaide Gualberta Beccari, founder of the women's journal *La Donna*, had already collected 3,000 women signatories for an abolitionist petition. The 1860 measure was repealed in 1888, but Italian abolitionists' success was brief because regulation returned in 1891. In France, the advocacy of Émilie de Morsier, a Protestant, paved the way for the energetic Ghénia Avril de Sainte-Croix (1855–1939), a feminist who devoted four decades to the abolitionist cause, nationally and internationally, beginning in the 1890s. In Germany, an early IAF branch was suppressed in 1885, but other groups took up the cause. Hanna Bieber-Boehm's Association for the Protection of Young Persons petitioned the legislature in 1894, and Lida Gustava Heymann in Hamburg and Anna Pappritz in Berlin started new groups with IAF ties in 1899. The German IAF branch had 1,200 members (mostly women) and chapters in 14 cities by 1913.

A related organization, the International Union of Friends of Young Women, founded in 1877 and also headquartered in Switzerland, tried to protect young women who left home and traveled to other cities or countries to find work. Volunteers went to train stations and docks in port cities, hoping to protect young and presumably naive women from the grasp of procurers who might promise respectable work but then force their prey into prostitution. By 1914, the Union had 16,530 members and chapters in 52 countries, and its branches operated 518 refuges and 118 job-placement bureaus, annually assisting about 19,000 young women.

The campaign against legalized prostitution and the white slave trade drew support from across national, religious, political, and class lines, but some participating organizations were identified by religious affiliation, Christian or Jewish. In London the Jewish Ladies' Society for Preventive and Rescue Work was founded in 1885, with two women from the Rothschild banking family as president and honorary secretary. Later opting for a male supervisory committee and renamed the Jewish Association for the Protection of Girls and Women, it became the international center for Jewish opposition to white slavery. Yet in Paris, concerned Jews long preferred to work with the nondenominational Association for the Repression of White Slavery, and many Viennese Jews supported a comparable Austrian league.

Bertha Pappenheim (1859–1936), from a wealthy, religiously observant Viennese family, favored organizing specifically Jewish women's groups. She was also the subject of a famous psychological case study, as patient "Anna O.," although that identity was not revealed until 1953. Dr. Josef Breuer, whose "talking cure" interested Sigmund Freud, had treated her for hysteria. Pappenheim moved to Frankfurt in 1890 to live with relatives and became active in poor relief and the founding of the Frankfurt Women's Welfare Organization. Berlin already had forty-eight Jewish women's volunteer groups by 1892, their leaders including Lina Morgenstern. At a time of anti-Semitic backlash against Jews' recently improved legal status and against an influx of Jews fleeing Russian pogroms, many Jewish leaders resisted openly discussing problems in Jewish communities, but Pappenheim frankly addressed the dilemmas of unwed mothers and illegitimate children. Separate women's groups were needed, she argued, because Jewish social services led by men "underestimated the value of women's work and trifled with their interest by refusing to admit them as equal partners." She also exposed Jews' involvement in prostitution rings preying upon young women in eastern Europe and Russia, where Jews were more numerous than in Germany or western Europe. Touring Galicia in 1903 with Dr. Sarah Rabinowitch, she reported on officially registered Jewish brothels. She attributed prostitution to legal and economic disadvantages faced by women and to "the concept of the inferiority of the female sex."[12] In communities in Austrian Galicia and Russian Poland, she spurred the creation of anti-prostitution committees, homes for "endangered" girls, and job counseling. Pappenheim also brought the anti-prostitution campaign into the Jewish Women's Federation (JFB, Jüdischer Frauenbund) that she created in 1904, at a time when German Protestants and Catholics already had national women's organizations. Philanthropic and feminist, the JFB joined the Federation of German Women's Associations (BDF, Bund Deutscher Frauenvereine) and by 1913 had 160 affiliates with 32,000 members – one-fifth of German Jewish women. Pappenheim's ability to inspire followers has been likened to that of Josephine Butler, and they were only two of the many persuasive women reformers who broadened the dimensions of women's volunteer work in the later nineteenth century.

---

[12] Quotations in Marion Kaplan, *The Making of the Jewish Middle Class: Women, Family, and Identity in Imperial Germany* (New York: Oxford University Press, 1991), 210; and Edward J. Bristow, *Prostitution and Prejudice: The Jewish Fight against White Slavery 1870–1939* (Oxford: Oxford University Press, 1982; reprint, New York: Schocken Books, 1983), 102.

Philanthropy and the state: saving children
and war readiness

In 1889, as part of celebrating the centennial of the French Revolution, the Third Republic sponsored an international congress on "assistance." Eleven years later, another Paris congress held in conjunction with the 1900 international exposition used the title "public assistance and private charity" to highlight governments' and charities' cooperation and sharing of many goals. Charities sought public subsidies and philanthropists sometimes served on government advisory councils or testified before legislative committees; and public officials joined, and sometimes led, charities. Although philanthropists, including many in Britain's COS, might resent government intrusion into areas where they believed that volunteers were more effective and caring than public employees, they increasingly concluded that tackling some huge problems required public revenues. At the 1913 international women's congress in Paris, a woman from Berlin declared that the phrase "from charity to social policy" was now common usage in Germany.[13] Children's health and safety loomed large among concerns that bridged private charity and the beginning of a welfare state in various countries by 1900, for national leaders saw in children the key to a country's future prosperity and ability to defend itself.

Concern for the welfare of poor children and their mothers was not novel, but some newer preoccupations reflected definitions of national interest. The loss of the Franco-Prussian War and territory in Alsace-Lorraine in 1871 spurred French politicians from various ideological camps to worry about "depopulation." In 1901, France's population was 38 million, as compared to 56 million in its rival Germany; and France's birthrate was 22 per 1,000 population, as compared to Germany's 35.6 per 1,000. Would France have enough young men for future armies, either for a war of revenge or defense against invasion, leaders asked? To combat the perceived menace of depopulation, charities and government agencies sought to reduce infant mortality rates. For example, after the 1874 Roussel law imposed new regulations on wet-nursing, to which many working mothers resorted, women created organizations to help needy mothers and improve infant nutrition. Both charities and French municipal authorities operated *crèches* for infant day care and supported milk dispensaries. The Society of Crèches' first facility dated from 1844, but its Catholic leaders refused to accept illegitimate infants until late in

---

[13] *Dixième Congrès International des Femmes, Oeuvres et Institutions Féminines*, ed. Ghénia Avril de Sainte-Croix (Paris: Giard et Brière, 1914), 52.

the century. Milk dispensaries developed as doctors recommended that needy infants be fed with sterilized milk in bottles rather than by uncaring wet-nurses. Indeed, abandoned infants sent by public authorities to rural wet-nurses had much higher mortality rates than children living with their mothers. Milk depots, publicly or privately funded, also existed in other countries, and women volunteers often helped staff them.

Among the new French women's organizations spurred by the Roussel Law was the Society for Maternal Breastfeeding, founded in 1876 by the young Marie Bequet de Vienne (1854–1913), wife of a lawyer with republican ties. Its subsidies allowed nursing mothers to remain at home with their infants, and unlike older religious charities, it helped needy mothers regardless of marital status or religion. A decade later Bequet de Vienne, in conjunction with the Society of Philanthropy led by politician Paul Strauss, created her Maternal Shelter for homeless pregnant women and new mothers. It offered advice on child care and help in finding jobs, and during its first twenty years assisted more than 12,000 women and children. With her mother's aid, Bequet de Vienne, childless until she adopted a daughter in 1894, poured her energies and her own money into helping other women. The secular Paris Maternal Society opened its "Pouponnière" in a western suburb in 1891 for a dual purpose: working mothers could leave children up to the age of three and visit twice a week, and single mothers in residence breastfed their own babies and nursed or bottle-fed two others boarded there. Dr. Blanche Edwards-Pilliet, who worked with Bequet de Vienne, used private donations and public subsidies to found the League of Mothers of Families in 1901. The League's nurses assisted midwives and advised new mothers, and if women gave birth away from home, League volunteers ensured that their other children received care.

Charities' activities and facilities sometimes became models emulated by public authorities. Recounting charitable women's contributions since the 1860s, one speaker at the 1913 women's congress credited Bequet de Vienne's initiatives with spurring the Paris Public Assistance Administration's creation of two shelters for pregnant women during the 1890s. The city also opened a shelter for homeless women in 1894, naming it after George Sand. At a time when France lagged behind Germany in providing maternity leaves, the combination of private and public aid was important. Whereas Germany mandated maternity leaves for women factory workers as of 1878 and supported paid leaves in 1903, France did not legislate leaves until 1909, or promise paid leave until 1913. By then, some women workers' groups, as well as philanthropies, had created maternity funds (*mutualités maternelles*), to which women workers and benefactors contributed, and from which women drew childbirth allocations before returning to work.

Large state subsidies to private facilities in France, as elsewhere – important when public welfare programs were still limited – entailed periodic inspections by state and local officials. Inspectors did not eliminate volunteer visitors' activity, and philanthropists often agreed that more coordination among private agencies was desirable. Yet many Catholic leaders and some secular philanthropists resisted government projects for additional monitoring of charities receiving public funds. At a 1908 French congress on public assistance and private charity, interior ministry inspectress general Hélène Moniez, wife of an education official, faced a storm of controversy over this issue. Nonetheless, many philanthropists and state officials shared a sense of serving the same public interests, as Bequet de Vienne's friendship with interior ministry inspectress general Olympe Gevin-Cassal demonstrated, and philanthropic women and men were advocates of expanding women's employment in public assistance administration.

Beyond France, preoccupation with child welfare and national strength, surfacing at somewhat later dates, also engaged women. For Great Britain the catalyst was the Boer War in South Africa (1899–1902), which prompted outpourings of anti-British sentiment across Europe and raised British awareness that many young men were not physically fit for military service. The ensuing public policy measures included mandatory physical examinations for school pupils, more nutrition and cooking lessons for girls, and free school meals for the needy. Local authorities and philanthropists also established more facilities to aid pregnant women and new mothers, relying on women volunteers to assist paid staff. In Italy, before the National Maternity Fund began operating in 1912, women's organizations and workers' groups sponsored voluntary maternity funds, modeled on French *mutualités* and usually more heavily funded by private donations and municipal subsidies than by poor workers' contributions. The League for the Protection of Women's Interests led the way in Turin in 1898 and in Milan in 1905. The National Council of Italian Women founded the Maternity Assistance and Provident Fund in Rome, and independent funds for women workers were created in Florence, Naples, and other cities as well.

Against a backdrop of international tensions, German officials, doctors, and an interested public also frequently discussed national health. To combat the high infant mortality rate – 229 per 1,000 live births in 1900, as compared to 160 in France and 154 in England – doctors enlisted support from the empress, who had seven children. She was the patron of the Berlin Crèche Association and a national symbol of the good mother, speaking to the Patriotic Women's Association (VFV, Vaterländischer Frauenverein) about the importance of breastfeeding and lessons in child care. In 1909 the Kaiserin Auguste Viktoria Haus for Combating Infant Mortality opened as a model institution for infant care. Urged by the empress, VFV members also volunteered at state-subsidized child welfare clinics, started in 1904 and numbering 1,000 by 1915. Different in tone was the League for Protection of Motherhood, founded in 1904 and also providing advice and aid to needy mothers and mothers-to-be. Some League members provoked conservatives' ire by advocating single women's right to become mothers, if they wished. Preoccupation with the health of the nation or "the race" also drew some men, and a lesser number of women, to eugenics. Eugenicists in Germany, England, and elsewhere, building on the ideas of Charles Darwin's cousin Francis Galton, advocated measures to improve the quality of a population. Their support for physical education and better hygiene, nutrition, and medical care resembled other public health programs, but eugenicist notions about preventing the "unfit" from marrying or reproducing were controversial well before the Nazis carried them to ghastly extremes.

In country after country, as arms races and imperialist rivalries raised the specter of future wars, women also joined Red Cross organizations, received short courses in nursing, and promised to volunteer as nurses if they were needed. The International Red Cross, headquartered in Switzerland, dated from 1864. Its founder, Henri Dunant, witnessed the bloody battlefield of Solferino during the Austro-Sardinian War of 1859, a prelude to Italian unification, and he persuaded envoys of various governments to meet and agree to the 1864 Geneva Convention standards for treatment of the wounded in wartime. Many national Red Cross groups emerged. The Russian Red Cross, founded in 1867 with support from the empress and other women in the court, worked with the nursing sisters organized during the Crimean War by grand duchess Elena Pavlovna and by 1913 supported nursing training in ninety-seven of the sisters' communities. The VFV affiliated with the Red Cross, already based in individual German states before the all-German Red Cross Association, ready to mobilize nurses during wartime, was formed in 1869. On the eve of World War I, nearly 900,000 German women participated in Red Cross groups, and the VFV alone had at least 500,000 members. France's three Red Cross organizations reflected political and religious differences, and the republican government turned in 1906 to the most secular one, the Union des Femmes de France, when it first appointed a woman to the advisory Higher Council of Public Assistance, comprised of politicians, administrators, doctors, and philanthropists.

Training for social action

Some philanthropists who valued volunteers' dedication nonetheless became convinced that women, and men, could more effectively help the needy if they received specialized training. That conclusion dovetailed with contemporary demands for improving young women's formal education. Whereas groups like the Charity Organisation Society first emphasized practical training, later efforts joined theory and practice. The emerging field of sociology, the "science of society" so named by the positivist Comte, provided theory and data for understanding urban problems in industrial societies. The first courses to train social workers were private initiatives, and early connotations of the term "social worker," like those for "nurse," did not necessarily imply a salaried professional employee. In England, the COS and the Women's University Settlement (WUS), founded in 1887, promoted training through formal lectures as of 1896. The settlement movement began when philanthropic men established themselves in group residences in working-class areas, hoping to create a sense of solidarity with people they wanted to help by offering practical instruction. At least thirty English women's settlements existed by 1909, most located in London or other large cities. The COS-WUS course was absorbed by the COS School of Sociology in 1903 and then by the Department of Social Administration at the London School of Economics in 1912.

Alice Salomon (1872–1948), the founder of modern social work in Germany, titled the school that she started in 1908 the Women's Social School (Soziale Frauenschule) (Figure 4.2). From a middle-class Jewish family in Berlin, Salomon became bored when her schooling ended at age fourteen and her family opposed her wish to become a teacher, deeming that occupation inappropriate for their social status. She found a way out of what she termed "the unnatural lives of wealthy girls" by attending the first meetings of the Girls' and Women's Groups for Social Assistance Work in 1893.[14] The founders included Minna Cauer, who admired American women's social activism, and Jeanette Schwerin, wife of a doctor practicing in a working-class district. The Groups' afternoon meetings gave volunteers theoretical and practical information useful for work with the poor. Sociologist Max Weber was among the lecturers on social change. The Groups also hoped to help bridge divisions between social classes, a concern as the Socialist Party's appeal to workers increased. In 1899 the Groups organized a formal

---

[14] Letter from Salomon to Jane Addams, in *Social Justice Feminists in the United States and Germany: A Dialogue in Documents, 1885–1933*, ed. Kathryn Kish Sklar, Anja Schüler, and Susan Strasser (Ithaca, N.Y.: Cornell University Press, 1998), 171.

ELVIRA,   MÜNCHEN.

Jede Art der Vervielfältigung vorbehalten. Copyright.

Hof-Atelier ELVIRA
v.d. Tann-Str.15, MÜNCHEN

Figure 4.2 Alice Salomon, pioneer in German social work education and active in German and international feminism.

one-year course, and Salomon became a leader after her mentor Schwerin died. Hundreds of Berlin women joined the Groups, and in 1912 at least 1,000 women belonged to 140 Groups located across Germany. In some localities women also assumed the traditionally male role of volunteer guardian of the poor: 40 women, as compared to 4,000 men, did so in Berlin in 1907. The Groups' secular nature separated them from the Protestant Women's Federation, founded in 1899, and the Catholic Women's Association, dating from 1904.

By the time that Salomon started the nondenominational Social School in Berlin, she had remedied gaps in her own education. Permitted to audit university courses when women still could not formally enroll in Prussian universities, she obtained a doctorate in political economy in 1906 with a thesis analyzing why men and women workers were paid at different rates. Salomon's school became a training ground for volunteer social workers, who expected little or no pay, and for women seeking jobs with municipal bureaus that had begun hiring women in subordinate posts as public welfare offices expanded. By 1913, 17,960 women worked in welfare offices in 559 localities, but only 1,021 held paid positions. The Social School enrolled many more Christians than Jews and remained self-supporting even as other schools opened elsewhere. Although Protestant women in Hanover had started social service training in 1905, most of the thirteen other social schools opened between 1909 and 1913 used Salomon's curriculum as a model. Salomon's visit to Jane Addams's Hull House in Chicago in 1909, after the meeting of the International Council of Women in Toronto, gave her additional ideas about urban social work. Soon known as the German Jane Addams, she wrote a preface to the German translation of Addams's *Twenty Years at Hull House*, terming the autobiography "religious and secular at the same time ... in the sense that faith needs to be converted into action." Of her own conversion to Christianity in 1914, she later wrote that firmly guiding others required religious precepts and Christianity seemed "the strongest motivating force of applied brotherhood, of charity and social reform."[15] Salomon also became prominent in the BDF, the German feminist organization, and like many BDF members, phrased views on women's issues cautiously. Distancing herself from women wanting "equal rights in every department of life," she underscored "the difference of capacities and gifts of men and women" and argued that women, if given additional rights, could bring "unique" talents into public life.[16]

The first French schools to train social workers, volunteer or paid, were also private efforts, albeit with a more religious tone than in Salomon's school. Formal training for Catholics developed in conjunction with new

[15] Salomon's preface in Sklar et al., ed., *Social Justice Feminists*, 174; Alice Salomon, *Character is Destiny: The Autobiography of Alice Salomon*, ed. Andrew Lees (Ann Arbor: University of Michigan Press, 2004), 103.
[16] Quoted in Richard J. Evans, *The Feminists: Women's Emancipation Movements in Europe, America and Australasia 1840–1920* (London: Croom Helm, 1977), 200.

types of engagement with social problems. Social Catholics were moved by Pope Leo XIII's encyclical *Rerum novarum* (1891), a call for addressing working-class problems to counter socialist gains. The first French settlement house (*maison sociale*) was created in 1896 in a poor area of Paris by the marquis Albert Costa de Beauregard and Marie Gahéry (1867–1932), a professor's daughter. Gahéry was its first general secretary, aided by a committee of patronesses and eighty-five women supporters, many of them aristocratic, but she soon turned leadership over to a nun, Mother Mercédès Le Fer de la Motte, who relocated the settlement. Two more "social houses" opened in other districts in 1903. After the expulsion of many religious orders and imposition of new restrictions when France separated church and state, Catholic laywomen took over the Social House Association in 1905. Other Catholic women supported the Joan of Arc Congress, a coalition of Catholic women's charities dating from 1902 and supported by bishops. Henriette Brunhes, wife of a prominent geographer, drew Catholic women to the Consumers' Social League, which focused attention on the poor pay and working conditions of women in the garment trades.

Catholic women's involvement with settlement houses proved more controversial than their many other charitable endeavors, as the much-publicized case of Jeanne Bassot (1878–1935), a general's daughter, demonstrated. Her extended "social house" work angered her family, who disapproved of a young woman of their social status leaving home and mingling with potentially dangerous elements of the Parisian population. In 1908 they had Jeanne seized as she left mass and sent her to a clinic in Geneva, claiming that she was mentally unbalanced. This occurred after General Bassot failed to secure religious leaders' assistance. The Geneva clinic director refused to confine her against her will, and she returned to Paris, soon bringing a lawsuit against her mother and a former policeman involved in her kidnapping. Although she eventually dropped the suit because of her parents' distress, the public prosecutor pursued it to win a symbolic verdict against her mother. After much page-one newspaper publicity, many Catholics concluded that Jeanne was a bad daughter who did not respect her family, and Catholic interest in "social houses" waned, especially after Pope Pius X condemned "social modernism" in 1910.

Other French social Catholic projects continued, including new schools providing training for charity work. Gahéry founded the School for Social Training in 1907, followed in 1908 by the Abbé Viollet's School for Familial Action, and by the Social Normal School of Andrée Butillard and Aimée Novo in 1911. The competing Practical School of Social Service, founded by pastor Paul Doumergue in 1913, attracted a

Protestant or nondenominational clientele. An alternative to the informal mentoring received by previous generations of charitable workers, these schools, like Salomon's in Berlin, eventually trained not only volunteers but also women hoping for paid positions.

Conclusion

The benefits that nineteenth-century women volunteers derived from charitable work loom large in recent historical studies. Women gained awareness of pressing social problems and a heightened sense of being able to contribute to the larger society. Contemporaries frequently described women's charitable efforts as extensions of their maternal and caring qualities to the community, claiming that women made unique contributions that men could not make. For some women needing to work, charities offered paid employment as well, setting the stage for certain public agencies' hiring of women for welfare work shortly before and after 1900. Historians of feminism also have drawn attention to the bridge between women's philanthropic and reform efforts and later feminist projects. Helping others was certainly an end in itself for many women, but philanthropic activism led some women to feminist organizations when they recognized links between the suffering of disadvantaged women and legal inequities affecting all women. Among 2,000 British women signers of an 1889 suffrage petition, there were 93 women identified as social and philanthropic workers, 23 Poor Law guardians, and 22 wives of clergymen. The International Council of Women (ICW), founded in 1888, put great emphasis on social action through volunteerism, as did its national affiliates, such as the BDF. At the ICW congress in Rome in 1914, Chrystal MacMillan's report thus noted Great Britain's "extraordinary" number of voluntary associations run by women, but also addressed job access and the vote.

Further reading and reference works

Adams, Christine. "Maternal Societies in France: Private Charity before the Welfare State." *Journal of Women's History* 17 (Spring 2005): 87–111.

Bock, Gisela, and Pat Thane, eds. *Maternity and Gender Policies: Women and the Rise of the European Welfare State, 1880s–1950s*. London: Routledge, 1991.

Bristow, Edward J. *Prostitution and Prejudice: The Jewish Fight against White Slavery 1870–1939*. Oxford: Oxford University Press, 1982. Reprint, New York: Schocken Books, 1983.

Burns, Arthur, and Joanna Innes, eds. *Rethinking the Age of Reform: Britain, 1780–1850*. Cambridge: Cambridge University Press, 2003.

Clear, Caitriona. *Nuns in Nineteenth-Century Ireland.* Dublin: Gill and Macmillan, 1987.

Cunningham, Hugh, and Joanna Innes, eds. *Charity, Philanthropy and Reform: From the 1690s to 1850.* Basingstoke and New York: St. Martin's Press, 1998.

Curtis, Sarah A. "Charitable Ladies: Gender, Class and Religion in Mid-Nineteenth-Century Paris." *Past and Present*, no. 177 (2002): 121–56.

"Emilie de Vialar and the Religious Reconquest of Algeria." *French Historical Studies* 29 (Spring 2006): 261–92.

Fuchs, Rachel G. *Gender and Poverty in Nineteenth-Century Europe.* Cambridge: Cambridge University Press, 2005.

Poor and Pregnant in Paris: Strategies for Survival in Nineteenth-Century France. New Brunswick, N.J.: Rutgers University Press, 1992.

Huber-Sperl, Rita. "Organized Women and the Strong State: The Beginnings of Female Associational Activity in Germany, 1810–1840." Translated by Andrew Spencer. *Journal of Women's History* 13 (Winter 2002): 81–105.

Kaplan, Marion A. *The Making of the Jewish Middle Class: Women, Family, and Identity in Imperial Germany.* New York: Oxford University Press, 1991.

Koven, Seth, and Sonya Michel, eds. *Mothers of a New World: Maternalist Politics and the Origins of Welfare States.* New York: Routledge, 1993.

Lannon, Frances. *Privilege, Persecution, and Prophecy: The Catholic Church in Spain 1875–1975.* Oxford: Clarendon Press, 1987.

Lewis, Jane. *Women and Social Action in Victorian and Edwardian England.* Stanford, Calif.: Stanford University Press, 1991.

Lindenmeyr, Adele. *Poverty is Not a Vice: Charity, Society, and the State in Imperial Russia.* Princeton, N.J.: Princeton University Press, 1996.

"Public Life, Private Virtues: Women in Russian Charity, 1762–1914." *Signs: Journal of Women in Culture and Society* 18.3 (1993): 562–91.

Luddy, Maria. *Women and Philanthropy in Nineteenth-Century Ireland.* Cambridge: Cambridge University Press, 1995.

Magray, Mary Peckham. *The Transforming Power of the Nuns: Women, Religion, and Cultural Change in Ireland, 1750–1900.* New York: Oxford University Press, 1998.

Mandler, Peter, ed. *The Uses of Charity: The Poor on Relief in the Nineteenth-Century Metropolis.* Philadelphia: University of Pennsylvania Press, 1990.

McCarthy, Kathleen D., ed. *Lady Bountiful: Women, Philanthropy, and Power.* New Brunswick, N.J.: Rutgers University Press, 1990.

McNamara, Jo Ann Kay. *Sisters in Arms: Catholic Nuns through Two Millennia.* Cambridge, Mass.: Harvard University Press, 1996.

Midgley, Clare. *Women Against Slavery: The British Campaigns, 1780–1870.* London: Routledge, 1992.

O'Brien, Susan. "French Nuns in Nineteenth-Century England." *Past and Present*, no. 154 (1997): 142–80.

Parker, Julia. *Women and Welfare: Ten Victorian Women in Public Social Service.* New York: St. Martin's Press, 1989.

Prelinger, Catherine M. *Charity, Challenge, and Change: Religious Dimensions of the Mid-Nineteenth-Century Women's Movement in Germany.* New York and Westport, Conn.: Greenwood Press, 1987.

"Prelude to Consciousness: Amalie Sieveking and the Female Association for the Care of the Poor and the Sick." In *German Women in the Nineteenth Century: A Social History,* ed. John C. Fout, 215–29. New York: Holmes and Meier, 1984.

Preston, Margaret. *Charitable Words: Women, Philanthropy, and the Language of Charity in Nineteenth-Century Dublin.* Westport, Conn.: Praeger, 2004.

Prochaska, F. K. *Women and Philanthropy in Nineteenth-Century England.* Oxford: Clarendon Press, 1980.

Quataert, Jean H. *Staging Philanthropy: Patriotic Women and the National Imagination in Dynastic Germany, 1813–1916.* Ann Arbor: University of Michigan Press, 2001.

Salomon, Alice. *Character is Destiny: The Autobiography of Alice Salomon.* Edited by Andrew Lees. Ann Arbor: University of Michigan Press, 2004.

Schor, Laura S. *The Life and Legacy of Baroness Betty de Rothschild.* New York: Peter Lang, 2006.

Shiman, Lilian Lewis. *Women and Leadership in Nineteenth-Century England.* New York: St. Martin's Press, 1992.

Sklar, Kathryn Kish, Anja Schüler, and Susan Strasser, eds. *Social Justice Feminists in the United States and Germany: A Dialogue in Documents, 1885–1933.* Ithaca, N.Y.: Cornell University Press, 1998.

Smith, Bonnie G. *Ladies of the Leisure Class: The Bourgeoises of Northern France in the Nineteenth Century.* Princeton, N.J.: Princeton University Press, 1981.

Tyrrell, Ian. *Woman's World/Woman's Empire: The Woman's Christian Temperance Union in International Perspective, 1880–1930.* Chapel Hill: University of North Carolina Press, 1991.

Van Drenth, Annemieke, and Francisca de Haan. *The Rise of Caring Power: Elizabeth Fry and Josephine Butler in Britain and the Netherlands.* Amsterdam: Amsterdam University Press, 1999.

Watts, Ruth. *Gender, Power and the Unitarians in England 1760–1860.* London and New York: Longman, 1998.

5   Extending education: learning and teaching

The education of girls and young women increasingly commanded attention during the nineteenth century. In 1800, many girls never entered a classroom. By 1914, nearly all did so in western and northern Europe, where compulsory education laws prevailed. In southern and eastern Europe illiteracy remained common, but more schools were being opened. Publicly funded schools, rare in many places before 1800, became far more common by 1900, especially at the elementary level.

Why did so much expansion of schooling, for both sexes, occur during the nineteenth century? What impact did it have on women's lives, and what role did women play in the process? After a brief review of past educational traditions and general explanations for the expansion of education, this chapter examines changes in primary and secondary education – including women's roles as teachers and advocates of educational reform – and, finally, women's entry into universities.

Educational traditions and expansion

The unprecedented nineteenth-century growth in schooling stemmed from a combination of government action and increasing demand for education from individuals and families. Fundamental economic and political changes, and the weight of religious and cultural traditions, all influenced the availability of formal schooling for both sexes. Cities and towns long had more schools, private or public, than did rural areas. In urban areas with commercial and industrial economies, employers increasingly sought literate workers, although early industrialization sometimes negatively affected school attendance because children often worked. Families, in turn, recognized uses for literacy not evident in traditional agricultural economies and wanted girls as well as boys educated. As more men gained voting rights, government leaders viewed schools as instruments for molding male citizens' opinions, and they expected schools to help shape women's beliefs and values as well, recognizing mothers' influence on children. Religious history also affected schooling, as previously noted. Protestants more often favored educating girls and boys together, at least at the elementary level, than did Catholics, and Protestant clergy frequently provided instruction. Catholic moralists sometimes feared that reading and writing encouraged immoral thoughts and deeds. Typically, boys and young men had more educational opportunities than girls and young women, a situation reflecting common notions about the purposes of education for each sex.

Realities of social class, as well as gender, influenced ideas about what people needed to know and where they learned. Latin and Greek, coupled with ancient history and philosophy, long remained central to the education of upper-class European men and, eventually, of the newer middle classes, who aspired to emulate aristocrats' tastes even as they sought to supplant their political dominance. Indeed, classical learning provided European elites with what the recent French sociologist Pierre Bourdieu termed "cultural capital," but was unavailable to most children.[1] It was also not traditionally provided to many upper-class girls. Instruction at home – by parents, male tutors, governesses, or older siblings – still prevailed for many upper- and middle-class girls around 1800, as women's biographies reveal. Parental priorities and children's age and sex shaped upper-class families' educational strategies. Sons might have male tutors, and daughters governesses, but some brothers and sisters learned together. Parents themselves often gave lessons before hiring tutors or sending children – more often sons than daughters – to private single-sex schools. Typically families wanted children to attend schools with their social peers.

Numerous comments on the inadequacy of girls' education color accounts of the lives of many nineteenth-century women who sought activity and achievement outside the home. Critiques targeted the limited nature of what was taught, at home or in schools, faulting teachers' inadequate knowledge and also prevailing beliefs about what subjects were morally or socially appropriate for young women. Some recent historians offer more nuanced views of earlier girls' schooling, however.

In the case of France, revolutionary leaders after 1789 advocated universal primary education for both sexes, to prepare men to exercise their new rights as citizens and to enable women to transmit new political values to children. But other pressing concerns limited educational advances, and the Revolution's new institutions of higher learning for male elites, the *grandes écoles*, took definitive shape only under Napoleon.

---

[1] Pierre Bourdieu, *Distinction: A Social Critique of the Judgement of Taste*, trans. Richard Nice (Cambridge, Mass.: Harvard University Press, 1984).

The first French public post-primary schools for girls, Napoleon's several Legion of Honor schools founded in 1807 for daughters of army officers and officials, were stratified by social class and less academically rigorous than the new secondary schools (*lycées*) for boys. Yet many Legion of Honor girls, especially orphans, needed to work and often became governesses or teachers, thus countering Napoleon's assumptions about women's domestic destiny and intellectual inferiority. Although nuns taught some classes, the supervision of Legion of Honor schooling by Campan and other laywomen provided a model for schools elsewhere, including a prestigious boarding school created in Tuscany by the Grand Duke in 1825.

The later activities of many young women who attended private boarding or day schools help explain why some historians have become less critical of the girls' schooling that existed before governments standardized curricula, improved teachers' training, and added advanced instructional options for young women. More sympathetic views of the competency of nuns who taught in private schools or in public schools in Catholic states have also emerged. However limited in scope or intent, many earlier nineteenth-century schools did enable young women to find employment or continue learning after leaving school.

From this standpoint, critical reminiscences about schools by writers like Sand, d'Agoult, or the Brontë sisters appear as understandable expressions of frustration by women whose intellectual accomplishments and insights made them aware of just how much more they might have learned in schools. Achievement in many fields required more than minimal formal instruction and, without advanced schooling, considerable will power and commitment to self-education and learning from others in one's milieu. For many young women, advanced learning long depended upon not only parental resources to finance it – in the absence of public secondary schools for girls – but also exposure to more than the "accomplishments" curriculum of literature, modern languages, the arts, and needlework deemed adequate for society's "ladies."

What role could individual women play in the expansion of education, so often determined by large political, economic, social, and cultural forces? Through advocacy and personal example some women tried to influence not only their own families and social circles but also government policymakers and a larger public. They published articles and books about the benefits of better education for women and created organizations to plead their cause. Women's advocacy mixed the practical and the idealistic. By the 1860s, reformers in many countries increasingly focused public attention on the plight of single women, widows, and married women who needed to work and would profit from better educational preparation. In a changing economy, middle-class women wanted to avoid the miseries of the industrial workplace, and one traditional option, work as a governess, could be fraught with insecurity. Daughters, wives, and sisters of men with elite social status usually did not expect to earn a living, of course, but some pushed for better education not only for less fortunate women but also for themselves. In the continuing discussion since the Renaissance and Enlightenment about whether women were or could ever be the intellectual equals of men, many women authors had bridled at the notion that their mental powers were inherently inferior and insisted, like Wollstonecraft, that until women's education improved, their intellectual abilities could not be fairly assessed. Published compilations of women's past and recent achievements also promoted arguments for better education. In due course, women teachers working in expanded school systems became important professional role models for other women, as did the first generations of women university students.

Trends in primary schooling

Class-based traditions in education meant that nineteenth-century public primary schools were typically considered places for children of "the people" rather than for offspring of the upper or middle classes. Lessons in Sunday schools or the English "ragged" schools where women volunteers often taught were also for poor children. Well into the twentieth century many Europeans assumed that a rigorous academic education did not suit children of the "popular" classes because it had no practical value for their work lives, which often began at a young age, or because more learning might provoke dissatisfaction with their place in society. Germans termed the primary school a *Volksschule* (people's school) and Norwegians, the *Folkeskole*. For girls, especially middle-class girls, concerns about the appropriateness or safety of leaving the home to attend school also arose. Thus *Jeanne et Madeleine* (1902), a popular French textbook for girls, featured a working-class heroine who walked to a public primary school with younger brothers, and a middle-class heroine who walked to a different school, accompanied by a maid. Fee-paying elementary classes attached to some public secondary schools in France and other countries also enabled middle-class pupils to avoid mingling with workers' children.

Primary schooling expanded considerably as families recognized its economic value and governments wanted an informed, law-abiding citizenry. Concurrently, the Catholic Church, alarmed that anticlerical men increasingly shunned churchgoing in France, Italy, and elsewhere, advocated that religious orders staff public as well as private schools, hoping that nuns' education of girls would maintain its influence in family life. In France, for example, nuns teaching in public schools were twice as numerous as lay women teachers in 1840 and outnumbered laywomen in private schools after mid-century. Jewish communities tradi-tionally attached more importance to men's than to women's education, but as states removed legal restrictions on Jewish minorities, rabbis worried about Judaism's survival in increasingly secular societies where assimilation was possible and so also emphasized women's role in preserving Jewish identity. Where economic development was slow and political and religious leaders did not push to improve schooling, primary education lagged.

Nineteenth-century literacy statistics reflect national, class, and gender variations in access to education. In 1871, Prussia, the new German Empire's largest state and a pioneer in compulsory schooling, was approaching universal literacy (men, 90 percent; women, 85 percent), although Catholic illiteracy rates were double those of Protestants. Sweden passed a compulsory education law in 1842, as did Austria (half of the empire renamed Austria-Hungary after the Austro-Prussian War) in 1869. In England, primary education, long religiously based, became compulsory in 1870, as it did in Scotland in 1872, but England did not guarantee free schooling until 1891. France's primary education laws of 1881–82, sponsored by the democratic Third Republic and education minister Jules Ferry, made school compulsory for children between the ages of six and thirteen, and made public primary schools free. Although most French boys and girls already received some schooling by the 1870s, republican curricular reform and improved training of teachers enhanced the quality of instruction. Around 1850, before the drive for universal education intensified, 30 percent of English grooms and 45 percent of brides were unable to sign a marriage register, and neither could 31 percent of French grooms and 46 percent of brides. By 1900, only 5–6 percent of French newlyweds could not sign, and in England in 1913, only 1 percent.

The length of primary schooling varied considerably from country to country: eight years in most German states and seven years in France or England by 1900, but, for some time, only two or three years in much of Italy, Spain, or Russia, where literacy lagged. Before Italy's unification, Austria had fostered many schools in northern provinces under its control. Piedmont's Casati Law of 1859, extended to other parts of the newly unified Italy in 1861, required towns to provide free public schools for children aged six to eight, but it was poorly enforced, as was the 1877 Coppino Law extending compulsory schooling to three years. Italian leaders saw schooling as a means for integrating citizens of previously independent states into one nation, but many poor communities could not fund schools adequately, and families were sometimes resistant. Indeed, standard Italian long remained a second language for many people. In 1861, 78 percent of Italians were illiterate, as were nearly half in 1901, when regional illiteracy rates varied from a low in the industrializing north – men, 14 percent; women, 21 percent – to a high in Sicily – men, 65 percent; women, 77 percent. Spain, lagging economically, recorded 65 percent male and 86 percent female illiteracy in 1860, and still 56 percent and 72 percent, respectively, in 1900. In Russia both the tsarist regime and the Orthodox church retarded schooling, the government considering illiterate subjects more docile and the church fearing that knowledge of western literature and science would divert people from religion. Peasants themselves often initiated the push for schooling after Russia emancipated serfs in 1861, but in 1897 only 35 percent of males and 13 percent of females were literate in rural areas, as compared to about 64 percent of urban dwellers. In the Balkans, Bulgarian literacy in 1900 was as limited as in rural Russia, and in Greece in 1910 women's literacy rate was only 17 percent, while men's was 50 percent.

Anticlericalism colored late nineteenth-century French and Italian educational policy because new governments feared Catholic teachers' influence on pupils' political leanings. Ferry, in a much quoted speech, had pronounced that "woman must belong to science or else she belongs to the church."[2] Amidst continuing conflict between republicans and Catholic monarchists, French leaders removed religion from public school curricula and replaced religious teachers with lay personnel. Secularization had greater impact on girls' schools, required to have women teachers, because nuns were a majority of teachers in girls' public schools before 1870, whereas lay men long predominated in boys' schools. After the 1850 Falloux Law urged towns with populations of 800 or more to maintain a separate girls' school, nuns' presence in public schools increased because nuns were less costly for communities. Many French families also preferred Catholic education for girls: in 1901, 31 percent of primary schoolgirls, but only 14 percent of boys, attended private Catholic schools. Italy's anticlerical policies countered papal antagonism to the new nation, whose creation entailed the demise of the independent Papal States. Camillo di Cavour wanted religious orders out of public schools, and in 1877 religious lessons were removed. In Spain,

[2] Jules Ferry, "Discours sur L'Égalité d'Éducation," in Antoine Prost, *Histoire de l'Enseignement en France, 1800–1967* (Paris: Armand Colin, 1968), 269.

however, the 1857 Moyano Law mandated religious lessons in public schools and allowed clerical inspection.

In areas where populations dreamed of gaining national independence, education was prized as a means to preserve and extend linguistic and cultural traditions. Austria granted its subjects the right to instruction in a native tongue in 1867–69, and Czechs in Bohemia used language to challenge Austrian Germans. Similarly, Norwegians used language to protest Swedish control before independence in 1905. In Russian Poland, especially after Alexander III required that most teaching be in Russian, women and men, at home and in schools, kept Polish alive for the next generations. Marie Sklodowska Curie, educated in Warsaw, described how teachers quickly switched from Polish to Russian if an inspector entered her school. Russia allowed Finns instruction in Finnish, as an alternative to Swedish, but blocked compulsory education before 1905. In Ireland, the Catholic Church symbolized an alternative to British domination, and British leaders abandoned a push for nonsectarian schools and permitted religious control.

Gender differences in literacy and schooling often reflected preferences for separate boys' and girls' schools, not only for elites but also for the urban working classes. Where public finances were limited, as in many rural areas, maintaining boys' schools or small coeducational schools took priority. Protestant states typically favored coeducation in primary, if not secondary, schools but varied in preferences for men and women teachers. Coeducational primary schools largely taught by women prevailed in late nineteenth-century Britain, as in the United States. In Prussia, where two-thirds of all elementary classes – particularly in rural areas – mixed the sexes in 1906, male teachers predominated. The French Third Republic retained Catholic preferences for single-sex primary schools, mandating them in communes with a population of 500 or more and requiring women teachers in girls' schools. Coeducation was the norm in European infant or nursery schools, located in cities where many mothers worked outside the home, and women teachers were strongly preferred for their very young pupils. In coeducational primary schools, women often taught lower grades and men the upper grades. French policy specified women teachers for one-room coeducational schools, but many villages still demanded a man.

For both sexes, primary schools taught reading, writing, and arithmetic, and also the work ethic, patriotism, and moral values. They reinforced gender norms and social divisions as well. French textbooks for girls' schools, often written by women, stressed women's domestic and maternal roles, typically featuring role models who were nurturing and gentle, but also watchful of their children's and husbands' behavior. Thus good housekeepers were depicted diverting men from cafés and excessive drinking, and loving wives dissuaded working-class husbands from participating in disruptive strikes. The textbook *Tu Seras Ouvrière* (1892, You Will Be a Woman Worker) was unusual because its heroine not only survived but also prospered in the workplace, rising from humble seamstress to successful owner of a Paris dressmaking business. Lest her example inspire unrealistic ambitions, a preface by a former education minister cautioned girls that the odds were 100 to one that they would remain workers. An 1878 Spanish textbook written by an archbishop's sister depicted Queen Isabella I as pious, intelligent, and also skilled in sewing shirts for her husband. Comparable differences in gender attributes and roles figured in German pedagogical materials, although the prevalence of coeducation minimized the number of feminine images. Across Europe, curricula often devoted fewer hours to math and science for girls than for boys, and sewing and needlework were also staples in girls' schools.

Secondary schools

Secondary education for girls generated far more controversy than primary schooling. As with primary education, proposals for reform provoked disputes over curricular content and who should teach – men or women, religious or lay personnel. But girls' secondary education also provoked debate over whether it should even exist outside the home, the extent to which the curriculum should match that for boys, whether it should be publicly funded, and what social groups it should serve. While primary school in educationally advanced countries extended to ages twelve or thirteen, what people then called secondary school might start by age ten or eleven. Indeed, the label "secondary" often covered "intermediate" or "middle" schools for young adolescents. The divide between primary and secondary schools was as much one of social class as of age and curricula. Most children never entered post-primary schools because their parents wanted them to work and could not pay fees charged even for public secondary schools. Social class differences also explain why, in response to lower-middle-class or artisan demands for more education for children, some governments created post-primary school options without the classical focus of traditional boys' secondary schools. French higher primary schools (*écoles primaires supérieures*) dated from 1833, and German technical or "modern" schools (*Realschulen*) offered alternatives to boys' classical *Gymnasia*. Academic secondary schools prepared graduates for universities; other post-primary schools usually did not. In 1891, only 2.7 percent of German boys aged ten to fourteen were in secondary schools, and the figures for France, Spain, and Italy were 2.6 percent, 2 percent, and 1 percent respectively. Post-primary schools were typically single-sex, in both Protestant and Catholic states, and were often private or local government ventures rather than national projects. While girls' access to secondary schools lagged, debates about boys' education weighed whether future businessmen or technical innovators benefited from classical studies. Many who questioned their practicality still favored their perpetuation, in combination with mathematics, science, and modern languages, as essential for giving new economic elites "cultural capital" signifying higher social status.

Dispute over whether girls should be able to study all of the subjects in the most rigorous education for boys was central to debates on girls' secondary education. Privileged adolescent girls already attended finishing schools, but should they have access to something more academic? Even many supporters of creating or extending girls' secondary schooling shied away from arguing that it should be fully identical to boys' schooling because curricular content had implications for what students might subsequently do. If middle- and upper-class women did not work, did they need a secondary education that could broaden employment opportunities in areas traditionally reserved for men? As of the 1860s, that question figured in new debates in many countries. Advocates of extending girls' schooling often cited both its utility and the value of learning for its own sake, but also adjusted emphases to suit particular publics. Unmarried middle-class daughters or widows might need to earn a living, and education could prepare them for respectable employment as governesses or teachers. For women not seeking paid work, instruction could provide the pleasure of mastering what fathers and brothers learned and, advocates argued, make them better-informed wives and mothers. Because secondary school was the route to study at universities, concerns also inevitably arose about the appropriateness of women attending universities and entering professions to which university degrees gave access. Frequently young women gained access to universities before secondary schools actually prepared them for university entry simply because, in some countries, women who studied privately could take exams to obtain secondary degrees required to enter universities: the French *baccalauréat*, German *Abitur*, or Austrian *Matura*, among others.

Individuals and private groups, rather than governments, often initiated the efforts to create or improve girls' secondary education. English demand for better-educated governesses contributed to the founding in

London of Queen's College in 1848 and Bedford College in 1849. Both also initially admitted young teenagers. Elizabeth Reid, a wealthy widow, provided funding for Bedford. In Denmark, Nathalie Zahle, a governess since the age of fifteen, borrowed money to open a higher course for girls in 1851, and after public primary school teaching opened to women, she started the first training college for women teachers in 1862. Successful private initiatives did not necessarily spur local or national governments to new investment in girls' secondary education, however. The landmark English legislation providing public funds for secondary schools for both sexes came only in 1902; Denmark opened upper-level public secondary schools to young women in 1903 and delayed funding women teachers' training until 1918.

By the 1860s, English local and regional associations were catalysts for secondary education and access to universities for young women. Donations enabled Emily Davies (1830–1921) to open a small women's college near Cambridge in 1869 and move it to Cambridge in 1873. Maria Shirreff Grey (1816–1906) was a driving force behind the National Union for Improving the Education of Women, founded in 1871, and the Girls' Public Day School Company (GPDSC). GPDSC shareholders supported a mission of "fitting girls for the practical business and duties of life" as well as forming "character by moral and religious training."[3] Headmistresses Frances Mary Buss (1827–94) and Dorothea Beale (1831–1906), who had studied at the new Queen's College, provided early models for better secondary schooling. Buss began teaching (with her mother) at the age of fourteen, and in 1850 started the North London Collegiate School for Ladies, heading it until 1894. Evidently the first woman to call herself a headmistress, she persuaded colleagues to start the Association of Headmistresses in 1874 and was its president for twenty years. Beale, the next president, taught at Queen's College and in 1858 became principal of the recently founded Cheltenham Ladies College, which she enlarged and improved. A contemporary verse mocked both women as unfeminine: "Miss Buss and Miss Beale/ Cupid's darts do not feel/ How unlike us/ Miss Beale and Miss Buss."[4] Their schools were, nonetheless, models for the GPDSC, which also opened a teacher training school in 1878 and had 37 secondary schools with over 7,000 students by 1900.

---

[3] Paul Monroe, ed., *A Cyclopedia of Education*, 5 vols. (New York: Macmillan, 1913), III: 114.
[4] Quotation in *Larousse Dictionary of Women*, ed. Melanie Parry (New York: Larousse Kingfisher Chambers, 1996), 112.

As long as English secondary education remained essentially private, most headmistresses and headmasters opposed creating official secondary diplomas like those in continental Europe, even though local examinations sponsored by Cambridge and Oxford universities had become a kind of public testing of secondary pupils. Headmasters argued that elite schools like Eton and Harrow already conferred a mark of learning and social distinction, even when their students did not go on to universities. The 1902 law on secondary education created competition for private schools, and by 1913 the GPDS Trust had closed six schools and transferred five others to public authorities or the Church Schools' Company. Girls' schools could still, after 1902, substitute domestic subjects for part of the science and mathematics curriculum.

English women's secondary school initiatives had parallels in Ireland, first among Protestants and then Catholics. Margaret Byers, widow of a Presbyterian missionary, opened the Ladies' Collegiate School (later named Victoria College) in Belfast in 1859, after heading another girls' school. In Dublin Anne Jellicoe helped found Alexandra College, modeled on Queen's College in London. Feminist Isabella Tod lobbied in London for young women's right to take the exams created by the Intermediate Education Act for Ireland in 1878 and also to obtain degrees from the new Royal University of Ireland (RUI). Because the RUI was an examining body and did not offer courses, Victoria and Alexandra Colleges and other girls' schools began providing university-level instruction. In turn, some families in the emerging Irish Catholic middle class demanded more advanced courses for daughters. In Dublin a Dominican convent school added Latin and advanced mathematics in 1885, and St. Mary's University College opened in 1893.

In France, which long had more private day and boarding schools for girls than did England, two secondary education milestones marked the 1860s. Julie Daubié (1824–74), a former governess, became the first woman to pass examinations for the secondary school *baccalauréat* in 1861. She had limited formal education but learned Latin and Greek from her brother and studied on her own, encouraged by praise for the essay she entered in an 1859 competition. She gained permission to take the exams from the regional education administration in Lyon, after being refused in Paris and Aix. Daubié's book, *La Femme Pauvre au XIXe Siècle* (1866, The Poor Woman in the Nineteenth Century), joined the debate on women's work and education, countering republican Jules Simon's much-quoted assertion in *L'Ouvrière* (1860) that "a woman who becomes a worker is no longer a woman."[5] In 1867, Victor Duruy, the

---

[5] Jules Simon, *L'Ouvrière*, 2nd edn. (Paris: Hachette, 1861), v.

Second Empire's liberal education minister, introduced "secondary courses" for girls, provoking a storm of controversy orchestrated by Catholic bishop Dupanloup, who contended that "public" education would divert young women from their maternal role. Because men taught these new courses, clergy also warned of moral dangers, citing the medieval example of Peter Abelard's seduction of pupil Héloise. In reality, men had taught advanced courses in some convent schools and many secular boarding schools for girls since the eighteenth century, their presence reflecting a lack of qualified women and a belief that male teachers enhanced a school's prestige. In 1867, however, both sides often assumed that no girls' secondary schools even existed because *all* girls' schools had been classified as primary in 1853. Catholics saw a threat to private girls' schools in state sponsorship of girls' secondary education, started just before the also controversial admission of women to the Paris Faculty of Medicine. Amidst the uproar, many of the fifty Duruy courses had limited appeal and most closed after the Second Empire fell in 1870.

When the French Third Republic started public secondary schools for girls in 1880, sponsoring deputy Camille Sée presented their purpose as better education for future republican wives and mothers, not professional preparation. Although Daubié had also obtained a university degree (*licence*) in literature in 1871, republicans planned a different trajectory for middle-class girls. The curriculum for the new girls' *lycées* and *collèges* was two years shorter than that for boys' schools and until 1924 did not include Latin or advanced mathematics and philosophy, all necessary to obtain the *baccalauréat* required by universities. Young women needed private tutoring to cross that degree hurdle, accomplished by about 300 before 1900, and by 1,749 between 1905 and 1914. When some competing Catholic girls' schools began offering *baccalauréat* subjects, certain public schools also provided that option. By 1914, 190 girls' public secondary schools enrolled 33,282 students, less than 2 percent of the total of 2,127,000 girls in public primary schools.

In Belgium, Isabelle Gatti de Gamond (1839–1905) became celebrated as the creator of girls' secondary education. Her mother, Zoé de Gamond (1812–54), a lawyer's daughter and wife of an artist, had written on French socialism and been appointed Belgium's first inspectress of nursery schools in 1847. Isabelle, after her mother's death, spent five years with a Polish family as a governess, also learning Latin and Greek, and studying science and philosophy. Returning to Brussels, she proposed to create a girls' secondary school and gained support from the new Belgian League for Education, whose advocacy of secular public schools was a model for the French League founded in 1866. The Brussels city government provided partial funding for her "courses of education," opened in 1864 and soon enrolling 318 girls aged 12 to 15. Gatti de Gamond headed the school for 36 years, fending off Catholic criticism of its secular orientation, which liberals supported. Her success inspired other schools in Brussels and provincial cities, her younger sister directing one of them. Marie Popelin, later a prominent feminist, taught for Gatti de Gamond in Brussels and headed a school in Mons. Only in 1881 did the national government create comparable girls' schools. Gatti de Gamond also added training courses for teachers, and after the government stiffened requirements for university entry in 1890 but did not add advanced courses to girls' public schools, she opened a "higher" course offering mathematics and classics for students aged fifteen to eighteen. That course was unique in pre-1914 Belgium, for ambitious young women were barred from male secondary schools, and as of 1910, public authorities supported only forty intermediate girls' schools, as compared to ninety-two for boys. Unsurprisingly, Gatti de Gamond, who retired in 1899, was also a feminist and socialist, following in her mother's footsteps.

Russian girls' education received an official boost in 1858, early in Alexander II's reign, when girls' *progimnazia* with a three-year curriculum and *gimnazia* with six-year programs were created after deliberations spurred by a surgeon impressed by nurses' work during the Crimean War. As of 1876 *gimnazia* offered an optional extra year of pedagogical training, and by 1883 285 girls' secondary schools (100 of them *gimnazia*) enrolled 50,000 students. Most girls' schools lacked a curriculum equivalent to that for boys until 1916, however. Russian Poland had 55 advanced girls' schools, public and private, by 1863, but in the wake of new repression after a massive Polish uprising that year many private schools closed, and courses other than those in the Polish language or religion had to be taught in Russian.

The major educational issues engaging German women reformers, including the German Women's Association (ADF) founded in 1865, were improving higher girls' schools and expanding women teachers' employment at all levels. Most girls' post-primary schools were then private or run by municipalities, and the more numerous private schools hired more women teachers than did the public schools. Because individual German states retained control of education after unification in 1871, variety in schooling and its religious affiliations continued, but Prussia's predominance in the Empire centered many reform efforts there. The reform of German girls' high schools brought Helene Lange (1848–1930) national prominence (Figure 5.1). Daughter of an Oldenburg merchant, she had lost her mother when she was six. After her father's death when she was sixteen, she lived with a minister's family

Figure 5.1 Helene Lange, reformer of German girls' education and organizer of women teachers.

and then worked as a teacher and governess. Moving to Berlin in 1871 to prepare for a teaching credential, she gave private lessons until named head of a private school in 1876. She also made contacts with reformers and professional women who supported her later campaigns. Henriette Schrader-Breymann, wife of a liberal politician, introduced Lange to Crown Princess Victoria, daughter of England's queen and supportive of educational reforms. Women reformers petitioned the Prussian education ministry and legislature in 1887, hoping for results while Crown

Prince Frederick, ill with cancer, and Victoria still wielded influence. No immediate changes ensued, but Lange's brochure supporting the petition became famous. During Frederick's brief reign in 1888, Victoria facilitated her trip to England to meet women educators. Lange organized the General German Women Teachers Association in 1890, heading it until 1921 and affiliating it with the BDF early on.

Against the backdrop of pressure from women's groups, Prussia finally set official standards for the upper three grades of girls' high schools in 1894, and reformers intensified demands for improving women's education to qualify them to teach these grades. Lange had tried to minimize controversy by not advocating a full classical curriculum leading to university study because critics alleged that it could lure women away from the home and into masculine professions. But she also recognized that ambitious German women were already enrolling in Swiss universities and so eventually started a course to prepare them to meet Swiss admissions standards. In 1893 it became a four-year program including classics, so that graduates could pass the *Abitur*, opened to women in 1895. Although women could not yet enroll formally in German universities, they might audit courses if individual professors approved. Women in Baden also founded a girls' classical high school in 1893, taken over by the city of Karlsruhe in 1897; and Leipzig women emulated Lange's course in 1894. In 1914, six years after Prussia opened universities to women, 540 Prussian *Gymnasia* prepared young men for university study, but only 43 girls' academic high schools (*Lyzeen*) did so.

In Austria, the development of private higher girls' schools also preceded the setting of official standards for them. Marianne Hainisch (1839–1936), active in the new Women's Employment Association, urged local authorities in Vienna to open a girls' *Realgymnasium* in 1870, and when that effort failed, the Association started a school for girls aged ten to sixteen. Similar ventures began in Prague and Graz. Unlike women in Germany, who were barred from the *Abitur* before 1895, women in Austria could take the exam for the *Matura* from 1872, although only twenty-five had obtained it as of 1895. Czech author Eliska Krásnohorská (1847–1926), editor of the *Women's Gazette* in Prague, launched a campaign in 1882 to secure young women's access to classical secondary studies. The daughter of an artisan, she always wished that her own formal education had been more extensive, even as her authorial career profited from Karolina Svetlá's encouragement. Publicizing women's educational progress in other countries was one of her strategies. In 1890 Krásnohorská and allies in the society Minerva (named after the Roman goddess of wisdom) opened the first private school in Austria with a curriculum adequate to prepare young women for the *Matura*. Its supporters expected that well-qualified graduates would promote the argument for access to the University of Prague. In Vienna, the Association for Extended Women's Education, founded in 1888, opened a girls' classical high school in 1892, with support from prominent men and women, including writers Ebner-Eschenbach, Suttner, and Emilie Mataja (pseudonym Emil Marriott). Local demand, as well as Prussia's 1894 regulations, influenced Austria's formulation of a six-year curriculum for girls' public secondary schools (*Lyzeen*), started in 1900. Yet, like the French counterpart, it was shorter than that for boys and did not prepare pupils for universities. The government in 1910 also halted some provincial towns' admission of girls to boys' secondary schools for that purpose. Private initiatives thus helped fill the void. Bestselling author Marie von Najmájer's 40,000-crown donation bolstered the Vienna Association's school, and by 1903 the Association had 650 members.

In traditionally Catholic Italy, as in France and Austria, families able to afford advanced schooling for girls usually favored single-sex institutions, but national policy differed in one respect. Because funding public primary schools had priority after unification, the government in 1878 allowed girls to attend boys' academic secondary schools: the five-year *ginnasio*, followed by the three-year *liceo*. New normal schools for training primary teachers were single-sex institutions, however, and some anticlerical parents sent daughters there, without expecting them to become teachers. Intermediate girls' public schools existed but did not offer Latin. Yet most middle- and upper-class families still preferred sending daughters to private, largely Catholic day or boarding schools. In 1888, nearly 106,000 girls attended 4,090 private day schools, and another 53,000 were in 848 boarding schools, which often resembled convents and typically did not stress preparation for employment. Italy's experiment in public secondary coeducation drew only 44 young women to *liceos* in 1888 and 791 in 1910, when they were 5 percent of *liceo* students and still faced unkind comments.

To the extent that coeducation figured in secondary schooling, it was most common in northern Europe. Its defenders argued that society benefited when young people got to know the opposite sex in a supervised setting, but as in Italy, limited funding was also a key reason for its adoption. In the Netherlands, eleven girls entered boys' schools in 1871 because their towns had no girls' secondary school. The first girls' secondary school opened in Haarlem in 1867, but the state and many localities were reluctant to fund others. Coeducational traditions in Protestant primary schools and lack of boarding schools also contributed to Dutch acceptance of secondary coeducation. Whereas eight of every nine secondary school girls attended an all-girls' school in 1885, only one out of three did so by 1914. The majority of Dutch Protestant secondary schools became coeducational, and in 1914 young women numbered 24 percent of students in the classical secondary schools which, unlike girls' schools, prepared for university admission. Dutch Catholics, a third of the population, largely opposed coeducation. Secondary coeducation also developed in Scandinavian states, but was resisted in Swedish state grammar schools. In England, local authorities made some schools coeducational after the 1902 Education Act. English headmistresses and most German women teachers lacked enthusiasm for coeducation, however, because single-sex schools served their professional interests, especially in Germany where teaching jobs for women were not plentiful.

In sum, girls' secondary schools, public and private, were increasingly common in much of Europe by 1900, but they enrolled limited numbers of pupils, as compared to primary schools, and their curricula typically differed from what rigorous academic high schools offered boys. Girls' programs were usually shorter and often lacked the classics, mathematics, and science needed to pass examinations for degrees required for university admission.

Teachers and school directresses

New schools required teachers, and during the nineteenth century more women taught classes than ever before. Contemporaries, in turn, regarded the increasingly well-trained teachers as the first professional women, believing also that maternal qualities ideally suited women for teaching. As an English clergyman's wife wrote in 1884, teaching "was for many years looked upon as the only bread-winning resource for poor ladies; but is now, happily, considered as a noble profession, not beneath the acceptance of any," regardless of whether one taught in a high school or a primary school for poorer children.[6] Her optimism notwithstanding, teachers' status continued to mirror the social divisions separating primary and secondary schools. Many primary teachers followed an educational path from primary school to higher primary school to normal school, without studying at more prestigious secondary schools. And before the multiplication of normal schools or training seminars later in the century, many primary teachers trained simply by assisting in established teachers' classrooms.

---

[6] Henrietta O. Barnett, "Women as Philanthropists," in *The Woman Question in Europe*, ed. Theodore Stanton (New York: G. P. Putnam's Sons, 1884), 109.

Striking national variations in training and hiring women teachers were tied to past precedents, religious and cultural preferences, and contemporary politics, as James Albisetti has demonstrated. Although women had long taught in private homes and in schools, official qualifications for public-school teaching and regulations on institutions training teachers were new during the nineteenth century. Bavaria initiated the first German state training for women teachers in 1814, preferring them for girls' schools, but a devout Catholic king ended that institute in 1826, leaving Bavaria without another until 1872. When Bavaria began state certification of women teachers in 1836, it was for women trained by other teachers or in convents. In Prussia, with a Protestant majority and large Catholic minority in Rhineland territory acquired in 1815, the first training "seminars" for women were designated by religious denomination. Prussia's early lead in compulsory education and certification had produced a tradition of male teachers, including clergy, and no women taught in Berlin public schools until 1863. Sweden opened public school teaching to women in 1853 and 1859, as did Denmark for rural schools in 1859 and in Copenhagen in 1861. Swiss practices varied by canton. Bern started training for women around 1840, and 24 percent of its primary teachers were women by 1861. Yet no women taught in Zurich until 1874. Dutch women had long taught but were first under state regulations in 1857. German-speaking women in Austria could teach in public schools as of 1869, and Russian women, by 1871. In Germany, the weight of traditions and greater prestige accorded to teaching careers there, as compared to elsewhere, help explain why women were still only 15 percent of Prussia's primary school teachers in 1901.

France first issued regulations on public primary school teaching in 1819, requiring a teaching certificate for lay men and women but allowing nuns to provide simply a "letter of obedience" from a superior. Under the Second Empire, nuns outnumbered laywomen in public girls' and nursery schools, but the Third Republic wanted lay women teachers. Whereas many departments funded normal schools for men by 1850, only a few did so for women, who usually trained privately or in courses run by nuns. The Republic in 1879 required each of France's eighty-seven departments to provide a normal school to train laywomen, as well as one for men, and compliance necessitated opening sixty-four new women's normal schools but only six for men (Figure 5.2). Two women's normal schools were in Algeria, where nuns and some laywomen had taught since the French conquest and where authorities now wanted lay teachers for public schools attended by daughters of European parents. A "higher" normal school (*école normale supérieure*) was also created at Fontenay-aux-Roses near Paris to train women

Figure 5.2 Young student teachers at the Women's Normal School in the Loiret department, 1880s.

professors for departmental normal schools. As conflict continued over secularizing public schools, the state assumed responsibility for paying teachers' base salary in 1889. With its preference for sex-segregated primary schools, France's 50:50 ratio of women to men teachers in 1900 was unique among large European countries but similar to Belgium and Portugal. Women also headed all French girls' schools (Figure 5.3). Although French women teachers, like most counterparts elsewhere, earned less than men at some levels of the official pay scale before 1914, the number of women applicants exceeded the availability of posts in many locales by 1900. To justify hiring lay women teachers, the Republic emphasized their maternal qualities – allegedly lacked by nuns – and unlike most nations did not make women leave teaching if they married or became mothers. At least a third of French women teachers were married before 1914, as compared to about 8 percent in the United States or 12 percent in England (countries where localities' marriage regulations varied) and still fewer in Germany and Austria.

France's most prestigious teaching posts for women were in the two higher normal schools at Fontenay-aux-Roses and Sèvres. The Sèvres school, created in 1881, trained women professors for the new girls' secondary schools. Although Fontenay was less elite than Sèvres and drew students largely from departmental normal schools, Lucie Saffroy's

Figure 5.3   A French teacher's science lesson on birds, 1903.

experience at Fontenay illustrates how women from humble backgrounds faced problems when advancing in the educational hierarchy.
Already a teacher before her training at Fontenay, Saffroy (1855–1944)
became its directress in 1890 and had protracted disputes with the
school's male chief and several instructors. Some critical peers also
judged her an unsuitable role model, scorning her as a rustic woman with
common manners. A baker's daughter from the Yonne department, she
was proud of her origins, "resolutely antiworldly," and uninterested in
fashion.[7] Educational authorities reassigned Saffroy to primary school
inspection in Paris in 1897, replacing her with Mme Jeanne Adèle
Dejean de la Bâtie, also humbly born but with an accommodating personality and better sense of the style expected of women educational
leaders. The Sèvres school enjoyed a more elite reputation but had difficulty attracting students from middle-class Catholic families that
favored private schools. By 1900, after a generation of public secondary
schooling for girls, perhaps a quarter of women secondary school
teachers were Protestants – at a time when Protestants were 2 percent of
the population.

[7] Yvonne Oulhiou, *L'École Normale Supérieure de Fontenay-aux-Roses, À Travers le Temps
1880–1980* (Fontenay-aux-Roses, 1981), 79.

Italy and Spain also favored women teachers for girls' schools, and Italy's shortage of male teachers often led to women's assignment to small rural coeducational schools or lower grades in boys' schools as well. By 1907, 42,000 women teachers held 70 percent of public primary school posts, and they also predominated in private schools, where nuns often taught. The late development of mass primary education in Italy, low pay, and male emigration contributed to the decrease in numbers of men teaching after 1875. Women greatly outnumbered men in normal schools created after unification, and some prepared to teach in women's normal schools by attending the higher training institutions for women in Rome and Florence. In Catholic Spain, with a population three-fifths that of Italy, about 12,000 women and 14,100 men taught in primary schools after 1900, and 37 women's normal schools provided training. Nuns or governesses typically taught upper-class girls, however.

Teaching was also undergoing feminization in Great Britain, Sweden, and Russia. In both Britain and the United States, teaching was overwhelmingly feminized by 1900 – about 75 percent of teachers were women – and it became stereotyped, especially in primary schools, as a "woman's profession" because men sought better-paid work. Almost half of British women elementary teachers were still "uncertified" before 1914, a situation linked to lower status, as compared to Germany, which required state certification. Many British residential training facilities for teachers had operated privately – thirty of forty-three identified in 1888 were under the Church of England – but during the 1890s universities opened day training departments for teachers. Some teachers moved to the colonies, usually to instruct British pupils. Only 2 percent of Indian girls attended school during the 1880s. In Sweden, women were 58 percent of elementary teachers in lower grades by 1889, and 65 percent by 1899, but men often resisted their teaching of higher grades. In Russia clergy had once dominated primary teaching, but shortages of male teachers led the government to hire women in 1871 and to add optional pedagogical training to girls' *gimnazia*. Yet until 1903 only men could teach the two upper grades in girls' *gimnazia*.

The feminization of primary school teaching was least evident in Germany and Austria-Hungary, where authorities preferred hiring men and men still found teaching relatively prestigious. Women had more teaching opportunities in urban girls' schools than in rural coeducational schools, where men were preferred. In 1911, women were still only 21 percent of German elementary teachers; 27 percent in Hungary; and about 30 percent in Austria. In the newer nation of Bulgaria women then comprised about a third of elementary teachers. Germany and Austria also lagged in training and allowing women to teach math, sciences, and classical languages at the secondary level.

The predominance of coeducation in public primary schools in much of Scandinavia and the Netherlands, as in Germany, similarly limited women's teaching because authorities favored men for upper grades. Women were 34 percent of Norway's primary teachers after 1900. They were 31 percent of Dutch public primary teachers by 1910, a major increase from a mere 5 percent in 1870, but still rarely headed schools. In the East Indies, where the Dutch government sent the first women teachers in 1875, 155 of 186 public schools serving a growing European population were coeducational in 1909 and the others were for girls. Teacher training also developed there. Although Muslim children in the colony entered some Dutch schools, girls were only 4 percent of the Muslim cohort because parents resisted letting them attend school. Nonetheless, the young Javanese princess Raden Ajeng Kartini opened a girls' school in 1903.

In sum, by 1914 women teachers were far more numerous in primary schools than at the more restricted secondary level, but their presence varied considerably from country to country, the well-known feminization of teaching notwithstanding. Women were at least 70 percent of primary teachers in Britain and Italy; around 50 percent in France, Belgium, Portugal, and Finland; over 40 percent in Russia, Spain, and Sweden; 30 percent or more in Austria, Denmark, the Netherlands, Norway, and Switzerland; 27 percent in Hungary; but just 21 percent in Germany. These variations reflected political, economic, cultural, and religious realities. Single-sex educational traditions provided jobs for women teachers and school directresses, where governments or parents invested in girls' schooling, but limited women's teaching of boys. Coeducation, outside Great Britain, often limited posts for women teachers.

Women educators' advocacy

Many influential advocates of improving women educators' professional status emerged from primary school ranks, although primary schools and most normal schools lacked the prestige of academic secondary schools. In France, inspectress general Pauline Kergomard (1838–1925) was probably the best-known woman educator by the 1890s. Daughter of a Protestant school inspector hounded out of his job in Bordeaux by Catholic clergy during the 1850s, she was closely identified with the Third Republic's secularizing policies. She was educated in a private school run by her aunt, a pastor's wife and mother of anarchists Élisée and Élie Reclus. After marriage she went to work because her husband, who had authorial ambitions, could not support their household and two sons. Obtaining credentials to inspect nursery schools, she was so appointed by Ferry's primary education director in 1879. Kergomard was one of the inspectresses general active in reforming nursery schools, renamed "maternal schools" (*écoles maternelles*) in 1881, and in 1886 became the first woman elected to the Higher Council of Public Instruction, the education ministry's influential advisory body. Promising to bring the perspective of "the mother and the woman" into deliberations on educating children, she served on the Council with men largely from secondary schools, universities, and inspectorates. Her arguments on women educators' behalf typically began with safe assertions that most women wanted to be wives and mothers, but then added that women needing to work deserved better pay and should face no barriers to additional opportunities. She advocated equal pay for women teachers, who were paid less than men at many ranks. More controversially, she called for appointing women primary school inspectors, citing inspectresses' accomplishments for nursery schools since the 1830s. Furious male teachers objected to competing with women for promotion to inspector rank, and the public controversy, dating from an education congress in 1889, doomed her bid for reelection to the Higher Council in 1892. She later headed the education section of the National Council of French Women. In 1911, when the Paris newspaper *Le Matin* profiled such pathbreaking career women as composer Chaminade, lawyer Maria Vérone, and aviatrix Hélène Dutrieu, Kergomard was featured for education. Energetic and assertive as one of four inspectresses general of nursery schools before 1914, she could not overcome male teachers' and inspectors' opposition to primary school inspectresses, who numbered only 5 in a corps of 450 in 1913.

Italy's tradition of sex-segregated schools also prompted the new national government to name a limited number of inspectresses, expected to defend its secularizing policies. Erminia Fuà Fusinato (1834–76) was temporarily assigned in 1871 to visit schools in Rome and Naples. From a politically liberal Jewish family in Venice and educated at home, she had defied her parents by converting to Catholicism to marry a nationalist poet. Felicita Morandi (1827–1906), an experienced teacher and school directress from a less privileged background, inspected schools from 1879 to 1893. Based in Milan, she wrote widely on pedagogy and wielded influence that angered clericals opposed to the public policies and reforms she represented. She was a role model for later inspectresses, numbering eight by 1895, and for women normal school teachers, dozens of whom wrote textbooks and pedagogical tracts, as did their French counterparts.

The issue of unequal pay for equal work drew women teachers to collective action in various countries. English women teachers, whose numbers increased noticeably after the Education Act of 1870, established an Equal Pay League in 1896, renamed the National Federation of Women Teachers in 1906. As about three-fourths of primary school-teachers by 1890, women also joined and sought support from the National Union of Teachers (NUT). The male-dominated NUT repeatedly rejected most of their demands, however, and at an NUT meeting in 1913 an insistent woman teacher was physically attacked – an incident akin to attacks on determined women's suffrage advocates. In Italy, women teachers, as two-thirds of the 32,000 members of the National Teachers' Union by 1904, did sway their Union to advocate equal pay. When the national congress of French teachers' groups (*amicales*) took the same step in 1909, it was less because of a small feminist teachers' group than because male teachers recognized that raising women's pay served their own self-interest by eliminating financial incentives for preferring women teachers. In Denmark, Anne Bruun (b. 1853), a Copenhagen teacher, began demanding equal pay for women teachers in 1898. She persuaded 229 women colleagues to petition the government for equal pay, seconded by the Danish Women's Society. She complained as well about the lack of a public normal school for women, when four existed for men. Also active in the Women's Society and editor of its periodical, Bruun became the first woman elected to the executive committee of the Danish Union of Teachers (DUT) in 1902. When she left the committee in 1915, women teachers' highest pay levels were still two-thirds those of men, but in the DUT women had gone from only 17 percent of members in 1900 to 41 percent of 7,200 members in 1913 and held 4 of 15 executive committee slots.

In Spain, Concepión Sáiz y Otero (1851–c. 1930), positioned centrally at the women's normal school in Madrid, became one of the determined advocates for girls' schooling and women teachers' interests. She belonged to the Association for Woman's Education and the Institute for Education, both products of the brief liberal reform era after 1868 that stimulated discussion of inadequacies in women's education, thanks to rector Fernando de Castro of the Central University of Madrid and to Concepión Arenal. The Institute started a school for governesses that became a catalyst for advances in women's education, holding evening classes at the Central Normal School. Women's normal schools opened since 1857 had a poor reputation, and the Association school's high quality spurred improvements in the Central School after 1880. The Association also spearheaded the creation of special women's schools for business, postal and telegraph work, and librarianship. Sáiz studied at the Central Normal School, received teaching certification in 1877, and soon qualified as an advanced teacher. While teaching in a private school, she attended evening classes to obtain a governess's diploma. She began teaching at the Central School in 1882, received a regular appointment in language and literature in 1884, and was tenured in 1889. Coauthor of a book on educational psychology, she also published an influential book on pedagogical theory and practice in 1908. Her articles in the review *Escuela Moderna* (Modern School) revealed the feminist ideas which led sociology professor Adolfo Posada to include her in his book *Feminismo* (1899). Sáiz credited the Central School, which graduated 313 women between 1882 and 1901, with providing cultural missionaries to provincial Spain. Carmen de Burgos (1867–1932), better known by her pen name "Columbine," was among the Madrid normal school instructors. In 1909, Sáiz became professor and assistant director at the new Escuela de Estudios Superiores de Magisterio, a coeducational, university-level center for advanced pedagogical training in sciences and letters, partly inspired by French precedents. Her later autobiographical account praised women teachers for directly or indirectly influencing pupils to develop political and feminist awareness. Commentators in other countries could make similar observations about women teachers' significance.

Universities

During the 1860s and 1870s middle-class women made demands for access to universities in most European countries, their interest paralleling a noticeable increase in men's pursuit of university degrees and professional status. For women, access posed more than one problem. Sometimes no laws or rules prevented their enrollment, but lack of a classical secondary education left them without the degree required for entry unless they were tutored privately to obtain it. In other cases, laws or administrative rulings barred access, often causing a lag between women's presence as auditors and formal admission. Delays between women's earning of university degrees and ability to use those degrees to enter certain professions also were common. Unlike Great Britain, most European continental nations did not create separate women's institutions of higher education, and some barred women from universities until long after the founding of pioneering English and American women's colleges. Although continental states usually favored single-sex secondary and normal schools, they accepted university coeducation because of the initially limited public demand and costs of starting new institutions. Many women also thought that separate women's universities would be judged inferior.

Switzerland and France led in offering university admission and degrees to women during the late 1860s, even as they delayed creating academic secondary schools for girls. Indeed, foreign women, admitted from states barring them from universities, long outnumbered Swiss and French women students in their country's universities. The University of Zurich accepted women auditors in 1864, and in 1867 a Russian medical student became the first woman awarded a degree. At the 1870 thesis defense of Elizabeth Frances Morgan, the second woman to obtain a Zurich degree, one professor lauded her as a "worthy model" for other women, proving "the success of the social experiment being made quietly here" and affecting "the whole world." The universities in Bern and Geneva admitted women in 1872, but Basel, the oldest Swiss university, and Lausanne did not until 1890. Swiss cantons rather than the central government set university policy, and in Geneva women were accepted when its academy, founded in 1559, was converted to a university. Marie Goegg and thirty other women petitioned Genevan authorities for women's admission, stating that they acted as mothers concerned about their daughters' future. Because Switzerland had a small population of only three million from which its six (later seven) universities could draw, cantonal governments and many professors welcomed fee-paying foreign students. Foreign women often entered with lesser credentials than were required of the Swiss. Only after 1900, for example, did a higher girls' school in Geneva, opened in 1847, add Latin to prepare pupils for the university. Enrollment at five Swiss universities was 23–27 percent female by 1900–10, but in 1906, the pre-1914 peak for women's enrollment, the 1,840 women students included only 138 Swiss women, and 1,539 of the foreigners were from Russia. Other governments watched Swiss precedents with interest, particularly German states and Austria-Hungary, long resistant to women's formal admission to universities. The international women's congress in Chicago in 1893 celebrated the Zurich milestone, one speaker noting: "The women of the world owe it to the University of Zurich that she has struck the keynote of justice to women, thus making the false note of injustice more distinctly heard around the world."[8]

Russian women flocked to Swiss and French universities because of barriers in Russia. After the abolition of serfdom, many young aristocratic and middle-class men and women wanted to do socially useful work and sought appropriate training, but in 1863 Alexander II excluded women auditors from universities. In 1872 his regime ordered the 108

---

[8] Quotation on Morgan in Thomas Neville Bonner, *To the Ends of the Earth: Women's Search for Education in Medicine* (Cambridge, Mass.: Harvard University Press, 1992), 39; Helen D. Webster, "Our Debt to Zurich," in *The World's Congress of Representative Women*, ed. May Wright Sewall, 2 vols. (Chicago: Rand, McNally, 1894), I: 694.

Russian women studying in Zurich to return home, claiming that the free circulation of ideas there fueled political radicalism. Yet Russia also opened advanced medical courses and other "higher courses" for women, responding in part to demands from women like journalist Evgenia Konradi and the philanthropic triumvirate of Trubnikova, Filosofova, and Stasova. In 1868, 178 St. Petersburg women, largely from the gentry class, petitioned the government, and soon collected 220 additional signatures, including that of the wife of war minister Dmitri Miliutin, himself linked to Filosofova's husband. Private donations of 50,000 rubles helped finance women's medical courses from 1872 to 1882. Russian women thereby gained access to more advanced education than many other European women of the 1870s, but a backlash occurred under Alexander III, who attributed his father's assassination in 1881 to liberal policies. His government closed women's medical courses – and higher courses other than some lectures in St. Petersburg – and also introduced quotas of 3 to 5 percent for Jewish students. Subsequently Nicholas II approved the opening of the St. Petersburg Medical Institute for Women in 1897 and allowed other "higher courses" in the capital and Moscow, and, after the 1905 Revolution, in nine additional cities. Yet Russian women could not enroll formally at the regular universities before 1914, and permission to audit, granted in 1905, was withdrawn in 1908.

In Great Britain, the separate women's institutions of higher education founded during the 1870s and 1880s were a response to existing universities' refusal to admit women. Pioneering women students in Cambridge moved into permanent quarters at Girton College in 1873, as did Newnham College students in 1875. Oxford's Somerville College and Lady Margaret Hall dated from 1879. The independent London School of Medicine for Women opened in 1874. The University of London admitted women to degree examinations in 1878, but a half-century elapsed between the founding of Girton and Newnham and Cambridge University's awarding of "titles" of degrees to women in 1923, which was still not the full status finally conferred in 1948. Yet women had long before gained admission to examinations at both Cambridge and Oxford. By 1895 Oxford and Cambridge were the only English universities *not* admitting women to degrees. Oxford granted women degrees as of 1920. Newer, less prestigious "red brick" universities in provincial towns typically admitted women when they opened. All four Scottish universities admitted women to degrees in 1892. Degree access and the opening of twenty-one day teacher-training departments in universities during the 1890s considerably increased women's enrollment: 16 percent (2,670) of students in 1900 in England,

Scotland, and Wales, and nearly 21 percent (4,644) in 1910. In Ireland, women prepared for Royal University exams at girls' schools until Trinity College, Dublin, opened to women in 1904 and the Universities Act of 1908 broadened access.

When British universities incorporated previously separate women's colleges, coeducation did not necessarily eliminate all discomfort with women's presence. At the University of Glasgow, for example, Queen Margaret College, founded in 1883 by a women's organization, merged with the university in 1892, but women students had to use a separate library reading room, sit apart from men during university ceremonies, and, if studying medicine, attend separate anatomy classes. When members of Cambridge University deliberated in 1897 on whether to award degrees to women, opponents placed an effigy of a woman student, wearing bloomers and mounted on a bicycle, near the Senate House.

Social custom, not official policy, delayed women's enrollment in French and Italian universities in large numbers. Custom dictated telling women to enter lecture halls only when professors arrived and to sit separately. The University of Paris was the second European university to admit women, with support from Duruy, the medical faculty dean Adolphe Wurtz, and also Empress Eugénie. Four women began medical studies in 1868, and the first degree was awarded to a woman in 1870. France's *grandes écoles*, more prestigious than universities, remained closed to women, however. Furthermore, for a long time more foreign than French women enrolled: in 1890 the University of Paris had 99 French women students and 111 foreigners; by 1902 French women numbered 276, but foreigners, 336. After 1900, French women's enrollment rose noticeably at all French universities, for the woman student had become less an oddity and more a familiar presence, as was also true elsewhere. By 1914, 2,547 French women studied at universities, as compared to 1,707 foreign women. Fully 55 percent of the French women studied in faculties of letters, 22 percent in sciences, 18 percent in medicine, and the rest in pharmacy and law. The Italian government declared universities open to women in 1875, but two decades later only 121 women were enrolled. By 1914, they were far more numerous.

Other nations also admitted women to universities ahead of the major central European powers. Sweden allowed women to obtain secondary degrees and begin medical studies in 1870, opening faculties other than theology and law in 1873. Denmark followed suit in 1875 (also excluding theology), as did Norway in 1882. Individual women's requests prompted the openings in Finland, the Netherlands, and Denmark. The Russian regime in Finland allowed a woman to enroll in Helsingfors

(Helsinki) in 1870 but treated every admission of a woman as a special exemption until 1901. The Dutch government granted Aletta Jacobs an exceptional admission to medical studies in 1871, generalizing the policy in 1880. The Free University of Brussels accepted women in 1881 and Belgium's two public universities, Ghent and Liège, soon followed, but not the Catholic University of Louvain. A resistant Belgian government responded to women students by tightening entry requirements in 1890. By the late 1870s a few women also studied in Barcelona and Madrid, but Spain, too, imposed obstacles after a woman received a medical degree. Women were barred from classrooms from 1882 until 1888, when they could again audit courses if professors agreed. Only fifteen women received Spanish university degrees by 1900, but in 1910, when formal barriers were lifted, there were eighty women students, largely in humanities and medicine. In the Balkans, Romania's universities admitted women to some faculties during the 1880s, followed by Serbia's University of Belgrade in 1888, the University of Athens in 1890, and Bulgaria's Sofia University in 1901. Some Serb and Bulgarian women also studied medicine at foreign universities while their own countries lacked medical schools.

In Austria-Hungary and Germany, the first women university graduates, like many Russians, obtained degrees in Switzerland, and their wish to utilize diplomas at home spurred demands for opening universities to women. Czech and German women applied pressure toward that end in Austria. Before the 1890s, two Czech women had earned medical degrees outside Austria, and in 1889 Krásnohorská published an open letter to Dr. Anna Bayerová, stating the hope that one day she could return from Switzerland to practice. Seven hundred women signed that letter, and in February 1890 Krásnohorská published a petition to the Austrian legislature in the *Women's Gazette*, asking that universities be opened to women. The Czech Women's Industrial and Commercial Training Association collected 4,810 signatures for it, and six Viennese women's groups with a combined membership of 3,500 made a similar request. Although the legislature did not act, Emperor Franz Josef allowed a Swiss-educated ophthalmologist to practice with her husband in Salzburg. The women campaigners took heart, and started private schools to prepare young women to pass the *Matura*, as previously noted. Hungary opened university philosophy and medical faculties to women in 1895, and Austria soon followed suit. Its education ministry ruled in 1896 that Austrian women with foreign medical degrees could practice if they also passed Austrian examinations. Women gained access to Austrian philosophy faculties in 1897 and to medicine in 1900 – despite some male students' protests – but law faculties were inaccessible until after the World War. Baden in 1900 became the first German state allowing women's matriculation in universities. Prussian universities, including Berlin, opened fully in 1908, with all German universities accessible by 1909. A majority of German women students enrolled in humanities programs, as in other countries. Jewish women were also noticeable among pioneering Austrian and Prussian women students: about a third of women enrolled at the University of Vienna in 1914, and at Prussian universities, 18 percent of women in 1908 and 28 percent of women medical students in 1911. Jews were then about one percent of Prussia's population.

In sum, on the eve of World War I, women were over 20 percent of university students in Great Britain, 16 percent in Finland, 10 percent in France, 8 percent in Austria and Romania, 6–7 percent in Germany and Italy, and 3 percent in Belgium. The comparable Russian figure was 27 percent, but women were restricted to special higher courses and not part of the established universities.

Once graduated from universities, women faced both formal and attitudinal obstacles to entering prestigious professions, such as medicine and law, or gaining access to higher-level civil service ranks, as is noted in Chapter 6. Access to university professoriates was also problematical. Here the familiar arguments about the value of women teachers' maternal and feminine qualities for instructing young children or female students were not helpful and, indeed, could be turned against ambitious women hoping to demonstrate that their intellectual abilities equaled those of men. Although women students attended many universities by 1914, women in a professorial capacity were rare exceptions. Certain research appointments and subordinate posts proved less difficult to obtain, but many male colleagues resented the award of such posts to women. For feminists eager to highlight women's contributions to advancing knowledge in universities, mathematician Sofia Kovalevskaia and physicist Marie Curie became the most widely cited examples.

Kovalevskaia (1850–91), born in Moscow, obtained a post in mathematics in Stockholm in 1883. The daughter of an aristocratic Russian general, she was taught at home by tutors and studied higher mathematics because a family friend who taught at the St. Petersburg naval school recognised her aptitude. During the 1860s, she shared with other young Russians the dreams of "liberty and universal enlightenment," described in her later memoir.[9] She married Vladimir

---

[9] Sofia Kovalevskaia, *Recollections of Childhood*, trans. Isabel F. Hapgood (New York: Century, 1895), 161.

Kovalevsky in order to escape parental control and accompanied him to Germany to study. From Heidelberg she went on to Berlin, where Karl Weierstrass tutored her privately from 1871 to 1874 because she could not formally enroll. Three highly original papers enabled her to receive a doctorate in absentia from the University of Göttingen. She published her important study of partial differential equations in 1875 and the other two papers in 1883 and 1884. In the meantime, she returned to Russia, reconciled with her husband, and gave birth to a daughter. After Vladimir's suicide in 1883, Weierstrass recommended her appointment to the new University of Stockholm, which granted her tenure in 1889, making her modern Europe's first woman university professor. Her advancement provoked controversy, however, for traditionalists objected to a woman becoming a professor. Tenure came after the French Academy of Sciences awarded her a major prize for a paper also honored by the Swedish Academy of Sciences and the Russian Academy of Sciences, which made her a member. A brilliant mathematician, she was a complex woman who wrote autobiographical novels as well.

Most women teaching at universities before 1914 were not tenured professors like Kovalevskaia, but their exceptional appointments still attracted attention. Switzerland was a leader in appointing women to lectureships, including the rank of *Privatdozent*, a traditional stepping stone to higher posts. As in Germany, the rank carried no official pay but enabled ambitious scholars to demonstrate their ability to attract students who paid for instruction. The University of Zurich designated Emilie Kempin, its first woman law graduate, a lecturer in 1892, and in 1896 the University of Geneva so appointed Austrian-born Ida Welt, whose doctorate was in physical sciences. Geneva had four women lecturers in 1913. The Russian Anna Tumarkin was the first woman promoted in Switzerland to the rank of "extra-ordinary" professor of philosophy, at the University of Bern in 1906, but never reached the top rank of "ordinary" professor before retirement.

Elsewhere in Europe women with doctorates also occasionally gained lectureships or research appointments. By 1910, there were at least four women lecturers in the Netherlands, at Leiden, Utrecht, and Groningen; two in Sweden; and one in Greece. In Rome, Teresa Labriola lectured on law, and Maria Montessori was on her way to international fame for work on early childhood education. Josephine Joteyko, a Polish physician trained in Paris, headed research at a psychology laboratory at the Free University of Brussels as of 1903. Marie von Linden, awarded a doctorate in Tübingen in 1896, became director of a university parasitology laboratory in Bonn in 1908 but was not allowed to teach. A few other

German women scientists also had special academic posts but were excluded from the *Habilitation* and university teaching. Imperial Germany had no woman *Privatdozent*, unlike Austria.

Elise Richter (1865–1943), Austria's first woman university lecturer, began setting milestones in 1897 when, at the age of thirty-two, she was one of the first three women enrolled at the University of Vienna. Daughter of an affluent Jewish physician, she had been taught at home by governesses and tutors. In 1901 she became the first woman awarded an Austrian doctorate and soon received faculty support to become a *Privatdozent* in Vienna, but she had to wait until 1907 for the education ministry to authorize her course in Roman philology. Although never a full professor, she was promoted in 1921. She denied having any "ambition to be a fighter for women's rights" but certainly paved the way for others.[10]

Great Britain had the largest number of women teaching in various capacities at universities, especially because of appointments at women's colleges, but most were tutors, assistant lecturers, or lecturers, often in education or the humanities. By 1913, about 250 women taught at English, Scottish, or Welsh universities, including four at professorial rank. Edith Morley (1875–1964), the first woman to achieve the rank of full professor, was so designated by the University College of Reading in 1908. Her promotion came seven years after the fledgling institution hired her to teach English and only after she threatened to resign if not given the title accorded to other department heads. Yet she still faced controversy over whether men in junior rank should report to a woman. Better known to scholars was classicist Jane Ellen Harrison (1850–1928), educated at home, Cheltenham Ladies College, and Newnham College, Cambridge. Mastering nine modern languages and five "dead" ones, she eventually built a career in the women's college setting, lecturing on classical archaeology at Newnham from 1898 to 1922. She first published books on Greek art and literature while working at the British Museum during the 1880s and, after holding Newnham's first research fellowship, published her famous work on the origins of Greek religion and drama, *Prologomena to the Study of Greek Religion* (1903) and *Themis: A Study of the Social Origins of Greek Religion* (1912). Neither Harrison nor Morley married, nor did most other women lecturers at residential colleges. British universities also employed women supervisory "principals" or "superintendents" at women's colleges and often expected tutors to help monitor students' nonacademic life. Obstacles to gaining research or teaching appointments, other than in universities' teacher-training departments or

---

[10] Quoted in Ernst Pulgram, "*In Pluribus Prima*: Elise Richter (1865–1943)," *Cross Currents* 5 (1986): 430.

Figure 5.4 Marie Curie, Polish-born physicist and winner of two Nobel prizes, in her University of Paris laboratory, 1912.

women's colleges, spurred women to start the British Federation of University Women in 1907.

Polish-born Marie Sklodowska Curie (1867–1934) was the first woman university professor in France (Figure 5.4). She and her husband Pierre were famed for their pioneering work on radioactivity and discovery of radium, which led to their Nobel prize for physics in 1903, shared with Henri Becquerel. Marie's father taught math and her mother ran a girls' school until her early death. One of five children, Marie completed school in Warsaw and worked as a governess for four years, continuing to read widely. In 1891 she moved to Paris to study at the Sorbonne and live with her older married sister, a medical student. She earned degrees in physics and mathematics, and in 1895 married Pierre Curie, an instructor at the School of Industrial Physics and Chemistry. Two daughters were born in 1897 and 1904 – the older, Irène, later a noted physicist. In the meantime, Marie continued research, taught physics at Sèvres, and completed her doctorate. The Nobel prize led to Pierre's appointment to a new chair in physics at the Sorbonne in 1904, with Marie designated his research assistant. She occupied the chair after his sudden death in 1906 and within two years became a titled professor. Her achievements made Curie "known all over the world," a Dutch feminist reminded the International Council of Women in 1909, and French feminists like Hubertine Auclert emphasized the "anomaly" that a woman could teach at the University of Paris but not be allowed to vote.[11]

Dubbed the "mother of radium," Curie also published a pathbreaking treatise on radioactivity in 1910, and in 1911 received the Nobel prize for chemistry, thus becoming the first two-time Nobelist. Yet earlier that year the French Academy of Sciences refused to grant her membership, and some hostile newspapers dismissed her candidacy as an effort to claim credit for her husband's work. The nationalist press was also pleased that someone foreign-born was denied the honor. Negative publicity intensified when, several days before the Nobel announcement, a Paris newspaper published details about her affair with the married physicist Paul Langevin. Although some feminists felt that the scandal harmed their cause, Marguerite Borel, wife of a professor at the École Normale Supérieure, encouraged academicians to support her, and British physicist and suffragist Hertha Ayrton welcomed her for a lengthy private visit in 1912.

Curie's Nobel prizes and Sorbonne status inspired other women in science, providing a powerful example for taking women's intellectual abilities seriously. In 1900, when French feminists and male supporters gathered to celebrate the intellectual accomplishments of the largely self-taught and aged Clémence Royer (1830–1902), translator of Darwin's *Origin of Species*, only 36 French women were enrolled in university science faculties. In 1913, 508 did so. From different generations, both Royer and

---

[11] Anna Polak, "Women as Scientific Investigators," in *Report of the International Council of Women held in Toronto, Canada, June 24–30, 1909*, 2 vols. (Toronto: G. Parker and Sons, 1910), II: 287; Hubertine Auclert, *Le Vote des Femmes* (Paris: Giard et Brière, 1908), 191.

Curie provided refutations of Darwin's contention in the *Descent of Man* (1870) that women's brains were less developed than those of men. Austrian-born Lise Meitner (1878–1968) was among the women recognizing the importance of Curie's example for her own pursuits. Depressed when her schooling ended at the age of fourteen, Meitner later took advantage of the opening of universities to women, in 1906 becoming the second woman awarded a doctorate in physics by the University of Vienna. She moved to Berlin, where Max Planck made her his assistant in 1912 and facilitated her becoming a paid associate at the new Kaiser Wilhelm Institute for Chemistry. Her research appointments and postwar teaching permitted a 31-year collaboration with chemist Otto Hahn on radioactivity, until the Nazis made her remaining in Berlin unsafe.

Conclusion

The push for more substantial teacher training, secondary education, or access to universities that women initiated in most European countries during the 1860s and 1870s produced significant gains for later generations by 1914. Women teachers were half or more of the primary school teachers in many countries and as such less likely to accept lower pay without protest. New public and private secondary schools had opened, and others were reformed and extended. Furthermore, women admitted to universities were no longer isolated individuals. Although still a minority among university students, after 1900 they saw their presence in lecture halls as secure, even if they also sometimes sensed themselves less than fully accepted by male peers. Historians studying social mobility have contrasted the impact of more educational opportunity on women with that on men, arguing that it gave men more chances for upward mobility but essentially let middle-class women maintain their status. Such sociological analysis does not, of course, weigh what education clearly contributed to broadening intellectual interests and thereby enriching individual lives. Many issues of occupational access and professional equality certainly remained to be addressed, as the next chapter also indicates, and some women who encountered discrimination in education or the workplace would join new feminist organizations.

Further reading and reference works

Albisetti, James C. "The Feminization of Teaching in the Nineteenth Century: A Comparative Perspective." *History of Education* 22 (1993): 253–63.
Schooling German Girls and Women: Secondary and Higher Education in the Nineteenth Century. Princeton, N.J.: Princeton University Press, 1988.

Anderson, R. D. *European Universities from the Enlightenment to 1914*. Oxford: Oxford University Press, 2004.

Bakker, Nelleke, and Mineke Van Essen. "No Matter of Principle: The Unproblematic Character of Coeducation in Girls' Secondary Schooling in the Netherlands, ca. 1870–1930." *History of Education Quarterly* 39 (Winter 1999): 454–75.

Burstyn, Joan. *Victorian Education and the Ideal of Womanhood*. New Brunswick, N.J.: Rutgers University Press, 1984.

Clark, Linda L. *Schooling the Daughters of Marianne: Textbooks and the Socialization of Girls in Modern French Primary Schools*. Albany: State University of New York Press, 1984.

Copelman, Dina. *London's Women Teachers: Gender, Class, and Feminism, 1870–1930*. London: Routledge, 1996.

Cullen, Mary, ed. *Girls Don't Do Honours: Irish Women in Education in the 19th and 20th Centuries*. Dublin: Women's Education Bureau, 1987.

Curtis, Sarah A. *Educating the Faithful: Religion, Schooling, and Society in Nineteenth-Century France*. De Kalb: Northern Illinois University Press, 2000.

Dudgeon, Ruth A. "The Forgotten Minority: Women Students in Imperial Russia, 1872–1917." *Russian History / Histoire Russe* 9.1 (1982): 1–26.

Dyhouse, Carol. *Girls Growing Up in Late Victorian and Edwardian England*. London: Routledge and Kegan Paul, 1981.

   No Distinction of Sex? Women in British Universities, 1870–1939. London: University College of London Press, 1995.

Frago, Antonio Viñao. "The History of Literacy in Spain: Evolution, Traits, and Questions." *History of Education Quarterly* 30 (Winter 1990): 573–99.

Freidenreich, Harriet Pass. *Female, Jewish, Educated: The Lives of Central European University Women*. Bloomington: Indiana University Press, 2002.

Gemie, Sharif. *Women and Schooling in France, 1815–1914*. Keele: Keele University Press, 1995.

Gold, Carol. *Educating Middle Class Daughters: Private Girls Schools in Copenhagen, 1790–1820*. Copenhagen: Royal Library Museum Tusculanum Press, 1996.

Graff, Harvey J. *The Legacies of Literacy: Continuities and Contradictions in Western Culture and Society*. Bloomington: Indiana University Press, 1987.

Grew, Raymond, and Patrick Harrigan. *School, State, and Society: The Growth of Elementary Schooling in Nineteenth-Century France, A Quantitative Analysis*. Ann Arbor: University of Michigan Press, 1991.

Harvey, Joy. *"Almost a Man of Genius": Clémence Royer, Feminism and Nineteenth-Century Science*. New Brunswick, N. J.: Rutgers University Press, 1997.

Hunt, Felicity, ed. *Lessons for Life: The Schooling of Girls and Women, 1850–1950*. Oxford: Basil Blackwell, 1987.

Johanson, Christine. *Women's Struggle for Higher Education in Russia, 1855–1900*. Kingston, Ont.: McGill-Queen's University Press, 1987.

Johansson, Ulla, and Christina Florin. "Order in the (Middle) Class! Culture, Class, and Gender in the Swedish State Grammar School, 1850–1914." *Historical Studies in Education / Revue d'Histoire de l'Éducation* 6 (Spring 1994): 21–44.

Jordan, Ellen. "'Making Good Wives and Mothers'? The Transformation of Middle-Class Girls' Education in Nineteenth-Century Britain." *History of Education Quarterly* 31 (Winter 1991): 439–62.

Margadant, Jo Burr. *Madame le Professeur: Women Educators in the Third Republic.* Princeton: Princeton University Press, 1990.

Mazón, Patricia M. *Gender and the Modern Research University: The Admission of Women to German Higher Education, 1865–1914.* Stanford, Calif.: Stanford University Press, 2003.

Meyers, Peter V. "From Conflict to Cooperation: Men and Women Teachers of the Belle Époque." In *The Making of Frenchmen: Current Directions in the History of Education in France, 1679–1979,* ed. Donald N. Baker and Patrick J. Harrigan, 493–505. Waterloo, Ont.: Historical Reflections Press, 1980.

Oram, Alison. *Women Teachers and Feminist Politics, 1900–1939.* Manchester: Manchester University Press, 1996.

Perrone, Fernanda. "Women Academics in England, 1870–1930." *History of Universities* 12 (1993): 339–67.

Purvis, June. "Towards a History of Women's Education in Nineteenth-Century Britain: A Sociological Analysis." *Westminster Studies in Education* 4 (1981): 45–79.

Quartararo, Anne T. *Women Teachers and Popular Education in Nineteenth-Century France: Social Values and Corporate Identity at the Normal School Institution.* Newark: University of Delaware Press, 1995.

Quinn, Susan. *Marie Curie: A Life.* Reading, Mass.: Perseus Books, 1995.

Rendel, Margherita. "How Many Women Academics, 1912–76?" In *Schooling for Women's Work,* ed. Rosemary Deem, 142–59. London: Routledge and Kegan Paul, 1980.

Rogers, Rebecca. *From the Salon to the Schoolroom: Educating Bourgeois Girls in Nineteenth-Century France.* University Park: Pennsylvania State University Press, 2005.

Ruane, Christine. *Gender, Class, and the Professionalization of Russian City Teachers, 1860–1914.* Pittsburgh: University of Pittsburgh Press, 1994.

Schmuck, Patricia A., ed. *Women Educators: Employees of Schools in Western Countries.* Albany: State University of New York Press, 1987.

Shils, Edward, and Carmen Blacker, eds. *Cambridge Women: Twelve Portraits.* Cambridge: Cambridge University Press, 1996.

Tullberg, Rita McWilliams. *Women at Cambridge.* Revised edn. Cambridge: Cambridge University Press, 1998.

Van Essen, Mineke. "Strategies of Women Teachers 1860–1920: Feminization in Dutch Elementary and Secondary Schools from a Comparative Perspective." *History of Education* 28 (1999): 413–33.

Winiarz, Adam. "Girls' Education in the Kingdom of Poland (1815–1915)." In *Women in Polish Society,* ed. Rudolf Jaworski and Bianka Pietrow-Ennker, 91–110. Boulder, Colo.: East European Monographs / Columbia University Press, 1992.

6   From education to other professions

In 1888 Caroline Schultze, a medical student at the University of Paris, concluded her thesis on nineteenth-century women doctors by situating their achievement within "a general movement of intellectual and professional emancipation for women" since the 1850s. The movement had attracted women from all "civilized countries," she wrote, and everywhere they faced – and overcame – obstacles.[1] Schultze, born in Warsaw in Russian Poland in 1867, was but one of the thousands of European women who enrolled in universities during the later nineteenth century and also among the many who sought advanced education in a foreign country when denied it at home.

Extended education enabled ambitious women to look beyond teaching and consider entering professions that were traditionally masculine preserves. The defining features of a profession include specialized knowledge acquired through academic preparation and an occupational ethos understood to benefit the public. As better-educated women, often but not always from the middle classes, gained access to university faculties of medicine, science, humanities, and law, they faced struggles for acceptance when they tried to enter certain professions. Not only deeply entrenched cultural values concerning appropriate gender roles but also laws and institutional rules created obstacles. During the nineteenth century many middle-class professionals – notably doctors, lawyers, and engineers – campaigned to improve their status by advocating stiffer educational standards and formal licensing procedures to control access to their professional corps. Although members of a profession typically prized independent control of its standards, many professionals also pressured governments to preserve and broaden standards or to introduce them if not already in place. Whether imposed by self-regulating professional organizations or by governments, such requirements could disadvantage women, for even when women met educational criteria they might find themselves excluded simply because they were women.

[1] Caroline Schultze, *La Femme-médecin au XIXe siècle* (Paris: Ollier-Henry, 1888), 76.

To cross professional barriers ambitious women often marshaled the same two-pronged arguments that women used in other pursuits. Assertions of intellectual competency equaling men's might be combined with insisting that, for certain functions, women could make distinctive contributions that men presumably could not make. By 1914, women doctors, lawyers, and civil servants with significant responsibilities epitomized a new kind of professional woman, although they were fewer in number than teachers and nurses. Nursing, like teaching, was seen as an extension of women's traditional nurturing and caring roles, but it had not previously been considered professional work. From women's philanthropic activities there also emerged programs with training for what became the new profession of social worker, employed by public agencies or private charities, as noted in Chapter 4. The emphasis on the utility of women's distinctive qualities or abilities could be a double-edged sword, however, justifying their access to some work but also providing reasons to exclude them from certain endeavors or to pay them less than men. Nonetheless, professional women, like male colleagues, typically enjoyed both higher status and more remuneration than most of the female labor force, largely employed in agriculture, industry, or domestic service. The rise of professional women during the later nineteenth century was part of the growth in white-collar work in the tertiary sector of the economy, a service sector that also included women clerical and commercial employees. This chapter treats some of the new professional women working in areas other than education.

Medical careers: professionalizing nursing

In medicine the two major developments in women's work during the second half of the nineteenth century were the professionalization of nursing and the credentialing of women as doctors. Previously nurses who worked for pay were often seen as little different from servants, and hospitals were deemed refuges for destitute patients rather than centers for the best medical care. Governments, professional organizations, and enterprising individuals all played roles in expanding women's employment in medicine. Governmental action was often decisive for enabling women to become doctors because many medical men did not welcome women as competitors. For nursing, traditionally done by religious orders, family members, or charities, the establishment of professional standards by law or government decree typically came late and in response to private groups' extensive lobbying.

As medicine became more professionalized, the midwives traditionally involved with childbirth found their competence increasingly questioned by doctors, even as some public officials alarmed by high infant mortality rates pushed for improving their training because their services remained in demand. France, like German states, had regulated midwifery since the Old Regime, and in 1892 stiffened regulations. Great Britain in 1902 set new standards for midwives, of whom there were 6,800 in 1911, as compared to 6,205 in the United States, 13,500 in France, 14,641 in Italy, 28,400 in Germany, and over 10,000 in Russia. These statistical differences reflected doctors' greater role in managing childbirth in Britain and North America than in continental Europe.

Historians of nursing, for good reason, have long treated Florence Nightingale's efforts as a watershed in nursing in the Anglo-American world, noting also her international influence. More recently, however, nursing done by religious orders and charities has received greater attention and respect (see Chapter 4), as historians situate the mythic figure of Nightingale within a larger social context. Nightingale wanted to make nursing an attractive and respectable occupation for middle-class women, recognizing that elevating its status required better training. Yet when some nurses encouraged by her efforts began terming their work a "profession," she insisted on using the term "calling," religiously inspired and more in keeping with nursing's past than its future.

Nightingale (1820–1910), the daughter of wealthy English parents who named her after the city of Florence where she was born, craved a sense of purpose in life that socializing or the possibility of marriage could not satisfy. She believed, as a teenager, that God had a different plan for her, but she faced opposition from her parents and sister. She was a complex personality, as the subtitle of one book about her – *Saint, Reformer or Rebel?* – well indicates.[2] Eventually in 1850–51 the family allowed her to go to Kaiserswerth, where German Protestant deaconess-nurses were trained. Kaiserswerth reinforced her belief that good nursing required a vocational commitment, in a quasi-religious sense. Yet Nightingale always rated good training as more important than religio-sity. Back in London, she took charge of a facility for invalid gentlewomen, some of them former governesses. Publicity and fame came to her during the Crimean War (1853–56), when England and France fought to support the Turks against the Russians. As English casualties mounted, some commentators asked why England could send no equivalent of the French Sisters of Charity, already in the Crimea. With support from war ministry officials, Nightingale took 38 nurses to the Black Sea area, organizing a field hospital in November 1854

---

[2] Raymond G. Herbert, ed., *Florence Nightingale: Saint, Reformer or Rebel?* (Malabar, Fla.: Robert E. Krieger, 1981).

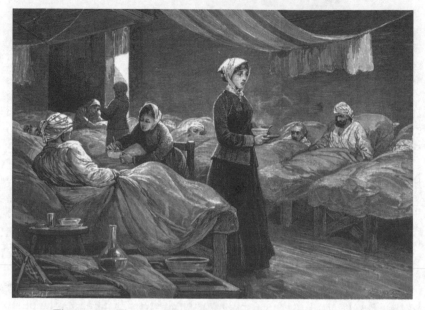

Figure 6.1 Florence Nightingale, organizer of British nursing during the Crimean War (1854–56) and reformer of nursing education, depicted in the barrack hospital at Scutari.

(Figure 6.1). Through better sanitation and discipline she hoped to reduce mortality rates. Her first nurses included 10 Catholic nuns, 14 Anglican sisters, and a Jamaican woman. Some military commanders objected to the women's presence, but other nurses followed. On the opposing side, at least 160 Russian women volunteered as nurses. Although historians debate whether Nightingale's organizational work as "Superintendent of the Female Nursing Establishment in the English General Military Hospitals in Turkey" contributed significantly to lowering casualty rates, her work made her a national heroine in a conflict costing many thousands of lives. Her supporters raised funds, ultimately £50,000, to establish a nurse training facility that opened in 1860 at St. Thomas's Hospital in London and inspired other efforts. Nightingale's report to the Army Sanitary Commission on military medicine and nursing was published and spurred creation of a small Army Nursing Service in 1861. Although in poor health after the war, she managed, as a semi-invalid, to conduct a massive correspondence, attract backers, and use social and political connections to further her goals. She also wielded influence through her *Notes on Nursing* (1859), published in multiple editions.

Nightingale wanted nursing to be controlled by women. She insisted that nurses should not question doctors' medical judgment, but she wanted experienced women to supervise nurses carrying out doctors' orders and oversee hospital support staff doing cleaning and cooking. Citing familiar feminine attributes like compassion and gentleness to emphasize nursing's suitability for women, she also recognized that some women had considerable organizational and leadership skills. She envisioned the ideal relationship between doctor and nurse as a partnership, where each had a defined sphere of activity, much like the division of labor in an idealized Victorian marriage, the husband as breadwinner and the wife as home manager. Because she gendered the division of medical labor, Nightingale was unenthusiastic about younger women's efforts to become doctors. She also thought that, ideally, nurses should remain celibate and live in a residence attached to their hospital, so as to be fully committed to their work. Those preferences did not appeal to many nurses, but single women often valued the chance to do meaningful work with ties to a community of women, and most appreciated nursing's improved reputation. For more ambitious women, the chance to lead other women was appealing. Although large British hospitals had employed "matrons" to run wards in the past, in the new Nightingale era head nurses gained a reputation for being well trained and cultured. As Nightingale hoped, nursing did attract more middle-class women, yet a majority continued to come from humbler backgrounds.

By the 1880s, the nursing staff in many large British hospitals was no longer primarily comprised of untrained, poorly paid women. The training period, combining formal courses and hospital practice, was standardized over time at about three years. Nightingale nurses went to Scotland to reorganize the Edinburgh Royal Infirmary in 1871, five nurses chosen by Nightingale having gone to Australia on a similar mission in 1867. In Liverpool Agnes Jones and other nurses, with support from philanthropist William Rathbone, sought in 1865 to improve workhouse infirmaries, hoping to show other municipalities that trained personnel made a difference. Florence Lees, among the first nurses trained at St. Thomas's, started a campaign to improve district nursing (visiting the poor and infirm at home), especially in rural areas. In some hospitals, however, doctors, not the nurse directors envisioned by Nightingale, controlled new nursing schools.

Issues of professional autonomy, as well as wages and hours, thus remained of concern, and in 1887 Ethel Gordon Fenwick (1857–1947), experienced as a nurse and matron at St. Bartholomew's Hospital, spearheaded the formation of the British Nurses Association (BNA) – over the objections of Nightingale and Mrs. Wardroper, the widowed matron at St. Thomas's Hospital. Within a year the BNA had 1,000 members, and Queen Victoria soon allowed the adding of "Royal" to its title. Fenwick and her husband, a doctor whom she married in 1887, also began a long campaign to secure state licensing of nurses. She saw this goal as vital for securing nurses' professional status, by distinguishing between the qualified and unqualified, but Nightingale and other opponents argued that state requirements for knowledge or length of training would likely be so minimal as to be worthless and could not, in any case, provide guarantees of personal morality. Many male hospital administrators thought state registration would lead to increased costs and less manageable nurses. Doctors divided over licensing, even as Fenwick's husband secured support from many in the British Medical Association. Fenwick herself also pushed the argument that the nation needed trained nurses in wartime, but many military leaders were unenthusiastic. The small army nurse corps of 72 increased only because of the Boer War, during which 900 nurses served. Fenwick, unsurprisingly, believed that "the Nurse question is the Woman question, pure and simple" – the "Woman question" then a familiar label for debates on women's status. To publicize her views, she used *The Nursing Record*, later retitled *The British Journal of Nursing*. After the International Council of Women met in London in 1899, Fenwick and American nursing leader Lavinia Dock created the International Council of Nurses (ICN). Fenwick told its meeting in 1901 in Buffalo, New York, "our profession, like every other, needs regulation and control, and we claim that this power of control should rest in our own hands."[3] She became the first president of the National Council of Nurses for Great Britain and Ireland in 1908. Although state registration of professional nurses began only after the World War, the census by 1881 no longer placed nurses in the same category as domestic servants, and after 1900 classed them among professional occupations. More than 77,000 nurses worked in England and Wales in 1911.

English improvements in training nurses and organizing services attracted international attention. Americans impressed by Nightingale included the mental asylum reformer Dorothea Dix and Clara Barton, both organizers of Union army nurses during the Civil War. Swiss Protestant philanthropists Agénor and Valérie de Gasparin started a nursing school in Lausanne in 1859, wanting to demonstrate that trained

---

[3] Quotations in M. Adelaide Nutting and Lavinia Dock, *A History of Nursing: From the Earliest Times to the Present Day with Special Reference to the Work of the Past Thirty Years*, 4 vols., vols. III and IV by Lavinia Dock (New York: G. P. Putnam's Sons, 1907–12), III: 33; and Margaret Breay and Ethel Gordon Fenwick, *A History of the International Council of Nurses 1899–1925* (Geneva: International Council of Nurses, 1931), 22.

lay women were as proficient as nuns or deaconesses. Mme de Gasparin had written *On Monastic Corporations within Protestantism* (1855) to denounce deaconesses' "glorification of celibacy" and separation from the world.[4] Other European women went to London to learn from St. Thomas's program. Nightingale herself recruited some foreigners, hoping especially to influence Scandinavian countries where the deaconess model was important. To offer a Swedish woman a place at St. Thomas's, she contacted *Home Magazine* editor Sophie Adlersparre, who recommended Emmy Rappe. After eight months in London in 1866, Rappe brought the Nightingale model to Sweden, becoming nursing director at a hospital in Uppsala. The model of the salaried professional nurse reached Germany partly because of Crown Princess Victoria, patroness of the Society of Domestic Hygiene and supporter of nondenominational nurses' training at the Victoria House, started in 1881. Louise Fuhrmann was sent to St. Thomas's to prepare for its reform and attachment to a Berlin public hospital, but other models of nursing still prevailed in Germany. Henny Tscherning, trained at the Copenhagen Municipal Hospital and later its lady superintendent, sought more training at St. Thomas's in 1883. Anna Broms, trained at the Royal Infirmary in Edinburgh, became the first head of Finland's leading nursing school, attached to a new hospital, in 1889, and the Helsinki hospital matron Sophie Mannerheim trained at St. Thomas's and often consulted Nightingale.

Across northern Europe advocates of improved nursing training – philanthropists, doctors, and government officials – argued that knowledgeable nurses could contribute to public health and help doctors make medicine more modern and scientific. Women, in particular, also emphasized that for women needing to work, hospitals or clinics were more desirable workplaces than factories. When poor working conditions or low pay disappointed better-trained nurses, they, like teachers, formed professional organizations, as Fenwick had done. Finnish nurses founded an association in 1898, and Danish nurses, in 1899. The Dutch group Nosokomos, started in 1900, drew members unhappy with doctors' and hospital directors' domination of the older Dutch Association for Sick Nursing. Comparable groups appeared in Germany, Sweden, Switzerland, Norway, and British India. Yet because such groups often linked membership to nursing credentials, they by no means represented

---

[4] Quoted in Jean Baubérot, "The Protestant Woman," trans. Arthur Goldhammer, in *Emerging Feminism from Revolution to World War*. ed. Geneviève Fraisse and Michelle Perrot, vol. IV of *A History of Women in the West*, 5 vols., ed. Georges Duby and Michelle Perrot (Cambridge, Mass.: Harvard University Press, 1993), 204.

a majority of nurses, as situations in Germany and France indicated. By 1907, the ICN included 8,500 members in 17 nursing associations in the United States, 4,300 in 14 English associations, and 1,400 in a German group. Dutch, Danish, and Finnish nurses joined in 1908.

In Germany older nursing traditions competed with the Nightingale model of training and practice. An 1876 survey of 8,681 "trained" nurses revealed that two-thirds were Catholic sisters (5,673); a fifth, Protestant deaconesses (1,760); and 525, Red Cross volunteers. Only 7 percent (633) worked for pay. The increasingly influential Red Cross had trained volunteer nurses during the wars leading to German unification by 1871, and its nurses were the first secular women nurses serving the state. Advocacy of a professional nursing alternative came from women's groups and some doctors. Doctors wanting more control over medical practice often found religious nursing orders' autonomy a nuisance and could also be uncomfortable with upper- and middle-class Red Cross volunteers who were not necessarily docile. Nurse reformer Agnes Karll, trained by the Red Cross, complained that because "religious and charitable bodies" had monopolized nursing, "the importance of professional knowledge was often quite overlooked and religious motives and duties were given front place, naturally resulting in collisions with the claims of science and hygiene."[5]

Karll, a Berlin nurse with independent means and experience in hospital and private duty work, led German efforts to raise salaried nurses' professional status. Aware that nurses not in religious orders greatly feared contracting illness on the job, she and feminist Adele Schreiber arranged a health insurance policy for independent nurses in 1899. Karll and other nurses proposed state licensing of nurses, recommending three years of training – far longer than what religious and Red Cross groups offered – and a qualifying examination. The Women's Federation (BDF) endorsed the proposal, and Karll and allies started the Professional Organization of German Nurses in 1903, with Karll as president. Although some charitable groups and public officials opposed requiring a nursing license, chancellor Bernhard von Bülow supported optional testing, introduced in Prussia in 1907 and adopted by most other German states. Karll arranged for experienced nurses to obtain state certification without a test. By 1909, when a survey identified 55,937 trained German nurses, about half were Catholic or Protestant sisters (38 percent were Catholic), but salaried nurses then numbered 12,000, 22 percent of nurses. State-certified nurses saw themselves as the vanguard of professional nursing. Although some nurses and doctors preferred designating a

[5] Quoted in Nutting and Dock, *History of Nursing*, IV: 22.

trained nurse as a *Pflegerin*, to distinguish her from a traditional *Schwester* (sister), others believed that using the familiar term sister better facilitated public acceptance of professional nurses.

In France efforts to professionalize nursing were often intertwined with conflicts between anticlerical republicans and Catholics during the early Third Republic. As the state moved to replace nuns teaching in public schools with laywomen, republicans on the Paris city council pushed for replacing nuns with lay nurses in public hospitals. Critics of nuns cited congregational rules forbidding them to see unclothed male bodies, even those of infants; unwillingness to deal with venereal disease, many obstetrical and gynecological cases, or unwed mothers; and attempts to impose religious views on unwilling patients. Hospitals often employed male attendants for male patients and laywomen to help with female bodily care. Recent historians have suggested, however, that doctors' complaints about nuns' competence as nurses or hospital managers were also rooted in dislike of their independence. Dr. Désiré Bourneville, a neurologist and Paris city councillor later elected to the legislature, took a delegation to London to study improvements in nursing. Paris secularized seven hospitals between 1878 and 1882, and by 1907 all twenty-seven hospitals and clinics under the Public Assistance administration. Nursing courses for staff and trainees were introduced in 1878 at two hospitals already run by lay staff – Salpetrière (for women) and Bicêtre (for men) – and the Pitié hospital added another. Students in these courses, taught at night because many attendees worked during the day, often needed instruction in basic literacy before medical lessons could begin. Such students were usually working-class women or men, not the middle-class nurses prized by Nightingale. Indeed, Bourneville believed that "women of the people" could better relate to poor patients likely to go to public hospitals, for people with means still preferred home care or private facilities. One veteran employee feted in 1891 for fifty years of service at Salpetrière, Marguerite Bottard, came from a peasant background and was a servant at the hospital before being promoted to nursing and some supervisory duties because of her ability to deal with mentally ill patients. Bourneville and allies also did not envision authoritative women supervisors like the English matrons. Efforts to improve nursing training for young lay women intensified after 1902, amidst heightened conflict over the impending separation of church and state. Although many envisioned the ideal lay nurse as a single woman, resident in a hospital, Bourneville insisted in this politically charged context that married nurses, especially if mothers, could provide more compassionate care, as well as better physical care, than could celibate nuns.

Figure 6.2   Anna Hamilton, French advocate of the Nightingale nursing model and director of nursing at Protestant Hospital, Bordeaux, defending her medical thesis, University of Montpellier, 1900.

By 1900, Dr. Anna Hamilton (1864–1935), part of a second gener-ation of women physicians, was the best-known French advocate of nursing reform on the Nightingale model (Figure 6.2). The daughter of an Anglo-Irish father and French mother, she grew up in Nice. A brother had studied medicine, a sister took nurse's training, and her mother had her read Nightingale's *Notes on Nursing*. After a conventional adolescence, she obtained a *baccalauréat* at the age of twenty-six and began medical study. Family financial reverses interrupted her studies, and she helped run a charitable clinic for children before completing a degree at the University of Montpellier in 1900. As a medical student she saw how doctors' orders were carried out in hospitals and concluded that better care would improve patients' recuperation. Her thesis, a comparative study of hospital nursing, presented information compiled during trips to England, Switzerland, and Italy, as well as to Paris. English hospitals strongly influenced her views. Like Nightingale, she wanted a new gendered division of hospital work, insisting that well-trained women should supervise nurses and aides, and thus challenging a masculine hospital hierarchy. Her emphasis on improved medical training for women supervisors also produced conflict with some philanthropic women involved in training nurses. Hamilton put her ideas into practice after 1901 as head of Bordeaux's Protestant hospital, funded by private donations and municipal subsidies. She reorganized its nursing course, recruiting a London nurse whose family was partly French, Catherine Elston. Bordeaux's mayor laicized the city hospital in 1903, aided by Elston. Republican officials in some other cities also recruited nurses from Bordeaux to reorganize and secularize nursing training. Hamilton headed the Protestant hospital until 1934, publicizing her work at national and international congresses and linking her efforts to the National Council of French Women in 1909. With Bordeaux colleagues she started the journal *La Garde-malade Hospitalière*. Its title – literally, hospital sick guard – was a traditional term for a nurse, her efforts to bring the word *neurse* into French vocabularies not succeeding. After the ICN meeting in Paris in 1907, Hamilton helped found the National Council of Hospital Directresses.

The Nightingale professional model, with leadership by well-trained nurses, did not strike deep roots in France before 1914. A movement associated with France's Protestant minority, English influences, and anticlerical politics clashed with Catholic support for traditional nursing sisters. On the republican side, many doctors resisted empowering a nursing hierarchy in hospitals. When the Paris Public Assistance Administration opened a modern nursing school at the Salpetrière Hospital in 1907, a trained midwife oversaw nursing education and was not allowed to supervise pupils' work in wards. Funds for secularizing hospital nursing were also limited because localities bore the major costs of public facilities. After stormy controversies over secularizing schools and church-state separation, many government leaders urged, but did not insist on, laicizing nursing staff. In Lyon nursing sisters retained support from doctors and many republicans. Secular initiatives did spur changes in nuns' nursing training, just as better-trained public school-teachers and pupils' desire to pass state examinations prompted Catholic schools to make improvements. In Paris the most notable private efforts to reform nurses' training were those of Gabrielle Alphen-Salvador, a feminist, and Léonie Chaptal (1873–1937), a devout Catholic. Influenced by teachers who saw nursing as an alternative to the overcrowded teaching field, the widowed Alphen-Salvador headed a small school opened in 1900. The wealthy Chaptal, sister of a priest, supported charities and decided, as she neared age thirty, to obtain nursing certification from the Pitié hospital and teaching credentials. In 1905 she took charge of a private nursing school which attracted many middle-class Catholics. Like Hamilton, Chaptal advocated state licensing of nurses, pushing that goal after her appointment to the interior ministry's Higher Council of Public Assistance in 1913. As in England, however, state licensing came only after World War I highlighted both the importance of nurses and deficiencies in their training. The French army's nursing service for military hospitals started in 1908, attracting 421 applicants for the first 29 job openings. As medical services grew significantly, the number of Catholic sisters in nursing rose from about 11,000 in the 1870s to 15,000 in 1911, but lay hospital staff (including men and aides other than nurses) grew from about 14,500 in 1880 to 95,000 in 1911, and women's representation in the lay category became proportionately greater.

European nurses also worked in colonial settings, first sent by Catholic orders or Protestant missions, as previously noted. Improving public health in India was on Nightingale's agenda, and by the 1880s both missionary groups and secular philanthropists started hospital training there for nurses. Recent historians often term such efforts a kind of medical imperialism which, like the cultural imperialism in schools, imposed western standards on other peoples' societal norms. Both missionaries and secular donors certainly recognized that if colonized peoples appreciated medical care or schools, they might also value, or at least accept, other aspects of European control. For European women, medicine offered a route to reach colonial women that European men might not be able to travel and thus a way to help reinforce imperialism. Yet medical reformers' professed humanitarian goals were not simply cynical rationales for controlling the colonized.

The sponsors of nursing and midwifery training in India included the Church of England's Zenana Mission Society, eager to reach upper-class women in *purdah* (seclusion in women's quarters, the *zenana*). It supported programs at hospitals in northern India, and Anglican Sisters of All Saints trained European and Indian women in Bombay. Some

English nurses learned local languages. Another Bombay nursing school, opened in 1886 and linked to the Cama Hospital for women and children, was long directed by nurse Edith Atkinson and trained at least 220 Indian nurses by 1910. The Dufferin Fund supported training Indian women as nurses and midwives, as well as doctors and hospital assistants, the training initially run by British professional women. Unlike medical missionaries, the Fund's backers did not want to mix medicine and religious proselytizing because the latter deterred Indians from utilizing facilities. Although skin color and social class usually separated Europeans from most Hindus and Muslims, the English nurses who founded the Trained Nurses Association in India in 1910 rejected creation of a separate section for Indian women as contrary to the goal of professional unity. But the English professional model did not attract many upper-class Indian women to nursing, which was still seen as undesirable menial work.

The London-based Colonial Nursing Association helped British nurses obtain overseas posts, which often paid more than work at home, and some government posts provided pensions. Contributing to a book on women's occupations, the matron of the Colonial Hospital in Trinidad stated in 1914 that colonial nursing required an adventurous spirit and liking of novelty. Yet "the most important part of an English nurse's work," she wrote, was "to make the native nurses, of whatever race ..., see the dignity and possibilities of their profession, and be stirred with the desire to become proficient themselves."[6] The urge to do something different also motivated some of the 178 women sent to Africa by the German Women's Association for Nursing in the Colonies between 1888 and 1907, although most of them returned home after limited periods of service usually spent treating European patients. French nurses, religious and later lay, worked in North African and sub-Saharan territories. Jeanne de Joannis, a marquis's daughter trained under Alphen-Salvador, directed Red Cross nurses at a Casablanca hospital in 1912–13.

Across Europe and in European colonies, increasing numbers of professional nurses thus joined women religious and volunteers in work dominated by women, but not necessarily administered by them. The 1911 English census recorded 77,060 nurses, 86 percent of them single or widowed, and only 1,257 men. A threefold increase had occurred since 1861. Censuses for other major countries revealed a larger masculine presence, often because other hospital workers were included.

[6] A. Fricker, "Nursing in the Colonies," in *Women Workers in Seven Professions*, ed. Edith J. Morley (London: Routledge, 1914), 205.

Women were 80 percent of 89,127 nursing personnel counted in Germany in 1907; 77 percent of 62,740 in France in 1906; and 56 percent of 18,084 in Italy in 1911, a total excluding thousands of nuns doing nursing. Like teaching, nursing had become a significant occupation for women.

Becoming doctors

Women doctors of the late nineteenth century received considerable attention from commentators highlighting recent changes in women's lives and ambitions. The exceptional instances of women credentialed as doctors in previous centuries were often forgotten, although Italian precedents had set the stage for the career of Maria Dalle Donne (1778–1842). Educated by tutors, she obtained a medical degree in 1799 from the University of Bologna, which then had her train midwives, often in her home. Dorothea Erxleben (1715–62), daughter of a doctor who taught her and her brother, was the first woman to receive a full medical degree from a German university, Halle, in 1754, and practiced until her death. Josepha von Siebold (1771–1849), trained by her brother-in-law and licensed in 1807 to deliver babies, later sought a university credential that would command more respect from patients. Her University of Giessen degree in 1815 was the first German obstetrics degree awarded to a woman, and her daughter Charlotte, whom she trained, received a degree two years later. The next generations of women faced more rigid German university barriers, however.

During the 1860s and 1870s, when arguments for women's admission to physicians' ranks multiplied, the precedents cited were often not earlier European cases but rather American examples, starting with Elizabeth Blackwell (1821–1910), who was admitted to a small medical school in Geneva, New York, and graduated in 1849. Born in England, the daughter of a businessman who emigrated to the United States, she had to earn a living after he died, leaving a widow and nine children. The daughters began teaching, which Elizabeth disliked. Nor did she wish to marry. After earning her degree, she sought more training in midwifery at hospitals in Paris and London, returning in 1851 to New York City, where she opened a dispensary, backed by private donors, that became the Infirmary for Women and Children. Her younger sister Emily and German-born Marie Zakrzewska, both with medical degrees from Western Reserve University in Ohio, assisted her. The Blackwells added a medical college in 1868, inspired by the Woman's Medical College in Philadelphia, founded in 1850. When Elizabeth returned to England to practice, Emily oversaw the college, which was open until 1899.

Elizabeth Blackwell's much publicized achievement inspired the first generation of American and British women doctors, and many on the continent. In Copenhagen, teacher Nielsine Nielsen read about American women doctors and initiated requests that led to her becoming Denmark's first woman medical student in 1876 and then the first woman to practice. At an international women's congress in 1889, French doctor Victorine Benoît credited Blackwell with opening doors for women doctors "in both worlds." Like Blackwell, many pioneering women doctors specialized in obstetrics and gynecology or pediatrics.

Elizabeth Garrett (1836–1917), the first English woman doctor, read about Blackwell in the *Englishwoman's Journal* and met her in London in 1859, a contact facilitated by Emily Davies and Barbara Bodichon. Blackwell was the first woman to be listed in the British Medical Register. Garrett's determination to become a doctor met resistance from her parents, who thought it disgraceful, but she eventually won over her father, a businessman. Because no medical school would admit her, she studied privately after first remedying gaps in her boarding school education, gained hospital experience as a surgical nurse, and finally resorted to the alternative of being licensed in 1865 by the Society of Apothecaries. With her father's financial help, she opened a dispensary for women and children, staffed by women. Yet she still wanted a formal degree to validate her status, especially after pharmacists closed the loophole she had used to enter medical practice. Mary Putnam, an American urged by Blackwell to go to Paris after training in Philadelphia, told Garrett that the Paris medical faculty would admit women in 1868, and both enrolled. Garrett wrote a thesis and took final examinations in March 1870, the first woman to receive a French medical degree. Having signed a famous women's suffrage petition in 1866, she took advantage of women's new opportunity to run for school boards, winning election in London in 1870. She married James Anderson, a hospital board member and shipping company employee, and between 1873 and 1877 gave birth to three children, two of whom survived. Garrett thus defied the contemporary belief, shared even by many professional women, that a demanding career was incompatible with marriage and motherhood.

Because of British refusals to admit women to medical study, the activist Sophia Jex-Blake (1840–1912) and Garrett Anderson founded the London School of Medicine for Women (LSMW) in 1874, enlisting Blackwell as professor of gynecology. Garrett Anderson preferred university coeducation, which she experienced in Paris, but agreed that a single-sex school was better than nothing. Jex-Blake and six other women had taken medical courses at the University of Edinburgh, but after male students rioted to protest their presence in 1870, the university refused to let the women graduate. Earning a degree in Switzerland, Jex-Blake continued legal battles to open British medicine to women. Her campaign influenced passage of an 1876 law allowing women to take the physician's licensing exam, provided that a regional medical board, of which there were nineteen, agreed. The Irish College of Physicians formally admitted her to practice in 1877. Students at the LSMW gained experience at the New Hospital for Women, an outgrowth of Garrett Anderson's dispensary, and at the Royal Free Hospital, opened to them in 1877. The University of London also admitted women to examinations for degrees in 1877. Yet the British Medical Association (BMA) voted in 1878 against admitting women, recognizing only Blackwell and Garrett Anderson, who were already members. Men's resistance to women as professional competitors was evident, particularly since 16,000 women had signed a petition stating a preference for women doctors, but opponents often justified resistance with such arguments as women's presumed lack of physical stamina. Edith Pechey, Garrett Anderson, and other women doctors then founded the Registered Medical Women's Association (RMWA), which continued after the BMA ceased excluding women in 1892. The RMWA had 200 members in the London area by 1910, coexisting with two other women's medical societies in northern England and Scotland until the three formed the Medical Women's Federation in 1917.

The LSMW was the only place where women doctors could train in Great Britain until 1886, and about 80 percent of pre-1914 British women doctors trained in a women's medical college. London's other medical schools continued to reject women, even as some provincial universities became more welcoming. Garrett Anderson became dean of the LSMW in 1883, succeeding the first dean, a male doctor, and oversaw fundraising and expansion of the New Hospital. Her quiet persistence and social skills suited her for administrative roles. The more confrontational Jex-Blake left to practice in Edinburgh, where she founded a women's hospital in 1885 and then a women's medical school, taken over by the University of Edinburgh in 1898. The LSMW joined with the University of London in 1948. As LSMW dean until 1903, Garrett Anderson avoided much public advocacy of women's suffrage, the controversial cause prominently engaging her sister Millicent. In retirement, however, she was elected mayor of a Suffolk village in 1908 – the first woman mayor in England – and with her daughter Louisa, a doctor, openly embraced the suffrage movement, endorsed by 538 of 553 British women doctors practicing in 1909.

In France, women's early access to the University of Paris medical faculty set a precedent for provincial universities, and no separate women's medical school was established. Indeed, the separate institutions to which women initially resorted in Britain and the United States were often judged inferior to older and better-funded facilities, although they educated significant numbers of women doctors. The Paris opening came after Madeleine Brès (1839–1925), a trained midwife, asked to enroll in 1866 and was told to first obtain the *baccalauréat*. Drawn to medicine since childhood when she often accompanied her father, a wheelwright, to a hospital in Nîmes where he worked, Brès had married at fifteen and had three children. She, Garrett, Putnam, and Catherine Goncharova, a Russian, entered the medical faculty in 1868.

Already in December 1867 the University of Zurich had awarded a medical degree to Nadezhda Suslova (1843–1918), daughter of a former Russian serf. Her father's aristocratic employer had facilitated education for her and siblings in schools from which their low social status otherwise would have excluded them. After attending a provincial boarding school and the St. Petersburg Institute for Young Noblewomen, she began auditing courses at the Medical Surgical Academy in 1861, her ambitions spurred by her friend Maria Obrucheva, a general's daughter. When women auditors were excluded, Suslova took a professor's advice and went to Zurich, later followed by Bokova-Obrucheva, who entered a "fictitious" marriage to a friend of her brother to overcome parental opposition to her goals. Two British women preceded Bokova-Obrucheva: the widowed Louisa Atkins and Elizabeth Frances Morgan (1843–1927), who had hoped for licensing by the British apothecaries before that possibility closed after Garrett used it. Morgan and her husband, Dr. George Hoggan, established a joint practice, Britain's first husband-wife team of physicians. The first Swiss woman enrolled in Zurich, Marie Voegtlin (1845–1916) was a minister's daughter from a conservative rural area and faced familial, local, and even national opposition to her enrollment. Unlike the other six women at Zurich by 1868, she lacked previous medical training and told a friend, "I feel that I stand here in the name of my entire sex and if I do poorly I can become a curse to my sex."[7] Marrying Dr. Albert Heim, she maintained a successful practice for women and children. Swiss professional women like Voegtlin were exceptional for several decades, however, because most Swiss women lacked secondary degrees required by universities, even as the enrollment of foreign women, particularly Russians, surged.

When Russia barred women from its universities in 1863, only one woman, Varvara Kashevarova (1842–99), could continue medical

---

[7] Quoted in Thomas Neville Bonner, *To the Ends of the Earth: Women's Search for Education in Medicine* (Cambridge, Mass.: Harvard University Press, 1992), 42.

studies there. A poor Jewish orphan and unschooled servant, she became interested in medicine after being hospitalized with typhus. She learned to read with her St. Petersburg employer's children, and at age fifteen married an older merchant, whom she soon left because he opposed her ambitions. Completing a midwifery course in 1862, she worked in the Orenburg military region where Muslim soldiers refused to let their wives see male doctors. So that she could better treat women, the military governor and the war minister facilitated her enrollment in the St. Petersburg Medical Surgical Academy and enabled her to finish her studies. She then faced controversy over whether she could receive a physician's diploma which carried entitlement to academic rank, obtaining it without the rank in 1868. Marrying Professor Mikhail Rudnev, Kashevarova assisted in his pathology laboratory and, heartened by the opening of women's medical courses, pursued a higher degree, for which she learned Latin. She completed a thesis on uterine cancer, in 1878 becoming the first woman awarded the degree of doctor of medicine in Russia, but Rudnev's death soon left her without the protection his status provided. Faced with vicious personal attacks, she moved to Kharkov and treated peasants for eight years before settling in a village near St. Petersburg, opening a private practice, and writing a brief autobiography.

Russia's acceptance of women doctors seemed assured by the late 1870s. At least 40 women doctors served in the Russo-Turkish War of 1877–78, after which their formal title of "learned midwife" was changed to "woman doctor." By 1881, the St. Petersburg medical courses for women – restricted to specialities in obstetrics, gynecology, and pediatrics – had attracted nearly 800 students, 691 of them graduates by 1887. But after Alexander II's assassination, Alexander III closed the women's courses and reinstated the title "learned midwife" for women doctors. Although women already enrolled could complete studies, the empress reportedly said, "We must return these poor souls to their families."[8] Russian women students again flocked to Swiss and French universities, and when women's medical courses reopened in 1897, many Jewish women, facing Russia's quotas on Jewish students, continued studying abroad. After the 1905 Revolution, new women's courses opened in Moscow, Kiev, Odessa, and Kharkov, and by 1914 Russia had more women doctors than any other European country: 1,600 women, about 7 percent of physicians.

---

[8] Emilia Pimenova, "Bygone Days," in *Russia through Women's Eyes: Autobiographies from Tsarist Russia*, ed. Toby W. Clyman and Judith Vowles (New Haven, Conn.: Yale University Press, 1996), 334.

Russian women doctors often worked for local governments, treating poor patients, especially women and children, and usually paid less than male doctors. Dr. Ekaterina Slanskaia published an article in 1894 about one grueling day when she saw forty patients in her St. Petersburg office and then made afternoon house calls in the slums. Anna Shabanova (1848–1932), from a military family with limited resources, also developed a lifelong concern about injustices besetting the poor and women. She went from a boarding school education to the youthful radicalism well portrayed by novelist Chernyshevsky, but after six months in jail she opted to work for reform within the system. Shabanova was the first woman medical student in Helsinki but left to enter the new women's medical courses in St. Petersburg. As a successful pediatrician affiliated with a major children's hospital, she published articles on children's health, promoted first-aid courses for girls' schools, and worked with charitable societies. Shabanova also used philanthropic organizations as a cover for feminist efforts. A. F. Zhegina, a celebrated colleague, was the first woman doctor appointed to a hospital staff, a step in 1885 that she likened to casting "at least one more stone amidst the countless stones that have begun to fill the immense chasm that continues to separate one half of humanity from the other."[9]

French women doctors, despite early access to degrees, also faced professional obstacles. Brès, the first French woman doctor, worked at a Paris hospital while still a student during the Franco-Prussian War, yet after the war was barred from competing for the *externat* – equivalent to an internship. Completing her thesis in 1875, she specialized in pediatrics. She also published books on child care and edited a journal on women's and children's health, her expertise prompting invitations to speak to nursery school teachers. Blanche Edwards (1858–1941) and American-born Augusta Klumpke (1859–1937), medical students since 1878, became the first women *externes* in 1882. Edwards, daughter of a doctor born in England and educated in France, often accompanied him on visits to patients' homes when she was young, and until his death he escorted her to the Sorbonne. After receiving degrees, Edwards and Klumpke asked to compete for the *internat*, a hospital residency. A storm of controversy ensued, and when the Paris city government intervened in their favor in 1885, students in the Latin Quarter burned an effigy of Edwards. Klumpke was appointed to a hospital where male residents refused to let her eat meals with them. Anna Hamilton faced no significant resistance until ready to defend her thesis on nursing at

[9] Quoted in Barbara Alpern Engel, *Mothers and Daughters: Women of the Intelligentsia in Nineteenth-Century Russia* (Cambridge: Cambridge University Press, 1983), 170.

Montpellier in 1900. The defense drew an audience of 200, word having circulated that her director found it controversial, but another initially skeptical examiner praised her for a thesis likely to be widely read. Edwards and Klumpke, like Brès, had lengthy careers. Klumpke specialized in neurology with her husband Jules Déjerine. Edwards, married to Dr. Henri Pilliet, was widowed in 1898 with three children. Aided by a loyal servant, she managed to combine a private practice primarily for women and children with teaching nurses at the Salpetrière hospital, seeing pregnant women and new mothers at one of Bequet de Vienne's facilities for poor women, serving as doctor for a girls' secondary school, and instructing Red Cross volunteers. She also became a familiar presence at feminist congresses and joined the League for Women's Rights.

The early examples of successful French women doctors encouraged others to overcome obstacles posed by social custom and lack of *baccalauréat* preparation in girls' schools. Although foreign women studying medicine in France's universities long outnumbered French women, by 1904 more than half of the 540 women medical students were French, and about 200 women doctors were practicing, a third of them in Paris. By 1914, 657 French women studied medicine, and 573 women were among France's 20,000 doctors. There were also 326 women dentists and 609 women pharmacists or pharmacy assistants, but far more – 13,500 – were midwives.

Imperial Germany's first women doctors, Emilie Lehmus and Franziska Tiburtius, obtained degrees in Zurich, where about 150 German women studied medicine before women's study in Germany became possible. Both were encouraged by Henriette Hirschfeld-Tiburtius (1834–1911), the first German woman dentist. A pastor's daughter employed as a housekeeper after being widowed, Hirschfeld became interested in dentistry because of experiencing painful tooth problems and poor treatment. She studied in Philadelphia, received a degree in 1869, and opened a practice in Berlin. Lehmus (1841–1932) was the daughter of a Bavarian pastor who tutored her in Latin when she decided to leave teaching for medicine. Tiburtius (1843–1927), also a certified teacher, was a farmer's daughter and sister of a doctor, Hirschfeld's second husband. After completing degrees, Lehmus in 1874 and Tiburtius in 1876, each gained experience at a maternity clinic in Dresden, recommended to its chief by their Zurich friend Voegtlin who had worked there. They could not, as women, take a certifying examination for German doctors, but they could legally give medical advice, so long as they did not claim to be certified doctors. They opened a women's clinic in 1877, with funds raised by Hirschfeld-Tiburtius and other women involved in the charitable work that she undertook in addition to her dental practice and caring for two children. For fifteen years, Lehmus and Tiburtius were Berlin's only women doctors, treating many women and children, even though male doctors had to sign their prescriptions. Similarly, the English-born Hope Adams-Lehmann, who began practicing in Frankfurt in 1881 after receiving a Bern degree, had her doctor husband sign documents. When male doctors resentful of the successful Lehmus-Tiburtius practice questioned their credentials, they countered by advertising that their degrees were from Zurich, which enhanced their reputation. Lehmus retired around 1900. Tiburtius continued practicing and later published a memoir. She also supported the BDF's educational agenda and advocated hiring women doctors for girls' schools because they well understood the "highly developed nervous organism of girls" and so could influence "capricious and often strange dispositions."[10]

The extensive campaigning of German women's groups to secure women doctors' certification also utilized gender-specific arguments. They claimed that women doctors would promote better national health because many women patients were more comfortable with women doctors and so would seek treatment more often. One petition to the Reichstag in 1891 had 55,000 signatories, 15,000 of them men. Changes in German policy came after important decisions in neighboring Austria-Hungary, where Emperor Franz Josef allowed Swiss-educated Rose Kerschbaumer to practice in her husband's eye clinic in 1890 and placed two Swiss-trained women doctors on the Austrian state payroll in 1892. Anna Bayerová (1852–1924), the first Czech woman doctor, and Polish doctor Teodora Krajewska (1854–1935) took new posts in remote Bosnia-Herzegovina, their duties including treatment of Muslim women. Austria allowed certification of women with foreign medical degrees in 1896 and opened medical study to women in 1900. As of 1897, women could also practice in Hungary, where previously the first woman doctor, Countess Vilma Hugonay (1847–1922), had been restricted to midwifery after receiving a Zurich degree in 1879. Germany finally permitted women who had audited German medical courses or earned foreign degrees to take the physicians' certifying examination in 1899. After women could formally enroll in German universities, including Prussia's in 1908, more took up medicine. By 1914, only Russia had more women medical students: 4,414, as compared to 1,027 in Germany. About 200 German women doctors then practiced, a quarter of them Jewish.

---

[10] Franziska Tiburtius, "The Development of the Study of Medicine for Women in Germany, and Present Status," in *Report of the International Council of Women held in Toronto, Canada, June 24–30, 1909*, 2 vols. (Toronto: G. Parker and Sons, 1910), II: 297.

The pioneering Dutch woman doctor, Aletta Jacobs (1854–1929), fascinated by the medical conversations of her father and an older brother, both doctors, decided to become a doctor before realizing the problems that posed for a woman. The eighth of eleven children, five of them girls, she was educated at a local school in Sappemeer and at home. Her mother, annoyed by her adolescent indifference to housekeeping, tried apprenticing her to a dressmaker, but her father taught her French, German, Latin, and Greek, and arranged for her to audit courses at the local boys' high school, their town lacking one for girls. He also persuaded the prime minister to allow her to study medicine, on an exceptional basis, at the University of Groningen in 1871. As the first Dutch woman university student, Aletta was the subject of "considerable commotion" in the press.[11] After receiving her degree and visiting London in 1879, she practiced in Amsterdam, where her fee-paying patients were mostly women. Under Trades Union Council auspices she also gave talks on infant care and offered free clinics twice a week for poor women and children. She married the progressive reformer Carel Gerritsen in 1892 and continued working, a solace after their only child died soon after birth. Jacobs paved the way for other Dutch women in medicine. Her older sister Charlotte became the country's first woman pharmacist in 1881. The second Dutch woman doctor, Catherine van Tussenbroek (1852–1925), was a former teacher who entered the University of Utrecht in 1880. At least ninety women doctors were practicing by 1913.

Jacobs also became known as a medical pioneer in birth control. When women patients requested advice on preventing conception, Jacobs believed that for medical, economic, and ethical reasons she should do more than advise abstinence. Too frequent pregnancies could endanger women's lives, she argued, and children born into dire poverty might "handicap both their parents and the community." In 1882 she began fitting women with the diaphragm developed and publicized by the German doctor Wilhelm Mensinga. Her birth control activity, like that of the Dutch Neo-Malthusian League, was controversial, however, and the Netherlands was not unique in this regard (see Chapter 7). Critics claimed that birth control promoted sexual activity outside of marriage, and Catholics objected to interfering with natural processes. Jacobs also published *Woman, Her Structure and Internal Organs* (1898), explaining that nothing about female anatomy was available for general readers like her patients. Steady demand for the illustrated book led to a fifth

---

[11] Aletta Jacobs, *Memories: My Life as an International Leader in Health, Suffrage, and Peace*, ed. Harriet Feinberg, trans. Annie Wright (New York: Feminist Press, 1996), 16.

Figure 6.3 Aletta Jacobs, first Dutch woman doctor, advocate of birth control, and feminist, 1904.

reprinting in the 1920s. After Gerritsen's death, she retired from medicine and devoted herself to feminist causes. In 1904 admirers celebrated her 25-year medical career, one newspaper opining that women "are now generally considered to be men's intellectual equals ... largely due to the campaigns and personal example of Dr. Aletta Jacobs"[12]

---

[12] Quotations from *European Women: A Documentary History, 1789–1945*, ed. Eleanor S. Riemer and John C. Fout (New York: Schocken, 1980), 216; and Jacobs, *Memories*, 132.

(Figure 6.3). Yet some pioneering Dutch women doctors found van Tussenbroek a less controversial role model.

Madeleine Pelletier (1874–1939), a bold younger doctor, advocated birth control in France at a time when many politicians, obsessed with the threat of depopulation vis-à-vis Germany, called for more, not fewer, births. From a poor Parisian family, she reacted strongly against her mother's religiosity and the nuns who taught her, preferring the beliefs of her anticlerical father, who was disabled by a stroke. The family lived behind the shop where her mother sold vegetables. Writing later about her mother's sloppy housekeeping, she linked her mother's many miscarriages to unhygienic habits. Pelletier left school at age twelve and worked at various jobs. She also discovered anarchism and feminism, eventually concluding that to gain personal freedom she needed further education and more agreeable employment. She studied on her own for the *baccalauréat* and, with a city scholarship, entered medical school in 1898. She wanted to specialize in psychiatry but, as a woman, was initially denied permission to compete for a residency in a psychiatric hospital. The feminist newspaper *La Fronde* took up her cause, contending that women nurses' presence in psychiatric asylums negated arguments about their dangers for women doctors, and she prevailed. Pelletier began a general practice but, with few patients, also continued working for the public mental health service. After failing an exam for a permanent position in that service in 1906, she became a doctor for women in the Post, Telegraph, and Telephone administration. In 1911 she published a book advocating women's right to contraception and abortion, and she eventually performed abortions. Not only feminist and socialist beliefs but also her appearance made Pelletier controversial. Favoring very short hair and male garb, she was committed to celibacy, considering sexual activity distasteful.

In Italy, Maria Montessori (1870–1952) was for a time the best-known woman doctor, although not the first. Only five women received medical degrees between 1876 and 1890, and not all practiced. Mary Valleda Farne, recipient of a University of Turin degree in 1878, was a medical assistant at Rome's main hospital and, with support from Queen Margherita, became a court physician, but she had difficulty attracting patients to private practice. Giuseppina Catani, with a Bologna degree, followed Dalle Donne's earlier path and became a lecturer in pathology at the university in 1889. Montessori, daughter of a middle-class civil servant, attended public schools in Rome and entered the University of Rome in 1890 to study science in preparation for the medical program, becoming the university's second woman medical graduate in 1896. Her mother supported her ambitions, but her father long thought a medical career inappropriate for women. Nonetheless, he walked her to university classes and took pride in her achievements. After completing a thesis on paranoia, Maria worked in the women's wards of a hospital, started a private practice, and also volunteered at a psychiatric clinic linked to the university. Her presentation at an international women's congress in Berlin in 1896, like her later addresses at Italian medical and pedagogical conferences, received much press coverage. Many of the 200 articles about her between 1892 and 1900 reported not only on what she said but also her attractive appearance. One of 29 women doctors in 1901, she was one of 83 in 1911.

Montessori's work at the psychiatric clinic and research on the learning ability of children deemed mentally deficient shaped her future, professionally and personally. She audited pedagogy courses, worked with the National League for Education of Retarded Children, and with Dr. Giuseppe Montesano became co-director of the Orthophrenic School, opened in 1900 to train teachers of retarded children. She also lectured on hygiene and anthropology at Rome's Higher Institution for Women Teachers from 1899 to 1906 and 1911 to 1916. Although increasingly involved in pedagogy, she did not fully abandon medical practice until 1910, when she was forty and better-known for her approach to early childhood education. In 1907 she began applying her methods for improving retarded children's learning to a larger population of young children in Rome's impoverished San Lorenzo district, site of the first *casa dei bambini* (children's house) which made her famous. She stressed letting children discover things for themselves, recommending – like earlier French pedagogues Marie Pape-Carpantier and Kergomard – that activities promoting physical coordination and sensory awareness should precede intellectual training. Recent biographers also link a hidden aspect of Montessori's life to her concerns with early childhood education, suggesting that the latter was compensation for neglect of her own child. Never married, she gave birth to a son, Mario, in 1898 and sent him to live with a rural family, visiting secretly. After the father, Montesano, married in 1901, she left the Orthophrenic School and refocused her pedagogical interests, while still practicing medicine and lecturing at the University of Rome. She brought Mario to Rome only after her mother's death in 1912, introducing him as an adopted child. In the meantime, her "children's houses" in various Italian cities attracted international visitors, especially after 1909 when her book on methods appeared. It was translated into English as *The Montessori Method* (1912) and into twenty other languages. During her first lecture tour in the United States in 1913, the *New York Tribune* hailed her as "the most interesting woman in Europe," and magazine publisher

Samuel McClure introduced her in Carnegie Hall as "the greatest woman educator in history."[13] Her emphasis on letting children individually choose their learning activities struck proponents of competing kindergarten methods as inadequate for helping them become part of a group, however. As doctor and then teacher, the successful Montessori projected an image of professional expertise in Italy and internationally.

Women doctors, like nurses and teachers, also pursued careers in overseas empires, for reasons that included religious vocation, family ties, and seeking opportunities or adventure unavailable at home. The need for women doctors in British India figured in parliamentary debates preceding the 1876 law enabling women doctors to practice, because women in purdah, more often Muslim than Hindu, shunned male doctors. The first woman missionary doctor in India, the American Clara Swain, arrived in 1869, and British women medical missionaries followed. The Zenana Mission Society sent Fanny Butler, an early LSMW graduate. Mary Ann Scharlieb (1845–1930), wife of an attorney, convinced a British governor in 1875 to allow her and three other women to enter the Madras Medical College, despite its superintendent's opposition. One of the first women qualified for a medical license in India, Scharlieb obtained more training at the LSMW. Issues of caste and class, as well as gender, influenced British approaches to medical care and training for Indian women. Because medical missionaries were often associated with lower-class patients, some women, philanthropists, and officials pressed for other options for Indian women of higher status and, like Dr. Frances Morgan Hoggan writing in the *Contemporary Review*, affirmed Indian women's right to shun male doctors. Parsi philanthropists, notably Pestonji Cama, funded a women's and children's hospital in 1883. Scharlieb and medical missionary Elizabeth Bielby spoke to Queen Victoria, who asked Lady Harriot Dufferin, wife of the viceroy for India, to take an interest in women's health. In 1885 English and Indian benefactors started the National Association for Supplying Medical Aid to the Women of India, soon known as the Dufferin Fund. Edith Pechey (1845–1908), graduated from the University of Bern after participating in Jex-Blake's failed effort in Edinburgh, left an English practice to work in Bombay and became senior medical officer at the Cama Hospital, also establishing a nursing school. Bielby, with an LSMW degree, headed a hospital in Lahore. Scharlieb helped start the Victoria Hospital for Caste and Gosha women in Madras in 1884 and taught at the Madras Medical

---

[13] Quoted in Rita Kramer, *Maria Montessori: A Biography* (Reading, Mass.: Perseus Books, 1988; first pub. 1976), 186, 194.

College before returning to London and becoming chief surgeon at the New Hospital for Women.

Indian women's pursuit of medical degrees began with Anandibai Joshi (1865–87), who trained in Philadelphia but died soon afterwards. Dr. Kandambini Ganguly (1861–1923) studied at the Calcutta Medical College, opened to women in 1883. Rukhmabai (1864–1951), a Hindu, risked imprisonment when she rejected a marriage agreement made by her family and went to London to study medicine in 1889. Her well-publicized story also heightened British feminists' anger about child-marriages. Returning to India as an obstetrician, she later oversaw a women's hospital. The widow Haimavati Sen (1867–1932) benefited from the Dufferin Fund, which provided scholarships for study in Britain or India and paid staff salaries. Trained at a school for women hospital assistants, she later ran a women's hospital in Bengal.

By 1900, the Dufferin Fund's regional and local branches helped sponsor 94 hospitals employing at least 100 women doctors, 35 of them with European or American diplomas and the others graduates of Hindu medical schools or the new Ludhiana Medical College for Christian Women, started in 1894 by Dr. Edith Brown (1864–1956). Also receiving government aid, the Fund's 160 hospitals and clinics treated, by 1910, more than 2 million Indian women each year, out of a population of 100 million women. To promote professional interests, British women doctors in India formed a medical women's association in 1907 – paralleling the nursing superintendents' association – and because Britain's Indian Medical Service employed only men with military rank, they lobbied for a comparable women's service. The government refused to create an official service but, under Dufferin Fund auspices, subsidized the Women's Medical Service. It began in January 1914, and Dr. Margaret Balfour soon became Assistant to the Inspector General of Civil Hospitals in India.

Women also pursued medical careers in other European empires. Charlotte Jacobs (1847–1916), the first Dutch woman pharmacist, worked for two years at a Utrecht hospital before going to Djakarta in the East Indies, where she worked until 1913 and advocated education for Indonesian girls. At least eleven women doctors practiced in Dutch colonies by 1909. In French North Africa, the government sent Dorothée Chellier, the first woman graduate of the medical school in Algiers, to report on women's health in remote areas. Because Muslim women shunned male doctors, authorities employed women in public facilities for women and children. Dr. Françoise Entz Legey directed the first such clinic in Algiers and later established one in Marrakesh, Morocco. The Algiers clinic treated thousands of patients after 1900, and by 1913 women doctors also headed eight other clinics. Dr. Angeliki Panajiotatou (1875–1954), one of the first two women doctors to graduate from the University of Athens in 1896, moved to British-controlled Egypt for hospital appointments unavailable to her in Greece.

Despite public skepticism, the hostility of many male medical students and doctors, and extended opposition from certain governments, by 1914 women had become established as doctors, dentists, and pharmacists – even if only as a small percentage of professionals in these categories. Their numbers as doctors ranged from about 1,600 in Russia, to nearly 600 or more in Great Britain and France, about 200 in Germany, between 50 and 100 in Italy, Denmark, the Netherlands, and Bulgaria, to fewer elsewhere. The last prewar British and French censuses each recorded over 250 women in dentistry. The pioneering medical women, born before 1860 or educated before the 1890s, typically faced more resistance, formal or informal, than a younger prewar generation. Scharlieb, later commenting on the reception of British women doctors by the medical profession and general public during the 1880s, put it starkly: "No one welcomed us, no one wanted us."[14] When private practices were difficult to establish, some women doctors welcomed working for governments in public clinics or girls' schools. To justify their professional status, many emphasized the distinctive contributions that they, as women doctors, could make in treating children and other women, a strategy used by contemporary women in many other positions.

The legal profession

The woman lawyer appeared noticeably later than the woman doctor in most European countries and aroused greater controversy. Even when women could study law and earn degrees, they often faced barriers to practicing law or entering professional civil service ranks open to men with law degrees. Yet many pioneering women law students had hoped for a different outcome, not foreseeing their exclusion from practice in many nations until after World War I, often for reasons similar to those used to deny women the vote. Whereas contemporaries might regard women doctors' work as an extension of women's traditional caring roles, many objected that legal practice would take women into courts or

---

[14] Mary Scharlieb, "Foreword," to *The Work of Medical Women in India*, by Margaret I. Balfour and Ruth Young (Bombay: Humphrey Milford at Oxford University Press, 1929), ix.

other public spaces inappropriate for them. Why did some women want to enter this traditionally male profession, and why did certain countries admit women to the bar before 1914?

By the time that the first European women sought admission to legal practice, some American states had set precedents. In 1869 Iowa became the first state to admit a woman to the bar, and by 1890 nineteen more states, the District of Columbia, and one territory had done so. In London Eliza Orme (1848–1937) attended law lectures at University College by 1871 and established a business drawing up documents for lawyers, but she did not receive a degree until 1888 and the English bar remained closed to women until after 1918. At least five other European women held law degrees by 1888: the Russian Anna Evreinova, on an exceptional basis from the University of Leipzig in 1873; Lydia Poët from the University of Turin in 1881; Emilie Kempin-Spyri from the University of Zurich in 1887; Marie Popelin from the Free University of Brussels in 1888; and Romanian Sarmisa Bilcesco with a *licence* from the University of Paris in 1887 and a doctorate in 1890. But they could not practice law. The bar in Turin actually admitted Poët before Italian courts blocked her in 1883 and later. She then worked in her brother's law office. Kempin-Spyri, married and mother of three, lectured on Roman law in New York in 1890–91 and at the University of Zurich from 1892 to 1895, but by the time that a referendum in Zurich opened legal practice to women in 1898, she suffered from a fatal cancer. Zurich's first practicing woman lawyer was German-born Anna Mackenroth, who earned a degree in 1894 and acquired Swiss citizenship. The angry Popelin (1846–1913) took her advocacy for women lawyers to international feminist meetings, and she, two male lawyers, and Isala Van Diest, Belgium's first woman doctor, founded the Belgian League for Women's Rights in 1892.

Before the canton of Zurich acted, Sweden had set a national precedent that France followed. Elsa Eschelson became Sweden's first woman lawyer after the legislature opened the legal profession to women in 1896. France admitted women to the bar in 1900, through a law that owed much to the efforts of Jeanne Chauvin and other women, as well as to key male politicians ready to brave controversy over letting women into another public arena. Chauvin (1862–1926), from a middle-class family, studied privately to pass *baccalauréat* exams in 1884–85 and enrolled in the Paris law faculty, as did her younger brother. After their father's death, Jeanne needed to work. She was the first French woman to earn a *licence* in law (1890) and a law doctorate (1892) (Figure 6.4). Male students' protests disrupted her scheduled defense of a thesis on the history of professions open to women, and when it later took

Figure 6.4 Jeanne Chauvin, pioneering woman lawyer who instigated a campaign to permit French women to practice law.

place, hostile students applauded professors' objections to her statements about women's rights. Then followed Chauvin's widely publicized campaign to practice law after the Paris bar refused to admit her. For income, she began teaching a special law course in Paris girls' *lycées* and published a law manual for women.

Chauvin and feminist supporters used a familiar two-pronged approach in advocacy for women lawyers. On the one hand, they cited an

1848 law regarding the right of all persons to work, and they noted precedents elsewhere. *La Fronde* reported, for example, that the United States had at least 120 women lawyers. On the other hand, in keeping with contemporary rationales used by many employed women, they also insisted that women could make distinctive contributions to the legal profession. Chauvin stated that her personal goal, and by extension one for other women lawyers, was advocacy for poor children and needy mothers in cases of "homelessness, larceny, divorce, separations" where her "role as defender will seem wholly natural – even to my colleagues." She also insisted that women lawyers could have better rapport with women clients. Opposition took the form not only of speeches and publications but also of caricatures, including Adolphe Willette's vulgar and widely reproduced image drawn for *Le Courrier Français* in 1897. It featured Chauvin flinging open a lawyer's robe to expose her breasts and was captioned her "final and best arguments."[15] After the Paris bar's rejection of Chauvin was upheld in court, her campaign, endorsed by politicians René Viviani and Raymond Poincaré, received at least 7,000 press notices in 1898 alone. The law of 1 December 1900 enabled women to become lawyers. Chauvin was the second woman admitted to the Paris bar. The first was the less controversial and politically well-connected Olga Balachowsky-Petit, Russian-born and married to a lawyer working for the minister of Commerce.

Chauvin, like Popelin, became a familiar figure at feminist meetings. Her reports at an international congress on women's organizations in Paris in June 1900 criticized French husbands' exclusive right to make decisions regarding children and also unmarried fathers' lack of obligations to children they refused to recognize. She helped organize the September 1900 international women's rights congress. Her first court case in 1901 in a provincial town entailed representing a woman corset maker accused of copying another maker's design. After a 1912 law allowed unmarried mothers to pursue legal action against their child's father, she and other women lawyers took on cases involving proof of paternity. Chauvin's controversial public image evidently deterred potential clients, however. Her major source of income was *lycée* teaching, and that limited her availability to clients.

Chauvin paved the way for other French women lawyers, but their numbers remained small before 1914. Most women university students chose other areas of study. Only in 1912–13 did French women law

---

[15] Quotations in Sara Kimble, "Justice Redressed: Women, Citizenship, and the Social Uses of the Law in Modern France, 1890–1939" (Ph.D. diss., University of Iowa, 2002), 147, 117.

students at the University of Paris outnumber the foreign-born, forty-three to forty-one. After university study, an aspiring lawyer did an apprenticeship (*stage*) with a practicing lawyer, many of whom did not welcome women *stagiaires*. Only thirty-one women lawyers were at work in France in 1914, most of them (twenty-four) based in Paris and nineteen still finishing a *stage*. Problems with attracting clients and gaining respect from peers caused many women to shun legal studies until after World War I, when some government offices opened higher-level posts to women, making law degrees more useful.

Despite their small numbers, women lawyers' very existence intrigued the press. The daily newspaper *Le Temps* featured ten women lawyers in February 1914, including Agathe Dyvrande, daughter of a judge who had sometimes brought her to court and encouraged a law career. She called her work intellectually challenging and stated that the satisfaction of doing it well compensated for the hostility still exhibited by many male lawyers or the general public. Other interviewees included Maria Vérone and the younger Hélène Miropolsky, Germaine Picard, Suzanne Grinberg, and Marie Galtier. Picard revealed that a photograph of Miropolsky in a lawyer's robe, published in the popular women's magazine *Femina*, helped inspire her ambition, admitting that publicity and fame attracted her. Indeed, more than one journalist commented on the elegant appearance and femininity of Miropolsky, wife of a lawyer. Miropolsky's path to the law had involved conflict with parents, both foreign-born doctors trained in Paris who urged her to study medicine. Like Chauvin, she insisted that women lawyers more readily understood women clients' feelings and motives than did men, and thus better represented them, and she bemoaned many male jurors' unfairness to women accused of crimes.

Vérone (1874–1938) was also well known as a feminist, having joined the League for Women's Rights and become its secretary-general in 1904 (Figure 6.5). The child of freethinking parents of modest means (her father was an accountant, her mother a shopworker), she attended a public school in a Paris suburb, made decorations for women's clothing after her father died, and was a substitute teacher from 1894 to 1897, when she was dismissed for political activities. Her next jobs included singing in a theater chorus and writing for newspapers. A divorced mother with two children when she entered law school, she received a degree at the age of thirty-three. Her first case in 1908 showed her readiness to take on controversial issues, for she secured the acquittal of a woman arrested for participating in a pacifist protest and obtained a light sentence for a male co-defendant. The first woman to plead at the Paris Assizes court, she also defended a woman reporter who ran, illegally, for

Figure 6.5 Maria Vérone, French lawyer and feminist.

a seat on the Paris Municipal Council in 1908. Vérone told *Le Temps* in 1914 that a capable woman lawyer could expect appropriate professional treatment in the largely masculine legal world, but elsewhere she reported encountering great animosity when she began practicing. Vérone, Chauvin, Dyvrande, and Grinberg all participated in the 1913 international women's congress in Paris. Although Miropolsky stated that voting was not the most important issue for women, she also asserted that if most women realized how much current laws disadvantaged them, "they would all be feminists."[16]

Beyond France, several other European countries had small numbers of women lawyers by 1914, but women remained excluded from practicing law in Great Britain, Germany, Austria-Hungary, Russia, Italy, Belgium, Spain, Portugal, and Balkan nations. In the United States, by comparison, the 1910 census counted 558 women lawyers or judges. More women studied law at universities than actually completed degrees, as was also true in medicine, and not all who earned law degrees sought admission to the bar or practiced very long. Adolphine Kok, the first Dutch woman lawyer, was admitted to the bar in Rotterdam in 1903, without government action being required. The Netherlands had twenty women lawyers by 1909. Kok's colleagues included Mrs. Werker-Beaujon, who promoted the introduction of women police assistants after studying Swiss precedents, and Mrs. Bakker van Bosse and Miss Nenn, authors of law manuals for women. Norway, following Sweden's example, opened legal practice to women in 1904, as did Denmark in 1906. At least three Norwegian women were lawyers by 1909, and the first, Sofie Conradine Schjött, later became a judge. Denmark had four women lawyers in 1914. The Swiss canton of Geneva allowed women to practice in 1904 and had four women lawyers by 1913, when Zurich had three.

A few women utilized law degrees in European colonies. Blanche Azoulay was the first woman lawyer in Algiers, her achievement recorded in the Paris press in 1908. Cornelia Sorabji (1866–1954), daughter of an Indian Christian minister, set a precedent for Indian women by studying law in Oxford and Bombay and passing qualifying examinations. Her father, a convert from Poona's Parsi community, and his wife, head of a girls' school, brought up their six daughters and one surviving son to respect both Indian and British customs, and the mother's concerns about women in purdah influenced Cornelia's desire to fight for women. The first woman student at Deccan College, Cornelia earned a degree in 1886, taught in Ahmedabad, and with friends' help entered Somerville College in Oxford in 1888. She was the first woman to take Oxford's examination for the Bachelor of Civil Law in 1892 but was not awarded a degree until 1922. After reading law at a solicitors' firm, she returned to India in 1894, eventually presuming to appear in court as a private person defending women. She passed examinations for a law degree in Bombay and for court pleader in Allahabad, but the Allahabad High Court refused to register her to practice law. The enterprising Sorabji then obtained a unique official appointment. Visiting England again, she

[16] Quoted in Charles Dawbarn, *Makers of New France* (New York: James Pott, 1915), 173.

persuaded the India Office of the value of assigning a woman liaison to the court of wards, which handled property issues affecting widows and their minor children. In 1904 she undertook this advisory post in Bengal. She traveled to visit hundreds of secluded women, writing detailed reports and prizing her role interpreting their lives to the English, as in her *Between the Twilights: Being Studies of Indian Women by One of Themselves* (1908) and later memoirs. Sorabji exemplified one kind of "hybrid identity" that resulted from contacts between colonizers and colonized in an imperialist age. She wore the traditional Indian sari but criticized Indian nationalists seeking independence. After finally obtaining her Oxford degree and admission to the bar, she practiced in India before retiring in England.

For qualified women blocked from legal practice before 1914, like Popelin in Belgium or Poët in Italy, feminist congresses provided a forum for protesting against inequities facing women. Some well-known feminists obtained law degrees to enhance their advocacy for changes in law and government, even if their countries did not allow women to practice law. Anita Augspurg (1857–1943), dismayed by Germany's law code of 1894, followed other German women to the University of Zurich and earned a law degree in 1897. Christabel Pankhurst, daughter of a deceased English lawyer, obtained a degree in Manchester before emerging, like her mother, as a leading suffrage militant. Her application for admission to the bar was rejected, as was that of Bertha Cave, whose effort drew much publicity in 1903. Augspurg, like Mackenroth, set an example for German women, who by 1909 could enroll in all German law faculties even though barred from private practice and public administrative posts for lawyers. Several dozen women studied law in German universities before the Empire collapsed in 1918. Marie Munk, a Berlin judge's daughter, overcame his objections to her legal studies and was the only woman law student in Bonn in 1907. After earning a degree in 1912, she gained experience as an unpaid clerk in a law office and then worked in a legal aid clinic in Munich, offering women advice on divorce, child custody, property, or the rights of unwed mothers and their children. Marie Berent followed a similar path in Berlin. Feminist Marie Stritt had started the first women's legal protection agency in Dresden in 1894, and by 1914, ninety-seven such agencies existed.

Public sector employment

Working for national and local government agencies added options for better-educated women, including some doctors and lawyers, during the later nineteenth century. The great expansion of government functions in education, health, welfare, communication, and transport multiplied jobs in the public sector, at a time when civil service reforms were tying jobs to specific qualifications rather than political patronage. Administrative hierarchies mirrored both the social stratification and the gender divisions in school systems. Primary schools could qualify women for teacher training in normal schools and for white-collar clerical work once reserved for men. Women's access to posts requiring advanced educational credentials was far more limited. Indeed, the first women in positions with significant administrative responsibility usually had jobs officially defined as suited to women's presumably natural abilities, and some obtained them because of charitable or teaching experience rather than advanced education. Allocating positions by gender limited women's opportunities but also countered numerous objections that women should not hold public positions of responsibility because they lacked the vote. School inspectresses Chevreau-Lemercier in France and Gatti de Gamond in Belgium or prison inspectresses Lechevalier in France and Arenal in Spain set precedents for later generations.

Clerical positions for women were more common than those carrying significant administrative responsibility, however. New telegraph and telephone services, and post offices to which these were often linked, were typically the first government agencies offering many openings to women, and there was much competition for such work. Traditions of restricting jobs by gender carried less weight when services were new. Indeed, telegraph equipment and telephone switchboards, like office typewriters, were seen as utilizing the same female finger dexterity and attention to detail as needlework. Moreover, as in the expanding banking, insurance, or retailing segments of the private sector, women clerks might be preferred because limited job options meant that many accepted less pay than men. Yet in central government offices traditionally staffed by men, officials often resisted hiring women clerks, frequently objecting that mixing the sexes in workplaces posed moral dangers. The introduction of French women as clerk-typists in a ministry's central government offices came a generation later than in England, where Inland Revenue offices hired a few women typists after 1878. By 1914, fewer than 300 women worked in French central government offices, as compared to about 1,700 in England. When the Swedish legislature's upper house brought in a woman stenographer in 1909, her very presence "caused a great sensation."[17] In general,

[17] Miss Thorstensen, "Shorthand and Typing in Sweden," *Report of the ICW 1909*, II: 338.

women's employment in offices, public or private, was less controversial in countries offering men a wide range of work opportunities but, as with teaching, more restricted where men preferred even low-paying public jobs to other limited options.

Whether consigned to separate work areas, as was common, or sharing work spaces with male colleagues, women employees quickly became a familiar presence in many European post, telegraph, and telephone offices. In industrialized England, girls and women worked for private companies as telegraphers by the 1850s, and when the Post Office took over telegraphy in 1870, officials retained women. Similarly, women already worked for private telephone companies in France when the state purchased these in 1889. In largely agrarian Denmark, author Mathilde Fibiger, a former governess, became the first woman telegraphist in 1866, paving the way for 1,500 women in post or telegraph offices by 1914. Women worked in Swedish and Finnish post and telegraph offices by 1870. French women often had run one-person rural post offices in the past, but they faced opposition in cities and male clerks blamed them for keeping men's wages depressed. Austrian women began working in post and telegraph offices between 1869 and 1871, and in Germany Crown Princess Victoria supported introducing women in telegraph centers, terming this respectable employment. Although "violent opposition" reportedly greeted the first Italian women in telegraph offices,[18] by 1888 Italy employed nearly 500 women as postal and telegraph clerks. Spain also opened telegraph work to women during the 1880s. By 1911, women in post, telegraph, and telephone services numbered 36,621 in England and Wales, 21,457 in France, and 22,523 in Germany. These large contingents comprised 90 percent of all women working for the English central government and 80 percent of French counterparts other than teachers. To protest discriminatory pay scales, English women organized the Association of Post Office Women Clerks in 1901 (later merged into the Federation of Women Civil Servants), but French women clerks favored the General Association of Postal Agents rather than a small women's group.

The employment of lower-level women clerks raised the issue of appropriate monitoring of their work, sometimes leading to appointment of women supervisors. In England in 1876 Maria Constance Smith, daughter of a university professor, became the superintendent of women clerks in the Post Office Savings Bank department, whose staff grew to more than 3,000 by the time she retired in 1913. Women employees'

---

[18] Aurelia Cimino Folliero de Luna, "Italy, A General Review," in *The Woman Question in Europe*, ed. Theodore Stanton (New York: G. P. Putnam's Sons, 1884), 315.

presence also led to new government posts for women doctors, such as Edith Shove, hired in England by 1882, or Pelletier. The final salaries of Smith and the English Post Office's chief woman doctor exceeded most school inspectresses' pay, and twenty other women supervisors in post, telegraph, and telephone offices had salaries on a par with school inspectresses.

The most prestigious administrative posts for women before 1914 were often in inspectorates for schools, factories, prisons, and public assistance facilities. Working in services benefiting women, girls, or young children, inspectresses had roles usually defined in gender-specific terms, with which they concurred. British factory inspectress Hilda Martindale (1875–1952), for example, reported to the International Council of Women in 1909 that "Women have special qualities, discernment, intuition, sympathy, and understanding ... needed in this work, and if to these be added tact and courage and a determination to carry through what they have undertaken, I am convinced that the woman worker, the child in the school, and the inmate of the workhouse, will ... reap the benefit of the woman inspector."[19] Yet inspectresses' appointments often proved controversial, as Kergomard learned in France. Men who resented women's access to well-paid posts voiced opposition by questioning the propriety of women's travel to do inspections or their interviewing of male employers and public officials.

Nonetheless, women inspectors became a familiar presence, even if in limited numbers. France, which first placed a nursery school inspectress on the national payroll in 1837, had 23 school inspectresses in 1914, but only 5 (limited to Paris-area girls' schools) belonged to the corps of 450 primary school inspectors. England's first regular appointment of a school inspectress dated from 1896, and in 1914, forty-four inspectresses, including a Chief Woman Inspector, worked for the Board of Education. Italy had eight school inspectresses by 1895. The Seine department, which included Paris, hired inspectresses for factories and workshops employing women in 1879, and some Seine appointees entered the French national inspectorate that replaced departmental units in 1893, with posts designated for fifteen women and seventy-seven men but limiting supervisory divisional posts to men. The English Home Office hired two factory inspectresses in 1893, and by 1914 employed twenty, including the Principal Lady Inspector, but unlike their nineteen French counterparts, they were not on the same pay scale as men. In Germany at least forty-seven assistant labor inspectresses then worked for various states but lacked the authority and civil service status of French

---

[19] Hilda Martindale, "Women Inspectors," *Report of the ICW 1909*, II: 344.

and English inspectresses. Marie Baum, hired in Baden in 1902, had studied chemistry in Zurich. Austria, Belgium, Finland, the Netherlands, Norway, and Swiss cantons also engaged labor inspectresses.

The expansion of public assistance and health care on the national and local levels also offered women new administrative and clerical opportunities, as well as nursing and social-work jobs. English women served as unpaid Poor Law Guardians after 1870, and 1,500 did so in 1914. The Local Government Board hired Jane Senior in 1873 to inspect facilities for children covered by the Poor Law, a decade before France employed any women to assess children's services, but after Senior resigned in 1874, England did not regularize an inspectress's appointment for welfare services until 1885. Harriet Mason, with a background in volunteer work, then became the inspectress of boarded-out children, and there were six more English inspectresses by 1914, along with one for Scotland and two for Ireland. The Home Office also assigned two others to prisons and girls' reform schools. Comparable French inspectresses general, employed by the interior ministry, numbered seven for prisons and children's services in 1900 but only three in 1914. French municipalities administering welfare funds added women for inspection roles, however. In the Paris area by 1900, more than 60 women were paid "visitors," monitoring infants placed with wet nurses or checking on recipients of public assistance funds for mothers, the aged, and the infirm. British local authorities also hired women "sanitary inspectors": in 1909, 124 worked in England, including 38 in London; 26 in Scotland; and 22 in Ireland. Germany had 1,021 women in paid posts in welfare offices in 1913. The four British women insurance commissioners hired for the new National Health Insurance Commission in 1912 enjoyed an exceptional position, with a salary of £1,000, higher than that of any other administrative women.

Yet many governments continued to block women's access to professional – as opposed to clerical – ranks in central government offices. Such posts often required a university degree, and when French women challenged the exclusion of women with requisite educational credentials, officials cited women's lack of military service to justify barring them. German lawyers, at least two-thirds of whom worked for public administrations or the courts, adamantly opposed opening the professional civil service to women. After World War I, new enactments in various countries reduced but did not eliminate discrimination in many administrative ranks.

Individual women often appreciated what prestigious public service posts added to their own lives. French interior ministry inspectress Olympe Gevin-Cassal (1859–1945), who went to work at the age of thirty-two because her troubled artist husband could not support their four children, confided to a friend that she enjoyed doing work that made her "someone." Twenty-six-year-old inspectress Marie Galtier chose government employment after earning a law degree because private practice posed difficulties for women. Interviewed by a Paris newspaper in March 1914 after her appointment by the Interior ministry, Galtier anticipated that inspecting hospitals, old-age homes, women's prisons, and child-care facilities would give her a virtually "unlimited" field of activity, and she called her position "the highest mission ... entrusted to a woman."[20] British factory inspectress Martindale found her work "interesting and all absorbing." Unlike French counterparts, however, most British women civil servants, as well as those in many other nations, could not retain positions if they married, because of a "marriage bar" existing until after World War II.

Conclusion

The notion of a professional woman was a development of the later nineteenth century. Yet while women became a majority of teachers in many countries and nursing was overwhelmingly feminized, only limited numbers of women entered the traditionally masculine professions of doctor, lawyer, or higher-ranking civil servant. More broadly, greater access to education, combined with growth in the banking, commercial, and public sectors, led to new opportunities in white-collar work for women, and young, single middle-class women increasingly joined the workforce. Most European working women on the eve of World War I did not have white-collar jobs, clerical or professional, however. Even in Great Britain and Belgium, where the importance of agriculture had declined more than in France or Germany, fewer than one out of every seven working women had a job other than in farming, industry, commerce, or domestic service.

Women's organizations long advocated improving women's access to better-paying jobs, insisting that work was an economic necessity for many women. Yet legal and organizational barriers often blocked women from professional fields, and adversaries questioned women's intellectual abilities and judgment, as well as the propriety of their working in various public settings. Unsurprisingly, professional women, including women

---

[20] Gevin-Cassal and Galtier quoted in Linda L. Clark, *The Rise of Professional Women in France: Gender and Public Administration since 1830* (Cambridge: Cambridge University Press, 2000), 97, 105.

administrators with significant responsibilities, attracted attention at national and international women's congresses. Exemplars of women's competence and intelligence, they successfully performed duties in arenas that were often public and thereby also furthered arguments that women were ready to become voters. Some women certainly feared that public identification with feminism could compromise their professional status, but after 1900 many well-educated women became more receptive to the idea that gaining the right to vote was necessary for eliminating unfairness in employment.

Futher reading and reference works

Adams, Carole Elizabeth. *Women Clerks in Wilhelmine Germany: Issues of Class and Gender.* Cambridge: Cambridge University Press, 1988.

Albisetti, James C. "The Fight for Female Physicians in Imperial Germany." *Central European History* 15 (June 1983): 99–123.

"Portia ante Portas: Women and the Legal Profession in Europe, ca. 1870–1925." *Journal of Social History* 33 (Summer 2000): 825–57.

Babini, Valeria. "Science, Feminism and Education: The Early Work of Maria Montessori." Translated by Sarah Morgan and Daniel Pick. *History Workshop Journal* 49 (Spring 2000): 44–67.

Balfour, Margaret Ida, and Ruth Young. *The Work of Medical Women in India.* Bombay: Humphrey Milford at the Oxford University Press, 1929.

Bek, Anna. *The Life of a Russian Woman Doctor: A Siberian Memoir, 1869–1954.* Translated and edited by Anne D. Rassweiler. Bloomington: Indiana University Press, 2004.

Blake, Catriona. *The Charge of the Parasols: Women's Entry to the Medical Profession.* London: The Women's Press, 1990.

Boigeol, Anne. "French Women Lawyers (*Avocates*) and the 'Women's Cause' in the First Half of the Twentieth Century." *International Journal of the Legal Profession* 10.2 (2003): 193–207.

Bonner, Thomas Neville. *To the Ends of the Earth: Women's Search for Education in Medicine.* Cambridge, Mass.: Harvard University Press, 1992.

Burton, Antoinette. *At the Heart of the Empire: Indians and the Colonial Encounter in Late-Victorian Britain.* Berkeley: University of California Press, 1998.

Dwelling in the Archive: Women Writing House, Home, and History in Late Colonial India. Oxford: Oxford University Press, 2003.

Clark, Linda L. *The Rise of Professional Women in France: Gender and Public Administration since 1830.* Cambridge: Cambridge University Press, 2000.

Clyman, Toby W., and Judith Vowles, eds. *Russia through Women's Eyes: Autobiographies from Tsarist Russia.* New Haven, Conn.: Yale University Press, 1996.

De Haan, Francisca. *Gender and the Politics of Office Work: The Netherlands, 1860–1940.* Amsterdam: Amsterdam University Press, 1998.

Dock, Lavinia L., and Isabel M. Stewart. *A Short History of Nursing: From the Earliest Times to the Present Day.* 4th edn. New York: G. P. Putnam's Sons, 1938.

Freeman, Stacey. "Medicalizing the Nurse: Professional and Eugenic Discourse at the Kaiserin Auguste Haus in Berlin." *German Studies Review* 18 (October 1995): 419–40.

Freeze, Karen Johnson. "Medical Education for Women in Austria: A Study of the Politics of the Czech Women's Movement in the 1890s." In *Women, State, and Party in Eastern Europe*, ed. Sharon L. Wolchik and Alfred G. Meyer, 51–63, 371–77. Durham, N.C.: Duke University Press, 1985.

Frieden, Nancy Mandelker. *Russian Physicians in an Era of Reform and Revolution, 1856–1905.* Princeton, N.J.: Princeton University Press, 1981.

Herbert, Raymond G., ed. *Florence Nightingale: Saint, Reformer, or Rebel?* Malabar, Fla.: Robert E. Krieger, 1981.

Holcombe, Lee. *Victorian Ladies at Work: Middle-Class Working Women in England and Wales 1850–1914.* Hamden, Conn.: Archon Books, 1973.

Howsam, Leslie. "'Sound-Minded Women': Eliza Orme and the Study and Practice of Law in Late-Victorian England." *Atlantis* 15 (Fall 1989): 44–55.

Jacobs, Aletta. *Memories: My Life as an International Leader in Health, Suffrage, and Peace.* Edited by Harriet Feinberg. Translated by Annie Wright. New York: Feminist Press, 1996.

John, Angela V., ed. *Unequal Opportunities: Women's Employment in England 1800–1918.* Oxford: Basil Blackwell, 1986.

Kimble, Sara Lynn. "Justice Redressed: Women, Citizenship, and the Social Uses of the Law in Modern France, 1890–1939." Ph.D. diss., University of Iowa, 2002.

Kramer, Rita. *Maria Montessori: A Biography.* Chicago: University of Chicago Press, 1976. Reprint, Reading, Mass.: Perseus Books, 1988.

Lovejoy, Esther Pohl. *Women Doctors of the World.* New York: Macmillan, 1957.

Marland, Hilary, and Anne Marie Rafferty, eds. *Midwives, Society and Childbirth: Debates and Controversies in the Modern Period.* London: Routledge, 1997.

McFeely, Mary Drake. *Lady Inspectors: The Campaign for a Better Workplace, 1893–1921.* New York and Oxford: Basil Blackwell, 1988.

McGann, Susan, and Barbara Mortimer, eds. *New Directions in the History of Nursing.* London: Routledge, 2005.

Nutting, M. Adelaide, and Lavinia L. Dock. *A History of Nursing: From the Earliest Times to the Present Day with Special Reference to the Work of the Past Thirty Years.* 4 vols.; vols III, and IV by Lavinia L. Dock. New York: G. P. Putnam's Sons, 1907–1912.

Roberts, Joan I., and Thetis M. Group. *Feminism and Nursing: An Historical Perspective on Power, Status, and Political Activism in the Nursing Profession.* Westport, Conn.: Praeger, 1995.

Schultheiss, Katrin. *Bodies and Souls: Politics and the Professionalization of Nursing in France, 1880–1922.* Cambridge, Mass.: Harvard University Press, 2001.

Simonton, Deborah. *A History of European Women's Work 1700 to the Present*. London: Routledge, 1998.

Summers, Anne. *Angels and Citizens: British Women as Military Nurses 1854–1914*. London: Routledge and Kegan Paul, 1988.

Tuve, Jeanette E. *The First Russian Women Physicians*. Newtonville, Mass.: Oriental Research Partners, 1984.

7   Organizing for women's rights: leaders and supporters

Nineteenth-century women formed organizations for a variety of purposes. Groups promoting charitable activity, moral and social reform, educational access, job access, and professional interests have figured in previous chapters. Organizations dedicated explicitly to securing women's political rights dated largely from the last third of the century, multiplying during the 1890s and after 1900. Although discussion of women's rights arose during the French Revolution, for several generations relatively few women ventured to claim the privileges of citizenship that Wollstonecraft or Gouges envisioned for women. Rather, demands for improving married women's legal status and providing better educational and employment opportunities long dominated contemporary discussions of women's rights or the "woman question." Well before the words "feminism" and "feminist" entered European vocabularies, countless women writers, such as George Sand, furthered awareness of how society and laws often disadvantaged women. As women's reform groups multiplied after the 1860s and 1870s, the proliferation of newspapers and magazines enabled more women to be better informed about activities on behalf of women in their own countries and elsewhere. This chapter highlights the history of women's organizing that was termed "feminist" by the end of the nineteenth century.

Defining feminism before 1900 often proved problematical or controversial. Hence various subcategories of feminism – liberal, conservative, socialist, bourgeois, Catholic, social, or maternalist, among others – figure in both contemporary accounts and later historians' analyses. The variety of labels testifies to the variety in arguments used by nineteenth-century feminists to claim equal rights for women. Going beyond familiar dictionary definitions of feminism as the theory of "equal rights for women" or the "equality of the sexes," many recent historians highlight differences between feminist argumentation grounded in political theories about the inherent equality of individuals and argumentation where "equality in difference" was prominent. Feminists in the former category were often prominent in the Anglo-American world but many there, as in continental

Europe, also used assumptions about psychological differences between the sexes to argue that women, as women, could make distinctive contributions to society *if* they possessed equal rights. We have seen that women in creative and professional fields marshaled similar mixes of arguments, sometimes claiming to be as talented or intelligent as men, sometimes claiming that because of their different qualities of personality and temperament, their work offered something unique. Not surprisingly, then, many feminists often mixed arguments, claiming equality as individuals and also, as women, "equality in difference."

Reform work and protests, 1830s–1850s

Independent of governments, private charitable and reform associations thrived. By the 1830s British women were signing antislavery petitions and assisting the Anti-Corn Law League's campaign against grain tariffs which raised food prices. Some also supported Chartism, the working-class movement sparked by anger that the 1832 reform law still left more than 80 percent of men disenfranchised. Although most Chartists sought universal manhood suffrage, not voting for both sexes, some women who supported Chartism later became involved with women's rights issues, as did some from other reform campaigns.

In France after the 1830 Revolution, working-class women joined socialist reform groups inspired by the ideas of Count Henri de Saint Simon and Charles Fourier. Fourier had written in 1808 that "the extension of the privileges of women is the general principle of all social progress." Socialist disciples typically treated equality between the sexes in a "relational" sense, believing that women and men had different qualities and, therefore, different roles in life, but that neither sex possessed more intrinsic human value than the other. The Saint-Simonian leader Prosper Enfantin asserted that "God is male and female."[1] Some socialist women also demanded women's "emancipation" and created their own publications, particularly when disillusioned by certain male socialists. Seamstresses Reine Guindorf and Désirée Veret founded the Saint-Simonian *Tribune des Femmes* (Women's Tribune), published from 1832 to 1834 and edited by Suzanne Voilquin. Women perceived danger in some male socialists' advocacy of free love because under current conditions a woman alone faced great difficulty supporting the

---

[1] Quotations from Susan K. Grogan, *French Socialism and Sexual Difference: Women and the New Society, 1803–1844* (Basingstoke: Macmillan, 1992), 20; and Claire Goldberg Moses, "'Difference' in Historical Perspective: Saint-Simonian Feminism," in *Feminism, Socialism, and French Romanticism*, by Claire Goldberg Moses and Leslie Wahl Rabine (Bloomington: Indiana University Press, 1993), 34.

children born from a "free union." Middle-class women influenced by Saint-Simonianism started the *Gazette des Femmes* (1836–38), which advocated "political and civil rights for women" and urged women to petition the government on such matters as reestablishing divorce. Although the July Monarchy's laws on the press and associations soon restricted political dissidents' ability to organize and function, artisans remained attached to their working-class organizations. The bold Flora Tristan (1803–44) also started the Union Ouvrière (Workers Union) for men and women, and died while touring France to recruit members.

Such activities set the stage for new French women's groups formed after the Revolution of February 1848 ousted Louis-Philippe and ushered in the Second Republic. Women's concerns included education, jobs and better pay, reform of laws disadvantaging women, and political rights. Jeanne Deroin (1805–94), a seamstress, teacher, and mother, helped organize the short-lived Club for the Emancipation of Women, the Fraternal Association of Democrats of Both Sexes, and the Mutual Society for Women's Education. Eugénie Niboyet (1796–1883), an experienced journalist who was the granddaughter of a Protestant pastor and wife of a lawyer, edited the newspaper *La Voix des Femmes* (Women's Voice), published between March and June. Désirée Veret Gay and Elisa Lemonnier organized women workers, and Gay edited another short-lived women's paper, its last issue regretting women's banishment from political clubs after the June Days uprising in Paris shook the recently elected constitutional assembly. Deroin and Niboyet had tried, without success, to persuade George Sand to run for that assembly in April 1848, and Deroin herself tried to run in 1849 for the new legislature, prompting the government to rule women's candidacies unconstitutional. As editor of another newspaper until August 1849, Deroin also kept the women reformers' press alive.

Awareness of European revolutions was in the background when a group of American women and men, including Elizabeth Cady Stanton and Lucretia Mott, organized a women's rights meeting in Seneca Falls, New York, in July 1848. Some 300 people assembled, and more than 100 signed a declaration on women's rights, modeled on the Declaration of Independence of 1776. The vote for women proved the most divisive demand, causing many to refuse to sign.

Both French and American advocates of women's rights faced ridicule in the press in 1848, and some French women experienced official retaliation. In response to continuing urban and rural protests, the Second Republic adopted repressive policies that set the stage for Louis Napoleon Bonaparte's election as president and later creation of the Second Empire. Deroin and Pauline Roland were among the women activists jailed or exiled in 1850–52, along with many male republicans. In 1852 the government also barred women from editing newspapers. The intrepid Deroin, then in London, started a women's almanac in French and English but could not make it financially viable.

Political repression in German states also affected both men and women after rulers recovered from the shock of revolutionary crowds in March 1848. The Frankfurt assembly, elected to plan German unification and write a constitution, was disbanded by June 1849. To avoid jail, many rebels chose exile, often with their wives and daughters. Apart from supporting male reformers, some women had pushed educational issues to the forefront. Forty years later, Louise Otto-Peters (1819–95) and four other women told American feminists that "the woman movement in Germany" began in 1848 when "a great revolution went all over the world."[2] But in 1850 Prussia's Association Law barred women, as well as children, apprentices, and the mentally incompetent, from joining political organizations. It remained in effect until 1908, and other German states issued similar bans. Otto had started a women's newspaper, *Die Frauen-Zeitung*, in Saxony in April 1849, and after women's editing of newspapers was banned, she moved it to nearby Thuringia, halting publication in 1852. From a middle-class background, unlike Deroin, Otto was orphaned when she was seventeen and supported herself by writing novels and articles, sometimes using a male pseudonym. Her fiancé August Peters was a writer and weaver's son, politically active in 1848–49 and imprisoned until 1856.

In England Anne Knight (1792–1862), a Quaker and antislavery activist present in Paris in 1848, still hoped for reforms benefiting women, despite the demise of Chartism as crowds revolted across the continent in 1848. She persuaded Chartist women in industrial Sheffield to start the Female Political Association in 1851 and then the Women's Rights Association. Although these small groups were short-lived, their petition to the House of Lords was women's first demand for the vote since Mary Smith's request in 1832. An article on "The Enfranchisement of Women" also appeared in the influential *Westminster Review* in 1851, its author identified as John Stuart Mill, although his wife Harriet Taylor (1807–58) was the primary author.

Other women's issues commanded greater public attention in England during the 1850s, however. Married women's lack of legal rights had been dramatized since the 1830s by the travails of Caroline Norton, a socially prominent writer abused by a drunkard husband. Publicity

[2] *Report of the International Council of Women* (Washington, D.C.: National Woman Suffrage Association, 1888), 219.

concerning her lack of access to her young sons helped prompt the passage in 1839 of a modest but pathbreaking reform which enabled mothers to seek custody of children under the age of seven. Her *English Laws for Women* (1854) drew on her own experiences, including her husband's legal right to tap his estranged wife's inheritance and earnings. Theirs was among the individual cases fueling demands for reforming the laws on married women's property rights and divorce. The 1857 divorce act gave separated and divorced women rights to their own property and to earnings received after a marriage's breakdown, and it enabled women to sue for divorce.

Among English women engaged with legal reform and employment issues during the 1850s, Barbara Leigh Smith Bodichon (1827–91) and her Langham Place circle in London were especially prominent. Daughter of an independent-minded MP (Member of Parliament) and from a family of active reformers, she was educated at home and at Bedford College. Using an annual income provided by her father, she opened an innovative elementary school and published pamphlets on the *Most Important Laws Concerning Women* (1854) and *Women at Work* (1857). A women's committee, formed in 1855, petitioned for married women's property rights, and its successors continued efforts until 1882, when major reform occurred. Jessie Boucherett, Bodichon's friend, created the Society for Promoting the Employment of Women, seeking to prepare women for and improve access to jobs in the skilled trades and professions. It became a model for similar societies in other countries. Bodichon's circle also had a publishing outlet, the *Englishwomen's Journal*, started with funds from Bodichon and edited by Bessie Rayner Parkes.

Cautious demands for change, 1860s–1870s

In cities and towns on the continent, individuals and new organizations also addressed women's education, work, and legal rights during the 1860s, but did so cautiously. The widowed Otto-Peters, teacher Auguste Schmidt (1833–1902), and kindergarten promoter Henriette Goldschmidt launched the General German Women's Association (ADF, Allgemeiner Deutscher Frauenverein) in Leipzig in 1865. The first German women's conference, attended by 150 women, focused primarily on the plight of poorly trained and underpaid women workers and spurred the creation of day care for women workers' children. Like Bodichon's circle, the ADF also soon addressed middle-class women's educational needs and employment. Mindful of legal restrictions, ADF reformers tried to limit controversy by using "maternalist" language that emphasized women's traditional nurturing roles and jobs compatible with these, including teaching. Two other groups promoting job training were even more cautious. The Berlin-based Lette Association, eventually headed by the male founder's eldest daughter Anna Schepeler-Lette (1827–97), supported schools which instructed hundreds of pupils in craft and industrial skills deemed suitable for women and also in homemaking. Seventeen women's groups based in ten cities, including Berlin, formed the Union of German Women's Educational and Employment Associations in 1869. The ADF developed a national organization as well and endured beyond Otto's death, but in 1913 its 14,000 members were only a small part of the Federation of German Women's Associations (BDF).

The American Ladies' Club of Prague and the Czech Women's Trade Association also promoted women's access to jobs and training. The Club, started in 1865 by a man who spent time in the United States after Czech nationalist efforts were suppressed in 1848, attracted middle-class women, including the popular novelist Karolina Svetlá. She, in turn, helped found the Trade Association in 1871, supported by her sister, writer Sofie Podlipská. The Association opened a commercial school and was a base for the educational projects of Eliska Krásnohorská, hired as its secretary. In the meantime, German women in Vienna had started the Women's Employment Association in November 1866, allying with the men's Association for Economic Progress which sought reform after Austria's humiliating loss of the Austro-Prussian War.

In Britain, Parliamentary debate in 1866 on extending men's voting rights by lowering financial requirements led Bodichon and others to launch the Women's Suffrage Committee and persuade 1,498 women to sign a petition requesting women's inclusion in a new law. Although Liberal MPs John Stuart Mill and Henry Fawcett supported the demand, the reform law of 1867 excluded women. Nonetheless, other groups formed, some combining as the National Society for Women's Suffrage (NSWS) in late 1867. With members in London, Manchester, Edinburgh, Dublin, Birmingham, and Bristol, it added a London-based central committee in 1872. Lydia Becker (1827–90) of Manchester, daughter of a manufacturer and eldest of fifteen children, became the pivotal NSWS figure. Influenced by Bodichon, she helped found the Manchester Women's Suffrage Committee and started the *Women's Suffrage Journal* in 1870. She also joined the Married Women's Property Committee and Butler's campaign against the Contagious Diseases Acts. Women's voting, the *Journal* asserted, would help "purify our whole state" and "repress our two worst curses – drunkenness and prostitution."[3] In the

---

[3] Quoted in Philippa Levine, *Feminist Lives in Victorian England: Private Roles and Public Commitment* (Oxford: Basil Blackwell, 1990), 96.

meantime, Mill's influential *Subjection of Women* (1869) addressed women's secondary status in the family, education, and the workplace, and boldly asserted that women deserved political rights. The "legal subordination of one sex to the other ... ought to be replaced by a principle of perfect equality," wrote England's most famous theorist of liberalism.[4] At this juncture, women's suffrage found few supporters elsewhere in Europe, even as women on the continent started new organizations and translations of Mill's controversial book appeared.

In Switzerland, the creation of the International League of Peace and Freedom in 1867, after the Austro-Prussian War, prompted Marie Goegg (1826–99), wife of one of its founders, to champion a separate women's society, the Geneva-based International Association of Women. A clockmaker's daughter with limited education, Goegg worked in her father's shop from the age of thirteen and always read widely. Her husband Amand had fled from Baden to avoid imprisonment after the 1848 Revolution. Marie served on the League's council until 1896, but her women's group became a casualty of the Franco-Prussian War because of disputes among its French, German, and Swiss members. Although she revived her association in 1872, renaming it Solidarity, it drew mostly Swiss members and did not survive beyond 1880. Goegg's concerns also broadened considerably, as her essay in Theodore Stanton's *Woman Question in Europe* (1884) indicated. Her husband's departure heightened her awareness of problems faced by women left alone.

French women reformers were heartened by the liberalization of the Second Empire during the later 1860s. Publications by Juliette Lamber, Jenny d'Héricourt, Josephine de Marchef-Girard, and Daubié had drawn attention since 1858 to women's issues, and organizations and public meetings advocating educational and legal change drew support from the republican opposition and some socialists. Particularly important for the future were Maria Deraismes, journalist Léon Richer, and their associates. Deraismes (1828–94), an heiress, was the well-educated daughter of a Voltairean father who emphasized the positive aspects of the 1789 Revolution. Maria became confident that social problems had solutions, asserting in 1868, "Women's inferiority is not a fact of nature ... It is a human invention, a social fiction."[5] Her views on the social construction of gender thus presaged Simone de Beauvoir's famous *Second Sex* (1949). Richer, a freemason, encouraged Deraismes's public speaking and in

---

[4] John Stuart Mill, excerpt from *The Subjection of Women*, in *History of Ideas on Women*, ed. Rosemary Agonito (New York: G. P. Putnam's Sons, 1977), 225.
[5] Quoted in Karen Offen, *European Feminisms 1700–1950: A Political History* (Stanford, Calif.: Stanford University Press, 2000), 143.

April 1869 started a women's rights newspaper, *Le Droit des Femmes*, the law still necessitating that a man be the editor. Thirty-eight women, including Deraismes and the widowed author André Léo (pseudonym of Léodile Béra Champseix) published a manifesto in the paper. Léo soon spearheaded the Society for Claiming Woman's Rights, and in April 1870 Deraismes and Richer started the Association for Women's Rights.

The Franco-Prussian War and political upheaval soon checked toleration of and support for such reform activities, causing Richer and Deraismes to proceed cautiously. The postwar monarchist-dominated constitutional assembly met in Versailles rather than Paris, and angry Parisians' creation of an alternative government, the Commune, in March 1871 led to the army's recapturing of the rebellious city, killing 20,000 people. Richer and Deraismes revived their activity, but Léo and her key allies went into exile. As in 1848, some women's support for the Commune fueled a reaction against women reformers' demands, especially while monarchists led the interim constitutional assembly. Avoiding a controversial "women's rights" label, Richer and Deraismes retitled their paper *L'Avenir des Femmes* (Women's Future) and to garner publicity staged a banquet for 150 supporters in 1872. Their organization, now called Amelioration of Woman's Situation, was dissolved in 1875 and not revived until 1878. The political climate eased when monarchists, split between supporters of Bourbon and Orleanist claimants, finally opted to create the Third Republic in 1875, and republicans then won control of the lower legislative house, also defeating monarchist efforts to regain control. A women's rights congress in 1878 was emblematic of the new French political moment.

Other signs of interest in "the woman question" on the continent also surfaced during the 1870s. By 1872 Mill's *Subjection of Women* had appeared in French, German, Dutch, Danish, Swedish, Russian, and Italian translations. Jenny Hirsch, the Lette Association secretary, provided one German version, and Anna Maria Mozzoni, the Italian. In Copenhagen Matilde Bajer and her husband Fredrik founded the Danish Women's Society in 1871, inspired by Goegg's group. It grew slowly, from 121 members by 1880 to 1,000 in 1887, but became a model for other Scandinavian associations. In Sweden, the Organization for Married Women's Right to Property dated from 1873. German novelist Hedwig Dohm also began advocating women's right to vote, although she found few supporters.

In July 1878 the first international women's rights congress, organized by Deraismes and Richer, met at a Masonic hall in Paris. Privately funded, it was timed to coincide with an international exposition drawing many visitors. With sessions on education, work, public morality, and law, the congress attracted nearly as many men as women. Three-fourths (168) of 220 registered participants were French, and 400 other people reportedly attended. Among 113 women registered, 77 were French, 13 English, 10 American, and the others from Italy, Russia, Switzerland, Belgium, and the Netherlands. The foreigners included Goegg, Dr. Catherine Goncharova, and the American Mrs. Klumpke, accompanied by two daughters. Anna Maria Mozzoni (1837–1920), sent by the Italian government, gave one of the opening addresses. Although no Italian women's rights group then existed, Gualberta Beccari's periodical *La Donna* (The Woman) provided an outlet for women reformers as of 1868. Mozzoni, like many women of her generation, had left school by the age of fourteen but continued reading widely, her father, a Milan architect, recommending Fourier, and her mother Sand's novels. Dismayed by the post-unification Italian law code, modeled on the Napoleonic code, she wrote *Woman and Her Social Relationships* (1864), denouncing married women's subordination as "intellectual castration, perpetual minority, the annihilation of . . . personality." At the congress Mozzoni's comments matched many French attendees' views. She denounced traditional girls' schools and convents for inculcating "authoritarian and dogmatic ideas" that produced the female "passivity" and "intellectual sterility" often cited to justify women's subordination. She would seek different results with her own teaching of a secular moral philosophy at a girls' school. Criticizing women's status in laws bequeathed by the "despot" Napoleon to various nations, she also complained that free republics favored male citizens and allowed despotism within the family.[6]

The 1878 congress passed resolutions asking for free, compulsory, and secular education; women's equal rights to work and organize as workers; equal pay; equal rights for women within the family; and legalization of divorce and paternity suits. Yet it also occasioned disagreement among French women's rights advocates. Richer and Deraismes, aware of the delicate political balance in France, refused to let Hubertine Auclert (1848–1914) speak on women's suffrage. Auclert, from a provincial landowning family, had rebelled against her convent education, moved to Paris, and used her inheritance to found a small women's suffrage group in 1876, believing that political rights were the best means for also

[6] Quotations from Judith Jeffrey Howard, "Visions of Reform, Visions of Revolution: Women's Activism in the New Italian Nation," in *Views of Women's Lives in Western Tradition: Frontiers of the Past and the Future*, ed. Frances Richardson Keller (Lewiston, N.Y.: Edwin Mellen, 1990), 444; and *Congrès International du Droit des Femmes* (Paris: A. Ghio, 1878), 18–20.

obtaining full civil and economic rights. In 1879 she presented her message to the socialist French Workers Party.

Despite most French feminists' reluctance to discuss women's suffrage when it seemed untimely, developments elsewhere gave it somewhat greater currency, especially in Britain. Sweden granted women taxpayers the vote for municipal elections in 1862. Russia in 1864 allowed some women property owners an indirect role in selecting the new local government councils (*zemstvos*); they could choose a male proxy to cast their vote. Similar arrangements existed for some Austrian regional assemblies, as carryovers of certain noblewomen's previous privileges, and in 1861 some propertied Czech and German women in Bohemia gained direct and indirect voting rights for the regional assembly. England's Municipal Franchise Law of 1869 enabled qualified women householders to vote in certain local elections. Their inclusion owed much to the Quaker MP Jacob Bright who, with his wife Ursula, supported the Manchester women's suffrage group. Although a court ruling soon disqualified most married women, women eventually became about 17 percent of local voters. Women, single or married, also could run in school board elections as of 1870 and seek the post of Poor Law guardian. Scottish women gained local voting rights in 1882. Among the first women on school boards were feminists Elizabeth Garrett and Emily Davies, elected in London in 1870, and Lydia Becker in Manchester in 1874. By 1900, after the 1884 reform lowered financial requirements for voting, about one million women had local voting rights, women school board members numbered 270, and Poor Law counterparts, 1,147. The Poor Law total reflected the dropping of monetary requirements for an unpaid, time-consuming post now less appealing to men but which feminists saw as "essentially housekeeping on a large scale," for which women were "manifestly better fitted" than men.[7] Local education authorities coopted women after school boards were abolished in 1902. Unsurprisingly, local voting and officeholding also fueled British feminist arguments about women's fitness for electing or serving in the House of Commons. Yet some opponents contended that *only* local offices, focused on children and the poor, suited women.

Feminist diversity and international organization, 1880–1900

During the 1880s the terms *féminisme* (feminism) and *féministe* (feminist) became familiar labels for advocacy of equal rights for women in

---

[7] Margaret Nevinson, quoted in Levine, *Feminist Lives*, 121.

France. Although author Alexandre Dumas (the younger) made the word *féministe* a pejorative in 1872, Auclert proudly embraced its usage in her newspaper *La Citoyenne* (Woman Citizen), started in 1881. The general press noted the usage, and during the 1890s it became more familiar in other languages: *feminism* in English, *femminismo* in Italian, *feminismo* in Spanish, *Feminismus* in German. German women, however, usually preferred the terms "women's movement" (*Frauenbewegung*) or "women's emancipation." Antifeminists, early on, degraded the term feminism by equating it with such negative connotations as unwomanly ideas and actions, or nasty competition and "war" between the sexes. Auclert's suffragism put her among the "radicals" of French feminism before 1900, even as more women embraced the term feminism. The French Catholic Marie Maugeret adopted the label "Christian feminism" in 1896 to separate it from the anticlericalism of Deraismes, Richer, and Auclert. Deraismes and Richer, in the meantime, took separate organizational paths in 1882, when Richer left Deraismes's Amelioration group and started the French League for Women's Rights (LFDF, Ligue Française pour le Droit des Femmes).

The need for distinctive labeling developed as more women's rights organizations appeared after 1880, often attracting women from philanthropies. Mozzoni founded the League to Promote Women's Interests in 1881 in Milan, short-lived and unable to gain local voting rights for women. Scandinavian women formed new associations in Sweden, Norway, and Finland in 1884, the Swedish group using Fredrika Bremer's name and all three calling the Bajers' Danish group an inspiration. In the Netherlands Wilhelmina Drucker (b. 1847) and Theodora van Campen Doesburg organized the feminist Free Women's Association in 1889, with special interests in women's employment and children's rights. Like Deraismes and Richer, most members of these northern European groups did not yet demand women's suffrage. In Norway, however, teacher Gina Krog (1847–1916), a founder of the Women's Rights Association in 1884, and nine other women started a small Women's Suffrage Association in 1885. The first Danish women's suffrage group emerged in 1888, and Drucker and her allies founded the Association for Women's Suffrage (VVVK, Vereeniging voor Vrouwenkiesrecht) in 1893. Already in 1883 Aletta Jacobs, influenced by British suffragists, had attempted, as a taxpayer, to register to vote.

In Britain, with older suffrage groups and some women voting locally, political parties found it useful to enlist women in party auxiliaries. The Conservative Party's Primrose League, formed in 1883, admitted both men and women. The Women's Liberal Federation began in 1886 and within a decade had 470 branches with 80,000 members – despite the exodus of women opposed to women's suffrage or opposed to Liberal Party support for Irish home rule, which also divided men.

International women's meetings in the United States and France in 1888 and 1889 set the stage for similar gatherings during the next twenty-five years. American suffragists Elizabeth Cady Stanton and Susan B. Anthony had traveled to England and France in 1882 and proposed creating an international association, as did Deraismes and Richer in 1878. To celebrate the fortieth anniversary of the Seneca Falls declaration, American feminists invited women from other countries to Washington, D.C., in 1888. Forty-nine delegates came, representing fifty-three organizations. Foreigners journeyed from Great Britain, France, Denmark, Norway, Finland, Canada, and British India. On behalf of the ADF, Otto-Peters, Schmidt, and three colleagues sent a brief history of the German "woman movement." They cited "the condition of our society" to explain why they dared not send delegates, but also explicitly identified the 1848 Revolution as their movement's starting point and praised the congress for demonstrating "that in every country there are women now ready to take part in such movements." Fanny Zampini Salazaro, editor of the *Woman's Review* in Rome, sent a paper on Italian women's status. Speaking in French, Isabelle Bogelot praised Deraismes, Richer, and Auclert for efforts to promote women's "political and social rights," including suffrage, and also reported on aiding women prisoners.[8] Pundita Ramabai Sarasvati discussed Indian women's recent educational gains.

The 1888 meeting launched the International Council of Women (ICW). Founders asked that women in each country desiring ICW affiliation form a single national council as an umbrella organization under which other groups furthering women's interests could unite. Although American suffragists spearheaded its creation, the ICW welcomed "all associations of women in trades, professions and reforms" as well as advocates of "political rights."[9] The subsequent membership of many charities and philanthropies in national councils made the ICW an exemplar of the "maternalist" feminism that emphasized women's distinctive contributions to social reform. But until 1893, when the Canadian council started, only the American council existed. Millicent Garrett Fawcett, elected president in absentia in 1888, declined the ICW post, citing her obligations in England. Lady Ishbel Aberdeen, a Scottish aristocrat and wife of the British governor general in Canada, became the

---

[8] Quotations from *Report of the International Council of Women* (1888), 219, 90.

[9] Leila J. Rupp, *Worlds of Women: The Making of an International Women's Movement* (Princeton, N.J.: Princeton University Press, 1997), 15.

ICW president in 1893, holding the post for thirty-six of the next forty-three years.

In the meantime, two international women's congresses met in Paris in 1889, as the French Republic hosted many international meetings to celebrate the centennial of the Revolution and showcase recent accomplishments, including the engineering of the Eiffel Tower. Legislator Yves Guyot, a member of Richer's LFDF, and Protestant philanthropist Émilie de Morsier persuaded the government to sponsor a Congress on Women's Charities and Institutions in July 1889. Deraismes and Richer initially helped with its planning, but after other organizers, including the congress's honorary president, resisted wideranging discussion of women's rights, the two veteran feminists organized a separate congress for June. Although their congress's title featured "women's rights," they still wanted to avoid resolutions on voting. Auclert, in Algeria with her husband since 1888, sent Deraismes a report on suffrage which was not read. Richer, like many republican men, believed "that at the present time, it would be dangerous" to give French women the ballot because they were, allegedly, "in great majority, reactionaries and clericals" likely to vote for monarchy and harm the Republic.[10] Although France was the first European nation to give all men voting rights, many republican politicians repeated that argument for the next fifty years. The Women's Rights congress, smaller than the official congress, drew 180 participants (130 women, 50 men). Although few foreigners attended, the well-known Elizabeth Blackwell and Marie Popelin were present, and Popelin, barred from practicing law in Belgium, chaired sessions on legislation. The official congress welcomed about 550 women and men, at least 400 of them French but also delegates from 19 other countries or dependencies. Most reports offered there were factual accounts of women's charitable, educational, and intellectual activities, but some pointedly demanded change – especially in civil legislation and education.

The ICW was represented at the official Paris congress by Americans May Wright Sewall and Frances Wright, but it had no European affiliate until 1897 when the new Federation of German Women's Associations (BDF, Bund Deutscher Frauenvereine) joined. A few German women had attended the World's Congress of Representative Women in 1893, which was organized by the ICW in conjunction with the Columbian Exposition in Chicago and drew more than 600 women – mostly Americans, but with 14 European countries represented. Thereafter Augusta Foerster and Anna Simson, representing the ADF and German

---

[10] Quoted in Patrick Kay Bidelman, *Pariahs Stand Up! The Founding of the Liberal Feminist Movement in France, 1858–1889* (Westport, Conn.: Greenwood Press, 1982), 155.

teachers, along with Käthe Schirmacher and Hanna Bieber-Boehm, spurred older groups to found a national federation, which began in 1894 with 34 affiliates and Schmidt as president. Working-class women in Socialist Party women's auxiliaries (discussed below) were not invited then to participate, BDF founders citing Prussia's ban on women in political associations. Within a year the BDF had 50,000 members in 65 affiliated groups. Schmidt focused on charity and education, and emphasized women's duties more than women's rights, terming rights valuable if they served the general welfare. Members wanting more pursuit of legal and political reforms soon challenged her. Marie Stritt (1856–1928) became the second BDF president in 1899, supported by Minna Cauer, Anita Augspurg, and Lida Gustava Heymann. Founder of the Dresden legal protection agency for women, Stritt had helped organize campaigns against some provisions in the new imperial law code affecting women. Augspurg, who held a law degree, and Cauer arranged a meeting in Berlin on the code in 1896, reportedly drawing 3,000 women. The widowed Cauer (1841–1922), head of the philanthropic Women's Welfare Association, also presided at the International Congress on Women's Work and Activities in Berlin in 1896 – with an attendance of 1,700 – and she edited *Die Frauenbewegung* (Women's Movement) until 1919.

Swedish, British, Danish and Dutch women's councils, also largely Protestant, joined the ICW in 1898 and 1899, and the ICW quinquennial meeting in London in 1899 attracted women from twenty-eight nations and spurred formation of other national affiliates. By 1904 the ICW added six more European councils – Italy, France, Austria, Switzerland, Hungary, and Norway – plus Australia, New Zealand, and Argentina. The French National Council (CNFF, Conseil National des Femmes Françaises) dated from 1901 and was led by Sarah Monod (1836–1912), a Protestant. Beginning with 21,000 members in 35 groups, it had 100,000 members by 1914. Ghénia Avril de Sainte-Croix, CNFF secretary-general, targeted state-regulated prostitution and also chaired the ICW standing committee on abolishing "white slave traffic." Marianne Hainisch (1839–1936), wife of a prominent Viennese liberal, attended the London meeting and helped create the Austrian national council (BOF, Bund Oesterreichischer Frauenvereine), which grew from 13 affiliates in 1902 to 80 affiliates with 40,000 members by 1914. It pursued a more moderate agenda than the small General Austrian Women's Association (AOF, Allgemeiner Oesterreichischer Frauenverein), started in 1892 by Auguste Fickert and teacher Marie Schwarz in reaction to withdrawal of propertied women's voting rights for a provincial assembly. In Hungary, the other half of the Dual Monarchy

(1867–1918), the national council united 52 societies in 1904, and over 100 by 1913. Balkan affiliates emerged in Bulgaria and Greece in 1908, and Serbia in 1911. Former teacher Callirhoi Parren (1861–1940) drew educational and philanthropic groups into the Greek council. Married to a French journalist, she had started the weekly *Ladies' Newspaper* in Athens, read by 5,000 subscribers from 1887 to 1916, and regularly attended international women's congresses. Tsarist policy prevented a Russian affiliation, despite reformers' hopes; the ICW named Russian philanthropist Anna Filosofova an honorary vice president in 1893 and conferred the title on Anna Shabanova after Filosofova's death. Until 1911 Russia also blocked a Finnish affiliation, long desired by Alexandra Gripenberg, present at the ICW's founding. By 1914 the ICW had 23 member councils, 17 of them European, but the contentious issue of voting had led to the founding of the separate International Woman Suffrage Alliance in 1904.

Beyond 1900: women's suffrage

Beyond the Anglo-American world, women's suffrage groups usually emerged well after associations pursuing better education and employment opportunities for women. The first English suffrage groups with continuing histories dated from 1867. In the United States in 1869–70 women disappointed by not being included in the constitutional amendment enfranchising former male slaves created two suffrage associations, combined in 1890 as the National American Woman Suffrage Association (NAWSA). But until the early twentieth century the voting issue divided many European feminists. Some who opposed women's suffrage believed that the public political arena was a masculine space where women did not belong. Others argued that it was more practical to pursue less controversial educational or legal reforms and delay demanding suffrage until their country's political environment became more hospitable. Suffragists also disagreed about whether to push first for women's inclusion under existing voting laws, which often set financial qualifications, or to demand votes for *all* women, which meant demanding votes for *all* men as well. Universal manhood suffrage did not exist in most European countries before 1900. France, with universal male suffrage since 1848, was exceptional among the major powers. In Germany after 1871 all men aged twenty-five and over could vote for the Reichstag, the imperial legislature's lower house, but its powers were limited; and in Prussia, the biggest state, the division of male voters into three classes enabled the wealthiest 15 percent to control the state legislature. Austria lacked universal male suffrage until 1907 and Italy until 1913, and Britain's 1884 reform still left about 20 percent of men disenfranchised.

Historians have long linked the start of women's suffrage activity to the growth of political liberalism, with its emphasis on individual rights, and also to the Protestant majorities in northern European countries where feminist and suffrage activity flourished. The political and religious correlations are apparent in Britain, Scandinavian states, and the Netherlands, where parliamentary governments were well established and many, if not all, men could vote. But in democratic France Auclert's early suffrage efforts drew few supporters, advocacy by large numbers of women came relatively late, and Catholic women shunned organizations led by Protestant or anticlerical women. Similar lags occurred in Italy and Belgium. In more authoritarian Germany, a majority of the BDF long resisted discussing voting, judging it risky when Prussia and other states banned women from political associations. Yet after 1900 interest in women's suffrage increased in Germany and other traditionally conservative nations.

German women frustrated by BDF silence on suffrage created the Union of Progressive Women's Organizations in 1899 and the German Union for Women's Suffrage (DVF, Deutscher Verband für Frauenstimmrecht) in 1902. Augspurg, Cauer, Heymann, Schirmacher, and nine allies started the DVF in Hamburg, a city-state that did not ban women's political organizing. Its first branches were also in states without bans: Baden, Württemberg, and Bremen. Stritt, BDF president, joined the DVF, which entered the BDF in 1903. The BDF general assembly, representing member associations, endorsed women's suffrage in 1907, yet DVF membership in 1908 was still under 2,500. Membership does not tell the whole story of public interest, however. When the ICW held its quinquennial meeting in Berlin in 1904, 4,000 women reportedly attended, and the *Berlin Illustrierte Zeitung*, Germany's biggest mass magazine, featured a cover photograph of the pro-suffrage Stritt, who presided at the meeting.

That 1904 ICW meeting was also the occasion when the BDF's progressive wing joined British, American, and Australian women in the new International Woman Suffrage Alliance (IWSA), led by an American, Carrie Chapman Catt. The ICW, in turn, created a standing committee on suffrage, under Anna Howard Shaw of the NAWSA. The ICW in 1904 had sixteen affiliates (eleven of them European) and the IWSA only six, including British, German, Dutch, and Swedish groups in Europe. The Swedish Women's Suffrage Association dated from 1902. Tours by IWSA leaders and a new English group's much-publicized use of militant tactics after 1905 gave women's suffrage greater international prominence. The IWSA added Norwegian, Danish, Austrian, Hungarian, Italian, and Russian groups in 1906, Bulgarian, Finnish, and Swiss groups in 1908, and French and Belgians affiliates in 1909. By 1914, twenty of twenty-six IWSA affiliates were European, and only the Chinese group stood apart from areas linked to European settlement.

In Austria-Hungary, campaigns to extend male suffrage prompted new efforts by women. Rosika Schwimmer (1877–1948) left the Berlin meeting in 1904 determined to start a suffrage association in Hungary. From a middle-class Jewish family, Schwimmer had needed to work at the age of eighteen because of her father's financial problems, and after attending a young men's commercial school, she did clerical work until 1904, when she tried journalism. Her family's return to Budapest in 1897 positioned the young but assertive Schwimmer to start the National Association of Women Office Workers and, in 1903, the Association of Working Women. She and Vilma Glücklich, one of the first women to study physics at the University of Budapest and later a teacher, founded the pro-suffrage Feminist Association (FE, Feministák Egyesülete) in 1904. In Austria, veteran feminists Hainisch and Schwarz joined with Ernestine von Forth to found the Committee for Women's Suffrage in 1906, titling it a "Committee" to skirt the 1867 ban on women in political organizations. In Bohemia-Moravia, Prague teacher Frantiska Plamínková (1875–1942) and twelve other women started a Czech women's suffrage committee in 1905. That committee, like a later Polish one in Galicia, posed a dilemma for international organizations. The ICW disappointed dissident ethnic minorities by recognizing only one council within an existing state, but the IWSA admitted the separate Czech and Galician groups.

Finnish and Russian women's ties to the IWSA developed during the brief period of political reform after the Russian Revolution of 1905. The Finnish legislature, regaining autonomy, voted in May 1906 for universal suffrage for both sexes, and Tsar Nicholas II accepted it. Finland thus became the first European country to let women vote in national elections, joining New Zealand, two Australian states, and four American western states. It was a victory for the Union of Women's Rights, formed in 1892 and led by Annie Furuhjelm. In 1907, 19 women (including 9 socialists) were elected to the 200-member legislature, including Lucina Hagman, a headmistress and first president of the Women's Union, and Hilda Käkikoski, a teacher active in the Finnish Women's Association. Although new Russian restrictions and repeated dissolutions soon hampered the legislature, subsequent elections continued to return women members.

The Finnish precedent influenced Norway, where women's support for nationalist campaigns also produced political benefits. Women meeting property qualifications could vote in local elections in 1901 and in national elections in 1907, two years after independence from Sweden. Social class divisions complicated suffragist organizing, however. Krog, Frederikke Marie Quam, and their allies broke with the older suffrage group that resisted universal suffrage, and started the National Association for Women's Suffrage in 1898. Quam (1843–1935), wife of a liberal politician, at one point headed three organizations: the Norwegian Women's Sanitary Association, formed in 1896 to train volunteer nurses in case war with Sweden erupted; the Women's Rights Association; and the newer suffrage group. She also became vice president of Norway's ICW affiliate. More Norwegian women received voting rights in 1910, and by 1913 universal suffrage existed for both sexes.

In Russia, women in Moscow formed the Union of Equal Rights (UER) during the spring 1905 upheaval. Its principal founders were born during the 1860s, but older supporters included Anna Evreinova, who held a German law degree. With several thousand members by autumn and branches in 54 localities, the UER pressed, unsuccessfully, for women's inclusion in a new election law. It next gathered 4,500 signatures on a suffrage petition sent to the new legislature (duma) shortly before the tsar dissolved it. Zinaida Mirovich and five other UER members also attended the IWSA conference in 1906 in Copenhagen, where Catt welcomed them as "daughters who had long been shut away in prison."[11] Later, Russian feminists used the IWSA journal *Jus Suffragii* to report mounting political repression. Although the UER lost members, it persuaded 20,000 women and men to sign a voting petition to the second duma in 1907. The Mutual Philanthropic Society, where Filosofova and Shabanova were prominent, also added a political rights section and used its connections with the tsarist government to secure approval to hold the first women's congress in Russia, albeit with restrictions. The regime tried to limit the agenda to philanthropy and education, and excluded foreigners. At least three-fourths of the 1,053 people registered for the congress in December 1908 were from St. Petersburg, and most women attending were middle-class and often worked. Subsequently the Russian League of Equal Rights for Women replaced the demoralized UER, maintaining international ties until 1917 but never attracting more than 2,000 members.

---

[11] Quoted in Linda Harriet Edmondson, *Feminism in Russia, 1900–1917* (Stanford, Calif.: Stanford University Press, 1984), 112.

Russia's momentary political liberalization also heartened Polish nationalists, women included. Repression since 1863 kept women's activities more surreptitious in Russian Poland than in Austrian Galicia, although they were more substantial than in Prussian Poland. Paulina Kuczalska-Reinschmit (1859–1921), from a landowning family, had organized a covert women's group after attending one of the congresses in Paris in 1889. Officially registered as a Circle of Working Women in 1891, it held a conference on women's work in Warsaw. The first such meeting for Polish women, it drew 198 participants. A second conference in Galicia in 1894 was timed to coincide with remembrance of a failed uprising in 1794 against foreign control. Women in Cracow staged a Polish Women's Conference in 1905, and in 1907 emboldened women formed the Association for Women's Equal Rights in Warsaw. Kuczalska-Reinschmit headed it before leaving, with older activists, to form the Union for Women's Equal Rights.

While most eastern European feminist and suffrage organizations were just starting, one part of the English suffrage campaign adopted more militant methods, its participants becoming known as *suffragettes* in 1906. Like the term *feminist*, *suffragette* was first coined as a pejorative, but after the mass-circulation *Daily Mail* used it to differentiate militants from other *suffragists*, many members of the Women's Social and Political Union (WSPU) embraced it. Emmeline Pankhurst (1858–1928), widow of a lawyer supportive of the Independent Labour Party, founded the WSPU in Manchester in 1903, hoping to attract more working-class women than the older National Union of Women's Suffrage Societies (NUWSS), formed in 1897 when fifteen groups united. The NUWSS leader was Millicent Garrett Fawcett (1847–1929), Elizabeth Garrett Anderson's younger sister, who devoted herself to suffrage work after her husband's death. Fawcett favored the traditional methods of lobbying and petitioning Parliament, and, eventually, peaceful demonstrations. The WSPU first drew national attention in October 1905, when Mrs. Pankhurst's daughter Christabel and Annie Kenney, a cotton-mill worker, disrupted a Liberal Party meeting in Manchester by asking what Liberals would do for women if they won the upcoming elections for the House of Commons. Both were arrested and, to dramatize their cause, opted for jail rather than pay a fine. The WSPU relocated to London to pressure the new Liberal government, organizing demonstrations in public squares and heckling unsympathetic politicians, including Herbert Asquith, the anti-suffrage prime minister as of 1908. In June 1908 the NUWSS organized a massive outdoor rally, attracting between 250,000 and 500,000 people, including members of the WSPU and the Women's Freedom League (WFL), which broke with the WSPU

Figure 7.1 "The March of the Women," composed by Ethel Smyth, 1911, for the Women's Social and Political Union (WSPU).

in 1907 to protest the Pankhursts' autocratic leadership. By 1909 the WSPU's escalated tactics included breaking shop windows. When punished with imprisonment, some suffragettes went on hunger strikes and endured force-feeding (Figure 7.1).

The WSPU methods were unladylike but gained publicity and, remarked WSPU members, resembled the contemporary street tactics used by both labor union militants and some Irish groups demanding home rule. Indeed, the WSPU drew the line at attacks on persons, unlike some radical Irish nationalists who resorted to political murders. The NUWSS rejected illegal action, but Fawcett also recognized suffragette achievements, telling the London *Times* that the WSPU had "done more to bring the movement within the region of practical politics within twelve months than I and my followers in the same number of years."[12] In terms of numbers, the publicity – positive and negative – that the WSPU brought the suffrage campaign helped the NUWSS more than the WSPU. In 1908, the NUWSS had 8,000 members, about double what the WSPU recorded; by 1914, NUWSS membership approached 55,000, in 600 affiliated groups, while the WSPU claimed only about 4,000, in 90 affiliates. The NUWSS also moved closer to the new Labour Party, which supported universal suffrage, while the WSPU pushed to enfranchise women under current law that excluded many men. The Pankhursts' frustration with the Liberal Party intensified in 1912–13, when the government moved forward on Irish home rule but not women's suffrage, two 1910 elections having ended the Conservatives' ability to block home rule indefinitely through the House of Lords. The WSPU added arson to its tactics in 1912, and the government responded with a law dubbed the Cat and Mouse Act, which enabled it to jail, release, and then rearrest WSPU militants.

The new momentum in British suffrage campaigning attracted much international attention and led some suffragists elsewhere to consider more assertive tactics than meetings and petitions. Women's militancy elsewhere was tamer, however. In France in 1904, the centennial year of the Napoleonic code, feminists protested its restrictions on women with a demonstration at the Vendôme column (topped by Napoleon's statue), and Auclert tore up a copy of the code. In 1908, she and Pelletier broke windows in a Paris polling place and overturned a ballot box, drawing much criticism (Figure 7.2). So did nine women's attempt to run for the legislature two years later. The nine included Marguerite Durand (1864–1936), founder of the feminist newspaper *La Fronde* (1897–1903), Auclert, and socialists Pelletier and Caroline Kauffmann. In Germany, the end of bans on women's political organizing in 1908 led Augspurg to propose street demonstrations. Indeed, she and thirty supporters participated in a demonstration in London in 1908, and English suffragettes visited Germany. Yet knowing that the general public associated street actions with socialists made most German suffragists dubious about militant methods. The BDF also became more cautious after a divisive internal debate on birth control and abortion,

[12] Quoted in Roger Ellis, *Who's Who in Victorian Britain* (Mechanicsburg, Penn.: Stackpole Books, 1997), 386.

Figure 7.2 Hubertine Auclert, early advocate of women's suffrage in France, campaigning in 1906.

and its assembly ousted president Stritt, deemed too radical, in 1910. Policy differences caused a three-way split in the ranks of Germany's 14,000 suffragists by 1913. Augsburg, Cauer, and Heymann left the DVF they had founded and joined the new German Women's Suffrage League. A third group, formed in 1911, was the most conservative, favoring the financial qualifications for voting used in many states' elections. Dutch suffragists were also wary of suffragette tactics, but under the urging of Jacobs, who had participated in London WSPU processions and was VVVK president from 1903 to 1919, they marched in 1910 on a day dedicated to women's suffrage. Schwimmer helped organize a mass meeting in Budapest in September 1912, reportedly drawing 10,000 people.

Czech suffragists sought to convince nationalist leaders that defending propertied women's political privileges, threatened by Austrian authorities after the granting of universal manhood suffrage in 1907, was as much a Czech as a feminist issue. A loophole in regulations for the Bohemian assembly seemingly permitted women's candidacies, which Plamínková now pushed. Tomáš Masaryk was sympathetic, his American-born wife Charlotte having translated Mill's feminist classic into Czech. In 1912 several parties nominated Bozena Viková-Kunetická, a successful writer, who won a seat after a male candidate withdrew. The provincial governor then barred her from the assembly, which was dissolved in July 1913 and never recalled because of World War I.

French suffrage organizing moved forward when the French Union for Women's Suffrage (UFSF) was formed in 1909, with support from some CNFF leaders. Earlier suffrage groups like Auclert's or Solidarity, dating from 1891, had dwindled to obscurity, each with fewer than 25 members. The LFDF, the most important older organization supporting women's suffrage, was won over by secretary-general Vérone but had only 200 members in 1901 and a few hundred more by 1910. The CNFF added a suffrage section in 1906, but not all affiliates favored it. Reporting to the IWSA in 1911, Cécile Brunschvicg (1877–1946), UFSF secretary-general, characterized earlier French suffragists as "a circle of feminists with advanced opinions," whereas the UFSF sought to reach the masses with "more moderate opinions."[13] Although probably unfair to some earlier suffragists, she reflected much middle-class opinion. Vérone's League affiliated with the UFSF but kept a separate identity. Brunschvicg, the daughter of a wealthy industrialist, wife of a philosophy professor, and mother of three, was also among the assimilated Jewish women who joined with Protestants and anticlericals or former Catholics in the CNFF and UFSF. The first UFSF president, the English-born Protestant Jeanne Schmahl (1846–1915), had orchestrated a campaign leading to the 1907 law on married women workers' control of their earnings. She was soon succeeded by the aging Eliska Vincent, an artisan's daughter, and then by Marguerite de Witt-Schlumberger, granddaughter of Guizot, wife of a rich businessman, and mother of six children. French feminists put suffrage on the agenda of the

[13] International Woman Suffrage Alliance, *Report of Sixth Congress, Stockholm, Sweden, 1911* (London: Women's Printing Society, 1911), 97.

International Congress on Women's Charities and Institutions in Paris in 1913, and in 1914 many believed that a first step, women's voting in local elections, was imminent because the new premier, René Viviani, was pro-suffrage. Just before the spring 1914 elections, the popular Paris newspaper *Le Journal* asked women readers whether they wanted the vote, and a half million sent affirmative responses. On 5 July, French feminists staged their largest prewar public action, as 6,000 women marched to honor the Marquis de Condorcet for his prophetic words on women's rights. The UFSF then had 12,000 members and the LFDF about 1,000, as compared to 100,000 in the CNFF.

Collective identities

Apart from women already identified, who were the leaders and members of the many feminist organizations existing by 1900 or soon thereafter when women's suffrage groups became more numerous? Only a small minority of any country's adult women joined such organizations. Many leaders and members were middle class and from urban areas, the middle class encompassing a range of income levels – from the prosperous to the more modest, including many teachers and clerks who worked for a living. Married women were probably at least half the membership in some groups – not surprising because they might have more leisure time than single working women to devote to reform causes. Feminist leaders and followers were more often Protestant than Catholic, and in central and eastern Europe Jewish women's involvement was also striking. After 1900, the older leaders were typically born between the 1840s and 1860s, the younger during the 1870s or early 1880s. Suffrage advocacy, in particular, required the psychological wherewithal to tolerate public scorn and raised eyebrows in middle- and upper-class social circles, as English feminist Gertrude Colmore knew from experience and conveyed in her novel, *The Suffragettes* (originally *Suffragette Sally*, 1911).

Two historians' analyses of four generational cohorts of British feminists offer similar findings. Olive Banks's study of 98 active women born between 1785 and 1891 found that 43 percent were married and another 11 percent widowed or separated; and Philippa Levine's survey of 194 women born between the 1790s and 1870s tabulated 45 percent as married. Compared to most contemporary married women, however, these married feminists usually had fewer children or none. Familial political leanings apparently influenced British women's participation in reform groups more than did social class or religious origins, the latter largely Protestant. Many feminists shared the sympathies of fathers, husbands, and other male relatives for the Liberal Party, at least until

Liberals' resistance to women's suffrage led to more feminist support for the new Labour Party. Among the personal experiences causing women to protest against their legal and societal subordination to men were disappointing marriages and problems in the workplace, such as difficulty in finding employment or earning less than men for comparable work. For women untouched by such adversity, a sense of having a mission to help others was often compelling, as with Josephine Butler. Few feminists had mothers who were employed, but 52 in Banks's group of 98 worked for pay at some point in life, as did 46 percent of the larger sample. Teaching, writing, and journalism were the most common sources of income, and nearly a third of Levine's group of 194 published books. The major difference between the two studies' findings is that nearly 90 percent (87) of Banks's 98 had some involvement in women's suffrage, whereas just 52 percent of Levine's 194 had "active ties" to it.

For the later British generations, a contemporary analysis in 1907 of women's signatures on a suffrage petition indicated considerable support from some working women, especially in white-collar occupations. The majority of 25,000 signers were employed, including 5,642 educators, 450 doctors, 1,100 clerks and secretaries, over 1,000 in the arts, 3,300 in trades and factories, and 2,769 domestic servants. British organizations enlisted more urban working-class women than did other European counterparts, partly because socialists on the continent rejected cooperation, as noted below. In addition to the well-known NUWSS, WSPU, and WFL, some suffrage groups were based on educational, professional, or religious identities, and might affiliate with the bigger organizations. For example, the Actresses' Franchise League claimed 900 members in 1914, a civil servants' group numbered 600, and women clerks formed a WSPU branch. The NUWSS drew support from 630 Cambridge University students and graduates, 850 from the University of London, and 330 from Scottish universities.

The largely middle-class and Protestant profiles of German feminists resembled those of the British. Of 40 German feminists prominent around 1900, 34 were middle class, and only 4 from the working class and 2 from the aristocracy. At least 40 percent were married. Teachers and former teachers among these leaders included Schmidt, Lange and Marie Loeper-Housselle, founders of the General Association of Women Teachers, Marie Lischnewska, and Gertrud Bäumer. Two-thirds became involved while in their thirties, and another quarter during their twenties. One-quarter were Jewish. In the large BDF, more than 100,000 women belonged to affiliated groups for white-collar workers in 1913, including nearly 43,000 teachers, 50,000 retail and office clerks, 6,800 postal and telegraph employees, 3,500 nurses, and 1,300 midwives. Unlike the conservative Protestant Evangelical Women's Federation, the Catholic Women's Association, founded in 1904, rejected membership in the BDF, judging its concerns too strictly secular. The Jewish Women's Federation with 32,000 members was among the larger affiliates of the Protestant-led BDF, although Jews were less than 2 percent of the population. As in Austria-Hungary, Jewish support also provoked anti-Semitic denunciations of feminism. Whereas membership in all BDF affiliates then totaled 470,000 (but was actually less because some individuals held multiple memberships), its suffrage affiliates had fewer than 14,000, despite BDF endorsement of suffrage in 1907.

Feminist groups elsewhere in Europe had similar middle-class profiles, and suffrage organizations, in particular, often attracted women in white-collar occupations. More than half of the members of the Norwegian Women's Rights Association were married, and over half lived in the capital city, Christiania (Oslo). Like Gina Krog, many unmarried and employed feminists were teachers. The Danish Women's Suffrage Federation, formed in 1898, recruited members from the Women's Society and associations of teachers, authors, artists, business and office workers, tailoresses, silverpolishers, and midwives. Many attendees at the Russian women's congress in 1908 were employed, and of 250 who completed a questionnaire, half indicated having a secondary education and a third had attended a higher course. The Hungarian FE appealed to women clerks and teachers. Similarly, in France in 1914, one-third of 180 UFSF leaders in Paris and provincial departments were teachers or directresses in primary, secondary, or normal schools.

An upper-class image for ICW leaders was certainly provided by Lady Aberdeen and a few other women, like German baroness Beschwitz who headed the ICW law commission from 1899 to 1908, but aristocrats were a minority among its leaders at the international level and in most affiliated national councils. Hungary, with a largely agrarian economy and small middle class, was an exception to the norm of middle-class leadership, for Countess Ilona Batthyány-Andrássy and then Countess Clotilde Apponyi headed the national council. Countess Gabriella Spalletti Rasponi presided over Italy's national council as of 1904. Baroness Alexandra Gripenberg twice led the Finnish Women's Association after 1888, although Russia barred a Finnish affiliation with the ICW until 1911. The unusual feminist trajectory of German aristocrat Lily von Kretschmann Braun (1865–1916), a general's daughter, ran from working with Minna Cauer to joining the socialists.

Feminists from working-class backgrounds were less numerous on the continent than in Great Britain. Banks identified 16 of 98 British feminist leaders (including 11 born after 1848) as working class, but Levine found that only 6 percent of her group of 194 ever did manual labor. British leaders certainly sought recruits from women workers' associations, such as the Women's Provident and Protective League started in 1874 by Emma Smith Paterson, a teacher's daughter who became a bookbinder. Textile workers in Manchester also gave noteworthy support. Yet many poor working women could not afford to pay organizational dues, lacked time to attend meetings, or felt uncomfortable with middle-class women. French seamstress Louise Saumoneau, who became a socialist, reported feeling out of place at a feminist meeting in Paris in 1897 because of her simple clothing and awareness that her way of speaking put off middle-class women. Socialist parties also discouraged working-class women from joining feminist organizations, as noted below. When leaders of the Russian women's congress in 1908 wanted to show solidarity across class lines, thirty-five women workers, urged on by Ekaterina Kuskova and socialist Alexandra Kollontai, denounced the meeting as "bourgeois" and staged a walkout.

At a time when relationships between church and state were often divisive in politics, religious allegiances also influenced women's attitudes toward feminism and suffrage in many countries. Protestant women's leadership of northern European associations has been noted. In France, where republicans and Catholics clashed over secular public schools, freeing Alfred Dreyfus, and separating church and state in 1905, Catholic women knew that Pope Pius X opposed women's direct involvement in politics. He asserted in 1909 that women were "under men's authority" and should not seek "the same rights and social role as men." Although a woman was "neither a slave nor a servant of men," her different and "unique" role was "to raise children and form a family."[14] To counter secular women's groups, French Catholic women formed Christian Feminism in 1897, Women's Social Action in 1900, and the Women's Patriotic League (LPF, Ligue Patriotique des Françaises) in 1902. Whereas Marie Maugeret and Jeanne Chenu, the creators, respectively, of the first two groups, envisioned a Catholic feminism engaged in social reform and Maugeret wanted women's suffrage, LPF leaders shunned the feminist label. Yet the LPF claimed half a million members by 1914, far outdistancing other French women's groups. Within the National Council of Italian Women, Catholic and secular women also clashed over the place of religion in public schools. Devout Italian women favored the Union of Catholic Women and shunned the National Committee for Women's Suffrage. When Italian suffragists,

[14] Quoted in Offen, *European Feminisms*, 199.

urged on by the indefatigable Mozzoni and Teresa Labriola, drew up their first petition to the legislature in 1907, they collected only 600 signatures, Montessori among them. But the Catholic hierarchy's resistance to women's voting, modified only after World War I, did not stop some Belgian Catholics from challenging Popelin's League for Women's Rights or the newer Union for Suffrage by starting the Society of Christian Feminism in 1902 and the Catholic League for Women's Suffrage in 1912. Similarly, some members of the German Catholic Women's Association were pro-suffrage, and the English Catholic Women's Suffrage Society, founded in 1911, quarreled with bishops. In Portugal the anticlerical republic that replaced the monarchy in 1910 and separated church and state provided the setting for groups led by women like Dr. Adelaide Cabete to affiliate with the ICW and IWSA, whereas neighboring Spain lacked feminist associations before 1914. The International Union of Catholic Women's Associations, founded in 1910, also shunned the ICW and IWSA, which were seen as Protestant and secular.

Organizational memberships tell only part of the story, of course, about public support for suffrage, as is indicated by the great difference between the membership of 14,000 in French suffrage groups in 1914 and the 500,000 women telling Le Journal that they wanted to vote. About 6 million women belonged to the ICW's national affiliates in 1914, as compared to perhaps 350,000 in IWSA affiliates. The American IWSA contingent was the largest – 75,000 in 1910, 100,000 in 1915 – followed by at least 60,000 in British groups. The memberships in women's suffrage organizations in Denmark (23,200), the Netherlands (18,800), and Sweden (15,000) – with populations of 3 million, 6 million, and 5.5 million, respectively – exceeded the 14,000 members in either Germany (population 65 million) or France (population 40 million). In southern, central, and eastern Europe, demanding votes for women was a more radical stance than in much of northern and western Europe where parliamentary traditions were firmly established and aspects of the larger culture, religious and secular, less resistant. In Hungary, for example, where fewer than 25 percent of adult men could vote, the ICW-affiliated Council had 45,000 members in 1914 but the pro-suffrage FE no more than 1,000. Yet the Budapest city council helped fund the 1913 IWSA meeting organized by the FE.

Reproductive rights: a marginal or unwelcome issue

Women's control of their own bodies, a central feminist issue since the 1960s, was a marginal concern, if that, for most feminists before 1914. As nations recorded declining birthrates, albeit to varying degrees, governments often called on married couples to produce more, not fewer, healthy offspring. For feminists using the maternalist argument that mothers deserved equal rights because they were rearing future citizens, asking for the right to control reproduction seemed both unimaginable and untimely. Campaigns against state-regulated prostitution certainly brought middle-class women into public debates entailing repeated references to sexuality, but many feminists thought discussion of birth control was unladylike, immoral, or likely to encourage irresponsible sexual behavior. When Jacobs became the Dutch suffragists' leader, she ceased discussing birth control in public. Similarly, Jacobs's friend Schwimmer tempered expression of her views when appointed to the National Board of Child Welfare in Hungary. Garrett Anderson evidently sometimes gave patients advice on contraception but was not a public advocate. Lady Florence Dixie, who wrote on women's "rights over their own person and the control of the birth of children" in 1891, was an exception to most British feminists' silence on the subject, as was novelist Mona Caird.[15] For Catholic women, birth control was contrary to church teachings. Before 1914, public debate about the desirability of limiting births was as much, or more, the concern of male reformers as it was of women. Yet some women entered this debate and linked it to feminism.

In England the trial of William Bradlaugh and Annie Besant for publishing a book about contraceptive methods drew attention to birth control in 1877 and led to the founding of the Neo-Malthusian League, named after Thomas Malthus, who had warned that overpopulation created poverty. Neo-Malthusians, like Dr. Charles Drysdale and his wife Dr. Alice Vickery, also emphasized that smaller families could be healthier families. Vickery founded the Women's Branch of the International Malthusian League in 1904. Stella Browne, a younger Malthusian, added the argument in 1912 that women, married or not, had a right to enjoy sex – a radical message for the day.

The Dutch Neo-Malthusian League dated from 1881, its members including Jacobs, who had met English Malthusians. Believing that "no child should come into the world" who was "not deeply desired," Jacobs also argued that contraceptive use would mean fewer abortions.[16] By the 1890s birth control probably had more public support in the Netherlands than in any other country, and the feminist Drucker favored

---

[15] Dixie quoted in Susan Kingsley Kent, *Sex and Suffrage in Britain, 1860–1914* (Princeton, N.J.: Princeton University Press, 1987), 112.

[16] Quoted in Ann Taylor Allen, *Feminism and Motherhood in Western Europe, 1890–1970* (New York: Palgrave Macmillan, 2005), 99.

it. Dr. Catherine van Tussenbroek dissented, however, contending that contraception gave men and doctors control over women's bodies. The advocacy of Neo-Malthusians Johannes Rutgers and his wife Marie Rutgers-Hoitsema could not prevent new Dutch regulations on selling contraceptives or stiffer anti-abortion laws in 1911.

French neo-Malthusians like the anarchist Paul Robin argued that the quality of a population was more important than the quantity, but such views clashed with emphasis on increasing the French population to withstand the larger Germany. A Protestant saddened by encountering many unwanted children when he headed an orphanage, Robin founded the League for Human Regeneration in 1896. French birthrates had been declining since the late 1700s, and France was, in fact, the first major European country where citizens limited births, many men apparently practicing withdrawal before ejaculation. The idea that French women might also control reproduction was another matter, but one which two very different women, Nelly Roussel and Pelletier, did not avoid.

Roussel (1878–1922) made birth control a national crusade. Born into a Catholic middle-class family in Paris, she had imagined an acting career but her parents disapproved. She married Henri Godet, a struggling sculptor fifteen years older, in 1898 and had three children by 1904, two of whom survived infancy. Godet's sister married Robin's son. Robin's comments on birth control at a feminist congress in Paris in 1896 had generated vehement opposition, but Roussel was not deterred. Gaining a reputation as a highly effective feminist orator well before she was thirty, she joined the moderate Union Fraternelle des Femmes, a pro-suffrage CNFF affiliate that included some *La Fronde* contributors. She protested against official celebration of the Napoleonic Code in 1904, speaking to an audience of 800 on how it disadvantaged women. But unlike most French feminists, she also publicly advocated birth control. An attractive middle-class wife and mother, Roussel cultivated an image of respectability, well described by Elinor Accampo, to soften a message otherwise judged extreme at a time when politicians railed against depopulation. Between 1901 and 1910, before tuberculosis weakened her, she made frequent speaking tours across France, sponsored by various groups: neo-Malthusians, feminists, teachers, Masonic lodges, freethinkers, socialists, and pacifists. When she was away from Paris, her mother, sister, and hired aides helped with child care; her husband ran the home; and her stepfather bolstered her finances.

Roussel saw birth control as consistent with a woman's right to take charge of her life but also shrewdly embraced other arguments to promote it. Thus she stressed that in smaller families each child could receive more maternal attention and, as a result, become a healthier and more productive adult. In her most famous lecture, "The Woman Always Sacrificed," delivered fifty times in 1905–06 alone, she artfully defined feminism as "the doctrine of *natural equivalence* and *social equality* of the sexes." Her talk on "The Freedom of Motherhood" proclaimed that "love and procreation are not inseparable" and asserted that "if both sexes had to give birth ... and share the pain of procreation equally," fewer men would oppose "voluntary birth control." She spoke frankly about women who looked like "human wrecks" because of "having too many children," adding that as "a woman and mother" she believed that she spoke "on behalf of all women and mothers, and of all men of heart."[17] Roussel's lectures often attracted hundreds of people, and her fees and sales of pamphlets financed the work that she likened to an apostolate. By not providing details about specific methods of birth control, she avoided prosecution for obscene speech, which several neo-Malthusians faced by 1909. She was not the only French woman to speak publicly about women's reproductive rights, but she had an aura of maternal and middle-class respectability that the unmarried and asexual socialist Pelletier or the socialist feminist Gabrielle Petit lacked.

Unlike Roussel and Jacobs, who presented birth control as a way to stop abortions, Pelletier insisted, controversially, that women should have the right to opt for abortion. The chapter "Motherhood Must Be a Free Choice" in her book *The Sexual Emancipation of Women* (1911) was republished separately as *The Right to Abortion* (1913). Pelletier contended that "Our right over our bodies is absolute," and a fetus "is part of the mother's body," not a person.[18] Calling for decriminalizing abortions, she argued that they were already common in large cities, and if legalized, doctors could safely perform them within the first trimester, the time limit she favored.

In Germany, a larger number of women than in France, albeit still a small minority, publicly addressed birth control and abortion law. In the background were the eugenics movement and new discussions of sexuality. Eugenicists wanted to improve the population by encouraging the fittest to reproduce and discouraging the supposedly less fit. The major women's group raising reproductive issues was the League for Protection of Motherhood (BFM, Bund für Mutterschutz), founded in Leipzig in 1904 but soon led by its Berlin branch and Helene Stöcker (1869–1943).

---

[17] Nelly Roussel, "She Who is Always Sacrificed," and "The Freedom of Motherhood," trans. Jette Kjaer and Jennifer Waelti-Walters, in *Feminisms of the Belle Epoque: A Historical and Literary Anthology*, ed. Jennifer Waelti-Walters and Steven C. Hause (Lincoln: University of Nebraska Press, 1994), 20, 243–45, 247.

[18] Madeleine Pelletier, "The Right to Abortion," trans. Lydia Willis and Jennifer Waelti-Walters, in Waelti-Walters and Hause, ed. *Feminisms*, 260.

The oldest of eight children, Stöcker had rebelled against a strict Calvinist upbringing and trained for teaching before receiving a doctorate in German literature in Bern in 1901. She believed that emancipating women "from economic subjection also involves emancipation from sexual subjection." On behalf of mothers and infants the BFM advocated birth control, compensation for maternity as a national service analogous to male military service, and the right of all women, married or not, to become mothers if they wished. Support for unmarried motherhood shocked moralists at a time when some contemporaries, including Freudians, had started an open discussion of women's sexual desires. The BFM campaign against current abortion law was also controversial. Insisting that motherhood "should no longer be forced on women by threats of imprisonment," it targeted the criminal code, section 218, which imposed prison terms of up to five years on women who deliberately aborted a fetus, resulting in about 400 women being jailed each year.[19]

Controversy over BFM goals also embroiled the large BDF. The BFM, with nearly 3,800 members by 1908, had joined the BDF, and Stritt, the BDF president, belonged to the BFM. Stritt urged the BDF Legal Committee to advocate abolishing section 218 so that women could take responsibility for themselves and refuse to be merely "the involuntary producers of cannon fodder." Asserting women's right to "freedom of the personality, to which above all belongs the disposal over one's own body," supporters of decriminalizing abortion also argued that it would reduce infant mortality and illegitimate births.[20] Opponents contended that women would become more vulnerable to men. BDF moderates and the conservative Protestant affiliate joined forces against Stritt and Stöcker at the BDF General Assembly in 1908. A small majority rejected the Legal Committee's comprehensive proposals yet did call for legalizing abortion in cases of rape, fetal defect, or protecting a mother's life. Thereby the BDF took a position on revising abortion law that had no parallel in major feminist organizations elsewhere. But the heated conflict over abortion and Stöcker's views on sexual morality doomed Stritt's continuation as BDF president. Gertrud Bäumer (1873–1954), a former teacher and Lange's assistant, succeeded Stritt in 1910, heading the BDF until 1919. German socialists also divided over reproductive rights, although some socialist doctors, including Hope Adams-Lehmann, evidently performed abortions.

Beyond Germany the BFM had small offshoots in Austria and in Sweden, where Frida Steenhoff started a branch, but birth control

---

[19] Quotations in Richard J. Evans, *The Feminist Movement in Germany 1894–1933* (London: Sage, 1976), 118, 132.

[20] Quotations in ibid., 133; and Allen, *Feminism and Motherhood in Western Europe*, 102.

advocate Katti Anker Moller failed to establish one in Norway. Feminist support for birth control elsewhere came largely from individuals rather than groups other than the neo-Malthusians.

Socialism and feminism

Large contingents of working-class women were missing from most European feminist organizations. In Britain many women in trade unions and the Labour Party, formed after 1900, did support women's suffrage, but differences in social class backgrounds and disputes over protective legislation often separated feminists and workers. During the 1890s England, France, and Germany passed new laws limiting the hours women could work, particularly in factories, and banning or restricting nighttime work. Other countries followed suit. Many feminists, especially in Anglo-American contexts, thought that protective laws unfairly restrained an individual's freedom to make economic decisions. In Germany and elsewhere on the continent, however, some feminists agreed with government claims, also supported by socialists, that such laws were needed to protect working mothers' health and allow them time for their children and household duties. Working women often appreciated limits on hours if they had family obligations, but many complained that fewer hours reduced their earnings, caused employers to prefer male workers with more flexibility, and were unfair because men did not face the same limits.

A divide also typically existed on the continent between feminist groups and working-class women who became socialists, despite socialists' theoretical commitment to equality between the sexes. August Bebel, a founder of the German Socialist Party, argued for the goal of gender equality in his *Woman and Socialism* (1879), and Friedrich Engels, Karl Marx's collaborator, blamed capitalism for women's virtual enslavement in the home. Engels's *Origin of the Family, Private Property and the State* (1884) envisioned women as both workers and homemakers in a future egalitarian, classless society. In 1889 Bebel and Wilhelm Liebknecht, in combination with French socialists and delegates from fifteen other European countries, met in Paris to found the Second International, the previous International Workingmen's Association that Marx and Engels helped create in 1864 not having lasted beyond 1876. The growth of the German Socialist Party (SPD, Sozialdemokratische Partei Deutschlands) after Bismarck's antisocialist laws were dropped in 1890 enabled Germans to dominate the Second International and impose Marxist doctrine on other parties. German socialists endorsed women's suffrage in 1891, first proposing it to the Reichstag in 1895, and they urged socialists elsewhere to do the same. Bebel's revised version of *Woman and Socialism* (1891) appeared in at least fifty editions and fifteen translations before 1914.

Yet the Second International also instructed socialist women to shun feminist organizations led by middle-class women, asserting that these benefited only the bourgeoisie, the upper middle class defined by Marx as the primary enemy of working-class liberation. Socialist women were told that after socialism triumphed, through elections or revolution, the elimination of economic inequality and class divisions would liberate women from the subjection caused by capitalism. Recognition of how working-class men also perpetuated women's subjection was usually missing from socialist statements. In practice, many socialists and men in labor unions resisted equal pay for women workers, convinced that it would depress their own wages; and many also believed that if they, as male breadwinners, could earn more, then their wives should remain at home, like middle-class women. Rejection of one class by another was not a one-way street, of course. Founders of the BDF initially refused to invite socialist women to meetings in 1894, and socialist Clara Zetkin had asserted by then that women could not be free until capitalism was destroyed.

In the German context, where many states barred women from political associations until 1908, some socialist women found opportunity. The SPD created separate women's groups during the 1890s, and Zetkin began editing the women's newspaper *Gleicheit* (Equality) in 1892. Born in Saxony, Zetkin (1857–1933) had attended the school in Leipzig headed by Auguste Schmidt and later worked as a governess. Her younger brother drew her to socialism, and in 1881 she followed her Russian partner into exile in Paris. His death in 1889 left her with two children to support, and she knew well the difficulty of having to make her "way in the world like a man." Speaking at the founding of the Second International in 1889, she stated that women needed economic independence to avoid remaining "socially dependent" upon men. Returning to Germany, she worked on organizing socialist women and saw *Equality*'s circulation increase to 124,000 by 1914. Zetkin agreed that socialism took primacy over feminism, but she attended the Berlin women's congress in 1896 and repeatedly criticized socialists in Belgium and Austria for giving the goal of universal male suffrage priority over women's suffrage. The 1907 International meeting endorsed her call for "complete equality" of the sexes and inclusion of women's suffrage wherever socialist parties campaigned for broader suffrage.[21] She also

---

[21] Quotations from Zetkin in Karen Honeycutt, "Clara Zetkin: A Socialist Approach to the Problem of Women's Oppression," in *European Women on the Left: Socialism, Feminism,*

organized the Socialist Women's International in 1907, and in 1910 proposed an International Woman's Day, taking the date (8 March) from a 1908 protest by working women in New York City. Beginning in 1911, such women's days featured women's suffrage, among other issues, for Zetkin believed that it helped attract working women.

The SPD viewed recruiting women as vital for winning over all members of working-class families, but after German women's exclusion from political associations ended in 1908, SPD leaders gradually dissolved separate women's groups. They marginalized Zetkin by choosing the less assertive Luise Zeitz for the seat on the party's executive council reserved for a woman, although Zetkin continued editing *Equality*. Zetkin's repeated defenses of women's interests also differentiated her from Rosa Luxemburg, who reportedly called feminism "old ladies' nonsense."[22] A famed Marxist theorist, Luxemburg (1871–1919), born in Russian Poland, held a doctorate in law and economics from Zurich and had German citizenship through marriage. By 1914, 174,751 women belonged to the SPD, comprising 16 percent of its membership and also outnumbering any single German feminist group, although the BDF affiliates' combined membership was larger. In no other country were socialist women so numerous or so visible. The SPD drive to amass large memberships also influenced party debate on birth control: supporters cited its benefits for working parents, but opponents argued that to gain power socialists needed a big working-class base, not reduced numbers. Zetkin concurred with male leaders opposed to birth control. Matters came to a head when some socialists proposed a "birth strike," a tactic French neo-Malthusians had suggested to show that workers did not want to produce future soldiers as cannon fodder for governments. After World War I started, SPD leaders threatened reprisals against birth control advocates and, like socialists elsewhere, then put national unity ahead of the class struggle.

Socialist women's groups in other countries faced similar pressure to subordinate women's issues to party dictates. Socialist women in Vienna created an "educational" society in 1892, skirting Austria's ban on women in political associations, and also started the *Working Women's Newspaper*,

and the Problems Faced by Political Women, 1880 to the Present, ed. Jane Slaughter and Robert Kern (Westport, Conn.: Greenwood Press, 1981), 32, 40; and Charles Sowerwine, "Socialism, Feminism, and the Socialist Women's Movement from the French Revolution to World War II," in *Becoming Visible: Women in European History*, 3rd edn., ed. Renate Bridenthal, Susan Mosher Stuard, and Merry E. Wiesner (Boston: Houghton Mifflin, 1998), 370–71.

22   Quoted in Richard J. Evans, *The Feminists: Women's Emancipation Movements in Europe, America and Australasia, 1840–1920* (London: Croom Helm, 1977), 161.

edited by Adelheid Popp. After the introduction of universal manhood suffrage in 1907, socialists, male and female, finally gave women's suffrage higher priority, and beginning in March 1911 socialist women organized an annual suffrage day, providing Vienna's first large street demonstration for women's voting. With 28,000 women in 312 groups by 1913, Austrian socialist women ranked second to German socialist women in numbers. In Italy, Anna Kuliscioff (1854–1925) and her partner Filippo Turati spearheaded the founding of a unified socialist party in 1892. Educated in Russia but fleeing in 1877 to avoid arrest, she earned a medical degree in Italy and practiced in Milan, supporting herself and a child. Although sometimes dubbed the Italian Zetkin, Kuliscioff deferred openly criticizing male socialists for neglecting women's suffrage until Italy moved to adopt universal male suffrage. She headed a new socialist women's group in 1912 but soon lost the post to Angelica Balabanoff, also Russian-born, who believed that for socialists a "feminist problem does not exist."[23] French women's role in socialist parties was also limited, and French socialism was highly factionalized until 1905, when German socialists and French Marxist allies forced the creation of a single party, the French Section of the Workers' International (SFIO), as a condition for staying in the International. The SFIO refused to recognize the small Feminist Socialist group started in 1899 by Saumoneau and Elisabeth Renaud, even when the party endorsed women's suffrage. Pelletier, active in the SFIO, did not push for a separate women's organization, and none was formally organized until 1913, under Marianne Rauze's lead. Marxist socialism exerted less appeal in republican France than in authoritarian Germany: the SFIO membership of 90,000 in 1914 was less than one-tenth that of the SPD, and women were only 3 percent of SFIO members.

As the backgrounds of Kuliscioff, Balabanoff, and Luxemburg indicate, Russian repression often drove the tsar's subjects who supported radical change underground or into exile. At a London meeting in 1903, Vladimir Ilich Ulyanov – better known as Lenin – split Russian Marxists into two wings, with himself as head of the more revolutionary Bolshevik wing, aided by his wife Nadezhda Krupskaia. Alexandra Kollontai (1872–1952), a general's daughter, started the Society for the Mutual Help of Working Women in St. Petersburg after the 1905 upheaval, and persuaded socialist women to shun cooperation with bourgeois women at the Russian women's congress in 1908. Yet she also knew, like Zetkin and Kuliscioff, that many socialist men ignored women's specific problems and did not treat their wives as equals. She had left her husband in 1898 and when she fled into exile after 1908, she left a teenaged son

---

[23] Quoted in Sowerwine, "Socialism, Feminism," 381.

behind. Kollontai's greater fame, like Lenin's, came with the Bolshevik takeover of the 1917 Revolution.

While repression in Russia fueled radical politics, in Great Britain traditions of parliamentary governance and reform inclined most working-class men and women to work within the existing system to effect change. Emma Paterson, an early suffragist and organizer of women workers, was evidently the first woman to attend a Trades Union Congress, in 1875, and after her death, Lady Emily Dilke, wife of a Liberal MP, led the Women's Trade Union League. The Labour Party sent women delegates to Zetkin's international meeting of socialist women in 1907 but avoided the Marxist dogmatism of Britain's small Social Democratic Federation (SDF), as did many trade unions, Labour's major supporters. The Labour Party and the older Independent Labour Party (ILP), SDF, and Fabian Society sent their own representatives, rather than a unified delegation, to the Second International. The Labour Party's Women's League, started in 1906, drew working-class members like Margaret Bondfield (1873–1953), who organized shop clerks, and some middle-class members. Its first leader, Margaret MacDonald, was a professor's daughter married to the working-class politician Ramsay MacDonald. By 1910, the League had 5,000 members. Keir Hardie's ILP backed women's suffrage at an early date and helped sway opinion in the larger Labour Party. When the Liberal government stalled action on women's suffrage, many NUWSS members found Labour, with a goal of suffrage for all adults, the most supportive party. The WSPU's deferral of universal suffrage caused a rupture with Labour, and Sylvia Pankhurst, who organized support for suffrage among women workers in London's East End, broke with her mother, sister, and the WSPU after 1912 and maintained her ILP membership. As in continental Europe, the rhetoric of class conflict could persuade many British working-class women to shun organizations led by middle-class women or to rate women's issues as secondary to working-class issues, but British suffrage groups attracted more working-class support than did their continental counterparts challenged by socialist parties.

Conclusion: in 1913–1914

On the eve of World War I the international dimensions of feminist and suffragist organizing were notable. The Budapest meeting of the International Woman Suffrage Alliance attracted 330 delegates from 22 countries, and total attendance by members and visitors reached 2,800. President Catt's formal report also included extensive commentary on interest in women's rights in North Africa, the Middle East, and Asia, for

Figure 7.3 Aletta Jacobs (left) and Carrie Chapman Catt (right), in South Africa, 1911.

she and Jacobs had made a world tour after the 1911 meeting in Stockholm (Figure 7.3). Welcoming a Chinese affiliate to the IWSA, Catt reported that "there is a serious woman's movement in Asia," bolstered in India and China by periodicals for educated women. Egyptian women, too, had started a society for the "emancipation of their sex," and in Indonesia Jacobs helped found nine affiliates of the Dutch suffrage association. Catt also cited serious problems in nonwestern lands, bemoaning the exploitation of child labor and the "Slave Traffic" which sold "white, brown, and yellow" girls and women into prostitution. "The women of East and West have a common cause," she stated, "in their common rebellion against every influence which robs them of their liberty."[24]

Catt's descriptions of women's lives in nonwestern lands echoed themes addressed by British feminists who wanted to help suffering nonwestern "sisters" but often sounded notes of cultural imperialism. "The responsibilities of Empire rest on women as well as men," wrote Helena Swanwick in the suffragist *Common Cause* in 1913.[25] While expressing heartfelt sympathy for unfortunate women in India and elsewhere, feminists also used the theme of the perpetually victimized women in the colonies to bolster their own cause by arguing that such women, suffering from lack of education and medical care, or male abuse, would not be helped substantially until women became voters able to influence British imperial policies. Auclert's *La Femme Arabe* (1900), based on her residence in Algeria, did include an egalitarian message. Exposing Arab women's sufferings at the hands of Arab men and chastising French colonial authorities for neglecting girls' education and allowing polygamy, she asserted that laws common to both French and Arabs should replace the "barbarous oppression" practiced since the 1830s. The idea that politically empowered women could help unfortunate women was not limited, of course, to nonwestern settings. It figured prominently in middle-class women's commentary on what they hoped to do for poor women and children in Europe, although working-class women often resented such interventions.

In May 1914 the International Council of Women convened its quinquennial meeting in Rome and drew at least 3,000 people (Figure 7.4). The mood, recalled some who attended, was optimistic. ICW leaders estimated that its national affiliates now totaled 6 million members. As in the past, many delegates reported on women's philanthropic and educational activities, and others cited recent professional and intellectual achievements as evidence of why women merited wider opportunities. Middle class in status, many ICW members nonetheless championed women needing or wanting to work. When Italian countess Daisy di Robilant reported on women's work and advised women to stay at home, she drew noisy protests. IWSA representatives also went to Rome, and Witt-Schlumberger presided at a large meeting on suffrage at

[24] Quotations in Adele Schreiber and Margaret Mathieson, *Journey Towards Freedom: Written for the Golden Jubilee of the International Alliance of Women* (Copenhagen: International Alliance of Women, 1955), 22–23.

[25] Quoted in Antoinette Burton, *Burdens of History: British Feminists, Indian Women, and Imperial Culture, 1865–1915* (Chapel Hill: University of North Carolina Press, 1994), 187.

Figure 7.4 International Council of Women meeting, Rome, May 1914.

the National Theater where women reported on accomplishments and continued struggles. Women could vote in national elections in Finland, Norway, New Zealand, Australia, and ten American states, and in local elections, under varying conditions, in Sweden, England, and Denmark. Prospects also seemed bright for obtaining municipal suffrage in France. About 1,500 British women served in 1914 as elected members of various local councils or boards, as did more than 200 Norwegian women and at least 67 Swedish women. Suffragists believed that securing the vote was the key to securing substantial changes in other areas, including family law and employment. Vérone from France and Regina Deutsch from Germany drew loud applause when they ended speeches with comments on women's role in maintaining world peace – an ICW standing committee concern since 1899. Less than three months later much of Europe plunged into a world war, and most feminist campaigning ceased, in the name of patriotic unity.

As with much else in the history of human experiences, feminist organizations and the women's achievements they celebrated in 1913–14 may be viewed from more than one perspective. Women had made many gains but also recognized that there was more to accomplish. Against a backdrop of economic and social change, campaigns to democratize governments, and secularization of ideas, European women had undertaken many activities, old and new, since 1789. More women engaged professionally in literature and the arts than their predecessors, had access to more formal schooling for longer periods of time, and as writers, teachers, nurses, doctors, and lawyers supplied models for the "new" women so much discussed by 1900. The extent of change varied from country to country, of course, and across the continent, social class typically limited educational access and, hence, employment possibilities. Western European women often considered themselves to be in a more favorable position than central or eastern European women, sensing that they lived in a freer political climate and that economic growth and urbanization created a wider range of opportunities. British women engaged in women's suffrage organizing sooner than women elsewhere in Europe. Yet women in Germany, Russia, and Austria-Hungary also sought more educational and professional opportunities, sometimes at an early date, and some became suffragists. To demand new rights and opportunities, many women emphasized that they, as women, could make distinctive contributions, while others argued that, as human beings, they deserved equal rights. Although feminists who continued to cite women's differences from men have been criticized, by other feminists and some historians, for perpetuating socially constructed gender differences that needed to be challenged, many feminists before 1914, as well as later, believed that they affirmed women's "equality in difference" and did not see emphasis on difference as indicative of women's inferiority.

Nineteenth-century European women challenged traditional constraints on women's lives more extensively than did women in previous centuries, and their achievements frequently generated a backlash, from angry men or from women disturbed by breaks in tradition. Postwar feminists would return to the continuing inequities in education, employment, the law, and political rights addressed by the last prewar women's congresses.

Further reading and reference works

Accampo, Elinor. *Blessed Motherhood, Bitter Fruit: Nelly Roussel and the Politics of Female Pain in Third Republic France*. Baltimore: Johns Hopkins University Press, 2006.

Allen, Ann Taylor. *Feminism and Motherhood in Germany, 1800–1914*. New Brunswick, N.J.: Rutgers University Press, 1991.

Feminism and Motherhood in Western Europe, 1890–1970. New York: Palgrave Macmillan, 2005.

Anderson, Bonnie S. *Joyous Greetings: The First International Women's Movement, 1830–1860*. New York: Oxford University Press, 2000.

Anderson, Harriet. *Utopian Feminism: Women's Movements in Fin-de-siècle Vienna*. New Haven, Conn.: Yale University Press, 1992.

Banks, Olive. *Becoming a Feminist: The Social Origins of "First Wave" Feminism*. Athens: University of Georgia Press, 1987.

Bidelman, Patrick Kay. *Pariahs Stand Up! The Founding of the Liberal Feminist Movement in France, 1858–1889*. Westport, Conn.: Greenwood Press, 1982.

Bosch, Mineke, and Annemarie Kloosterman, eds. *Politics and Friendship: Letters from the Woman Suffrage Alliance, 1902–1942*. Columbus: Ohio State University Press, 1990.

Boxer, Marilyn J. "Rethinking the Socialist Construction and International Career of the Concept of 'Bourgeois Feminism,'" *American Historical Review* 112 (February 2007): 131–58.

Boxer, Marilyn J. and Jean H. Quataert, eds. *Socialist Women: European Socialist Feminism in the Nineteenth and Early Twentieth Centuries*. New York: Elsevier, 1978.

Burton, Antoinette. *Burdens of History: British Feminists, Indian Women, and Imperial Culture, 1865–1915*. Chapel Hill: University of North Carolina Press, 1994.

Edmondson, Linda Harriet. *Feminism in Russia, 1900–1917*. Stanford, Calif.: Stanford University Press, 1984.

Engel, Barbara Alpern. *Mothers and Daughters: Women of the Intelligentsia in Nineteenth-Century Russia*. Cambridge: Cambridge University Press, 1983.

Evans, Richard J. *The Feminist Movement in Germany 1894–1933*. London: Sage Publications, 1976.

The Feminists: Women's Emancipation Movements in Europe, America and Australasia, 1840–1920. London: Croom Helm, 1977.

Fletcher, Ian Christopher, Laura E. Nym Mayhall, and Philippa Levine, eds. *Women's Suffrage in the British Empire: Citizenship, Nation, and Race*. London: Routledge, 2000.

Frevert, Ute. *Women in German History: From Bourgeois Emancipation to Sexual Liberation*. Translated by Stuart McKinnon-Evans, with Terry Bond and Barbara Norden. New York: Berg, 1989.

Gordon, Felicia. *The Integral Feminist: Madeleine Pelletier, 1874–1939*. Minneapolis: University of Minnesota Press, 1990.

Grogan, Susan K. *French Socialism and Sexual Difference: Women and the New Society, 1803–1844*. Basingstoke: Macmillan, 1992.

Hackett, Amy. "The German Women's Movement and Suffrage, 1890–1914: A Study of National Feminism." In *Modern European Social History*, ed. Robert J. Bezucha, 354–86. Lexington, Mass. : D. C. Heath, 1972.

Hause, Steven C. *Hubertine Auclert: The French Suffragette*. New Haven, Conn.: Yale University Press, 1987.

Hause, Steven C., with Anne R. Kenney. *Women's Suffrage and Social Politics in the French Third Republic*. Princeton, N.J.: Princeton University Press, 1984.

Herminghouse, Patricia A., and Magda Mueller, eds. *German Feminist Writings*. New York: Continuum, 2001.

Hollis, Patricia. *Ladies Elect: Women in English Local Government, 1865–1914*. Oxford: Clarendon Press, 1987.

Holton, Sandra Stanley. *Suffrage Days: Stories from the Women's Suffrage Movement*. London: Routledge, 1996.

Howard, Judith Jeffrey. "Visions of Reform, Visions of Revolution: Women's Activism in the New Italian Nation." In *Views of Women's Lives in Western Tradition: Frontiers of the Past and the Future*, ed. Frances Richardson Keller, 432–50. Lewiston, N.Y.: Edwin Mellen, 1990.

Kaplan, Marion. *The Jewish Feminist Movement in Germany: The Campaigns of the Jüdischer Frauenbund, 1904–1938*. Westport, Conn.: Greenwood Press, 1979.

Kent, Susan Kingsley. *Sex and Suffrage in Britain, 1860–1914*. Princeton, N.J.: Princeton University Press, 1987.

Kuzmack, Linda Gordon. *Woman's Cause: The Jewish Woman's Movement in England and the United States, 1881–1933*. Columbus: Ohio State University Press, 1990.

Levine, Philippa. *Feminist Lives in Victorian England: Private Roles and Public Commitment*. Oxford: Basil Blackwell, 1990.

Victorian Feminism 1850–1900. Gainesville: University Press of Florida, 1994.

Mayhall, Laura E. Nym. *The Militant Suffrage Movement: Citizenship and Resistance in Britain, 1860–1930*. New York: Oxford University Press, 2003.

Moses, Claire Goldberg. *French Feminism in the Nineteenth Century*. Albany: State University of New York Press, 1984.

Moses, Claire Goldberg, and Leslie Wahl Rabine. *Feminism, Socialism, and French Romanticism*. Bloomington: Indiana University Press, 1993.

Offen, Karen. "Defining Feminism: A Comparative Historical Perspective." *Signs: Journal of Women in Culture and Society* 14 (Autumn 1988): 119–57.

  European Feminisms 1700–1950: A Political History. Stanford, Calif.: Stanford University Press, 2000.

Paletschek, Sylvia, and Bianka Pietrow-Ennker, eds. *Women's Emancipation Movements in the Nineteenth Century*. Stanford, Calif.: Stanford University Press, 2004.

Pugh, Martin. *The March of the Women: A Revisionist Analysis of the Campaign for Women's Suffrage, 1866–1914*. Oxford: Oxford University Press, 2000.

Purvis, June. *Emmeline Pankhurst: A Biography*. London: Routledge, 2002.

Quataert, Jean H. *Reluctant Feminists in German Social Democracy, 1885–1917*. Princeton, N.J.: Princeton University Press, 1979.

Reagin, Nancy R. *A German Women's Movement: Class and Gender in Hanover, 1880–1933*. Chapel Hill: University of North Carolina Press, 1995.

Rendall, Jane, ed. *Equal or Different: Women's Politics, 1800–1914*. Oxford: Basil Blackwell, 1987.

Romero, Patricia W. *E. Sylvia Pankhurst: Portrait of a Radical*. New Haven, Conn.: Yale University Press, 1990.

Rupp, Leila J. *Worlds of Women: The Making of an International Women's Movement*. Princeton, N.J.: Princeton University Press, 1997.

Schirmacher, Kaethe. *The Modern Woman's Rights Movement: A Historical Survey*. Translated by Carl Conrad Eckhardt. New York: Macmillan, 1912. Reprinted New York: Kraus, 1971.

Scott, Joan Wallach. *Only Paradoxes to Offer: French Feminists and the Rights of Man*. Cambridge, Mass.: Harvard University Press, 1996.

Slaughter, Jane, and Robert Kern, eds. *European Women on the Left: Socialism, Feminism, and the Problems Faced by Political Women, 1880 to the Present*. Westport, Conn.: Greenwood Press, 1981.

Sowerwine, Charles. *Sisters or Citizens? Women and Socialism in France since 1876*. Cambridge: Cambridge University Press, 1981 (French edition, 1978).

  "Socialism, Feminism, and the Socialist Women's Movement: from the French Revolution to World War II." In *Becoming Visible: Women in European History*. 3rd edn., ed. Renate Bridenthal, Susan Mosher Stuard, and Merry E. Wiesner, 357–87. Boston: Houghton Mifflin, 1998.

Stanton, Theodore, ed. *The Woman Question in Europe: A Series of Original Essays*. New York: G. P. Putnam's Sons, 1884.

Stites, Richard. *The Women's Liberation Movement in Russia: Feminism, Nihilism, and Bolshevism, 1860–1930*. Princeton, N.J.: Princeton University Press, 1978.

Waelti-Walters, Jennifer, and Steven C. Hause, eds. *Feminisms of the Belle Epoque: A Historical and Literary Anthology*. Lincoln: University of Nebraska Press, 1994.

Biographical dictionaries

Banks, Olive. *The Biographical Dictionary of British Feminists*. 2 vols. New York: New York University Press, 1985, 1990.

Crawford, Elizabeth. *The Women's Suffrage Movement: A Reference Guide, 1866–1928*. London: UCL Press, 1999.

De Hann, Francisca, Krasimira Daskalova, and Anna Loutfi, eds. *Biographical Dictionary of Women's Movements in Central, Eastern, and South Eastern Europe: 19th and 20th Centuries*. Budapest and New York: Central European University Press, 2006.

Epilogue: looking beyond 1914

The long World War that began in August 1914 disrupted and changed the lives of millions of European women. While husbands, fathers, and brothers did combat, many women coped alone at home, and many assumed new work roles in factories, fields, and offices. Other mothers and daughters volunteered as nurses or aided refugees. In 1916 French feminist Jane Misme termed the war's mobilization of womanpower an "upheaval ... producing the social equality of women with men on a vast terrain," even though feminist campaigns were "almost totally suspended."[1] Most feminist organizations in countries at war encouraged followers to aid the war effort. In Germany, for example, Bäumer spearheaded the National Women's Service. Only a minority of feminists or socialist women challenged their nation's war effort and advocated ending hostilities short of victory. After an international socialist women's meeting in neutral Switzerland in March 1915, Zetkin was jailed for several months. Pacifists from the IWSA, including Jacobs and Jane Addams, met at The Hague in the neutral Netherlands in April 1915 and laid the basis for the Women's International League of Peace and Freedom.

Historians often disagree about the long-term significance of wartime changes for women's lives but typically note that the enormous need to replace men called to battle gave many women access, albeit often temporary, to jobs once reserved to men, thereby allowing women to demonstrate the abilities highlighted by prewar women's groups pressing for expanded employment opportunities. Many young single women and, to a lesser extent, married women worked before the war, and during the war many other married women and widows returned to work or entered the workforce for the first time. Some labored in heavy industries that seldom employed women before 1914, and thousands flocked to office jobs in government agencies and businesses. After the war women's participation in the workforce quickly declined as returning

---

[1] Jane Misme, "La Guerre et le Rôle des Femmes," *Revue de Paris* (November 1916): 204–05.

soldiers reclaimed jobs. Yet because of new wartime precedents, not all gains in employment disappeared, and women's role in economies' expanding service sector continued to grow.

Women's political rights returned to the forefront in some countries even before the war ended. Neutral Denmark and Iceland implemented women's suffrage measures in 1915. The Russian Revolution that toppled the tsar in March 1917 also promised votes to women. Britain's loss of more than 700,000 soldiers in combat, many of them working class, spurred passage of legislation in 1918 enfranchising all men aged 21 and over, and enabling women to vote at the age of 30. That gender disparity, designed to prevent women from becoming a majority of voters, lasted until 1928. As Germany faced defeat in November 1918 and experienced military mutinies and civilian strikes, the Socialist-led provisional government that replaced Emperor Wilhelm II endorsed women's suffrage, incorporated into the Weimar Republic's constitution in 1919. The French Chamber of Deputies also voted heavily in favor of votes for women in May 1919, and many people expected the Senate to follow suit. Against this European backdrop, where by early 1919 women's suffrage was also a reality or promised in Sweden, the Netherlands, Austria, Hungary, and the newly independent Czechoslovakia, Poland, Estonia, Latvia, and Lithuania, the United States Senate in June 1919 finally followed the House of Representatives' lead and approved the women's suffrage amendment to the Constitution, paving the way for states' ratification in 1919–20.

The many changes in women's employment and status prompted French jurist Henri Robert to call the war's impact on women revolutionary, a veritable "1789" for women. French Senate opposition, however, blocked votes for women in 1922 and throughout the interwar years. In Italy, political divisions and the rise to power of Mussolini's Fascist Party also doomed women's suffrage. French and Italian women gained voting rights only at the end of World War II. Where once the post-1918 period had seemed to offer both substantial gains for women and high hopes for new European democracies, there would soon be backlash, often from right-wing and fascist groups unnerved by postwar gains by the Left, socialist and communist. Some veterans' groups also resented women's new positions.

Feminist organizations' strength after the war varied from country to country. Where women could vote, feminist groups often lost prewar members. The British NUWSS retitled itself the National Union of Societies for Equal Citizenship (NUSEC) and promoted civic education and benefits for mothers, but its ninety affiliates in 1929 were less than one-sixth of the prewar total. In France, on the other hand, lack of voting rights led many more women, including Catholic women, into suffrage groups. In Germany, where women voted, the BDF, with its many philanthropic and professional women's groups, grew larger as well, but disbanded after Adolf Hitler's Nazi regime came to power in 1933.

European women also won election to postwar legislatures – Finnish women having set a prewar precedent – and occasionally were appointed to ministerial cabinets or ambassadorships. In 1919, 41 women were elected to the German constitutional assembly, including 25 socialists and the feminists Bäumer, a moderate democrat, and Adele Schreiber. Before 1933, 111 women served in Weimar legislatures, as compared to 38 women in Britain's House of Commons between 1919 and 1935. In Czechoslovakia, Plamínková went from the Prague city council to the legislature, continuing public service until the Nazi takeover.

The first woman cabinet minister served in revolutionary Russia, after Lenin and Trotsky overthrew the provisional government in November 1917. The independent-minded Kollontai was briefly the minister of social welfare before being reassigned to head a new communist women's group. As of 1923, ambassadorial assignments removed her from the Soviet Union, which she represented in Norway, Mexico, and Sweden. By the later 1920s, several other European countries had women cabinet ministers, appointed by parties of the Left. Socialist Nina Bang became Denmark's education minister in 1924 and commerce minister in 1926. Miina Sillanpaa was minister of social affairs in Finland in 1927. Labour Party activist Margaret Bondfield, elected to the House of Commons in 1923, became minister of labour in 1929, the only woman in a British cabinet before 1945. In 1933, twelve years after a Canadian precedent, the first woman cabinet member, Frances Perkins, was appointed in the United States. In France in 1936, when for the first time a socialist premier, Léon Blum, headed a cabinet (the Popular Front coalition of socialists and republican radicals, backed by communists), three women were designated undersecretaries, a rank just below cabinet minister. Republican feminist Cécile Brunschvicg served in the education ministry, as, briefly, did, Irène Joliot-Curie; and socialist Suzanne Lacore, a retired teacher, was undersecretary of health. Spain's new democratic republic (1931–39) enfranchised women, and in 1936, as civil war raged, Federica Montseny was briefly health minister in a leftist cabinet. Women's appointments to German and Italian cabinets had to await defeat of the Nazi and Fascist dictatorships.

Professional women were, of course, more numerous than women legislators or occasional women cabinet ministers. In some nations, women made notable gains in employment in public administration. French women entered the professional ranks of the central administration in 1919, although some ministries continued to exclude them, and others imposed hiring quotas and limited promotions. Denmark promised women equal access to civil service posts in 1921, as did Sweden shortly thereafter, Norway having done so for most offices in 1911. Italy's Sacchi law of 1919 also opened more administrative ranks to women. English women's advances in the civil service were checked by the continuation of a marriage bar, which Dutch women likewise faced. Weimar Germany gave some women, such as Bäumer, important administrative assignments but often dismissed married women. Victoria Kent, among the first Spanish women lawyers, became director general of prisons after 1931 and during the Civil War worked in the embassy in Paris, aiding refugees fleeing from Francisco Franco's forces that destroyed the republic.

The global economic Depression of the 1930s posed new threats to women's work, as did the dictatorships of Hitler, Mussolini, and Franco, opposed in principle, if not always in practice, to women's work, especially married women's work, outside the home. In democracies as well, some leaders reacted to the depressed economy by denouncing women workers for allegedly taking men's jobs, even if they did not impose new limits on employing women. The Nazi regime condemned feminism as something un-German and Jewish, and in place of dissolved feminist associations created the Frauenwerk, led by Gertrud Scholz-Klink and offering women social services and racist indoctrination. Mussolini imposed quotas on women civil servants and disbanded the remaining Italian feminist groups.

Women's advances in other professional and creative arenas did continue in many countries. Most nations which had barred women from legal practice changed policies after World War I, and newly independent states, other than Hungary and Bulgaria, also allowed women to practice law. Many women lawyers chose administrative employment, however, because in private practice they often had difficulty attracting clients. Unsurprisingly, some women lawyers continued efforts to improve women's legal status, particularly that of married women. Women doctors still outnumbered lawyers, and in many nations hundreds of women doctors practiced. Germany in 1929 counted 2,200. Only in the Soviet Union were women about half of the medical profession, the Communists expanding a prewar trend. The professionalization of nursing also continued as the English, Dutch, French, and Italian governments, among others, set new standards for training and registration during the early 1920s. Similar developments affected the credentialing of social workers.

Women writers and artists, who had helped pave the way for women to become familiar figures in European public culture during the eighteenth and nineteenth centuries, continued to win critical acclaim. Yet they received prestigious awards far less often than men. The Nobel prize for literature, awarded to one woman before 1914, went to three others by 1938: the Italian Grazia Deledda, Norwegian Sigrid Undset, and American Pearl Buck. The British Royal Academy, founded in 1768 with two women painters, finally inducted another woman as an associate member in 1922 and Laura Knight as a full member in 1936. The first woman elected to the Prussian Academy of Arts in 1919, artist Käthe Kollwitz, resigned to protest the Nazi takeover, as did author Ricarda Huch. Major orchestras still resisted hiring women musicians, although French women continued to win prizes for musical composition. The Académie Française did not welcome its first woman member until 1980, Marguerite Yourcenar then citing her debt to past generations of women writers, including de Staël and Sand. In the sciences, where Marie Curie's two Nobel prizes before 1914 had been heralded by feminists as confirmation of women's intellectual ability, only one woman, Joliot-Curie, won a Nobel award during the interwar years. The French Academy of Sciences, which had rejected Marie Curie, inducted a woman "corresponding" member in 1962 and awarded a full membership in 1979.

In the long run, access to educational opportunity and employment mattered far more for European women's professional advancement than the occasional well-publicized prizes and academy slots. Women comprised a quarter of university students in France, England, and Czechoslovakia by 1928, and more than 18 percent in Germany in 1932, although few women held university professorships. After World War II, access to academic secondary schools and universities was gradually expanded in western Europe, increasing notably during the often tumultuous 1960s.

The 1960s set the stage for what many historians call a "second wave" of feminism, when young and not so young women began gaining or regaining awareness of what foremothers before 1914 had sought and achieved. By the early twenty-first century, more women in the western world had entered professions traditionally gendered as masculine and become more visible as politicians. Yet debate about women's achieving genuine equality of opportunity continues, as women still wrestle with how to combine employment with motherhood and family responsibilities, finding more support for this combination in many European nations' public policies than in the United States.

Additional general studies and reference works

Bell, Susan Groag, and Karen M. Offen, eds. *Women, the Family, and Freedom: The Debate in Documents*. 2 vols. Stanford, Calif.: Stanford University Press, 1983.

Chaudhuri, Nupur, and Margaret Strobel, eds. *Western Women and Imperialism: Complicity and Resistance*. Bloomington: Indiana University Press, 1992.

Clancy-Smith, Julia, and Frances Gouda, eds. *Domesticating the Empire: Race, Gender, and Family Life in French and Dutch Colonialism*. Charlottesville: University of Virginia Press, 1998.

DiCaprio, Lisa, and Merry E. Wiesner, eds. *Lives and Voices: Sources in European Women's History*. Boston: Houghton Mifflin, 2001.

Engel, Barbara Alpern. *Women in Russia, 1700–2000*. Cambridge: Cambridge University Press, 2004.

Foley, Susan K. *Women in France since 1789*. Basingstoke: Palgrave Macmillan, 2004.

Fout, John C., ed. *German Women in the Nineteenth Century: A Social History*. New York: Holmes and Meier, 1984.

Fraisse, Genevieve, and Michelle Perrot, eds. *Emerging Feminism from Revolution to World War*. Vol. IV of *A History of Women in the West*, ed. Georges Duby and Michelle Perrot. Cambridge, Mass.: Harvard University Press, 1993.

Good, David F., Margarete Grandner, and Mary Jo Maynes. *Austrian Women in the Nineteenth and Twentieth Centuries: Cross-Disciplinary Perspectives*. Providence, R.I.: Berghahn Books, 1996.

Hendry, Maggy, and Jenny Uglow. *Dictionary of Women's Biography*, 4th edn. Basingstoke: Palgrave Macmillan, 2005.

Hutton, Marcelline J. *Russian and West European Women, 1860–1939: Dreams, Struggles, and Nightmares*. Lanham, Md.: Rowman and Littlefield, 2001.

Jaworski, Rudolf, and Bianka Pietrow-Ennker, eds. *Women in Polish Society*. Boulder, Col.: East European Monographs/Columbia University Press, 1992.

Margadant, Jo Burr, ed. *The New Biography: Performing Femininity in Nineteenth-Century France*. Berkeley: University of California Press. 2000.

McMillan, James F. *France and Women, 1789–1914: Gender, Society and Politics*. London: Routledge, 2000.

Melman, Billie. *Women's Orients: English Women and the Middle East, 1718–1918*. 2nd edn. Ann Arbor: University of Michigan Press, 1995 (1st edn. 1992).

290

Ogilvie, Marilyn, and Joy Harvey, eds. *The Biographical Dictionary of Women in Science: Pioneering Lives from Ancient Times to the Mid-20th Century.* 2 vols. New York: Routledge, 2000.

Parry, Melanie, ed. *Larousse Dictionary of Women.* New York: Larousse Kingfisher Chambers, 1996.

Perkin, Joan. *Victorian Women.* New York: New York University Press, 1993.

Riemer, Eleanor S., and John C. Fout, eds. *European Women: A Documentary History, 1789–1945.* New York: Schocken, 1980.

Robertson, Priscilla. *An Experience of Women: Pattern and Change in Nineteenth-Century Europe.* Philadelphia: Temple University Press, 1982.

Simonton, Deborah, ed. *The Routledge History of Women Since 1700.* London: Routledge, 2006.

Smith, Bonnie G. *Changing Lives: Women in European History Since 1750.* Lexington, Mass.: D. C. Heath, 1989.

Strobel, Margaret. *European Women and the Second British Empire.* Bloomington: Indiana University Press, 1991.

Vicinus, Martha, ed. *A Widening Sphere: Changing Roles of Victorian Women.* Bloomington: Indiana University Press, 1977.

Wildenthal, Lora. *German Women for Empire, 1884–1945.* Durham, N.C.: Duke University Press, 2001.

Index

Aberdeen, Lady Ishbel 251–2, 265
Abitur 168, 174
abortion 220, 260, 270–1
Académie Française 16, 18, 19, 27,
  59, 289
academies
  literary and women 18, 19, 27, 59, 70–1,
  78, 289
  of art, women members 12, 13–14, 18,
  27, 87, 289
  scientific, women members 18, 190, 193,
  289
"accomplishments" lessons 82, 162
actresses 20–1, 28, 30, 113–21
  British 21, 113–16, 120, 264
  French 28, 30, 113, 114–15, 116–17,
  119, 120
  German 113, 114
  Russian 115, 116, 119
Adams-Lehmann, Hope 217, 271
Addams, Jane 155, 285
ADF, *see* German Women's Association
Agoult, Marie d' 52–3, 59, 162
Aleramo, Sibilla 75–6
Algeria, French women in 131, 177, 223–4,
  230, 278
Alphen-Salvador, Gabrielle 208, 209
Amar y Borbón, Josefa 18–19, 31
anticlericalism
  and education policy 165, 177–8
  and nursing 205, 207
  Catholic responses to 130
antislavery societies, women and 136–7
Arenal, Concepción 138, 141–2,
  183, 232
aristocrats, and women's associations 265
Arnim, Bettina von 20, 51
art, genres seen as "feminine",
  "unfeminine" 15, 84, 85
artists, women 12–15, 26–7, 83–98, 288–9
  exhibitions 14, 15, 16, 27, 87, 89–90, 98
  government patronage 90–1, 98

numbers of 12–13, 83, 89–90, 98
organizations 86, 87, 89, 97–8
sculptresses 15, 84–5, 85–6, 97, 112
training 12, 14, 83–9
Association for Extended Women's
  Education (Austria) 68, 175
Association for Women's Suffrage
  (Vereeniging voor Vrouwenkiesrecht,
  VVVK) 250, 261–2
Association Law, Prussia 243, 253, 255
Aston, Louise 59
Auclert, Hubertine 193, 248–9, 250, 251,
  252, 255, 260, 262, 278
Augspurg, Anita 231, 253, 255, 260–1
Austen, Jane 47–8, 55, 64
Avril de Sainte-Croix Ghénia 147, 253

baccalauréat 168, 170, 171
Backer, Harriet 95, 113
Bajer, Mathilde, Fredrik 247, 250
Balzac, Honoré, de 53, 55, 57
Banks, Olive 263–4
Barat, Sophie 129
bas-bleus 9
Bashkirtseff, Marie 87, 96
Bassot, Jeanne 156
Bäumer, Gertrud 264, 271, 285,
  287, 288
Bayerová, Anna 188, 217
BDF, *see* Federation of German Women's
  Associations
Beale, Dorothea 169
Bebel, August 272–3
Beccari, Alaide Gualberta 147, 248
Becker, Lydia 245, 249
Bedford College 169
Beeton, Isabella 78
Belgiojoso, Cristina 46, 59
Bequet de Vienne, Marie 150,
  151, 216
Bernhardt, Sarah 115, 116–17, 119, 120
Bertaux, Hélène 85, 87–8, 90, 98

BFM, *see* League for Protection of
    Motherhood
Bieber-Boehm, Hanna 147, 253
birth control 218, 220, 260, 268–72, 274
Blackwell, Elizabeth 210–11, 252
Blau, Tina 89, 95
bluestockings 9, 52, 90
Bodichon, Barbara 64, 86, 211, 244, 245
Bogelot, Isabelle 141, 251
Bondfield, Margaret 276, 287
Bonheur, Rosa 84, 91–2, 95
Booth, Catherine 144
Boulanger, Lili 112
Bourdieu, Pierre 161
Bradlaugh-Besant trial 267
Braquemond, Marie 95
Braun, Lily 79, 265
Bremer, Fredrika 60–1, 250
Brès, Madeleine 213, 215
Bright, Jacob, Ursula 249
Brontë, Charlotte 46, 57, 162
Browne, Henriette 90
Browning, Elizabeth Barrett 46, 55
Brunschvicg, Cécile 262, 287
Bruun, Anne 183
Burney, Fanny 20, 47, 48, 83
Buss, Frances Mary 169
Butler, Elizabeth Thompson 93
Butler, Josephine Grey 145–6, 148, 264

Campan, Jeanne 16–17, 29, 30, 35, 162
Candeille, Julie 26
Capet, Gabrielle 85
Carpenter, Mary 140–1, 146
Cassatt, Mary 94
Catherine II ("the Great") 7–8, 15, 17–18,
    34, 132
Catholic Reformation, and women 11, 129
Catholic religious orders 22–3, 128–31
    charity 23, 128–31
    French Revolution and 22–3, 128
    nursing 23, 199, 204, 205, 207–8
    prison staff 140
    teaching 23, 129, 133, 162, 164, 165,
        175, 177, 180
Catholic women's associations 155, 156,
    265, 266–7
Catt, Carrie Chapman 255, 257, 276–8
Cauer, Minna 153, 253, 255, 261
Cavour, Camillo di 147, 165
Chaminade, Cécile 111, 182
Chaptal, Léonie 208
charities, women's role 125–57
    Catholic laywomen 132, 137–8, 156
    Jewish women 133, 147–8

Protestant women 133–6; *see also*
    deaconesses
Russian traditions 132, 138, 144
statistics 127
Charity Organisation Society (COS) 142–3,
    144, 149, 153
Chartism, women and 241, 243
Chateaubriand, François René, de 49, 128
Chauvin, Jeanne 225–7, 229
Chenu, Jeanne 266
Chernyshevsky, Nikolai 144, 215
Chevreau-Lemercier, Eugénie 134, 232
child welfare, women and 133–4, 140–1,
    149–52
Cinti-Damoreau, Laure 101–2
classical education 10, 11, 15, 161, 168,
    171, 172, 174, 176, 184, 185
Claudel, Camille 97
clerks, women 232–3
CNFF, *see* National Council of French
    Women
coeducation, *see* schools, coeducational
Collett, Camilla 61–2
Collot, Marie-Anne 15
Comédie Française 28, 30, 113, 116, 119
Comte, Auguste 64, 153
Concordat, 1801 36, 128
Condorcet, Marquis de 22, 24, 263
congresses, women's 78, 237, 251–2
    ICW 98, 145, 155, 157, 193, 234, 251,
        253, 255, 278
    International Congress on Women's
        Rights
        Paris 1878 247–8
        Paris 1900 227
        Paris 1889 252
    International Congress on Women's
        Charities and Institutions
        Paris 1889 127, 211, 252
        Paris 1900 142, 143, 227
        Paris 1913 149, 150, 229, 262–3
    International Congress on Women's
        Work and Activities, Berlin 221, 253
    IWSA 255–6, 257, 267, 276–8
    Polish 258
    Russia 257, 265, 266, 275
    World's Congress of Representative
        Women, Chicago 47, 119–20, 185,
        252
Conservatoire, Paris 29, 100–1,
    101, 103, 105, 110
conservatories, training women 29, 100–1,
    110, 111
consumers' movement, women and 156
COS, *see* Charity Organisation Society

Contagious Diseases Acts 145–6
Cottin, Sophie 46
Coudray, Mme du 17
Counter Reformation, *see* Catholic
    Reformation
Courths-Mahler, Hedwig 78
Craig, Edith 115, 120
Curie, Marie Sklodowska 166, 189,
    192–3, 289

Dalle Donne, Maria 210, 220
Darwin, Charles 152, 193–4
Dashkova, Princess Ekaterina 17–18, 34
Daubié, Julie 170, 171, 246
David, Jacques-Louis 14, 26, 27, 85
Davies, Emily 169, 211, 249
deaconesses 135–6, 140, 203, 204
Deken, Aage 20, 30, 41
Demont-Breton, Virginie 87, 92
dentists, women 216–17, 224
depopulation, French concern 149–50, 269
Deraismes, Maria 246–8, 250, 251, 252
Deroin, Jeanne 242–3
Dickens, Charles 57
divorce 24, 36, 50, 53, 244
doctors, women 171, 188, 197, 210–24,
    234, 288
    associations 212, 223
    numbers 214, 216, 217, 224
    Russian courses for 186, 214
Dohm, Hedwig 79, 247
Donna, La 147, 248
Droste-Hülshoff, Annette 53, 55, 72
Drucker, Wilhelmina 250, 268
Dufferin Fund 209, 222, 223
Duras, Claire de 49
Durand, Marguerite 120, 260
Duruy, Victor 170–1, 187
Duse, Eleonora 115, 117–19
DVF, *see* German Union for Women's
    Suffrage

East Indies, Dutch women in 181, 223,
    277
Ebner-Eschenbach, Marie von 67–8, 72,
    175
École des Beaux-Arts 86, 87–8
École Gratuite de Dessin 86, 91
Edgeworth, Maria 47, 48, 61
education at home, girls' 11, 43, 161
Edwards-Pilliet, Blanche 150, 215–16
Eliot, George 46, 57, 62–5, 77, 92
Ellenrieder, Maria 85, 91
Engels, Friedrich 272
Englishwomen's Journal 211, 244

Enlightenment, and women 8, 9–10, 11,
    16, 18, 28, 30, 163
Épinay, Louise d' 30
equality in difference 4, 87–8, 240–1,
    280–1
eugenics 152, 270
Eugénie, Empress 90, 92, 111,
    137–8, 187
Evreinova, Anna 225, 257
Expressionists, women 95–6

Falcon, Cornélie 100, 102
Farrenc, Louise 110
Fawcett, Henry 245
Fawcett, Millicent Garrett 212, 251, 258,
    260
FE, *see* Feminist Association
Federation of German Women's
    Associations (Bund Deutscher
    Frauenvereine, BDF) 148, 155, 174,
    204, 217, 252–3, 255, 260–1, 264–5,
    271, 273, 287
Femina 78, 228
feminism, defined 240–1
    nineteenth-century goals 2, 240–1
    term introduced 40, 71, 249–50
Feminist Association (Feminsták
    Egyesülete, FE) 256, 265, 267
Fénelon, François de Salignac de la Mothe
    9, 12, 43
Fenwick, Ethel Gordon 201–2
Ferry, Jules 164, 165, 182
feuilleton 58
Fickert, Auguste 253
Filosofova, Anna 144, 186, 254, 257
Fonseca Pimentel, Eleonora 34
Fontenay-aux-Roses, higher normal school
    178–9
Foucault, Michel 126
Fouqué, Caroline de la Motte 50
Fourier, Charles 241, 248
Fox, Eliza 86
French League for Women's Rights, (Ligue
    Française pour le Droit des Femmes,
    LFDF) 216, 228, 250, 262–3
French Revolution 1, 5–7, 21–37
    centennial 111, 149, 252
    education 24–5, 29, 161
    impact beyond France 5, 30–4
    impact on women 1, 5, 21–35, 37
    public assistance 22, 125, 128
    women's clubs 22, 23, 24, 27
French Union for Women's Suffrage
    (Union Française pour le Suffrage des
    Femmes, UFSF) 262–3

French Women's Patriotic League 266
Fronde, La 120, 220, 227, 260
Fry, Elizabeth 135, 138–40
Fuà Fusinato, Erminia 182
Fuller, Margaret 46, 64

Gahéry, Marie 156
Galtier, Marie 228, 236
Gan, Elena 56
Garrett Anderson, Elizabeth 211–12, 213, 249, 268
Gaskell, Elizabeth 56–7
Gasparin, Valérie 202–3
Gatti de Gamond, Isabelle 171–2
Gatti de Gamond, Zoé 171, 232
Gay de Girardin, Delphine 46, 52
gender, defined 1
    history of ideas on 10
    traits cited to promote women's activities 2, 4, 23, 37, 44, 87–8, 112, 127, 140, 157, 176, 178, 182, 198, 201, 217, 222, 224, 226–7, 228, 232, 234, 240–1, 244–5, 249, 280
Genlis, Stéphanie de 10, 15–16, 19, 21, 30, 40, 46, 48, 52
Gérard, Marguerite 83
German Socialist Party (Sozialdemokratische Partei Deutschlands, SPD) 272–4
German Union for Women's Suffrage (Deutscher Verband für Frauenstimmrecht, DVF) 255, 261
German Women's Association (Allgemeiner Deutscher Frauenverein, ADF) 172, 244–5, 251, 252
Gevin-Cassal, Olympe 151, 235–6
gimnazia, progimnazia (Russia) 172, 180
Gippius, Zinaida 76
Glümer, Claire von 59
Goegg, Marie 185, 246, 248
Goethe, Johann Wolfgang von 46, 49, 51
Gómez de Avelleneda, Gertrudis 55
Goncharova, Catherine 213, 248
Goncharova, Natalia 97
Gouges, Olympe de 5, 6, 22, 24, 26, 31
GPDSC, Girls' Public Day School Company 169, 170
Grand, Sarah 71
Greenaway, Kate 93–4
Gripenberg, Alexandra 254, 265
Grondahl, Agathe Backer 113
Groups for Social Assistance Work, Women's (Germany) 153–5
Gymnasia 167

Habermas, Jürgen 8
Hahn-Hahn, Ida 57, 59
Hainisch, Marianne 174, 253, 256
Hamilton, Anna 206–7, 208, 215–16
Hamilton, Cicely 112, 120
Harrison, Jane Ellen 191
Hensel, Fanny Mendelssohn 110
Herz, Henriette 9, 50, 51
Heymann, Lida Gustava 147, 253, 255, 261
Hierta-Retzius, Anna 143
high culture/popular culture divide 62–3
Hill, Octavia 142, 143
Hippel, Theodore von 33
Hirschfeld-Tiburtius, Henriette 216–17
Holmès, Augusta 111
Huch, Ricarda 72–3, 77, 78, 289
Hugo, Victor 48, 55, 69

Ibsen, Henrik 62, 75, 117
ICN, *see* International Council of Nurses
ICW, *see* International Council of Women
imperialism, women and 146, 208–9, 222–4, 230–1, 278; *see also* missionaries
Impressionists, women 94–5
Independent Labour Party (ILP) 276
India, British women and 131, 141, 146, 208–9, 222–3
Indian women, careers 208–9, 223, 230–1, 251
industrialization, impact on women 1, 37, 58
inspectresses 17, 232, 234–6
    factories 234–5
    prisons 140, 141, 235
    public assistance 151, 235
    schools 134, 171, 181–2, 234
International Abolitionist Federation (IAF) 146–7
International Association of Women 246
International Council of Nurses (ICN) 202, 204, 207
International Council of Women (ICW) 98, 157, 251–2, 252–4, 255, 256, 267, 278; *see also* congresses
International Union of Friends of Young Women 147
International Woman Suffrage Alliance (IWSA) 254, 255–6, 257, 267, 276–8, 280; *see also* congresses
International Woman's Day 274
Ireland, women's initiatives in 130, 170
IWSA, *see* International Woman Suffrage Alliance

Jacobins 23, 25, 26, 28, 29, 32
Jacobs, Aletta 188, 218–20, 250,
    261–2, 268, 270, 277, 285
Jacobs, Charlotte 218, 223
Javouhey, Anne-Marie 129
Jex-Blake, Sophia 211–12
Jewish women, in associations 133, 147–8,
    262, 263, 265
JFB, Jewish Women's Federation,
    Germany 148, 265
Joliot-Curie, Irène 193, 287, 289
Jugan, Jeanne 130
Julian Academy 87, 88
July Monarchy, France 51, 242

Kaiserswerth 135–6, 199
Kant, Immanuel 9–10, 21
Karll, Agnes 204
Kashevarova-Rudnev, Varvara 213–14
Kauffmann, Angelica 14, 83, 87
Kemble, Fanny 113, 114
Kempin-Spyri, Emilie 190, 225
Kèralio-Robert, Louise 21
Kergomard, Pauline 181–2, 221, 234
kindergartens 134, 222
Klumpke, Augusta 215–16
Kollwitz, Käthe 96, 289
Kollontai, Alexandra 266, 275–6,
    287
Kovalevskaia, Sofia 189–90
Krásnohorská, Eliska 174, 188, 245
Krog, Gina 250, 257, 265
Kuczalska-Reinschmit, Paulina 258
Kuliscioff, Anna 275

Labille-Guiard, Adélaïde 14, 27, 85
Labour Party, and women 276
Labriola, Teresa 190, 266–7
Ladies National Association for Repeal of
    Contagious Diseases Acts (LNA) 146
Lafayette, Countess Marie Madeleine
    Pioche de la Vergne 41, 52
Lagerlöf, Selma 73–4, 77, 78
Lamartine, Alphonse de 47, 56
Landes, Joan 6
Lange, Helene 172–4, 264
Langtry, Lillie 115, 120
La Roche, Sophie von 20, 41, 51
lawyers, women 224–31, 288
    feminism 225, 226–7, 228–30, 231
League for Protection of Motherhood
    (Bund für Mutterschutz, BFM) 152,
    270–1
League of Mothers of Families (France)
    150

Lechevalier, Antoinette 140, 232
Legion of Honor, girls' schools 35, 162
    awarded to women 92, 111, 119
Lehmus, Emilie 216–17
Leipzig Gewandhaus, women pianists at
    105, 108
Léo, André [Léodile Béra Champseix]
    247
Lette Association 244, 247
Levine, Philippa 263–4
Lewald, Fanny 50, 57, 59
Lewes, G. H. 55, 63
LFDF, see French League for Women's
    Rights
licence 171
Lind, Jenny 104
Lindegren, Amalia 86, 87
literacy, women's, men's 11, 41, 69, 77,
    164–5, 166
London Philharmonic Society, women
    performers 102, 105, 106–7, 108
London School of Medicine for Women
    (LSMW) 186, 211–12
Luxemburg, Rosa 274
lycées 35, 171

Macaulay, Catherine 19–20
MacDonald, Margaret 276
Mackenroth, Anna 225, 231
magazines, periodicals, women's 41, 66,
    78, 120, 147, 228, 244
Malibran, Maria 102–3
Mallet, Émilie 133
"March of the Women" 112, 259
Marie Antoinette, Queen 6, 7, 12, 15, 17,
    21, 24, 26, 29, 34, 132
Marholm, Laura 78–9
Marlitt, Eugenie 65–6
marriage bar 178, 236, 288
married women's property rights 35–6,
    243–4, 247, 248
Martindale, Hilda 234, 236
Martineau, Harriet 61, 146
Marx, Karl 272, 273
maternalism 37, 127, 157, 176, 178, 244–5,
    251, 268
maternity, charity support 132, 150–1,
    152
maternity leave 150
Matura 168, 174–5, 188
Maugeret, Marie 250, 266
McAuley, Catherine 130
Meitner, Lise 194
midwives 17, 198–9, 210, 214, 216
Mill, Harriet Taylor 114, 243

Mill, John Stuart 55, 64, 114, 243, 245
  The Subjection of Women 246, 247
Miropolsky, Hélène 228, 229–30
missionaries, women 129, 130–2, 208–9,
  222
Modersohn-Becker, Paula 96
Moens, Petronella 33
Montagu, Elizabeth 9
Montessori, Maria 190, 220–2, 266–7
Morandi, Felicita 182
More, Hannah 9
Morgan Hoggan, Frances 185, 213, 222
Morisot, Berthe 95
Morley, Edith 191
Morsier, Emilie de 147, 252
Mott, Lucretia 137, 242
Mozzoni, Anna Maria 147, 247, 248, 250,
  266–7
Münter, Gabriele 96
musicians, women 26, 29, 99–113, 289
  brass instruments 101, 107
  composers 26, 99, 103, 107–13
  critics' reception 105–6
  numbers 99, 110
  performers, piano 99, 104–6, 107–9
  performers, string instruments 101,
    106–7
  performers, vocal 99–104
  teachers 29, 99, 101, 103, 108–9
  training 100–1; *see also* conservatories
Mutual Philanthropic Society (Russia) 144,
  257

Napoleon 27, 29–30, 34–6, 42, 44, 46,
  161–2
  impact of regime on women 29–30, 34–6
  law codes 34, 35–6, 53, 248, 260, 269
Napoleon III (Louis Napoleon Bonaparte)
  59, 90, 242–3
National Council of French Women
  (Conseil National des Femmes
  Françaises, CNFF) 182, 207, 253,
  262, 263, 269
National Council of Italian Women 119,
  151, 253, 266
National Union of Women's Suffrage
  Societies (NUWSS) 258, 260, 276,
  286
nationalism 42, 46, 113, 165, 166, 182
  feminists and 256–7, 258, 262
  women authors and 42, 59–60, 66, 79
naturalism, literary 69–70, 96
NAWSA, National American Women's
  Suffrage Association 254
Necker, Jacques 8, 43, 44

Necker, Suzanne 8, 43
Negri, Ada 73, 75
Nemcová, Bozena 59–60
neo-Malthusians 218, 268–9, 270,
  272, 274
Neruda, Wilma 106–7
"new" biography 4
"new" woman 12, 71–7
Ney, Elisabeth 85–6, 91
Niboyet, Eugénie 242
Nightingale, Florence 136, 146, 199–202,
  208
  international influence 202–4, 206,
    207
Nobel prize winners, women 69, 73, 192,
  193, 289
normal schools, *see* teachers, training
Norton, Caroline 243–4
novel, emergence of 40
  deemed a woman's genre 40, 41,
    53, 57
nuns, *see* Catholic religious orders
nursing 134–6, 198–210, 288
  associations 201–2, 203–4, 207, 209
  in colonies 208–9
  military 200, 202, 208
  Red Cross 152, 204
  statistics 204, 209–10
  see also Catholic religious orders,
    deaconesses
NUWSS, *see* National Union of Women's
  Suffrage Societies
Nyström, Jenny 94

Offen, Karen 4
Old Regime 6
  exceptional women 7–21, 30
Oliphant, Margaret 64, 65
Orme, Eliza 225
Orzeskowa, Eliza 66–7
Osborn, Emily 92–3
Otto-Peters, Louise 243, 244, 251

Paape, Maria 33
Palm d'Aelders, Etta 22–3, 33
Pankhurst, Christabel 231, 258–60
Pankhurst, Emmeline 258–60
Pankhurst, Sylvia 276
Pappenheim, Bertha 148
Pardo Bazán, Emilia 69–71, 77
Parlaghy, Vilma 91
Parren, Callirhoi 254
Pasch, Ulrica 15, 83
Paterson, Emma Smith 266, 276
Patti, Adelina 104

Patriotic Women's Association
    (Vaterländischer Frauenverein, VFV)
    152
Pavlova, Karolina 56
peace organizations, women in 68, 246,
    280, 284
Pelletier, Madeleine 220, 234, 260, 270,
    275
pharmacists, women 216, 218
philanthropy, connotations of 126
    self-help emphasis 133, 142–3, 144
Pisan, Christine de 40
Plamínková, Frantiska 256, 262, 287
Pleyel, Marie 101, 105–6
Poët, Lydia 225
poor law guardians, women 143–4, 235,
    249
Popelin, Marie 172, 225, 227, 252, 267
Popp, Adelheid 274–5
post, telegraph offices, women in 232,
    233–4
Potter, Beatrix 94
Poullain de la Barre, François 30
Prince, Mary 137
prison reform, women and 138–40,
    141–2
professions, characteristics of 197
prostitution, women campaigning against
    146–8, 253
protective legislation 272
Protestant Reformation, and education 11
Protestant women, charities
    deaconesses missionaries and
    women's rights and 262, 263, 264
Protestant Women's Federation (Germany)
    155, 265
Prussia, education 11, 164, 166, 172, 174,
    177
pseudonyms, women using 52, 57, 63, 65,
    69, 75, 78, 90, 247
public administration and services, women
    in 91, 231–6, 287–8
public welfare, women's work in 155, 157,
    235
purdah 208
Putnam, Mary 211, 213

Quam, Frederikke Marie 257
Quarré, Antoinette 56
Queen's College, London 169

Rachel [Élisa Félix] 116
realism, artistic 90
realism, literary 51, 57
Red Cross, women in 127, 152, 204

Reign of Terror 22, 23, 27
    women and 6, 23–4
religion, feminization of 128–9
Renaissance, and women 7, 10, 30, 82, 163
Renoir, Pierre-Auguste 82
Restoration, Bourbon, politics of 48, 49
Reuter, Gabriele 72
Reval, Gabrielle 73
revolution of 1830 France 51, 241
revolution of 1905 Russia 67, 76, 113, 186,
    214, 256, 257, 275
revolutions of 1848, women and 58–9, 134,
    137, 242–3
Richardson, Samuel 41, 47, 60
Richer, Léon 246–7, 247–8, 250, 251,
    252
Richter, Elise 191
Robin, Paul 269
Robins, Elizabeth 120, 121
Roland, Manon 20, 24, 25–6, 67
romanticism 46, 48, 128
Romantics, German 46, 50, 51, 73
Rousseau, Jean-Jacques 9, 12, 16, 21, 22,
    31, 41, 43
    Émile 9, 10, 12, 43, 62
Roussel, Nelly 269–70
Royal Academy of Arts, Great Britain 14,
    86, 87, 89–90, 93, 289
Royal Academy of Painting and Sculpture,
    France 12, 13–14, 27
Royer, Clémence 193
Ruskin, John 93, 143

Saffroy, Lucie 178–9
Sáiz y Otero, Concepión 183–4
Salic law 7
Salomon, Alice 153–5
Salon, Paris, exhibitions 14, 15, 16, 27,
    89–90, 92
salons, women's role in 8–9, 35, 43, 44, 49,
    50, 56, 73, 103
Salvation Army 107, 144
Sand, George [Aurore Dupin Dudevant]
    46, 51–6, 57, 58–9, 77, 82, 103, 106,
    162, 242, 248
    Indiana 52, 53
Saumoneau, Louise 266, 275
Scharleib, Mary Ann 222–3, 224
Schirmacher, Käthe 253, 255
Schlegel, Dorothea Mendelsohn Veit 46,
    50, 51
Schlegel Schelling, Caroline Böhmer 33
Schmidt, Auguste 245, 251, 252–3, 253,
    264–5, 273
schooling, girls', before 1789 11–12

schools
    coeducational 161, 166, 180, 181, 184,
        187
    girls' private 29
    nursery 133–4, 166, 171, 182
    primary, girls' access 163–7
    secondary, girls' access 167–76
Schreiber, Adele 204, 287
Schröder-Devrient, Wilhelmine 100, 102
Schumann, Clara Wieck 100, 105, 107–10
Schwartze, Thérèse 91, 95
Schwarz, Marie 253, 256
Schwimmer, Rosika 256, 262, 268
Scott, Joan 1–2
Scott, Walter 48, 57
Second International 272–4
Seidler, Louise 85, 91
Seneca Falls, N.Y.,1848 women's rights
    meeting 242
separate spheres, rhetoric and reality 1–3,
    22, 58
Serao, Matilde 73, 117
Serova, Valentina 113
settlement movement, women in 153,
    155, 156
Sèvres, higher normal school 73, 178–9,
    193
Shabanova, Anna 215, 254, 257
Sharples, Ellen and Rolinda 83–4
Siddons, Sarah 21, 113–14
Sieveking, Amalie 134–5
slavery, abolition of 6, 129, 136–7; see also
    antislavery societies
Slessor, Mary 131
Smolny Institute 11
Smyth, Ethel 111–12
social work, origins 132–3, 153–7,
    198, 288
socialists, women 57, 79, 241–2, 253, 265,
    272–6; numbers 274, 275
Société des Concerts (Society of Concerts)
    102, 105, 106
Society of Female Artists (Britain) 86, 89,
    98, 104
Society of Maternal Charity 132
Society of Revolutionary Republican
    Women 22, 23
Society of Women Musicians 112
Sontag, Henriette 100, 102
Sorabji, Cornelia 230–1
SPD, see German Socialist Party
St. Cyr 8, 9, 11
Staël, Germaine de 8, 34–5, 42–7, 49, 52,
    53, 55, 83
    Corinne 45–6, 47

On Literature 34, 44, 46
Stanton, Elizabeth Cady 62, 137,
    242, 251
Stanton, Theodore, The Woman Question in
    Europe 62, 67, 142, 246
Stasova, Nadezha 144, 186
Stöcker, Helene 270–1
Stowe, Harriet Beecher 46, 68
Stritt, Marie 231, 253, 255, 260–1, 271
suffragettes, suffragists, differences
    258–60
Suslova, Nadezhda 213
Suttner, Bertha von 68–9, 79, 175
Svetlá, Karolina 60, 174, 245
Szarvády, Wilhelmine 106

Taylor, Helen 114
teachers, women 163, 164, 166,
    176–84, 194
    associations 174, 182–3
    training 73, 175, 176–80, 183–4
    women's rights and 264, 265
temperance, women and 145
Terry, Ellen 115–16, 119, 120
textbooks, children's books 78, 163, 166–7,
    182
Thérèse of Lisieux, Saint 130
Thornycroft, Mary 84–5
Tiburtius, Franziska 216–17
Tristan, Flora 56, 242
Trubnikova, Maria 144, 186
Tussenbroek, Catherine van 218, 220, 269
Twining, Louisa 144

UFSF, see French Union for Women's
    Suffrage
Union of Women Painters and Sculptors
    87, 98
universities, women's access 155,
    168, 169, 170, 171, 174, 184–94,
    211–13, 289
    teaching posts 71, 189–94
University of Paris, women at 171, 187,
    212–13
University of Zurich, women at 185, 190,
    213, 216–17

Valadon, Suzanne 97
Varnhagen, Rahel von 50
Verbitskaia, Anastasia 76–7
Vèrone, Maria 182, 228–9, 262, 280
VFV, see Patriotic Women's Association
Viardot, Pauline 102, 103
Vial'tseva, Anastasiia 104
Victoria, Crown Princess 173–4, 203, 233

Victoria, Queen 93, 104, 105, 113, 222
Vigie-Lebrun, Élisabeth 12, 13–14, 15, 16,
    17, 21, 26, 27, 34, 35, 45, 46, 83, 85
Voegtlin, Marie 213, 216
VVVK, *see* Association for Women's
    Suffrage (Dutch)

Ward, Henrietta 91, 92
Ward, Mary 78–9
Wegmann, Bertha 87, 95
Weill, Berthe 97, 98
Weiss, Rosario 85, 91
White, Maude Valerie 110
white-collar work, women in 198, 232–4,
    236
Wilhelm II, Emperor 91, 95, 96
Williams, Helen Maria 33, 47
Witt-Schlumberger, Marguerite de 262,
    278
Wolff, Betje 20, 30, 33, 41
Wollstonecraft, Mary 20, 31–3, 51, 64, 163
women rulers 7–8
Women's Employment Association
    (Austria) 174, 245
WFL, Women's Freedom League 258–9
women's rights congresses *see* congresses,
    women's
women's rights organizations 127, 157,
    240–81
    Austria 245, 253, 256
    Belgium 225, 256, 267
    Bulgaria 254, 256
    China 256, 277
    Czech 245, 256, 262
    Denmark 183, 247, 250, 253, 256,
        265, 267
    Finland 250, 254, 256, 265
    France 182, 247, 250, 253, 256,
        262–3, 267, 286–7
    Germany 148, 155, 172, 174, 244–5,
        252–3, 255, 260–1, 267, 287

    Great Britain 243, 244, 245–6, 253,
        255, 258–60, 264, 267, 286
    Greece 254
    Hungary 253–4, 256, 265, 266
    Italy 151, 250, 253, 255–6, 266
    Netherlands 250, 253, 255, 261–2, 267
    Norway 250, 253, 256, 257, 265
    Poland 256, 258
    Portugal 267
    Russia 256, 257
    Serbia 254
    Sweden 61, 247, 250, 253, 256,
        267
    Switzerland 246, 253, 255–6
Women's Social and Political Union
    (WSPU) 112, 258–60, 276
women's suffrage 22, 92, 98, 112, 120, 146,
    157, 193, 237, 243, 245–6, 248–9,
    250, 254–67, 280, 286–7
    local, municipal vote 249, 257, 280
    organization memberships 260, 262–3,
        265, 267
    professional groups and 98, 120, 212,
        264–5
worker-poetry 56
working-class women, and women's rights
    241–2, 264, 265–6, 272, 276
World War I, impact on women 285–6
writers, women 16, 18–20, 25,
    40–79, 288–9
    numbers 19, 25, 41, 58, 77
writers' organizations 58, 68, 77
WSPU, *see* Women's Social and Political
    Union

Yver, Colette 78

zenana 131, 208, 222
Zetkin, Clara 273–4, 285
Zhukova, Maria 56
Zola, Émile 70, 75, 96

NEW APPROACHES TO EUROPEAN HISTORY

4 ROBERT JÜTTE
  Poverty and Deviance in Early Modern Europe
5 JAMES B. COLLINS
  The State in Early Modern France
6 CHARLES G. NAUERT
  Humanism and the Culture of Renaissance Europe
9 JONATHAN DEWALD
  The European Nobility, 1400–1800
10 ROBERT S. DUPLESSIS
  Transitions to Capitalism in Early Modern Europe
14 W. R. WARD
  Christianity under the Ancien Regime, 1648–1789
15 SIMON DIXON
  The Modernisation of Russia 1676–1825
16 MARY LINDEMANN
  Medicine and Society in Early Modern Europe
19 JAMES R. FARR
  Artisans in Europe, 1300–1914
20 MERRY E. WIESNER
  Women and Gender in Early Modern Europe Second edition
21 CHARLES W. INGRAO
  The Habsburg Monarchy 1618–1815 Second edition
22 JULIUS R. RUFF
  Violence in Early Modern Europe
23 JAMES VAN HORN MELTON
  The Rise of the Public in Enlightenment Europe
24 DANIEL GOFFMAN
  The Ottoman Empire and Early Modern Europe
25 NIGEL ASTON
  Chritstianity and Revolutionary Europe, c. 1750–1830
26 LEONARD V. SMITH, STÉPHANE AUDOIN-ROUZEAU
  AND ANNETTE BECKER
  France and the Great War
27 ROGER CHICKERING
  Imperial Germany and the Great War, 1914–1918 Second edition
28 ULINKA RUBLACK
  Reformation Europe
29 JONATHAN SPERBER
  The European Revolutions, 1848–1851 Second Edition

30 R. PO-CHIA HSIA
    The World of Catholic Renewal 1540–1770 Second edition
31 DORINDA OUTRAM
    The Enlightenment Second edition
32 REX WADE
    The Russian Revolution Second edition
33 EDWARD MUIR
    Ritual in Early Modern Europe Second edition
34 DONALD QUATAERT
    The Ottoman Empire Second edition
35 RACHEL G. FUCHS
    Gender and Poverty in Nineteenth-Century Europe
36 MACK P. HOLT
    The French Wars of Religion Second edition
37 CHARLES G. NAUERT
    Humanism and the Culture of Renaissance Europe Second edition
38 KATHERINE CRAWFORD
    European Sexualities, 1400–1800
39 ANDREW LEES AND LYNN HOLLEN LEES
    Cities and the Making of Modern Europe, 1750–1914
40 MERRY E. WIESNER
    Women and Gender in Early Modern Europe Third edition
41 LINDA L. CLARK
    Women and Achievement in Nineteenth-Century Europe